National Perspectives on Russia

This book presents a ground-breaking comparative study of the bilateral relations of all 27 EU member states with Russia and an assessment of their impact on the EU's efforts to conduct a coherent and effective policy towards its most important neighbour.

While there has been a lot of research on European foreign policy, there has been much less on the role that national foreign policies play in it. Based on a common analytical framework, this book offers a detailed analysis of 'national perspectives on Russia' and how they interact with and affect policymaking at the EU-level. The authors provide deep insights into the relationship between individual states and Russia looking at a range of policy areas: economics, trade, energy, security, culture and education. They are not only interested in examining policy failure but also probing the possibilities of seeing national foreign policies and the bilateralism with third parties that they often entail as a potentially positive resource for the European Union.

As Russia is an example of a particularly hard case for EU foreign policy, this book yields important insights concerning the possibilities as well as limits of developing a common EU policy in the future. It will be of interest to students and scholars of European politics, EU Studies, Russian politics, foreign policy studies and international politics.

Maxine David is a Lecturer in European Politics in the School of Politics at University of Surrey, UK.

Jackie Gower is a Teaching Fellow in the Department of War Studies at King's College London, UK.

Hiski Haukkala is a Professor of International Relations at the University of Tampere, Finland.

Routledge Advances in European Politics

1 Russian Messianism
Third Rome, revolution,
Communism and after
Peter J.S. Duncan

**2 European Integration and the
Postmodern Condition**
Governance, democracy, identity
Peter van Ham

3 Nationalism in Italian Politics
The stories of the Northern League,
1980–2000
Damian Tambini

**4 International Intervention in the
Balkans since 1995**
Edited by Peter Siani-Davies

5 Widening the European Union
The politics of institutional change
and reform
Edited by Bernard Steunenberg

**6 Institutional Challenges in the
European Union**
*Edited by Madeleine Hosli,
Adrian van Deemen and Mika Widgrén*

7 Europe Unbound
Enlarging and reshaping the
boundaries of the European Union
Edited by Jan Zielonka

8 Ethnic Cleansing in the Balkans
Nationalism and the destruction
of tradition
Cathie Carmichael

**9 Democracy and Enlargement in
Post-Communist Europe**
The democratisation of the general
public in fifteen Central and Eastern
European countries, 1991–98
Christian W. Haerpfer

**10 Private Sector Involvement
in the Euro**
The power of ideas
*Stefan Collignon and
Daniela Schwarzer*

11 Europe
A Nietzschean perspective
Stefan Elbe

12 European Union and E-Voting
Addressing the European
Parliament's internet voting
challenge
*Edited by Alexander H. Trechsel and
Fernando Mendez*

**13 European Union Council
Presidencies**
A comparative perspective
Edited by Ole Elgström

14 European Governance and Supranational Institutions
Making states comply
Jonas Tallberg

15 European Union, NATO and Russia
Martin Smith and Graham Timmins

16 Business, The State and Economic Policy
The case of Italy
G. Grant Amyot

17 Europeanization and Transnational States
Comparing Nordic central governments
Bengt Jacobsson, Per Lægreid and Ove K. Pedersen

18 European Union Enlargement
A comparative history
Edited by Wolfram Kaiser and Jürgen Elvert

19 Gibraltar
British or Spanish?
Peter Gold

20 Gendering Spanish Democracy
Monica Threlfall, Christine Cousins and Celia Valiente

21 European Union Negotiations
Processes, networks and negotiations
Edited by Ole Elgström and Christer Jönsson

22 Evaluating Euro-Mediterranean Relations
Stephen C. Calleya

23 The Changing Face of European Identity
A seven-nation study of (supra) national attachments
Edited by Richard Robyn

24 Governing Europe
Discourse, governmentality and European integration
William Walters and Jens Henrik Haahr

25 Territory and Terror
Conflicting nationalisms in the Basque country
Jan Mansvelt Beck

26 Multilateralism, German Foreign Policy and Central Europe
Claus Hofhansel

27 Popular Protest in East Germany
Gareth Dale

28 Germany's Foreign Policy Towards Poland and the Czech Republic
Ostpolitik revisited
Karl Cordell and Stefan Wolff

29 Kosovo
The politics of identity and space
Denisa Kostovicova

30 The Politics of European Union Enlargement
Theoretical approaches
Edited by Frank Schimmelfennig and Ulrich Sedelmeier

31 Europeanizing Social Democracy?
The rise of the party of European socialists
Simon Lightfoot

32 Conflict and Change in EU Budgetary Politics
Johannes Lindner

33 Gibraltar, Identity and Empire
E.G. Archer

34 Governance Stories
Mark Bevir and R.A.W Rhodes

35 Britain and the Balkans
1991 until the present
Carole Hodge

36 The Eastern Enlargement of the European Union
John O'Brennan

37 Values and Principles in European Union Foreign Policy
Edited by Sonia Lucarelli and Ian Manners

38 European Union and the Making of a Wider Northern Europe
Pami Aalto

39 Democracy in the European Union
Towards the emergence of a public sphere
Edited by Liana Giorgi, Ingmar Von Homeyer and Wayne Parsons

40 European Union Peacebuilding and Policing
Michael Merlingen with Rasa Ostrauskaite

41 The Conservative Party and European Integration since 1945
At the heart of Europe?
N.J. Crowson

42 E-Government in Europe
Re-booting the state
Edited by Paul G. Nixon and Vassiliki N. Koutrakou

43 EU Foreign and Interior Policies
Cross-pillar politics and the social construction of sovereignty
Stephan Stetter

44 Policy Transfer in European Union Governance
Regulating the utilities
Simon Bulmer, David Dolowitz, Peter Humphreys and Stephen Padgett

45 The Europeanization of National Political Parties
Power and organizational adaptation
Edited by Thomas Poguntke, Nicholas Aylott, Elisabeth Carter, Robert Ladrech and Kurt Richard Luther

46 Citizenship in Nordic Welfare States
Dynamics of choice, duties and participation in a changing Europe
Edited by Bjørn Hvinden and Håkan Johansson

47 National Parliaments within the Enlarged European Union
From victims of integration to competitive actors?
Edited by John O'Brennan and Tapio Raunio

48 Britain, Ireland and Northern Ireland since 1980
The totality of relationships
Eamonn O'Kane

49 The EU and the European Security Strategy
Forging a global Europe
Edited by Sven Biscop and Jan Joel Andersson

50 European Security and Defence Policy
An implementation perspective
Edited by Michael Merlingen and Rasa Ostrauskaitė

51 Women and British Party Politics
Descriptive, substantive and symbolic representation
Sarah Childs

52 The Selection of Ministers in Europe
Hiring and firing
Edited by Keith Dowding and Patrick Dumont

53 Energy Security
Europe's new foreign policy challenge
Richard Youngs

54 Institutional Challenges in Post-Constitutional Europe
Governing change
Edited by Catherine Moury and Luís de Sousa

55 The Struggle for the European Constitution
A past and future history
Michael O'Neill

56 Transnational Labour Solidarity
Mechanisms of commitment to cooperation within the European Trade Union Movement
Katarzyna Gajewska

57 The Illusion of Accountability in the European Union
Edited by Sverker Gustavsson, Christer Karlsson, and Thomas Persson

58 The European Union and Global Social Change
A critical geopolitical-economic analysis
József Böröcz

59 Citizenship and Collective Identity in Europe
Ireneusz Pawel Karolewski

60 EU Enlargement and Socialization
Turkey and Cyprus
Stefan Engert

61 The Politics of EU Accession
Turkish challenges and Central European experiences
Edited by Lucie Tunkrová and Pavel Šaradín

62 The Political History of European Integration
The hypocrisy of democracy-through-market
Hagen Schulz-Forberg and Bo Stråth

63 The Spatialities of Europeanization
Power, governance and territory in Europe
Alun Jones and Julian Clark

64 European Union Sanctions and Foreign Policy
When and why do they work?
Clara Portela

65 The EU's Role in World Politics
A retreat from liberal internationalism
Richard Youngs

66 Social Democracy and European Integration
The politics of preference formation
Edited by Dionyssis Dimitrakopoulos

67 The EU Presence in International Organizations
Edited by Spyros Blavoukos and Dimitris Bourantonis

68 Sustainability in European Environmental Policy
Challenge of governance and knowledge
Edited by Rob Atkinson, Georgios Terizakis and Karsten Zimmermann

69 Fifty Years of EU-Turkey Relations
A Sisyphean story
Edited by Armagan Emre Çakir

70 Europeanization and Foreign Policy
State diversity in Finland and Britain
Juha Jokela

71 EU Foreign Policy and Post-Soviet Conflicts
Stealth intervention
Nicu Popescu

72 Switzerland in Europe
Continuity and change in the Swiss political economy
Edited by Christine Trampusch and André Mach

73 The Political Economy of Noncompliance
Adjusting to the single European market
Scott Nicholas Siegel

74 National and European Foreign Policy
Towards Europeanization
Edited by Reuben Wong and Christopher Hill

75 The European Union Diplomatic Service
Ideas, preferences and identities
Caterina Carta

76 Poland within the European Union
New awkward partner or new heart of Europe?
Aleks Szczerbiak

77 A Political Theory of Identity in European Integration
Memory and policies
Catherine Guisan

78 EU Foreign Policy and the Europeanization of Neutral States
Comparing Irish and Austrian foreign policy
Nicole Alecu de Flers

79 Party System Change in Western Europe
Gemma Loomes

80 The Second Tier of Local Government in Europe
Provinces, counties, départements and landkreise in comparison
Hubert Heinelt and Xavier Bertrana Horta

81 Learning from the EU Constitutional Treaty
Democratic constitutionalism beyond the nation-state
Ben Crum

82 Human Rights and Democracy in EU Foreign Policy
The cases of Ukraine and Egypt
Rosa Balfour

83 Europeanization, Integration and Identity
A social constructivist fusion perspective on Norway
Gamze Tanil

84 The Impact of European Integration on Political Parties
Beyond the permissive consensus
Dimitri Almeida

85 Civic Resources and the Future of the European Union
Victoria Kaina and Ireneusz Pawel Karolewski

86 The Europeanization of National Foreign Policies towards Latin America
Lorena Ruano

87 The EU and Multilateral Security Governance
Sonia Lucarelli, Luk Van Langenhove and Jan Wouters

88 Security Challenges in the Euro-Med Area in the 21st Century
Mare nostrum
Stephen Calleya

89 Society and Democracy in Europe
Oscar W. Gabriel and Silke Keil

90 European Union Public Health Policy
Regional and global trends
Edited by Scott L. Greer and Paulette Kurzer

91 The New Member States and the European Union
Foreign policy and Europeanization
Edited by Michael Baun and Dan Marek

92 The Politics of Ratification of EU Treaties
Carlos Closa

93 Europeanization and New Member States
A comparative social network analysis
Flavia Jurje

94 National Perspectives on Russia
European foreign policy in the making/
Edited by Maxine David, Jackie Gower and Hiski Haukkala

National Perspectives on Russia
European foreign policy in the making?

Edited by
Maxine David, Jackie Gower
and Hiski Haukkala

LONDON AND NEW YORK

First published 2013
by Routledge
2 Park Square, Milton Park, Abingdon, Oxfordshire OX14 4RN

Simultaneously published in the USA and Canada
by Routledge
711 Third Avenue, New York, NY 10017

First issued in paperback 2014

Routledge is an imprint of the Taylor & Francis Group, an informa business

© 2013 Maxine David, Jackie Gower and Hiski Haukkala for selection and
editorial matter; individual contributors their contribution.

The right of the editors to be identified as the authors of the editorial
material, and of the authors for their individual chapters, has been asserted
in accordance with sections 77 and 78 of the Copyright, Designs and
Patents Act 1988.

All rights reserved. No part of this book may be reprinted or reproduced or
utilised in any form or by any electronic, mechanical, or other means, now
known or hereafter invented, including photocopying and recording, or in
any information storage or retrieval system, without permission in writing
from the publishers.

Trademark notice: Product or corporate names may be trademarks or
registered trademarks, and are used only for identification and explanation
without intent to infringe.

British Library Cataloguing in Publication Data
A catalogue record for this book is available from the British Library

Library of Congress Cataloging in Publication Data
National perspectives on Russia European foreign policy in the making? /
edited by Maxine David, Jackie Gower and Hiski Haukkala.
    pages ; cm. – (Routledge advances in european politics ; 94)
    Includes bibliographical references and index.
    1. Russia (Federation)–Foreign relations–Europe. 2. Europe–Foreign
relations–Russia (Federation) I. David, Maxine. II. Gower, Jackie. III.
Haukkala, Hiski.
    DK510.764.N376 2013
    327.4704–dc23
                        2012046957

ISBN 978-0-415-53832-9 (hbk)
ISBN 978-1-138-89808-0 (pbk)
ISBN 978-0-203-49516-2 (ebk)

Typeset in Times New Roman
by Taylor & Francis Books

Contents

	List of illustrations	xiii
	List of contributors	xiv
	Preface	xvi
	List of abbreviations and acronyms	xviii
1	Introduction MAXINE DAVID, JACKIE GOWER AND HISKI HAUKKALA	1
2	Germany SUSAN STEWART	13
3	France RACHEL LE NOAN	30
4	Ireland and the United Kingdom MAXINE DAVID	48
5	Italy RICCARDO ALCARO	67
6	Poland BARTOSZ CICHOCKI	86
7	Portugal and Spain LICÍNIA SIMÃO	101
8	Belgium, Luxembourg and the Netherlands TOM CASIER	118
9	Denmark, Finland and Sweden TOBIAS ETZOLD AND HISKI HAUKKALA	132

xii *Contents*

10 Estonia, Latvia and Lithuania 149
AINIUS LAŠAS AND DAVID J. GALBREATH

11 Czech Republic, Hungary and Slovakia 169
MARTIN DANGERFIELD

12 Bulgaria 187
DIANA BOZHILOVA

13 Romania 197
MIRCEA MICU

14 Austria 209
MARTIN MALEK AND PAUL LUIF

15 Slovenia 222
JACKIE GOWER

16 Malta 231
ARSALAN ALSHINAWI

17 Cyprus and Greece 238
GEORGE CHRISTOU

18 Conclusion 255
MAXINE DAVID, JACKIE GOWER AND HISKI HAUKKALA

Index 267

Illustrations

Figures

5.1	Share of crude oil and natural gas imports from Russia in Italian gas and oil imports	75
5.2	Italy's crude oil and natural gas imports from Russia	75
10.1	Baltic–Russian trade dynamics (2000–10)	156

Table

11.1	Czech, Hungarian and Slovak trade with Russia 2004–10	177

Contributors

Riccardo Alcaro is Senior Fellow at the Istituto Affari Internazionali (IAI) of Rome and European Foreign and Security Policy Studies (EFSPS) Fellow.

Arsalan Alshinawi is a Lecturer at the Department of International Relations, University of Malta. He was previously at the Ministry of Foreign Affairs of Malta.

Diana Bozhilova is a Visiting Research Fellow at the Centre for Hellenic Studies at King's College London.

Tom Casier is Senior Lecturer in International Relations and Jean Monnet Chair at the Brussels School of International Studies of the University of Kent. He is also Visiting Professor at the University of Leuven.

George Christou is Associate Professor of European Politics at the Department of Politics and International Studies, University of Warwick.

Bartosz Cichocki heads the International Analysis Unit at the National Security Bureau of the Republic of Poland. Prior to this post he was affiliated with the Centre for Eastern Studies and the Polish Institute of International Affairs.

Martin Dangerfield is Professor of European Integration and Jean Monnet Chair in the European Integration of Central and East Europe at the University of Wolverhampton.

Maxine David is Lecturer in European Politics at the School of Politics, University of Surrey. She is Editor of *Journal of Contemporary European Research*.

Tobias Etzold is a Research Associate and Project Leader for Nordic and Baltic Sea Studies at the German Institute for International and Security Affairs (SWP).

David J. Galbreath is Reader in the Department of Politics, Languages and International Relations at the University of Bath. He is Editor of *European Security* and Treasurer of the University Association for Contemporary European Studies (UACES).

Contributors xv

Jackie Gower is a Teaching Fellow in the Department of War Studies, King's College London and a co-ordinator of the UACES EU–Russia Research Network.

Hiski Haukkala is Professor of International Relations in the School of Management, University of Tampere.

Ainius Lašas is Senior Research Fellow, ERC Project on Media and Democracy in Central and Eastern Europe at St Antony's College, Oxford.

Rachel Le Noan is completing a PhD focusing on Russia's national security policies and the strategic use of diaspora politics in the post-Cold War era at the University of Aberdeen.

Paul Luif is a member of the Austrian Institute of International Affairs and Senior Researcher at the Political Science Department of Vienna University.

Martin Malek is a (civilian) Researcher at the Institute for Peace Support and Conflict Management and also at the Institute for Strategy and Security Policy, both of the National Defence Academy (Vienna).

Mircea Micu is a doctoral researcher in politics and international studies at the University of Cambridge. He is also a Romanian diplomat, currently on secondment to the European External Action Service.

Licínia Simão is an Assistant Professor in International Relations at the University of Coimbra and Researcher at the Centre for Social Studies at the same University.

Susan Stewart is a Senior Associate in the Russian Federation/CIS Research Division of the German Institute for International and Security Affairs (SWP) in Berlin.

Preface

The book is based on a collaborative research project under the auspices of the UACES–BASEES EU–Russia Network. We are most grateful to UACES for their sponsorship of an early workshop that resulted in a common framework for the book being developed. We are grateful to all who participated at that workshop but who have not been involved in the later outcomes. We are particularly grateful for the encouragement we received at that workshop to move forward with the project. After all, mapping 27 states' relations with another actor is no small thing. The sheer scale of the enterprise was therefore daunting. However, the early workshop and the feedback then received at subsequent conferences, convinced us that there was a compelling need for a deep but comprehensive analysis of the subject matter. This imperative overrode any apprehensions we may have had about the undertaking.

For this encouragement and for all the other valuable comments and suggestions we received from our 'audiences' at conferences, we owe a debt of thanks. There are too many people to list individually but those who attended our presentations at the following conferences will know who they are: the European Consortium for Political Research (ECPR) Fifth Pan-European Conference on EU Politics, Porto, Portugal, June 2010; the University Association of Contemporary European Studies (UACES) Annual Conferences, in Bruges, 2010, and Cambridge, 2011; the European Union Studies Association (EUSA) 12th Biennial International Conference, held in Boston, Massachusetts, in March 2011; the Political Studies Association (PSA) Annual Conference, London, April 2011; and the European Union in International Affairs (EUIA) biennial conference, Brussels, May 2012. Without the generosity of input we received at these venues, our work would have been all the harder.

The early fruits of the project have already been published as a Special Issue of the *Journal of Contemporary European Studies* (Vol. 19, No. 2, 2011) and the permission to reprint the articles in a revised format here is gratefully acknowledged. We also want to thank the editors at Routledge, Heidi Bagtazo, Paola Celli, Harriet Frammingham, Alexander Quayle and Hannah Shakespeare for sharing our enthusiasm for this project and being so professional and helpful in the production of this book.

Preface xvii

It would be remiss of us not to acknowledge and thank all those people who have given up time to be interviewed by us and so many of our authors. The interest shown by practitioners in the project and their willingness to share their experience and views with us has greatly enriched the analysis. This book is the product of the authors and they alone are responsible for their ideas and conclusions. However, those ideas are themselves informed by the knowledge and experience of the many practitioners, in Brussels, in member states, and in Russia itself, without whose contributions in interviews, telephone calls and e-mail exchanges, this book would be the poorer. A special thank you is owed to Fraser Cameron, Director of the EU–Russia Centre, who has been an invaluable source of help and guidance throughout the project.

The subject matter is not without its sensitivities and one of the greatest challenges we faced was ensuring that a wide range of views and perspectives could be included and that the book was not a mere reflection of British or western European views on the bilateral relationships and on the EU's own relations with Russia. Thus, contributions to the book come from 19 authors located in 10 different countries, representing 13 different nationalities. This itself presented some problems of co-ordination and gave us, perhaps, more sympathy for the challenges faced by the EU in trying to bring 27 states together! Last but not least, therefore, we want to thank the group of excellent contributing authors to this book, all with competing demands and responsibilities, who have nevertheless stayed with the project and demonstrated impressive levels of dedication and professionalism to ensure this final outcome. We trust our authors have found this project to be as exciting and worthwhile as we have.

Maxine David, Jackie Gower and Hiski Haukkala
Farnham, London and Lavia, Finland, September 2012

Abbreviations and acronyms

ABM	Anti-Ballistic Missile
BLEU	Belgium–Luxembourg Economic Union
BMD	Ballistic Missile Defence
CDU	Christian Democratic Union (Germany)
CEE	Central and Eastern Europe
CEECs	Countries of Central and Eastern Europe
CEGH	Central European Gas Hub
CFE	Treaty on Conventional Armed Forces in Europe
CFSP	Common Foreign and Security Policy
CIS	Commonwealth of Independent States
CMEA	Council for Mutual Economic Assistance (also COMECON)
COEST	Council Working Group on Eastern Europe
COMECON	Council for Mutual Economic Assistance (also CMEA)
Cominform	Communist Information Bureau
Comintern	Communist International
COPS	Political and Security Committee (also PSC)
COREPER	Committee of Permanent Representatives to the EU
CSCE	Conference on Security and Cooperation in Europe
CSDP	Common Security and Defence Policy
CSTO	Collective Security Treaty Organization
CSU	Christian Social Union (Germany)
DfID	Department for International Development (UK)
DG	Directorate General (European Commission)
DG RELEX	Directorate General for External Relations
DTT	Double Tax Treaty
EA	Europe Agreement
EADS	European Aeronautic Defence and Space Company
EaP	Eastern Partnership
EC	European Community/ies
ECSC	European Coal and Steel Community
EDF	Electricité de France
EEAS	European External Action Service
ENP	European Neighbourhood Policy

Abbreviations and acronyms xix

ESDP	European Security and Defence Policy
EU	European Union
EUBAM	EU Border Assistance Mission (to Moldova and Ukraine)
FAC	Foreign Affairs Council
FCO	Foreign and Commonwealth Office (UK)
FDI	Foreign direct investment
FDP	Free Democratic Party (Germany)
FRG	Federal Republic of Germany
FSU	Former Soviet Union
G7	Group of Seven
G8	Group of Eight
GAERC	General Affairs and External Relations Council (of the EU)
GDR	German Democratic Republic
IAEA	International Atomic Energy Agency
IRBA	Ireland Russia Business Association
JHA	Justice and Home Affairs
KGB	Committee for State Security
LNG	Liquefied Natural Gas
MAP	Membership Action Plan (NATO)
MDS	Missile Defence System
MEP	Member of European Parliament
MFA	Ministry of Foreign Affairs
MoD	Ministry of Defence
NATO	North Atlantic Treaty Organization
ND	Northern Dimension
NGO	Non-governmental organization
NKVD	People's Commissariat for Internal Affairs
NRC	NATO–Russia Council
ODA	Official development assistance
OECD	Organisation for Economic Co-operation and Development
OPEC	Organization of the Petroleum Exporting Countries
OSCE	Organization for Security and Co-operation in Europe
PCA	Partnership and Cooperation Agreement
PCI	Partito Comunista Italiano
PCP	Portuguese Communist Party
P4M	Partnership for Modernization
PfP	Partnership for Peace
PSC	Political and Security Committee (also COPS)
SDI	Strategic Defence Initiative
SPD	Social Democratic Party (Germany)
START	Strategic Arms Reduction Treaty
TACIS	Technical Assistance to the Commonwealth of Independent States
TEP	Third Energy Package
UN	United Nations

xx *Abbreviations and acronyms*

UNSC	United Nations Security Council
USSR	Union of Soviet Socialist Republics
VG	Visegrad Group
WTO	World Trade Organization

1 Introduction

Maxine David, Jackie Gower and Hiski Haukkala

One of the key tensions in the development of a 'European foreign policy' is the interplay between the national foreign policies of the EU member states and the ambitions for a common policy line agreed at the EU level. At first sight this juxtaposition is somewhat artificial as almost by definition there can be no 'common' line at the EU level without the prior existence of national foreign policies from which this commonality should spring. In addition, this tension is also perhaps surprising because at least in principle the 'Grand Narrative' of the 2000s in the EU has been towards increasing institutionalization and hence ostensibly also growing commonality in foreign policy at the European level (Smith 2008; Keukeleire and MacNaughtan 2008). The Treaty of Lisbon (2009) and its institutional innovations – the President of the European Council, the new High Representative and the European External Action Service (EEAS) that has brought the external relations aspects of the Council and the Commission together – was specifically designed to facilitate the emergence of a more common and unified European foreign policy (Ashton 2010; see also Cameron 2012 and Missiroli 2010).

Against the background of this objective, it is hardly surprising that the extant analysis has mainly focused on the question of whether there is evidence of a common European foreign policy emerging. The majority of the literature naturally considered the various levels at which European foreign policy is made and envisaged the relationship between the national and EU levels in largely antagonistic or at least competitive terms (Vaïsse and Kundnani 2012; Keukeleire and MacNaughtan 2008). Important inroads have been made into assessing the impact of Europe on national foreign policies, primarily through the Europeanization literature (Wong and Hill 2011). However, what is less clear is whether and how the member states through their national policies impinge, both positively and negatively, upon the construction of a common foreign policy at the EU level (for early attempts see Hill 1996; Manners and Whitman 2000). Thus, good case studies are called for.

Russia is an interesting, significant and difficult case, both in respect of EU-level relations and member state–Russia relations. Speaking in his capacity as EU Trade Commissioner, Peter Mandelson (2007) said: '[n]o other country reveals our differences as does Russia. This is a failure of Europe as a whole,

2 *Maxine David, Jackie Gower, Hiski Haukkala*

not any Member State in particular. But it does our interests no good'. There are a number of reasons for this: the extent and intensity of the bilateral relationships and arrangements; the number of these which are characterized by poor relations; the uploading of disputes and the impact on the multilateral level; and a particularly sharp division between the member states as to the most effective way of conducting the relationship at the EU level. Thus, by reason of being a particularly 'hard case' for EU foreign policy, Russia can yield correspondingly important insights concerning the possibilities as well as limits of developing a common European foreign policy in the future.

For its part, Russia seeks to encourage, use and even abuse bilateral relations in its wider relations with the EU. These types of interactions may yield tactical gains for Russia and some member states but in the longer term they have undermined prospects for a successful and mutually advantageous EU–Russia strategic partnership (Haukkala 2010). That said, it should be pointed out that this book is not only interested in examining policy failure but also in probing the possibilities of seeing national foreign policies and the bilateralism with third parties that they often entail as a potentially positive resource for the European Union. To that end, this collection has three objectives. The first is to map the relations of each of the 27 member states with Russia, giving an exhaustive comparative account of these bilateral relationships. Here, we seek to provide the necessary analysis in order to draw conclusions in respect of our second objective, which is to consider the larger question of whether bilateral member state relations constitute a challenge to the development of a coherent and effective EU relationship with Russia. This arises from the dominant discourse that bilateralism has a negative impact on multilateralism (Ginsberg 2001; Smith 2008; Schmidt-Felzmann 2008). The final objective, therefore, is to achieve an understanding of whether there are grounds for challenging this discourse and looking for instances of what we have termed 'constructive bilateralism'. The need for such a comprehensive contribution is clear. While others have attempted to cover all bilateral relations, notably Leonard and Popescu's typology of member state relations with Russia in their *Power Audit of EU-Russia Relations* (European Council on Foreign Relations 2007), very little space, and certainly not recently, has been given to a fully comprehensive yet detailed account of these relations and their impact on the EU. This is therefore the first post-2004/07 enlargements account of the totality of these relations and the first since the newer member states have become embedded in the EU. This is of particular significance given the general assumption that it is the addition of these new states that has made European foreign policy-making particularly problematic in respect of Russia (Raik 2007; Light 2008).

At this juncture some definitional ground clearing is in order. By 'European foreign policy' we mean the common EU policy line adopted in, and increasingly also made by, the institutions in Brussels. By contrast, 'national foreign policies' – or 'perspectives' – alludes to the wide variety of approaches utilized by the 27 member states in their bilateral relations with Russia. It

Introduction 3

should be pointed out that we employ a broad understanding of foreign policy: instead of 'high politics' dealing with diplomacy and security policy alone, we are interested in the whole spectrum of relations that the member states entertain with Russia, be they economic, political, socio-cultural or security and defence-related. Therefore, our take on these relations is more akin to external relations than traditional foreign policy per se (Keukeleire and MacNaughtan 2008, see particularly Chapters 8 and 9; Manners and Whitman 2000).

Such an interpretation of foreign policy is essential because it is at the level of *all* these policy areas that the EU–Russia relationship has been developed and institutionalized: indeed, one might argue that the Common Foreign and Security Policy (CFSP) and Common Security and Defence Policy (CSDP) have been the least operationalized areas in the relationship. This extended policy field is not distinct to EU–Russia relations, of course. The blurring of the line between domestic and foreign policies is evident in national policies, as is an increasing need to see a range of policies and ministries as tools for the achievement of foreign policy goals. In the EU–Russia case, the driving force is trade and energy, albeit more recently other important matters have appeared on the agenda. Particularly important has been the question of visa liberalization, which has, in turn, brought the area of Justice and Home Affairs (JHA) into focus. With this diffusion of policy areas comes a diffusion of competence, thus key actors are located at the EU level in the Commission, the Council, the European Parliament and the new External Action Service. Adding to this already complex picture, member states conduct their relations with third parties through a range of domestic fora, numerous ministries, parliaments, courts, for instance, as well as through sub-state levels: media, business, public opinion and NGOs. The question of who has competence to do what therefore has enormous relevance.

Following the decision in the Lisbon Treaty to remove the pillar system that stressed the intergovernmental nature of the CFSP, the EU now has increased competence over all aspects of foreign policy that fall under the CFSP. This is not to deny the still-central role of the member states, whereby the European Council is tasked with identifying 'the strategic interests and objectives of the Union' (Art. 10b, 1 Lisbon Treaty). However, the CFSP has received a major boost to its EU-level resources, with the creation of new offices and bodies designed to ensure that the CFSP becomes more coherent and effective. In order to provide the continuity denied by a system of six month rotating presidencies, Lisbon created the office of President of the European Council, appointed for two and a half years to act as external representative of the EU on foreign and security policy matters. However, it was with the creation of the position of High Representative of the Union for Foreign Affairs and Security Policy (henceforth referred to as the High Representative) that Lisbon was perhaps most innovative. Appointed by the European Council, this person (currently Baroness Catherine Ashton) is responsible for the conduct and consistency of European foreign policy. The

4 *Maxine David, Jackie Gower, Hiski Haukkala*

High Representative heads the Foreign Affairs Council (FAC) and is also a Vice-President of the Commission, thus having a foot in both the Council and the Commission. She can submit joint proposals (with the Commission) for CFSP, and the Commission (jointly with the High Representative) for external actions-related matters. Ashton is assisted in her work by the EEAS that brings the external relations features of both the Council and the Commission under one roof. Thus, on paper at least, the Lisbon Treaty vastly extended the toolbox of the EU in relation to the CFSP.

The encounter and consequent enmeshing of member state perspectives and policies on Russia with the EU level largely takes place in Brussels. Here the key political fora for debate and decision-making are the gatherings of the European Council and the FAC but it is the intricate bureaucratic machinery operating under the political overlay that is of perhaps greater significance. The actual details of common policies are debated and prepared especially in the Working Party on Eastern Europe and Central Asia (COEST) that convenes under the Chairmanship of the EEAS. In the COEST the national diplomats prepare and agree issues and policies – in most cases wordings in documents and declarations – to be further debated and eventually decided at the Political and Security Committee (COPS) or the Committee of Permanent Representatives to the EU (COREPER II) that meet at an ambassadorial level. It is the deliverables flowing from this multifaceted machinery that prepare the EU's policy on Russia and they are often approved without much further political or strategic debate at the FAC or in the European Councils. That said, under Ashton the FAC has undertaken a new initiative to ponder the state of play and the strategic direction of EU–Russia relations at the ministerial level as well.

Despite the additions and innovations, questions continue to be asked about the sufficiency and efficiency of the EU's foreign policy resources. Most problematic is the question of how European foreign policy can be co-ordinated in a system that has such a plurality of actors, with a plurality of competences in areas which either reside directly in the foreign policy arena or in external relations-related areas whose activities impact on the CFSP. The problem of co-ordination applies both at policy and institutional levels. Institutionally-speaking, it would be fair to say that it is the member states who present the largest problem for they conduct 'their' foreign policy not only through the EU but also outside it in their bilateral relations. While the High Representative has responsibility for co-ordination, she is ultimately reliant on the member states and the problem this might present is not unanticipated in Treaty terms. The Lisbon Treaty requires that: '[b]efore undertaking any action on the international scene or entering into any commitment which could affect the Union's interests, each member state shall consult the others within the European Council or the Council' (European Council, Art 16(b), 2007/C 306/01). However, this consultation process most often represents an ideal rather than a reality (interviews with Commission officials July 2011) and it is not always obvious either that the member states' foreign policies

Introduction 5

evidence the 'mutual solidarity' that ensures that 'the Union is able to assert its interests and values on the international scene' (European Council, Art 16(b), 2007/C 306/01).

The mapping of the bilateral relationships in this collection provides valuable insights into why that solidarity has been so difficult to achieve. While there are many similarities in respect of each member state's historical and current experiences with Russia, there are also many points of difference. The extent of the differentiation was clear from the earliest stages of our discussions and presented its own analytical conundrum. The only really viable theoretical framework was that of Europeanization and indeed, the loose framework we propose incorporates elements of that. Following Wong and Hill (2011: 4) we understand Europeanization to be referring to the 'process of foreign policy convergence'. This implies increasing commonality between the member states and the EU level. There are three aspects to this process: top-down whereby changes in national foreign policies are identified and attributed to participation in the EU foreign-policy making arena (downloading); second, a bottom-up process whereby developments at the EU level are considered to be shaped by the member states themselves (up-loading); finally, a process of identity change in the participating states and the EU itself (cross-loading). (For a detailed argument on causality in Europeanization, see Exadaktylos and Radaelli 2012.) The contributors to this collection were directed to consider only the application of wider arguments rather than attempting to contribute to this literature by detailing, for instance, processes through which this has or has not occurred.

Multiple levels of analysis naturally had to be considered: the national, regional (i.e. European) as well as, in many instances, the systemic. It is, in certain cases, difficult to talk about a member state's relations with Russia without reference to NATO, for example in the case of Italy, or without reference to the USA, for example, the UK or the Baltic States. At the national level, authors were asked to identify and elucidate what makes 'their' state's or states' relations with Russia 'unique' and to consider what structures and constrains the relationship. Most importantly, authors had to consider what the main driver is behind national policies towards Russia: to decide whether these are accounted for by changes in the domestic environment, by changes in Russia or at the regional or systemic levels. In certain cases, it might be considered more appropriate to focus on agency and the role of specific individuals or groups of actors in decision-making processes. For others, a member state's vulnerability to external pressures might mean privileging structures and explanations centring on relative (in)vulnerability. Whether explanation centred on agency or structure, a variety of factors were likely to be of importance. For instance, the legacy of historical relations has to be considered in respect of understanding individual leaders' perceptions of and attitudes towards Russia. But such a legacy might pertain also at a more structural level, at least where broader definitions of structure were applied. Geographical location – relative proximity – matters, of course, although as some chapters go on to demonstrate, this cannot function as a sole predictor of the state of the bilateral relationship. For many of the member states, the economic relationship is inevitably what binds the states together, thus data relating to levels of energy dependence, trading figures, even tourism, is crucial to building an understanding of what functions as the glue in the relationship. However, all authors were directed to consider also the role of identity, including culture and religion, and results here have been surprising in some cases, as we go on to explore in the Conclusion to the book.

Ultimately, the brief to authors was to avoid crude typologies and to deliver instead a nuanced analysis that dealt with the complexities of the bilateral relationship(s). At base, authors were directed to identify, if possible, internal tensions and cleavages concerning Russia in their respective member states. However, having once delivered an understanding of the member state–Russia relationship, authors were asked to consider the impact of that upon the EU–Russia relationship. Here we were firstly looking for evidence of consistency: was there a shared analysis and policy line or were there perhaps meaningful differences? If so, did these differences constitute a problem or were they perhaps a resource, offering potential for fruitful change, for instance? *How* a member state implements decisions made at the national level are of relevance here. Thus, we asked authors to consider questions, for instance, about the extent to which member states attempt to draw on EU resources/capacities in order to achieve their national objectives; whether wider European discourses were invoked when member states defended their policies or their implementation; whether member states' policies towards Russia were consistent or inconsistent with EU-level policy.

Of particular relevance here, if nuance was to be achieved, was whether there was evidence or not of a pattern in relation to policy areas. Thus, in a policy area highly regulated at the EU level, was there a corresponding commonality at national level? Was there evidence that discourse or priorities changed over a period of time in a direct reflection of interactions within Brussels? We began with an expectation that this might be most evident in the cases of newer member states. We asked authors to consider also that it may be the case that multilateralism in fact 'funds' bilateralism in that EU membership grants member states a stake in and a level of understanding about Russia previously unknown, thus facilitating deeper interaction.

Other questions centred around the issue of whether it was the case that as enlargement occurred, certain issues fell within the domain of the EU with which some member states had a prior, deeply vested interest, concern and/or capacity. Human rights issues particularly came to mind here. Thus, we asked whether the EU could be seen as playing a role in terms of changing the ground rules of the national game concerning Russia. Was there any potential for identity change in this respect? Foreign policy analysts have long been preoccupied with the question of change versus continuity (Northedge 1968; Donaldson *et al.* 2002; Hill 2003). They demonstrate the need to understand the forces for continuities in any actor's foreign policy, variables such as belief

Introduction 7

systems, historical experience, identity (Johansen 1980; Larsen 1997) since beliefs, for instance, 'should be seen as something which constitutes a frame for action' (Larsen 1997: 7). However, there are equally persuasive arguments about the need to understand that foreign policies are mutable and that analysis of them 'is the analysis of the causes and effects of changes' (Modelski 1962: 102). Thus, we seek to understand the circumstances under which change occurs and to see that even a state's identity is susceptible to domestic and external forces which have the capacity to bring about change (Hopf 2005). Furthermore, increasing interdependence means that state identity must be seen as increasingly allied to the wider political context in which states function (Hill 2003: 175). While we begin with the assumption that foreign policy is about change *and* continuity, the high levels of interconnectedness felt between EU member states requires particular consideration of what, if anything, changes and why. Furthermore, we ask in our Conclusion: what needs to change in the future?

One final caveat is in order. Inevitably, given that this book is written from the perspective of the EU member states rather than that of Russia, judgments relate far more to the member states and Brussels than Russia. Thus, we do not claim to deliver any insights from the Russian point of view. In fact, this necessary omission suggests avenues for further research and comparison. Therefore, we would like to take this opportunity to present a challenge to our Russian colleagues and invite them to produce a commensurate volume where the Russian perspective(s) on individual EU member states is analyzed.

The plan of the book

We begin with Germany, arguably the pivotal member state in respect of Russia. Susan Stewart accentuates the economic and business relationship but also highlights the centrality of the German–Russian relationship for all aspects of the EU–Russia partnership. She assesses the justification for the widespread criticism that the closeness of the relationship undermines the EU's efforts to pursue an effective common policy towards Russia and concludes that the truth is rather more nuanced, with clear differences discernible both between the approaches of the Schröder and Merkel governments and between specific policy spheres. The chapter concludes with an assessment of the possible implications of the German–Polish rapprochement on the EU–Russia policy.

Considering the discourse about the existence of a Franco–German axis, a comparison of the chapters on these two states' relations with Russia is instructive. Both argue that business interests are central to the relationship. However, the French relationship with Russia, Rachel Le Noan argues, is best understood as a reflection of France's long-standing search for a post-imperial role and its desire to retain influence. She illustrates the tensions that exist in France's wider foreign policy, where it plays a prominent role within the EU but where those interactions often reflect a promotion of French values and interests rather than a desire to negotiate a European consensus. Paradoxically, the failure of the EU to agree a common foreign policy frustrates French interests, driving it to seek deeper relations with Russia as an alternative avenue for its ambitions, which in turn hinders the emergence of a common EU–Russia policy.

Ireland's relations with Russia are peripheral at best, based on small trading figures, relative energy independence, very minor geo-strategic manoeuvrings and little shared history to speak of. The under-developed state of this relationship is explained most obviously by geographic distance. However, that geography alone cannot be an indicator of relations is clear from the UK since it is nearly as remotely situated from Russia as Ireland. Here, however, Maxine David argues that (former) great power status comes into play and explains much of the intensity of the relationship as well as the conflicts. The UK presents as an example of a state that pursues pragmatic and strategic interests but which also attempts to promote the normative agenda. Neither case is particularly instructive in respect of wider lessons for the EU, although, other things being equal, the UK at least could play a more significant role in respect of the normative agenda.

It is the Italian case that is the most revealing, however, in respect of how a member state could usefully contribute more to the development of a more coherent EU Russia policy. In his chapter, Riccardo Alcaro explores Italy's story with Russia, revealing striking similarities with many other western European states: there is a perception of a shared history, an interest in culture, strong trading relations with Russia and a significant degree of energy reliance. Security issues also come into play, such that, as is argued elsewhere in this volume in respect of other EU member states, Italy's situation and interests mean that no assessment of the relationship can be made without reference to NATO as well as the EU. In delivering his assessment, Alcaro provides interesting insights into what should, versus what does, constitute Italy's foreign policy, its leverage over Russia, and its failure to use this as an effective means by which to achieve even its own objectives, never mind those of Europe.

Polish–Russian relations are analyzed next. In his contribution Bartosz Cichocki traces the evolution of relations during the post-Cold War era. According to him, the main driver for change in the relations has been Poland's growing realization that its place in the EU and indeed the wider Euro–Atlantic context is largely predicated on Warsaw's ability to normalize its relations with Russia. At times, it seems, this willingness has been reciprocated by the Russian side and the two have made some inroads in developing mutually beneficial relations as well as tackling some of the most painful problems. At the same time, the negative historical experiences as well as the lack of mutual trust between the two make the process of rapprochement very difficult and prone to crises and even sudden reverses.

Licínia Simão's examination of Spain and Portugal's relations with Russia is no less revealing of the effects that EU membership can have on its member states' relations with other actors, although she also argues that what might

Introduction 9

be termed the effects of Europeanization should not be seen as irrevocable. Both Spain and Portugal are examples of states for which attention to Russia has shifted as a result of EU membership. Despite similar orientations and interests in general foreign policy terms, there is clear blue water between them in respect of relations with Russia. It is true that both have sought to engage with Russia and act as promoters of good relations but Spain's relations are more extensive, reflecting Spain's relative size and status, which have served it well in building relations with Russia. However, Simão questions whether there is enough of substance in either state's Russia relations to ensure a continued interest, concluding that attention is as likely to take a turn away from Russia as to remain with it if other opportunities present themselves.

We then turn to consider the position of the majority of the smaller EU member states where clearly their relationship with Russia is very different compared to that of the larger states and also where there may be structural limitations on their capacity to be major players in European foreign policymaking. However, what is apparent from the chapters that follow is that size is not necessarily the most important factor when it comes to explaining the huge variations in the intensity and quality of the bilateral relationships of small states with Russia that our authors identify. Furthermore, the need generally to act on the basis of consensus with regard to EU-level foreign policy means that some small states, either acting as veto states or working together with like-minded states, have played a significant role in the development of the EU's Russia policy.

Tom Casier compares the policies of the three small founder EU members, Belgium, Luxembourg and the Netherlands, and explores the evolving balance between their traditional pro-integrationist disposition and a more pragmatic pursuit of national business interests, especially with regards to the energy sector. He concludes that in recent years commercial interests have tended to push the Benelux states to favour bilateral deals over EU co-ordinated actions and thus their credibility as impartial, pro-European actors in the development of EU policy towards Russia has been weakened. Casier is not the only author to deal with member states that share many characteristics but which operate quite different relations with Russia. Indeed, in their chapter, Tobias Etzold and Hiski Haukkala go so far as to challenge the notion of any substantial Nordic commonality concerning Russia. Instead, they argue that for various historical, geopolitical and economic reasons, Denmark, Finland and Sweden have all developed and had rather different relations with Russia. That said, recent years have witnessed an increasing convergence between the Russia policies of the three countries but it is too early to suggest that a Nordic EU caucus concerning Russia would be in the making in the North.

The Russia relations of the three Baltic States Estonia, Latvia and Lithuania are analyzed by Ainius Lašas and David Galbreath. According to them, the key issue in the Baltics' relations with Russia is the negative historical experiences and the mutual lack of trust between the three and Russia that it gives rise to. This lack of trust is then reflected in more concrete realms of

10 *Maxine David, Jackie Gower, Hiski Haukkala*

co-operation, such as trade and energy that end up easily being securitized. The Czech Republic, Hungary and Slovakia are also new member states for whom the communist-era legacy continues to cast a shadow on contemporary relations with Russia. However, Martin Dangerfield argues that the picture is not entirely negative and particularly in the economic and energy spheres there are increasingly important and constructive relationships at both the private and state levels. He explores the differences, as well as similarities, in attitudes towards Russia in the three countries and why there has been little formal co-ordination within the Visegrad framework on policy towards Russia at the EU level.

Bulgaria's relations with Russia are rooted in a long history, close proximity and total energy dependence. However, in her chapter, Diana Bozhilova shows how relations have been upset by Bulgaria's perceptions of where its economic and security interests lie after 1991, perceptions which took it into an EU and NATO orientation, at the expense of Russia. At the same time, Bulgaria has continued to seek close co-operation with Russia in areas consonant with EU interests: energy and conflict resolution. Failures identified here reflect less, Bozhilova argues, on Bulgaria's objectives than on its capacity to achieve those objectives, either within the EU or with Russia, not least because it is not viewed as a sufficiently weighty political player. Like Bulgaria, Romania is linked to Russia through history, albeit a far more antagonistic and conflictual one. Still, as Mircea Micu demonstrates, their close proximity presents a clear imperative to co-operate on security matters, particularly in relation to frozen conflicts in the region, and also in relation to energy. To a large extent, Romanian antipathy to Russia has been overcome both by the need to co-operate and the realization that it was failing to upload its concerns to the EU successfully because of a perception that it was not a constructive player. Micu considers the reasons for Romania's preference for conducting relations with Russia through relevant multilateral fora, and argues this is especially so where they might result in losses for Russia.

Situated in a part of Europe which would not necessarily warrant the development of strong contemporary relations with Russia, are Austria and Slovenia. Paul Luif and Martin Malek reveal an interesting multifaceted Austrian relationship in which political elites pursue a closer relationship with Russia than is publicly acknowledged. A familiar story unfolds in which energy is a pivot around which interactions between the two states turn, with serious consequences for the EU's energy policy, as Austria is revealed as a significant hub for what many judge to be two competing rather than complementary mooted projects: the EU-backed Nabucco and the Russia-backed South Stream projects. The relationship is about more than energy, however, with Luif and Malek showing the effects of the Chechen Wars on Austria and detailing some of the activities of the Russian secret services in this small but central European state. Slovenia is one of the smallest of the new member states and its foreign policy is primarily focused on its immediate neighbourhood, especially the western Balkans. But as Jackie Gower shows, it has in

Introduction   11

recent years developed quite an extensive and positive relationship with Russia, particularly with regard to trade and energy but also with an important cultural dimension. With the prospect of Croatia's accession to the EU in July 2013 and other candidate states in the region, she considers whether we are likely to see a distinctive Western Balkans perspective on EU–Russia policy.

Consideration of the member states' relations with Russia ends with two chapters examining the relationships of the three southern Mediterranean states, all geographically distant from Russia but each with surprisingly active bilateral relations with Russia. Arsalan Alshinawi discusses the relationship between Malta and Russia. Interestingly, despite its small size, Malta has been active in its relations with Russia and this activism has been reciprocated by the Russian side. For Malta, the key Russia-related interest seems to be economic and their political dialogue hardly goes beyond regional issues. In his chapter, George Christou debates the notion that Cyprus and Greece are Russian Trojan horses in the EU context. He argues that the certain commonality between Cypriot and Greek and Russian stances is based less on the former countries' willingness to placate Russian interests for its own sake and more on an actual correspondence of certain key interests between the three. Overall, according to Christou, both Cyprus and Greece are on their way towards increased Europeanization in their foreign policies.

In the Conclusion, we bring the individual country analyses together. On the one hand we consider what general conclusions can be drawn from a host of 'national perspectives' on Russia. On the other hand we will tease out the wider ramifications of bilateral relations on the making of common policies on the EU level with a view even to arriving at some policy-relevant conclusions concerning how to take the EU's policy on Russia forward in the future.

References

Ashton, C. (2010) 'Joint Debate on Foreign and Security Policy'. European Parliament, Strasbourg, 10 March 2010, available at http://europa.eu/rapid/pressReleasesAction. do?reference=SPEECH/10/82& format=HTML&aged=0&language=EN&guiLangu age=en (accessed 14 June 2012).

Cameron, F. (2012) *An Introduction to European Foreign Policy.* 2nd edn. London and New York: Routledge.

Donaldson, Robert H. and Nogee, Joseph L. (2002) *The Foreign Policy of Russia. Changing Systems, Enduring Interests.* 2nd edn. Armonk, NY: M. E. Sharpe.

Exadaktylos, T. and Radaelli, C. M. (eds) (2012) *Research Methods in European Studies: Research Design in Europeanization.* Basingstoke: Palgrave Macmillan.

Ginsberg, R. H. (2001) *The European Union in International Politics: Baptism by Fire.* Lanham, MD: Rowman & Littlefield Publishers.

Haukkala, H. (2010) *The EU–Russia Strategic Partnership: The Limits of Post-Sovereignty in International Relations.* London and New York: Routledge.

Hill, Christopher (ed.) (1996) *The Actors in Europe's Foreign Policy.* London and New York: Routledge.

12   Maxine David, Jackie Gower, Hiski Haukkala

Hill, Christopher (2003) *The Changing Politics of Foreign Policy*. Basingstoke: Palgrave Macmillan.

Hopf, Ted (2005) 'Identity, Legitimacy, and the Use of Military Force: Russia's Great Power Identities and Military Intervention in Abkhazia', *Review of International Studies*, 31: 225–43.

Johansen, Robert, C. (1980) *The National Interest and the Human Interest. An Analysis of US Foreign Policy*. Princeton, NJ: Princeton University Press.

Keukeleire, S. and MacNaughtan, J. (2008) *The Foreign Policy of the European Union*. Basingstoke and New York: Palgrave Macmillan.

Larsen, Henrik (1997) *Foreign Policy and Discourse Analysis. France, Britain and Europe*. London and LSE: Routledge.

Leonard, M. and Popescu, N. (2007) *A Power Audit of EU-Russia Relations*. Policy Paper, London: European Council on Foreign Relations, available at http://ecfr.3cdn.net/1ef82b3f011e075853_0fm6bphgw.pdf (accessed 23 June 2012).

Light, M. (2008) 'Keynote article: Russia and the EU: strategic partners or strategic rivals?', in U. Sedelmeier and A. R.Young (eds) *The JCMS Annual Review of the European Union in 2007*. Oxford: Wiley-Blackwell, 7–27.

Mandelson, P. (2007) 'The EU and Russia: Our Joint Political Challenge'. 20 April Speech, Bologna, available at http://trade.ec.europa.eu/doclib/docs/2007/april/tradoc_134524.pdf (accessed 4 July 2012).

Manners, I. and Whitman, R. (eds) (2000) *The Foreign Policies of European Union Member States*. Manchester: Manchester University Press.

Missiroli, A. (2010) 'The new EU "foreign policy" system after Lisbon: A work in progress', *European Foreign Affairs Review*, 15: 427–52.

Modelski, George (1962) *A theory of foreign policy*. London: Pall Mall.

Northedge, F. S. (1968) 'The Nature of Foreign Policy', in F. S. Northedge (ed.) *The Foreign Policies of the Powers*. London: Faber and Faber, 9–39.

Raik, K. (2007) 'A Europe divided by Russia? The new eastern member states and the EU's policy towards the East', in J. Gower and G. Timmins (eds) *Russia and Europe in the Twentieth Century: an Uneasy Partnership*. London: Anthem Press.

Schmidt-Felzmann, A. (2008) 'All for one? EU member states and the Union's common policy towards the Russian Federation', *Journal of Contemporary European Studies*, 16: 169–87.

Smith, Karen E. (2008) *European Union Foreign Policy in a Changing World*. 2nd edn. Cambridge: Polity Press.

Vaïsse, J. and Kundnani, H. (2012) *European Foreign Policy Scorecard 2012*. European Council on Foreign Relations, available at www.ecfr.eu/page/-/ECFR_SCORECA RD_2012_WEB.pdf (accessed 14 June 2012).

Wong, R. and Hill, C. (eds) (2011) *National and European Foreign Policies: towards Europeanization*. London and New York: Routledge.

2 Germany

Susan Stewart

Germany is arguably the EU member state with the most developed relationship with Russia. This is due to a complex mixture of historical, geographical, cultural, political and economic factors, not least among them the division of Germany into two states during the Cold War. Since unified Germany is also a major economic and political powerhouse within the EU, its potential to project its ideas and interests regarding Russia onto the European stage is significant. Germany is often reproached for being too tolerant of Russian flaws and too inclined to allow Russian interests to influence its agenda, as well as for pursuing specifically national interests which hinder the emergence of an effective EU line towards the Russian Federation.

In the following I focus on developments in German–Russian relations over the last 25 years, with a particular emphasis on the past decade. However, the analysis is prefaced by a section on the Cold War relationship, since several aspects of it are crucial for understanding Germany's contemporary Russia policy. I then utilize the conclusions from this analysis to embed Germany's relationship with Russia in the EU context. The overall conclusion is a nuanced one, which reveals differences both between the Schröder and the Merkel governments and between the economic and energy spheres on the one hand and the realms of security and rule of law on the other. These differences indicate that Germany tends to focus on national interests in the economic and energy fields, whereas in other areas the broader EU context is more likely to be taken into account.

West German–Soviet relations during the Cold War

The development of relations between West Germany and the Soviet Union is somewhat paradoxical. On the one hand, the Federal Republic of Germany (FRG) was poised to be a key opponent of Soviet power since it opted for clear integration into Western institutions, was dependent on Western powers (and the USA in particular) for its reconstruction efforts and was on the absolute frontline of the confrontation between the two blocs, having lost part of German territory to the Soviet-controlled Eastern bloc. On the other hand, exactly this frontline status placed West Germany in a situation in which regular communication with the Soviet authorities was necessary. This was particularly true with regard to West Berlin, which, although divided up among three of the four victorious powers (the USA, Great Britain, France), was an official part of West Germany. The territorial isolation of Berlin from the remainder of the FRG and its division following the construction of the Berlin Wall in 1961 meant that frequent negotiations with the Soviets were required to ensure the security and mobility of West Berlin's inhabitants. This recurring interaction between the West Germans and the Soviets inclined the German side to focus on building a working relationship with their inter-locutors, which discouraged a strong emphasis on a hard-line Cold War stance and fostered pragmatic co-operation on specific issues.

This 'working relationship' contributed to the evolution of a more general West German position that a serious attempt at a co-operative framework could result in more satisfactory outcomes for the West German side than the con-frontational stance pursued by Christian Democratic governments between 1949 and 1969. Thus, Ostpolitik was born under the chancellorship of Willy Brandt (1969–74). While not uncontroversial within the West German elite, Ostpolitik was firmly embedded within West Germany's broader policy of deepening integration in Western institutions, rather than challenging this policy. It drew on a phrase coined by Egon Bahr in 1963: 'Change through rapprochement' ('Wandel durch Annäherung'). The policy led to the signing of a treaty with the USSR in 1970, as well as one with Poland later that same year. In 1972 the FRG actually entered into a Basic Treaty with the German Democratic Republic (GDR), which implied the recognition of the GDR as a separate state and paved the way to its representation in the United Nations. Although extraordinarily controversial in the German parliament, the treaty was ratified in May 1973. The perception that Ostpolitik contributed to the eventual collapse of the Soviet bloc by creating openings for new ideas and types of interaction has significantly influenced foreign policy thinking in unified Germany with regard to German–Russian relations.

The second area which continues to have implications for the German approach to Russia is the energy field. Beginning in the 1970s the Soviet Union served as a key exporter of natural gas to the FRG. After the USSR collapsed, the Russian Federation took over the obligations of the Soviet side. West German political and business leaders experienced the Soviet Union as a reliable partner in the energy realm, while the Soviets were dependent on the hard currency brought in by their gas and oil exports. This co-operation set the stage not only for continued interaction following the collapse of the USSR, but also for the expansion of contacts and projects into other areas (e.g. energy efficiency, renewable energy sources) with Russian partners.

Thus, co-operation within the framework of Ostpolitik and in the energy sphere formed the basis for some elements of German policy towards Russia after reunification. However, during the original Ostpolitik the Cold War continued to rage despite certain forms of pragmatic co-operation. West German Chancellor Helmut Schmidt encouraged the stationing of mid-range nuclear missiles by NATO on West German territory to counter Soviet dominance in the nuclear realm. This led to the NATO *Doppelbeschluss* of 1979, which, after failed negotiations with the Soviets, resulted in the missiles being stationed in Germany in 1982, at which point Helmut Kohl (CDU) had taken over the chancellorship. Thus Kohl, who was to preside over German reunification and a rapprochement with the USSR, originally followed in the traditions of the Cold War. It was the domestic changes in the Soviet Union, initiated by Communist Party Secretary Mikhail Gorbachev starting in the mid-1980s that, coupled as they were with a radically different approach to Soviet foreign policy, convinced Kohl (and other key leaders) to change tack in their relations with the USSR.

One of the crucial implications of the new Soviet approach was a reduction in control over the satellite states of Eastern Europe. The Soviets had enormous domestic problems in the economic and social spheres and were too involved in managing their own *perestroika* (restructuring) to impose repressive measures on the satellites. Rather, the leaders of the Eastern European countries were encouraged to follow the Soviet line and begin their own reforms. While many of them eagerly responded to this offer, Erich Honecker and the political leadership of the GDR viewed potential reforms as a threat to their power and resisted any significant change.

For the West Germans the altered Soviet stance represented a chance to pursue their main foreign policy goal of German reunification. Certainly reunification was made possible in particular by domestic protest in the GDR, which revealed that the majority of the population did not support the Honecker regime. Equally important, however, was the decision taken by the USSR leadership not to deploy the Soviet troops stationed on East German soil against the protesters. In the end, Soviet approval for reunification was necessary. It was achieved – on the terms desired by West Germany – through a series of negotiations between Kohl and Gorbachev and their foreign ministers, Hans-Dietrich Genscher and Eduard Shevardnadze. A reunified Germany within NATO was a result which was not at all popular with the Soviet elite and was therefore a serious risk for Gorbachev. The gratitude felt by Kohl and others in the German foreign policy elite for Gorbachev's support played an important role in the formation of German policy towards the Russian Federation under its first president, Boris Yeltsin. This gratitude, as well as a sense of responsibility towards Russia due to the destruction wrought by German forces in the Soviet Union during the Second World War, still influences the attitudes of Germany policymakers to a certain extent today (Chivvis and Rid 2009: 114–16).

Relations between reunified Germany and the Russian Federation

In the end, reunification meant the integration of the GDR into the West German political, economic and security systems. The fall of the Soviet Union led to the emergence of a consensus within the EU to begin accession processes with

16 *Susan Stewart*

the three Baltic states and the Visegrad countries. Russia took a back seat to these developments, especially since the German elite (along with many others) assumed Russia would gradually become integrated into the Western order. Nonetheless, certain issues were crucial for Germany in its emerging relationship with the Russian Federation. First and foremost was the evacuation of Soviet troops from the territory of the former GDR, which was essential for the establishment of an independent unified Germany. For the evacuation process, and for many other aspects of the reform processes in the USSR and later in the Russian Federation, the German government was willing to contribute enormous amounts of financial assistance.[1] The evacuation was completed by 1994, although the broader transition ran into difficulties for many reasons.[2] By the mid-1990s the political transition to democracy had been largely derailed. Difficulties with the economic transition were compounded by the East Asian economic crisis, which spilled over into Russia and was exacerbated by the way certain reforms had been carried out (Stiglitz 2003). However, none of these problems prevented the emergence of a warm relationship between Kohl and Yeltsin, which was based more on the arrangements made regarding the German situation than on the developments in Russia itself.[3]

German policy towards Russia under Gerhard Schröder

The beginning of Schröder's chancellorship in 1998 coincided with a period of economic turmoil for Russia. Initially the trajectory on which Schröder eventually embarked seemed highly unlikely. Schröder was suspicious of the close friendship Kohl had developed with Yeltsin, and Russia did not appear poised to become an important economic partner (Stent 2010: 159–60). However, by the end of 1999 Boris Yeltsin no longer saw himself in a position to run the country and passed the reins of power to a former KGB colonel, Vladimir Putin. Thus, Schröder's developing relationship with Russia, which was unfamiliar territory for him, became intimately connected with Putin and his emerging leadership style. In the first years of Putin's rule it appeared that he was determined to carry out a series of urgently needed reforms in Russia, which made a close relationship with him seem advantageous for Germany. In addition, the German opposition to the US-supported war with Iraq ensured a certain degree of commonality between Russia and Germany (as well as France) on the foreign policy front. Putin's knowledge of German (due in part to his experience working for the KGB in Dresden) and his extremely well-received speech on German–Russian relations in the Bundestag in September 2001 helped to bolster his reputation in Germany. Not only did he give the speech in fluent German, but his expressed solidarity with the USA in the wake of the 9/11 terrorist attacks and his vision of Russia as part of a European system of values garnered him the enthusiastic support of many members of the Bundestag.

Although after the conclusion of Schröder's period in office his approach towards Russia appeared morally dubious, in the early years of his chancellorship

Germany 17

the advantages of intensifying relations with the Russian Federation seemed clear. He could build on the positive developments which took place under Kohl and Yeltsin, and expand the relationship to include a significant economic component, which was only logical if one assumed that Russia was on its way to becoming a large market economy with attractive export opportunities for German businesses. This also tallied with Schröder's previous position as Prime Minister of Lower Saxony, where Volkswagen has its headquarters.[4] Schröder's sensitivity to the needs of large enterprises combined with Russian interest in developing the country's automobile industry made a good match. Thus, Schröder and Putin decided to create a 'strategic economic partnership' between Russia and Germany (Meier 2004: 5). In 2003 Putin referred to economic issues as the cornerstone of the bilateral relationship (Meier 2004: 17).

Indeed, the economic aspect of German–Russian relations boomed, especially from the German perspective. Trade in goods increased 19 per cent between 2000 and 2003, rising from €21.3 billion to €25.5 billion.[5] German exports rose almost 75 per cent in this time period, whereas imports from Russia decreased. As is still the case today, in the early 2000s the bulk of Russian exports to Germany consisted of energy sources and raw materials, especially oil and natural gas. This category made up 73 per cent of Russian exports in 2003. The German side developed much more dynamically, with large increases in the amount of machines, electrotechnology and vehicles during the three years in question (Meier 2004: 7). These developments were strongly supported by the German and Russian governments. The so-called Hermes guarantees given by the German government encouraged investors to enter the Russian market by reducing their risk on capital investments. As the Russian Federation recovered from the 1998 economic crisis and became more solvent and capable of repaying its debt in a timely fashion, Germany raised and then abolished the limit on the amount of these guarantees (Meier 2004: 10). In addition, programmes of technical assistance and advice were organized in several Russian regions, and 'projects aimed at advancing economic co-operation between Russian and German enterprises had priority' (Meier 2004:13). This was complemented by a programme to provide training and continuing education opportunities for both established Russian business leaders and promising young management personnel. Finally, a large portion of the Soviet debt owed to the former GDR for trade in goods was forgiven by the German government in 2002 in exchange for Putin's assistance in resolving an outstanding issue concerning a Hermes investment guarantee (Meier 2004: 14). Thus, under Schröder the German–Russian economic relationship flourished on many fronts and was ensured the support of the federal government.

However, German–Russian relations in this phase were by no means limited to the business sphere. Arguably the most important additional component was the 'Petersburger Dialog', a forum intended to serve as an opportunity for discussions and networking among civil society actors from both Germany and Russia. It was called into being by Putin and Schröder in

18 *Susan Stewart*

2000, and the first session was held in 2001. The dialogue was located at a very high level in the political hierarchy from the very beginning. Having the blessing of the German Federal Chancellor and the Russian President, it was originally chaired by Mikhail Gorbachev on the Russian side and Peter Boenisch, previously spokesman for Kohl's government, on the German one. In addition, it took place at the same time and location as the German–Russian governmental consultations, a practice which has continued to this day. It has also become a tradition that the Chancellor and the President participate in the final session of the dialogue and hear its conclusions. This arrangement raised questions from the very beginning about the ability of such a format to reflect the needs of civil society and to provide a genuine opportunity for frank dialogue. Concerns were raised in particular about the dialogue being orientated towards high politics and the Russian side sending representatives closer to state structures than to civil society (Meier 2003). In fact, these issues have turned out to be persistent and remain problematic to this day (see below). In this way the Petersburg Dialogue is symptomatic of a larger problem in the German–Russian relationship. As Andrei Zagorsky has pointed out, the interactions in the Putin–Schröder period had an overtly top-down character and were overly dependent on the friendship between the two heads of state (Zagorsky 2005). These tendencies helped pave the way for Schröder's later move to Nord Stream and his strong reliance on individuals rather than institutions, which eventually inclined him to utilize his relationship with Putin for personal gain.

Other aspects of the relationship also played a role under Schröder and Putin. Hans-Joachim Spanger and Andrei Zagorsky point to the fact that 'Chancellor Schröder never tired of emphasizing that Germany and Russia were in accord on all important international issues' (Spanger and Zagorsky 2012: 231). Indeed, the Iraq war initiated by the USA and opposed by certain European states, including Germany and Russia, appeared to indicate compatibility regarding the international agenda. Not only were they united in their opposition to the war, but they, together with French President Jacques Chirac, called for a UN-led post-war order in Iraq.[6] This foreign policy line implied agreement on a critical stance towards the USA in general as well. Indeed, Schröder's tenure is seen as being a period during which German–US relations seriously deteriorated. This coincides to some extent with an increasing scepticism in Russia about the role of the USA and US–Russian relations, despite a temporary improvement following the 11 September terrorist attacks in the USA in 2001. However, seen in retrospect, the opposition to the Iraq war appears as more of an isolated case of agreement rather than the beginning of a pattern.

Difficult issues did arise during Schröder's chancellorship with regard to Russia, such as the Russian approach to separatism in Chechnya, which included massive human rights violations.[7] Schröder was reluctant to fault Russia on any account, and was heavily criticized for failing to take Russia to task on its human rights record, among other things. The criticism came not

Germany 19

only from the German opposition, but also from within Schröder's own party.[8] Thus, his characterization of Putin as a 'flawless democrat' is only one symptom of a general willingness to overlook disturbing developments within Russia and to focus solely on the positive aspects of the bilateral relationship. During his tenure official German policy towards Russia diverged more and more clearly from public opinion in Germany towards the Russian Federation (Zagorsky 2005: 8; Kaul *et al.* 2005: 191). In Russia as well Schröder's policy was interpreted by forces in opposition to the regime to mean 'that Germany has put its democratic values on the back burner and is instead pursuing a cynical 'realpolitik' consisting of unconditional support for Putin and lobbying in the interests of German business in Russia' (Zagorsky 2005: 8–9). Thus, some of those very members of civil society Schröder had once hoped to reach through the Petersburg Dialogue had become completely disillusioned with his approach. This disillusionment made his decision to accept the position of head of the Nord Stream consortium (at the nomination of Gazprom) only a few days after leaving his position as Chancellor even less palatable than it might otherwise have been. The fact that Schröder had been instrumental in initiating the Nord Stream project, and had even pushed through €1 billion in German governmental guarantees to cover the Russian contribution, made his accession to the new position morally highly suspect.

The Nord Stream (or Baltic Sea) pipeline has become associated with German-Russian relations like no other project in the past two decades. Similar to the business deals in other sectors, the project seemed quite sensible at its initiation. It fitted in with the German strategy in the energy sector, which foresaw a growing role for natural gas in the German energy mix, since the coalition of the SPD and the Greens opted for a gradual exit from nuclear energy as well as a significant reduction in the use of coal. As renewable energy sources were expected to develop only slowly, gas occupied a key place in the energy scenario which the government under Schröder accepted as the basis for its energy-related decisions. Since relations with Russia were good, nothing seemed more logical than to engage in a co-operative project which would address Germany's growing gas needs while further enhancing the relationship with the Russian side, thereby paving the way for yet more lucrative economic projects.[9] The importance of the energy sphere within the German–Russian relationship was indicated by the 'Declaration of Expansion of Business Contacts' in the energy realm concluded between the two countries in August 2004.

However, the co-operation created serious problems for Germany within the EU. It was frequently seen as evidence of a 'Russia first' policy which placed Germany's narrow national interests above broader European concerns in the energy sphere. Even the participation of the Netherlands (with a 5 per cent stake) and the designation of the project as part of the Trans-European Energy Network, implying its significance for energy security and the internal EU market, did not convince Germany's critics of the European nature of the project. The Poles in particular were disturbed by the planned pipeline, since

20 Susan Stewart

it would allow Russia to cut off gas to the former Eastern European satellite states while keeping it flowing to Western Europe. (For more discussion of Poland's reaction, see Cichocki in this volume.) Thus, the pipeline project was seen as evidence of Germany's failure to demonstrate solidarity with EU member states to the east.[10] The same line of argument held for Belarus and Ukraine, the importance of which as transit countries would be reduced due to Nord Stream, leaving them more vulnerable to Russian pressure.

During the Schröder period, Russia policy was largely concentrated in the Chancellor's office. The Foreign Ministry did not play a very large role. On the whole there was a division of labour between Schröder and Foreign Minister Joschka Fischer, who focused primarily on other issues, such as the situation in the Balkans (Kempe 2006: 6). Fischer was, however, active in the security realm, which included questions relevant to the relationship with Russia, such as NATO–Russia co-operation. The fact that Fischer and Schröder pursued different (if overlapping) dossiers in the foreign policy sphere helped to mitigate the impact of their various disagreements. (For example, the two disagreed vehemently with regard to the question of German support for the Iraq war.) Thus, potential criticism on Russia policy within Schröder's own ranks was dampened by the accepted division of labour between the Chancellor's office and the Foreign Ministry. Nonetheless, the position of 'Co-ordinator for German-Russian Intersocietal Co-operation' was created in 2003 and attached to the Foreign Ministry. Gernot Erler (SPD) was the first person appointed to the post, which was intended to reflect the importance the German government imparted to the civil society level in the German–Russian relationship, thereby complementing the Petersburg Dialogue.

In general the Schröder period has been seen as the beginning of a 'normalization' of German policy within the EU context, implying that Germany views European interests as subordinate to national interests, and that multilateralism becomes less instinctive (Kundnani 2010; Grant 2005; Bulmer and Paterson 2010). There are examples of Schröder acting in broader EU interests, for example by using his influence with Putin to convince him to agree to a third round of the Ukrainian elections during the 'Orange Revolution' (Grant 2005: 3). However, Nord Stream was understandably seen by several EU member states as contravening their interests in the energy sphere. The Nord Stream project came to be perceived as the hallmark of the German–Russian relationship during the Schröder period, in particular due to Schröder's assumption of the chairmanship of the Nord Stream consortium following his departure from politics. The attitudes towards Nord Stream in the new EU member states to the east coincided with their overall perception that Schröder's close relationship with Putin did not bode well for these states, and that the German government was ready to sacrifice their interests for its own (Grant 2005: 3; Kempe 2006: 12–13). Indeed, German diplomats tended to see energy policy as national policy rather than as embedded in a larger EU context (Bastian 2006: 183). In the economic realm more broadly Schröder acted first and foremost in the interest of German businesses, lending them governmental support for their expansion into the Russian market. While it is possible to see this as some sort of overarching EU interest, since if the German economy continues to flourish this is likely to benefit the EU as well, it nonetheless falls more directly in the sphere of specific German interests. Thus, the overall conclusion on the Schröder phase of German–Russian relations must be that relations were highly personalized, lacked transparency, were concentrated at the top of the political and economic hierarchy, and focused primarily on benefits for Germany, rather than for the EU as a whole.

Germany's Russia policy under Angela Merkel

Significant expectations for change in Germany's Russia policy were connected with the shift from Gerhard Schröder to Angela Merkel in 2005. Merkel's experiences in the former GDR, as well as the fact that she had joined in the CDU's criticism of Schröder's Russia policy, and her overall support for transatlantic relations, inclined many observers to posit that changes in that policy were likely. On the other hand, the appointment of Frank-Walter Steinmeier as Foreign Minister suggested continuity with regard to Russia. Steinmeier had worked directly with Schröder since 1993, including as his Chief of Office in the Federal Chancellery, and was known to share his general approach towards the Russian Federation.

Indeed, continuity ended up prevailing. Merkel and Putin retained a certain distance in their interactions, and Merkel openly brought up some human rights issues and made a point of meeting with Russian opposition figures, but on the level of substance very little changed. In particular, the German government continued to back the Nord Stream project, which was closely associated with Schröder. Business interest in Russia remained strong, and important deals between large German and Russian enterprises were concluded. The practice of significant economic delegations accompanying the chancellor to the annual intergovernmental consultations was maintained. So was the Petersburg Dialogue, although it has been subjected to increasing criticism for being too close to politics and failing in its original mission to be a forum for open discussion at the civil society level (Pörzgen 2010). In 2011 there were some indications that certain changes in the forum might be forthcoming. Merkel in particular hinted at the need to include some younger faces among the organizers. However, the Russian side appeared essentially satisfied with the current arrangement.

What did change in the new government were the relative roles of the Chancellor's office and the Foreign Ministry in Russia policy. Steinmeier played a much more significant part than Fischer had, although Merkel was also active on the Russia front. Thus, there was a shift from a division to a sharing of labour with regard to Russia policy. In 2006 Steinmeier introduced the idea of 'Annäherung durch Verflechtung' ('rapprochement through linkage'), which consciously connected to Willy Brandt's Ostpolitik and the idea of 'Wandel durch Annäherung' ('change through rapprochement'). This made

22 *Susan Stewart*

clear that an intensification of engagement with Russia was desired, both in the economic sphere and more broadly. In the international arena Germany continued its support for including Russia in important organizations. After having pushed for Russia to enter the Group of Seven (G7), turning it into the G8, the Germans further opted to postpone their G8 chairmanship scheduled for 2006 to allow Russia to chair the group, thereby helping to cement Russia's place in international affairs.[11]

In an interview with the *Frankfurter Allgemeine Zeitung* in December 2007, Steinmeier spoke very clearly about his position towards Russia, making three key points. First, Russia is a large neighbour with which Germany needs to develop good relations independent of the Russian form of government. Second, Russia is in a transition phase, the outcome of which is not yet clear. Third, Putin has made a major contribution to Russian stability.[12] These statements reveal much about the tenets of Germany's Russia policy in the past decade. They imply that one should value stability highly and appreciate those who provide it. Also, if the outcome of a transition is still unclear, it is possible to assume the best and to develop offers which make the 'best-case scenario' more probable. This assumption underlies both the idea of 'rapprochement through linkage' and the 'modernization partnership' introduced later (see below).

In the first half of 2007 Germany held the EU Council Presidency. The original German intention was to incorporate a significant focus on the post-Soviet space. This was to include upgrading the European Neighbourhood Policy (ENP), launching an EU Central Asia strategy, and pursuing a strategic partnership with Russia. In fact, concrete results were achieved only regarding Central Asia, on which a strategic document was agreed, even if implementation has been patchy (Schmitz 2010). The EU–Russia summit in Samara in May 2007 was difficult, given a series of problems connected with negotiating the successor to the Partnership and Cooperation Agreement (PCA) between the EU and Russia. However, the general consensus was that the German presidency, along with Brussels, demonstrated clear solidarity with the concerns of several new EU member states (Poland, Lithuania and Estonia) regarding their relations with Russia (see the chapters by Cichocki and Lašas and Galbreath in this volume). This earned Germany some frustration from the Russian side, with Putin in particular being clearly annoyed, but scored it points within the EU for standing up for the interests of other member states.[13] In general Germany has invested significant time and energy into developing a good relationship with Poland, including a regular German–Polish dialogue in various formats on Russia and the eastern neighbourhood, which have more recently been complemented by several German–Polish–Russian formats. Improvements in Polish–Russian relations in the past several years have been one factor in allowing for a certain amount of convergence between German and Polish positions on Russia (see Cichocki in this volume).[14] Indeed, the extent of this convergence was revealed when the German Foreign Minister Guido Westerwelle and his Polish counterpart

Radosław Sikorski sent a joint letter to High Representative Catherine Ashton in November 2011, accompanied by a 'non-paper' drafted by the policy planning units of the Polish and German foreign ministries. The letter encouraged the formation of a 'joint approach on the basis of shared interests and objectives vis-à-vis Russia' within the EU, while the non-paper was entitled 'Food for thought on the EU–Russia strategic relationship'.[15] It was discussed by the EU foreign ministers in December 2011 and found to reflect current EU thinking on the Russia dossier.

2008 was a key year for German–Russian relations for several reasons. First, in March Dmitry Medvedev was elected President of the Russian Federation. Significant hopes were attached to this development on the German side, as many German diplomats and politicians believed that improvements in rule-of-law issues and media freedom might be forthcoming in Russia based on Medvedev's pre-election rhetoric. As a result of Medvedev's emphasis on the need for 'modernization' in Russia, the German government suggested launching a 'modernization partnership' between the two countries, which Steinmeier officially announced in a speech at the state university in Ekaterinburg in May 2008. From the German perspective, this new format was to serve as an umbrella for a broad set of co-operative projects for example in the spheres of rule-of-law, efficient administration and health care. Essentially, this was a continuation of 'rapprochement through linkage' in a guise more closely tailored to Medvedev's rhetoric and Russian aims as Germany perceived them.

Second, the NATO summit in Bucharest in April 2008 played an important role in determining how Germany's relations with Russia were perceived both within and outside the alliance. At the summit Germany (and France) opposed granting a Membership Action Plan (MAP) to Georgia and Ukraine, over the strong objections of the USA, which was eager to see those countries move closer to NATO. The reason given by the German side was that the two countries were not ready for a MAP (Georgia due to its territorial issues and Ukraine because of significant popular opposition to NATO), but it seemed clear that the Germans were also seriously reluctant to antagonize Russia, which had made no secret of its clear opposition to any moves which advanced NATO expansion eastward. Although outside the EU context, the perceptions of many countries regarding Germany's veto on the MAP question carried over into the framework of EU–Russia relations and contributed to a sense of a 'Russia first' element in German policy towards the east.

Third, the brief war between Georgia and Russia in August 2008 was clearly relevant for German–Russian relations, as well as for Germany's reputation on Russia policy within the EU. In the run-up to the war, Steinmeier had taken a suggested plan regarding Abkhazia to Moscow, Tbilisi and Sukhumi in the hopes of beginning a new process of conflict resolution, but it was already too late for such an initiative. After the war, the Germans supported the mediation efforts of the French EU presidency and in particular pushed for a fact-finding endeavour to clarify the trajectory of the war itself and the larger context. The Germans were instrumental in ensuring the creation of the Tagliavini Commission, which was responsible for a thorough investigation of both the war and its background and eventually published an extended report on the case.[16] While Germany did not oppose the suspension of the NATO–Russia Council (NRC) in response to Russia's actions in Georgia, German diplomats later lamented the fact that the NRC was unable to provide a forum for dialogue in the critical days immediately after the outbreak of the war. In general, Germany was interested in returning to 'business as usual' soon after the war, both on the EU and on the national level. As time went on, disillusionment with the Georgians, and Saakashvili in particular, seemed to be greater than with Russian behaviour. However, Merkel did clearly describe the Russian reaction to the Georgian attack on Tskhinvali as 'disproportionate' and strongly condemned the Russian recognition of Abkhazian and South Ossetian independence (Pressekonferenz 2008). German–Russian governmental consultations in the autumn of 2008 took place largely as usual, as did the Petersburg Dialogue.

In September 2009, the 'grand coalition' between the CDU/CSU and the SPD was replaced by a coalition between the CDU/CSU and the FDP (the German liberal party or Free Democrats). Since this shift, very little has occurred in the way of policy towards Russia or the eastern neighbourhood in general. There are several reasons for this. First, German foreign policy was weakened as a result of the new coalition. The FDP took over the Foreign Ministry and its General Secretary at the time, Guido Westerwelle, replaced Steinmeier as Foreign Minister. Due to his lack of experience in foreign policy and his initial decision to remain deeply involved in other aspects of the FDP agenda, Westerwelle has come across as weak and inconsistent. Second, issues such as Afghanistan and later Libya (and the situation in the Middle East and North Africa on the whole) have occupied the attention of the foreign policy establishment, while Russia (except with regard to Syria) and the eastern neighbourhood have taken a back seat. Early statements by politicians such as Michael Link, FDP spokesperson for European policy and since January 2012 Minister of State in the German Foreign Ministry, that there would be a stronger emphasis on neighbourhood states such as Ukraine to counter the dominance of Russia in Germany's Ostpolitik have not been followed up by a concrete programme of action. Third, developments in Russia itself as well as in other countries of the region (Ukraine in particular but also Belarus) have not offered much hope that a strong foreign policy investment in the area would bring about positive results. The region has not been completely neglected, as Westerwelle has travelled to Ukraine, Moldova and (together with his Polish counterpart Sikorski) Belarus, but there has been no visible development of a coherent policy towards these states, despite the heightened interest in Ukraine due to the case of former Ukrainian Prime Minister Yulia Tymoshenko and the European Football Championship organized by Poland and Ukraine in June–July 2012. This lack of initiatives has

Germany 25

meant that the Nord Stream project has continued to dominate in perceptions of German Russia policy outside Germany, especially since the first gas was pumped into the pipeline in September 2011.[17] Neither the questionable legitimacy of Putin's election to a third term as Russian President in March 2012 nor the growing forms of opposition to the current regime within Russia appear to have triggered a review of Germany's Russia policy.[18]

However, one exception to the above trend is the so-called Meseberg initiative, an idea on which Merkel and Medvedev reached agreement in the Meseberg Castle near Berlin in June 2010. The German proposal foresaw a sequencing of events. First, Russia would demonstrate its willingness to make a constructive contribution to the process of resolving the conflict regarding Transnistria, a breakaway region of Moldova which is dependent on Russia for its security and much of its revenue. Second, Germany would push for the creation of an EU–Russia security dialogue at the level of Catherine Ashton and the 27 EU foreign ministers, who would meet regularly with Russian Foreign Minister Sergei Lavrov to discuss security concerns and find ways to deal with them jointly. Progress regarding Transnistria was to serve as a means of convincing potentially sceptical EU member states that the dialogue could bring tangible results. While Medvedev concurred with this initiative originally, since then the Russian side has distanced itself from the idea of sequencing and called for the creation of the planned dialogue independent of advances on the issue of Transnistria. Thus, the initiative has not been able to move forward in Brussels, where some officials were annoyed at the German decision to pursue such a plan without first conducting more extensive consultations within the EU. However, it has not been completely abandoned and there is some hope within EU circles that the Transnistria issue may be more open to resolution following the replacement of the long-term de facto Transnistrian President Igor Smirnov by Yevgeny Shevchuk in December 2011 and the election of Moldovan President Nicolae Timofti in March 2012.

Angela Merkel has been accused of failing to take a 'European view' of political issues and of focusing on narrow German interests in her foreign and EU policy. However, this is only true to a limited extent with regard to Germany's approach to Russia during her chancellorship. While Merkel did continue with the controversial Nord Stream pipeline project and thereby indicated her intention to preserve key economic and political ties to Russia, she also attempted to mitigate Polish concerns in particular. Even though these concerns were only partially addressed, the intensification of Germany's relationship with Poland on a variety of issues during Merkel's tenure improved Polish–German ties significantly and resulted in less vocal complaints regarding Nord Stream from the Polish side. While Merkel clearly indicated her preference for working with Medvedev rather than Putin, with both she has been willing to raise difficult questions such as human rights violations and concerns about rule-of-law issues within Russia. She also displayed unmistakable solidarity with new EU member states at the EU–Russia summit in 2007. Nonetheless, she has also been quite keen to bolster opportunities for German businesses in Russia, and was willing to downplay the significance of the Russian–Georgian war for the German–Russian relationship.

The desire for a relatively broad modernization partnership expressed by Steinmeier has now been parlayed up to the EU level. In general, however, Germany has not attempted to take the lead on developing an EU policy towards Russia, confining itself to individual initiatives such as Meseberg or to formats such as the German–French–Russian meeting in Deauville in October 2010, in which forum Medvedev announced his willingness to attend the NATO summit in Lisbon later that year. However, the joint letter to Catherine Ashton from Westerwelle and Sikorski and the accompanying non-paper on the EU's relationship with Russia may signify Germany's intention to pursue a more intensive discussion of Russia policy on the EU level by presenting a common front together with Poland. On the whole under Merkel parallel tracks are visible: in the economic and energy realms Germany's approach towards Russia has been guided primarily by German business interests, even when these ran counter to broader EU goals. However, with regard to security, rule of law and other spheres, Germany's Russia policy has tended to be more in line with EU aims and has been able to 'upload' certain ideas to the Brussels level.

Conclusion

Germany is without doubt a major player within the EU in general, but one which has recently been increasingly criticized for putting national interests above larger EU concerns. This debate has especially come to the fore in the context of the ongoing euro zone crisis. However, with regard to Russia policy this criticism is only partially justified. The above exploration of Germany's policy towards Russia under Chancellors Schröder and Merkel indicates a double conclusion. First, there are significant differences between Schröder and Merkel in terms of the degree to which they pursued national interests in their respective approaches to Russia. While under Schröder national interests usually took priority, under Merkel this has been the case to a lesser degree. Second, there have been two tracks in German–Russian relations. In the spheres of energy and the economy, national interests have generally prevailed, while in other realms Germany has kept the broader EU context more firmly in mind. In some areas, such as the Partnership for Modernization, Germany has been able to upload elements of its approach to Russia to the EU level. With regard to security considerations, the record has been mixed. While in the question of granting a MAP to Ukraine and Georgia Germany was inclined to give strong weight to Russian fears, the more recent Meseberg initiative reflects a different approach in which EU concerns about Transnistria are to be addressed before Russia is offered the option of a broader high-level security dialogue with the EU.

Considering its overall weight within the EU and its developed relationship with Russia, Germany is often seen as a potential motor for revitalizing EU–Russia relations. However, the perception of Germany as too inclined to cater to both Russian and its own national interests, fuelled in particular by the Nord Stream project, makes it unlikely that Germany could take on this role alone. The Polish–German rapprochement in recent years, which has included a certain degree of convergence on Russia policy, holds potential for joint efforts at the EU level in the future. A Russia initiative spearheaded by both Poland and Germany would have a significant chance of being palatable to most or even all EU member states. However, preoccupation with the euro zone crisis coupled with Poland's traditional (if currently frustrated) emphasis on Ukraine and Belarus and a growing disillusionment with the Russian regime all make the successful pursuit of such a joint initiative unlikely in the immediate future. Nonetheless, the wave of protests in Russia which has arisen since the Duma elections in December 2011, as well as new forms of opposition emerging in the wake of the presidential elections in March 2012, may give new impetus to the Russia dossier within the EU, in which case Polish–German efforts could play a decisive role. While there is some interest in reviving the Weimar Triangle for inter alia the purpose of co-operation regarding Russia, France has shown a more sporadic interest in Russia, and one limited to certain sectors, than has been the case with Poland or Germany (Barysch 2011).

Germany's strong pursuit of its economic interests in its relationship with Russia will likely remain constant, leaving it vulnerable to criticism within the EU. If, though, as appears increasingly possible, Russia becomes weaker internally due to its failure to modernize on a variety of fronts, it may grow less attractive as an economic partner for Germany. This could bring other aspects of Germany's Russia policy to the fore, ones that are more compatible with broader EU interests. In this scenario the idea of Germany (together with Poland) as a driver of the EU's Russia policy appears probable. In such a case there would also be a clear demand for a new approach to Russia on the Brussels level, as the Partnership for Modernization will cease to be an appropriate instrument if Russian plans to modernize largely fail to materialize (Stewart 2011). A German–Polish initiative could prove especially timely if the ongoing protests in Russia should result in the emergence of new actors who welcome offers of co-operation from the EU and are willing to respond to them in a more substantive fashion than the current Russian leadership has done.

Notes

1 This included more than DM 10 billion in (partly interest-free) loans and a payment of DM 12 billion. See Bastian 2006: 150–53.
2 The internal Russian transition cannot be addressed here, but see Treisman 2011 for a nuanced and well-researched account.
3 For a treatment of other issues in German–Russian relations under Kohl and Yeltsin see Stent 2010: 158–59.
4 Volkswagen was already active in Russia in the late 1990s and became much more so in the 2000s. See e.g. Meier 1999: 20.

28 Susan Stewart

5 This trend has continued, with allowances for the 2008–9 financial and economic crisis, to the present. See Stent 2010: 163.
6 www.pbs.org/newshour/updates/meeting_04-11-03.html (accessed 29 May 2012).
7 www.dw-world.de/dw/article/0,1548335,00.html (accessed 29 May 2012).
8 See e.g. Empörung über Schröders Freundschaftsdienst für Putin, *Spiegel* online, 1 September 2004, www.spiegel.de/politik/ausland/0,1518,316178,00.html (accessed 29 May 2012).
9 Later the amount of gas to be imported was corrected downwards as a result of rising oil (and therefore gas) prices, but this occurred in the scenarios prepared under the government of Angela Merkel.
10 See e.g. www.ag-friedensforschung.de/themen/oel/nordstream3.html (accessed on 29 May 2012).
11 This was part of a larger trend in German policy which aimed at including Russia in relevant international formats. See e.g. Rahr 2007: 138.
12 Im Gespräch: Bundesaußenminister Frank-Walter Steinmeier, *Frankfurter Allgemeine Zeitung*, 17 December 2007: 7.
13 http://euobserver.com/24/24094 (accessed 29 May 2012).
14 On convergence regarding Russia within the EU see Stewart 2012.
15 For the text of the letter and the non-paper see www.msz.gov.pl/files/docs/komunikaty/20111117LIST/joint_letter_sikorski_westerwelle_eu_russia.pdf (accessed 29 May 2012).
16 For a description of the Commission and the text of the report see www.ceiig.ch/ (accessed 29 May 2012).
17 See www.hs.fi/english/article/Russia+is+already+pumping+gas+into+Nord+Stream+pipeline/1135269169862 (accessed 29 May 2012).
18 On recent trends and possible upcoming developments in German–Russian relations see Meister 2012.

References

Barysch, K. (2011) *The EU and Russia: All Smiles and No Action?*. Centre for European Reform, Policy Brief, April 2011, available at www.cer.org.uk/publications/archive/policy-brief/2011/eu-and-russia-all-smiles-and-no-action (accessed 29 May 2012).
Bastian, K. (2006) *Die Europäische Union und Russland: Multilaterale und bilaterale Dimensionen in der europäischen Außenpolitik*. Wiesbaden: VS Verlag für Sozialwissenschaften.
Bulmer, S. and Paterson, W. E. (2010) 'Germany and the European Union: From 'tamed power' to normalized power?', *International Affairs*, 86: 1051–73.
Chivvis, C. S. and Rid, T. (2009) 'The Roots of Germany's Russia Policy', *Survival*, 51: 105–22.
Grant, C. (2005) *German foreign policy: What lessons can be learned from the Schröder years?* London: Centre for European Reform, 2 September 2005, available at www.cer.org.uk/publications/archive/essay/2005/germanys-foreign-policy-what-lessons-can-be-learned-schr%C3%B6der-years (accessed 29 May 2012).
Kaul, M., Kunath, M., Lievl, M. and Müller, A. (2005) 'Latente Probleme in den Beziehungen zu Russland und die Zukunft der Partnerschaftspolitik', in A. Niemann (ed.) *Herausforderungen an die deutsche und europäische Außenpolitik: Analysen und Politikempfehlungen*. Darmstadt: TUDpress, 191–214.
Kempe, I. (2006) 'From a European Neighbourhood Policy toward a New *Ostpolitik* – The Potential Impact of German Policy', *CAP Policy Analysis*. Munich, No. 3, May 2006.

Germany 29

Kundnani, H. *Germany's withdrawal symptoms*. European Council on Foreign Relations, 25 June 2010, available at http://ecfr.eu/content/entry/commentary_germanys_withdrawal_symptoms (accessed 29 May 2012).

Meier, C. (1999) 'The Russian economic crisis and its effects on German-Russian economic relations', in *The Russian Transition: Challenges for German and American Foreign Policy*. Conference Report, American Institute of Contemporary German Studies, The Johns Hopkins University, 9–10 June 1999, 7–24, available at www.aicgs.org/site/wp-content/uploads/2011/11/russia.pdf (accessed 29 May 2012).

——(2003) 'Deutsch-russische Beziehungen auf dem Prüfstand: Der Petersburger Dialog 2001–3', *SWP-Studie*. Berlin: Stiftung Wissenschaft und Politik, S10, March 2003.

——(2004) 'Deutsch-russische Wirtschaftsbeziehungen unter Putin: Praxis – Probleme – Perspektiven', *SWP-Studie*. Berlin: Stiftung Wissenschaft und Politik, S42, November 2004.

Meister, S. (2012) *An alienated partnership. German-Russian relations after Putin's return*. Helsinki: The Finnish Institute of International Affairs. FIIA Briefing Paper 105, 10 May 2012, available at www.fiia.fi/en/publication/263/an_alienated_partnership/ (accessed 29 May 2012).

Pörzgen, G. (2010) 'Dringend reformbedürftig: Der Petersburger Dialog auf dem Prüfstand', *Osteuropa*, 60/10: 59–81.

Pressekonferenz von Bundeskanzlerin Merkel und Bundesaußenminister Steinmeier, Brussels, 1 September 2008.

Rahr, A. (2007) 'Germany and Russia: A Special Relationship', *The Washington Quarterly*, 30: 137–45.

Schmitz, A. (2010) 'The Central Asia Strategy: An Exercise in EU Foreign Policy', in A. Warkotsch (ed.) *The European Union and Central Asia*. London: Routledge, 11–21.

Spanger, H.-J. and Zagorsky, A. (2012) 'Constructing a Different Europe: The Peculiarities of the German – Russian Partnership', in R. Krumm, S. Medvedev and H.-H. Schröder (eds) *Constructing Identities in Europe: German and Russian Perspectives*. Baden-Baden: Nomos, 221–46.

Stent, A. (2010) 'Germany–Russia relations, 1992–2009', in K. Engelbrekt and B. Nygren (eds) *Russia and Europe: Building Bridges, Digging Trenches*. London and New York: Routledge, 156–66.

Stewart, S. (2011) A *Weaker Russia: Serious Repercussions for EU–Russia Relations*. Stiftung Wissenschaft und Politik, SWP Comments 2011/C26, September 2011, available at www.swp-berlin.org/fileadmin/contents/products/comments/2011C26_stw_ks.pdf (accessed on 29 May 2012).

——(2012) 'Coherence in EU Policy toward Russia: Identities and Interests', in R. Krumm, S. Medvedev and H-H. Schröder (eds) *Constructing Identities in Europe: German and Russian Perspectives*. Baden–Baden: Nomos, 185–204.

Stiglitz, J. (2003) *Globalization and Its Discontents*. New York: Norton.

Treisman, D. (2011) *The Return: Russia's Journey from Gorbachev to Medvedev*. New York: Free Press.

Zagorsky, A. (2005) *Russia and Germany: Continuity and Changes*. Paris: IFRI Research Programme Russia/CIS, Russie.Cei.Visions, No. 6(a), September 2005.

3 France

Rachel Le Noan

Russia has always constituted a crucial feature in the European security landscape. With the end of the Cold War and the collapse of the Soviet Union, on the one hand the EU as an organization had to learn how to deal with a new neighbour bearing in mind that 'it would be a historic error to begin the next century by locking Russia out of European affairs' (Patten 1999: 2). On the other hand, it also meant that France, like any other European state, had to (re)evaluate its own relationship with Russia in a new strategic environment. In the post-Cold War world, France's main foreign policy objectives of 'grandeur' and independence, as well as its leadership role as a great European power, could be hindered by the increasing influence of a reunified Germany and by the weight of the EU itself as a more autonomous political player in the European security game.

For Gueldry, these transformations mean that France is confronted by a choice between a 'bad solution' and a 'very bad solution' regarding its current and future relations with the EU; either France accepts that it has to operate within the context of regional interdependence (i.e. the EU) to solve regional and international issues, or it has to face these challenges alone (2001: 7). Nevertheless, it is also important to consider that, as far as the French authorities are concerned, operating within the EU and making a successful contribution to European security can only be achieved if France's status as a leading European power is maintained and promoted within the organization. The current French national security strategy indeed indicates that one of France's objectives is to turn the EU into a major actor in crisis management (Ministère de la Défense 2008: 315).

Preserving and enhancing France's prestige in Europe and beyond have represented significant parameters of the country's security policies and objectives since Général de Gaulle's presidency (1958–69) which introduced the concepts of greatness and independence at the core of French foreign policy making. The latest national security strategy published in 2008 refers to de Gaulle's legacy by highlighting freedom of decision, nuclear dissuasion and independence as key determinants of France's foreign policy (Ministère de la Défense 2008: 316). Moreover, not only has Gaullism defined French foreign policy for decades but, as far as the Franco–Russian relationship is concerned, de

France 31

Gaulle was also the president who first initiated dialogue with the Soviet Union and strengthened what was to become a significant political and economic partnership between Paris and Moscow in the twenty-first century.

Nowadays, the French authorities are keen to explain that such a partnership is based on trust and that balanced and ambitious co-operation between Russia and EU member states is necessary. According to them, co-operation will enable Russia to use its power responsibly alongside the EU as both entities have in fact common security interests like the stabilization of Afghanistan, the fight against terrorism and the question of Iran and its nuclear programme (Ministère de la Défense 2008: 38). Nonetheless, it has been suggested that France, like Germany, Italy and Spain, favours the logic of a 'creeping integration' of Russia into the European Union. In opposition to a 'soft containment approach', this logic sees 'confrontation with Russia as a loss of time or a not very constructive desire of revenge' (Parmentier 2009: 53). These considerations therefore lead to the following question: to what degree has France actually tried to impose Russia upon the EU?

As well as strong historical ties, France and Russia are both fervent supporters of the concept of multipolarity in world affairs; they are keen on limiting the influence of the United States as a superpower, if not in the world, at least on the European continent. Moreover, this bilateral relationship represents an increasingly significant economic partnership which is growing stronger despite the current financial crisis. One of the most recent major deals is in fact the military agreement between the two countries over the selling of Mistral ships in 2011, when France became the first NATO member to finalize military co-operation with Russia since the end of the Second World War. This development seems to support the argument advanced by Arnaud Dubien from the Institut de Relations Internationales et Stratégiques (IRIS) that the relationship between Moscow and Paris is a quality relationship ('relation de qualité') (interview, February 2010).

The new agreement over Mistral ships certainly represents an important step in the Franco–Russian partnership. It is therefore essential to assess the extent to which France's Russia policy has actually impacted upon the EU foreign policy strategy. In order to answer these questions, this chapter will first highlight the main determinants of France's foreign policy before focusing on the development of the Franco-Russian partnership. It will then analyze the nature of these relations in more detail underlining the strong economic links between the two states and examining the Mistral agreement. Finally, this chapter will address the impact of the 'German factor' on the Franco–Russian relationship and on France's European strategy.

France's foreign policy in the twenty-first century

In order to preserve France's independence as a global actor, the 2008 French national security strategy emphasizes that the country's main objective is to maintain its status as a major military and diplomatic power in the twenty-

32   *Rachel Le Noan*

first century (Ministère de la Défense 2008: 10–11). According to the same document, today's geopolitical configuration is best illustrated by the existence of a strategic uncertainty ('incertitude stratégique') which explains why French foreign policy is focused on five crucial strategic functions: knowledge and anticipation, prevention, dissuasion, protection and intervention (Ministère de la Défense 2008: 314) that should preserve its autonomy of decision-making in world affairs and allow the president to ensure France's contribution to European and international security strategy (Ministère de la Défense 2008: 62).

As a founding member of the EU, France has always been a key player in European politics and the desire to contribute to European security can thus be considered as a natural objective of French foreign policy. French leaders have always been very keen on advancing their goals within the EU framework as long as it clearly benefited French national interests. Indeed, de Gaulle and his successors have all supported the role of the European Union as a platform from which to project national interest abroad. They have also always stressed that promoting the EU and supporting common policies should not become, or be perceived as, a weakening or a loss of national identity. The national security strategy, for example, points out that the ongoing progressive political unification of the EU is not synonymous with uniformity ('uniformisation') (Ministère de la Défense 2008: 81). France sees the EU as another relevant instrument to preserve its influence on the international scene. Ole Waever argues that 'for France the main issue is whether the sense of France and of its mission (and its economy) can be regained through the constitution of a Europe able to act and be respected by others' (1990: 482). From a French point of view, one may argue that the EU exists so that France can preserve its status as a great power internationally and increase its influence regionally to become *the* European leader.

Furthermore, ever since de Gaulle's presidency, the EC/EU has been exploited by the French authorities to promote the concept of multipolarity as an essential feature of contemporary world politics, and consequently as a way to counterbalance the influence of other powers. Among these powers, the USA certainly represents a serious concern for the French authorities, but crucially Paris has also always considered the EU as an effective framework within which it can counterbalance the rising influence of Germany as an economic and increasingly political European player. In theory, the Union therefore represents a great opportunity for France to retain and exercise political influence and project power beyond its borders. In practice, if the French approach towards the EU has sometimes led to conflicts between Brussels and Paris, the latter has nevertheless always been a fervent supporter and promoter of a common foreign and security policy.

Since the 1998 St Malo accord between then-President Jacques Chirac (1995–2007) and the British Prime Minister of the time, Tony Blair, the French authorities have supported the establishment of a common foreign policy as an imperative for the EU to fulfil a role successfully in the international security landscape. France's commitment to this project was explicitly reaffirmed by the former French President, Nicolas Sarkozy, who declared that 'France is back in Europe' shortly after his election in May 2007 (Sarkozy 2007). In doing so, France's strategy is also to promote and shed new light on the relations between Europe and Russia. France may indeed have 'flirted' with the Soviet Union under de Gaulle in order to gain more independence from the United States (Braithwaite 1999: 285), but Paris' objectives towards Russia under Sarkozy were focused on a more regional setting and the French president aimed at qualifying other EU member states' judgement on Russia which was, according to him, too often perceived as a source of concern in the EU (Sarkozy 2008a).

France's Russia strategy from De Gaulle to Sarkozy

Historically, diplomatic relations between France and Russia began as early as 1717 under the reign of Peter the Great when the first Russian ambassador was sent to France (RIA Novosti 2010a). Throughout this chapter however, our main interest lies with contemporary relations. In fact, France's approach towards the Russian Federation has not dramatically changed since the strategy of rapprochement initiated in the 1950s–60s. For de Gaulle, engaging in dialogue with Russia was a way to promote France as a partner in the conduct of relations between the two superpowers at the time, shedding new light on France's potential role on the international scene. This strategic move was therefore politically orientated but it also represented the beginning of an economic partnership with, for example, space co-operation between Paris and Moscow starting as early as 1966. That same year, de Gaulle travelled to Moscow for an official visit which constituted a founding event not only in the relationship between Moscow and Paris, but also between Moscow and the world according to Naoumova (2011). The two countries have thus shared a clear historical bond over past centuries.

Furthermore, some argue that Moscow and Paris also bear resemblance to each other in the way they have adapted to geopolitical developments, albeit decades apart. For Pierre Hassner,

> although France was no longer a great power de Gaulle's great game was to pretend that she still was and to get her to punch above her military and economic weight in the Great Powers League. Putin has been trying to do something similar with Russia.
>
> (Hassner 2008: 8)

As far as France's status is concerned, the situation faced then significantly differs from the one faced by the French presidency today. Nevertheless there is no doubt that a 'great power' mentality remains an important element of world politics. France has a role to play globally and regionally and if Hassner's comments about France's claims are certainly still relevant regarding the

34   *Rachel Le Noan*

country's influence internationally, within the European context, France remains a major if not great power by comparison to the remaining 26 member states. Because of this, it may be argued that Paris is convinced that French policies and objectives in terms of European security are the best for the EU and its members to implement, including in the formulation of a more coherent strategy towards Moscow.

Since 1989, all French presidents have in fact promoted and strengthened the role of the relationship with Moscow as a key element for EU and European security as a whole. As for the new President, François Hollande, it is unlikely that the French approach towards Russia will dramatically change under his presidency and one might expect some continuity in France's policy rather than a breaking-off with previous strategies (Gomart in Vaillant 2012). In December 1989, Francois Mitterrand highlighted the role of Russia in Europe by stressing the special responsibility of France and Russia for European stability. Incentives towards a strong partnership between France and Russia were certainly given by Putin's election as Russian President in 2000 and the friendship that flourished between him and Chirac, the then French president. The friendship was well illustrated by Putin's visit to Paris in March 2010 during which he met with the former French president and explained to a journalist that 'his relationship with Chirac had been of the highest calibre'. One could not help but notice the difference in tone when he talked about his relation with Sarkozy as 'when asked if he enjoyed such a bond with Sarkozy, Putin coolly replied that relationships between heads of state were sometimes dictated by national interests over personal friendships' (NATO 2010).

Chirac indeed described Moscow as a strategic partner and 'expressed the desire to "reinforce" EU–Russian relations' (Bowen 2005: 107). According to Glucksmann, 'the difference with Chirac is that Sarkozy prefers the new members of the EU to Putin' (in Donovan 2007). Glucksmann's statement may have been particularly relevant at the beginning of Sarkozy's presidency when it could be argued that the EU took precedence over Russia on the French security agenda. During the French presidency of the EU in the first term of 2008, Paris was also mostly expected to focus on the Mediterranean region as it had been supporting the implementation of a new neighbourhood policy with the 'Union pour la Méditerranée'. Opposed to the accession of Turkey to the EU, Sarkozy had actively campaigned for the establishment of a partnership between the EU and countries bordering the Mediterranean Sea. However, increasing tensions and the war between Russia and Georgia over Abkhazia and South Ossetia in the summer of 2008 dramatically put Russia back on the European and French agendas.

Sarkozy's holding of the EU's presidency in 2008 and mediation between parties during the Russo–Georgian conflict could have boosted the EU's capacity to build a common Russia policy and it could also have promoted the role of the Union as a guarantor of security in the region. He himself declared that 'the crisis in Georgia has shown for the first time that Europe can, if she wants to, be on the front line at the beginning of a conflict to

France 35

search for a peaceful solution' (Euractiv 2008). He did stress the role of the EU as a security guarantor and by doing so also wished to prove France's commitment and loyalty to the EU. At times though, France has been accused of being 'unwilling to make practical concessions to European cooperation that went beyond gesture politics' (Menon 1995: 23); for others like Daniel Vernet, 'France has a vision of what a European policy could be; if the others share it, it is up to them too to supply the necessary resources' (1992: 664). It may thus be argued that the French authorities were keen on demonstrating France's good influence on the EU, acting as a leader.

Rapidly however the weight of the Franco–Russian partnership emerged and Sarkozy's mediation was criticized as being too lenient towards Russia. Paris was 'blamed for his conciliatory tone' and 'neglecting to make any mention of sanctions' (Euractiv 2008). In particular, the EU's actions through the voice of Sarkozy did not seem to take fully into account more anxious reactions from Poland and the three Baltic states for example, whose presidents then accused Russia of 'imperialism' and 'revisionism' (Lobjakas 2008). According to Jauvert (2008), Sarkozy was criticized in both France and Europe for giving in to Russia, whether he acted by ignorance or out of self-interest. The issue of self-interest is highly relevant and it is worth noting that Sarkozy's mediation was mainly exploited by the French authorities to demonstrate their country's 'grandeur'. A few weeks before the war, Sarkozy even explained that 'France has imposed the EU as a major actor to facilitate the resolution of conflicts' (2008b). Last but not least, as far as Paris is concerned, the crisis in Georgia and its aftermath played a part in enhancing the President's own status and prestige as a great leader in that geostrategic environment. 'Presidential ego' constitutes a significant factor in the analysis of France's foreign policy in the European context and beyond, as in other EU member states, and certainly plays a part in the Union's difficulties agreeing a Russia policy.

As other chapters in this volume show, member states have different relationships with Moscow depending on their history, their location, and/or their national security priorities. Reconciling these interests represents a mammoth task for the EU in dealing with Russia and the crisis in Georgia illustrates well the extent to which bilateralism was exposed as an obstacle to a common policy. This is a relevant example of how multilateralism may be exploited for national pride. For some observers, the strong relationship established between Paris and Moscow has indeed damaged European cohesion by favouring Moscow and therefore neglecting new members (Gomart 2007a: 151). Such analysis supports the argument that bilateralism negatively impacts on multilateralism, consequently preventing the implementation of a common policy towards Moscow. However, it has been argued that 'a more assertive Russia might push the members of the EU into a more active co-ordination of their approaches' (Hoffmann 2000: 196).

Based on this argument, one could only assume that the conflict between Georgia and Russia would have triggered such co-ordination. Through the

36 *Rachel Le Noan*

voice of Sarkozy, the EU did react against the Russian intervention on Georgian soil and managed to bring parties to an agreement. However, the fact that the French leadership was criticized illustrates the ongoing and strong divisions between EU member states on the issue of Russia. It also emphasizes how national interests differ among the 27 and acts as a reminder that the achievement of national economic and strategic goals combined with national pride and the promotion of national interest still largely prevail over the establishment and implementation of a truly efficient common European Russia policy.

An interested partnership with military implications

According to Gomart (2007b), there are various interpretations of Russia in France. On one hand, the French press and academia are divided between the defenders of human rights, those who fear a revival of imperialism and those concerned about Russia's ambiguous position on proliferation and arm sales. On the other hand, the political elite seems divided between those who value Russia as a strategic partner, those who see Russia as an emerging market and thus a major opportunity to boost the economy and finally those who admire Putin as a defender of Russian interests and independence in the mould of Charles de Gaulle, the last 'real statesman' on the international stage. Gomart explains that the reference to de Gaulle in particular, although not entirely relevant in terms of policy, nonetheless influences perceptions of Russia as a country (2007a: 147–49). Indeed, in practice it is the value of Russia as an economic partner and the importance of maintaining a good relationship with Moscow in order to secure French strategic interests that have acted as the most important factors in France's foreign policy from the 1960s onwards. Stanley Hoffmann argues that: 'De Gaulle always sought to act in such a way that his successors would find themselves committed by what he had done, whether they liked it or not' (1964: 28). By promoting foreign policy as the president's 'domaine réservé', de Gaulle has without a doubt influenced his successors. Importantly, as far as Russia is concerned, he also initiated the economic partnership and thus political relationship with Moscow that each French president has since then developed.

From a partnership that began in the 1960s, areas of co-operation between France and Russia have significantly expanded and in 2012 the bilateral relationship focuses on many fields, from cultural exchanges and ministerial seminars to space and military co-operation. As far as diplomacy is concerned, in 1995 an inter-parliamentary commission was created by Philippe Seguin (Assemblée Nationale) and Ivan Rybkine (Duma). The Grande Commission Inter-Parlementaire France–Russie can be described as a common organ to both the French Assemblée Nationale and the Russian Duma which aims at maintaining and improving political, economic, social and cultural exchanges between the two countries through yearly meetings (Assemblée Nationale 2011). As an example, in November 2009, the two states signed an agreement

France 37

on economic migration (which came into force on 1 March 2011); the agreement simplifies visa rules for citizens from both countries working for private and public firms and professionals with high skill qualifications travelling between France and Russia for work purposes (Ministère de l'Economie, des Finances et de l'Industrie 2012a). Such developments reflect the position of France, and Germany, who would like the EU to progress talks on visa-free travel with Russia (Pop and Rettman 2011).

Furthermore, in 2010, the Year of France in Russia was celebrated in both countries and reaffirmed French support towards the modernization of Russia and the diversification of the economic partnership. A Franco–Russian Centre for Energy Efficiency was opened in Moscow in April 2010 and Paris also supports the project of establishing Moscow as an international financial centre as well as plans for a 'Russian Silicon Valley' (project Skolkovo). Importantly Paris and Moscow also hold intergovernmental seminars every year, the equivalent of high level ministerial meetings. During the seminar in Moscow in November 2011, the French Prime Minister François Fillon, described Russia as a great European nation and the French authorities also confirmed that France was willing to take part in the EU's 2010 Partnership for Modernization's initiative with Russia.

Moreover, significant contracts for French firms including Sanofi (pharmaceutical industry), Thales (telecommunication satellites), Alstom (electricity and coal energy) and Bouygues (construction of a Russian orthodox centre in Paris) were signed. These contracts offer a good illustration of the growing economic partnership between the two countries. Despite the current financial crisis, economic relations have strengthened: in 2010 French exports to Russia were worth €6.2 billion and Russian exports to France represented €12.1 billion. France is the fifth foreign investor in Russia and owns 4.5 per cent of the Russian market thanks to its presence in the aeronautic, pharmaceutical and cosmetic industries, including 'industrie du luxe' (Ministère de l'Economie, des Finances et de l'Industrie 2012b). Economic relations also emphasize the importance of history in the bilateral relationship. For example, the contract signed between Roskosmos and Arianespace in June 2010 confirmed the space co-operation project begun back in 1966. As the Centre National d'Etudes Spatiales[1] (CNES) explains, France was then the first Western European state to sign an agreement on peaceful exploration of space with the USSR; 'France and Russia have forged a uniquely close and extended scientific, technical and human partnership over 40 years' (CNES 2006). In 2003, space co-operation was brought to a new level with the decision to operate Russia's Soyuz launch vehicle from the French space base in French Guyana which is also a European Space Agency launch site.

The number of contracts in the fields of energy and aeronautics has also increased and represents another significant side of the Franco–Russian relationship. The declaration on atomic energy approved at the Economic Forum in June 2010 reaffirmed previous deals respectively signed in 1993 and 2000; while the deal signed between Gazprom and Total in July 2007 illustrates the

38   Rachel Le Noan

impact of energy policy on France's diplomatic relations with Russia (Kraft 2007: 5). Moreover, at the ministerial meeting in 2011, a common declaration on nuclear energy and energy policy was signed. According to Paris, it constitutes an important step for the old and exemplary co-operation between France and Russia in the post-Fukushima context. This declaration also highlights France's support of Russia for the creation of an international centre of formation for crisis management in that particular field. Importantly, other energy contracts have been signed by French firms which support projects known for running against EU interests.

Energy security was discussed at the 2009 Franco–Russian ministerial meeting when France decided to support the 'highly controversial South Stream project' (Dunn 2010) without, however, fully rejecting the Nabucco project. Electricité de France (EDF) indeed agreed to participate in South Stream along with the Italian company Eni among others. The main argument of the French government to justify their participation in South Stream is that France's energy policy is about the diversification of transportation of oil and gas (Fillon 2009). According to the EU Directorate-General for Energy, the main obstacles to Nabucco mostly lie with 'the complexity of transit issues and difficulties in coordinating investments in production and transit infrastructure' (European Commission 2007). Their research also emphasizes that 'improving the pan-European political context' and 'extending the EU-dialogue' may help overcome these obstacles (European Commission 2007). However, there is no mention of the weight of individual member state's national interest, like France, as a significant liability in the success of this enterprise. The intergovernmental agreement reached between Turkey and several EU member states (Romania, Bulgaria, Hungary and Austria) in Ankara in July 2009 did not prevent France from prioritizing its own economic interest over the EU's credibility only a couple of months later. Finally, as far as aeronautics is concerned, it is worth noticing that the Russian Vneshtorgbank bought a 5 per cent stake in the European Aeronautic Defence and Space Company (EADS) in 2006. Some fear that such deals allow Russia to acquire more power within the agency with France and Germany unable to counter it if necessary, although Putin said this was not to be seen as 'a sign of aggression'. As explained by Chris Noon,

> the push for closer defence and aeronautic ties is not one-way traffic. Chirac [had] long hoped to draw Moscow deeper into the EU's defence arm, believing that Russia's military might is necessary for Europe to match the U.S. as a global superpower.
>
> (Noon 2009)

Last but not least, from March 2010, Paris and Moscow had been discussing the possibility of an agreement on the selling of the French military ships, Mistral,[2] which was finalized in 2011. The transaction was concluded at the Economic Forum in St Petersburg on 17 June 2011 between the Direction des

Constructions Navales Systemes et Services (DCNS) and Rosoboronexport for about €1.2 billion (*Le Monde* 2011). Negotiations had been postponed in the winter of 2010/1 because of discussions regarding Moscow's demands for a transfer of technology to be sold with the ships. The deal signed in 2011 will have France delivering two vessels to Russia in 2014/5. Another agreement may be signed in the future regarding two more ships that would be built in Russia. This agreement brings a new dimension to the nature of the partnership between Paris and Moscow since military and defence issues have been confirmed as new fields of co-operation. The possibility of further co-operation between France and Russia at the military level has also been reported with Thales looking at the potential privatization of Russian Technologies (Russia's military industrial umbrella) (Stratfor 2011). Not only does the Mistral deal reinforce the links between the two countries, but it also puts renewed pressure on the EU regarding the building of a common Russian policy. Military transactions have so far remained a very sensitive subject in the EU, even more so if they include Russia. The French initiative therefore worries those member states that still perceive Russia as a potential and serious security threat: 'some believe it could be used in the future in potential conflicts with NATO and its allies' (RIA Novosti 2010b). The Latvian Minister of Defence, Artis Pabriks, said that 'if this deal changes the security balance in the Baltic Sea region, Latvia will demand compensation' in order to recreate the status quo. He explained that if the Mistral ships are deployed to the Baltic Sea, Latvia will ask for both military and political support from France and the rest of NATO. The support will have to be enough to restore balance in the region (Raudsepp 2011).The interest of Russia in acquiring Mistral ships has been explained as a gift from Medvedev to Sarkozy to thank him for his support during the Georgian crisis; as vessels that could be used for 'pacific explorations' like humanitarian operations or against piracy in Somalia (Fasciaux and Gornovskaya 2011); or as part of an ongoing campaign from Moscow to unsettle Central Europeans (Stratfor 2011).

Others, like Lilia Shevstova, are of the view that Sarkozy was manipulated by the Russian authorities in reaching such an agreement. Shevstova also describes France's Russia policy as 'based on only a vague understanding of what is going on in Russia and on the complicated network of interests around the Kremlin' (Shevstova and Wood 2011). But, as well as an important business contract for the French defence industry (Cabirol 11 June 2011), France's new step may also be considered as the natural evolution of a bilateral relationship that until then had touched upon every field from art to space. Twenty years after the disintegration of the Soviet Union, military co-operation with Russia was perhaps a matter of time. France is the first NATO member to agree on a transfer of military technology to Russia since the Second World War, and the agreement has sparked criticism from some in the USA; according to US Congresswoman Ileana Ros-Lehtinen, 'it is a profound mistake to arm our opponents for profit or for the mirage of cooperation that never materializes' (17 June 2011). The reaction of the Latvian Minister

40   *Rachel Le Noan*

detailed above also shows that while Moscow may be happy about the Mistral, EU states like the Baltics or Romania are not. However, it is important to note that neither Washington nor Brussels have explicitly and unambiguously opposed the agreement. This may suggest that the deal over Mistral might not be as threatening as claimed, or that other countries might have wished to conclude such (business) agreements sooner.[3] On the other hand, it may also emphasize France's own status within the EU as one of the leading powers, alongside Germany. Consequently, if neither Brussels nor Berlin strongly opposes such an agreement, one may argue that for Paris there is no imperative to discuss the issue with other EU members beyond assurances that the deal will not disturb current European security dynamics. The French authorities are perfectly aware of the concerns such an agreement will raise, however, the voices of smaller EU member states are not yet strong enough to influence the Franco–Russian relationship significantly.

Berlin over Brussels: France's competition with Germany

France sees its EU membership as an opportunity to promote its profile regionally and internationally. Geopolitical transformations worldwide and throughout Europe have impacted upon the development of French foreign policy that may be described as 'on the defensive in a global environment which weakens French prestige and authority and reduces her freedom of manoeuvre' (Manners and Whitman 2000: 41). The EU enlargement has also to some extent weakened what some analysts refer to as France's 'auto-proclaimed diplomatic vocation' (Weidmann Koop and Vermette 2009: 212). What is more, it has placed Germany, geographically and increasingly politically and economically, at the heart of the new European landscape. Historically, Germany has been a crucial factor in the development of French politics and since the 1950s France has perceived the European Community as a useful framework to address this issue. As Germany's weight increased following reunification, so did France's competitive instincts; Paris is to be a step ahead of Berlin in European and world affairs. In the post-Cold War period, Mitterrand thus worked towards promoting a vision of a European confederation where France was to lead the Ostpolitik of the European Community as a way to counterbalance German economic dominance (Waever 1990: 484). France's partnership with Russia represents a vector for Paris to keep up with Germany's own relationship with Moscow.

Berlin has not yet established any military co-operation with Moscow, and the Mistral agreement can to some degree be explained by the 'German factor' that undoubtedly influences Paris' relations with Moscow. For some, the strengthening of Franco–Russian relations would be France's response by 'ensuring that the evolving Berlin-Moscow relationship does not leave Paris unable to affect security issues on the continent' (Stratfor 2011). As analyzed in Stewart's chapter in this volume, Germany's relations with Moscow represent another significant partnership in the EU context and, to some degree, it may be argued that Paris feels compelled to react to the consolidation of another bilateral relationship by attempting to promote trilateral dynamics as seen in 1998 under Chirac or in 2010 at the summit held at Deauville.

The series of meetings between French, German and Russian leaders held under Chirac's presidency between 1998 and 2007 are also known as the 'Yekaterinburg Triangle' cycle and led, for example, to joint opposition to the US military intervention in Iraq in 2003. Chirac and Dominique De Villepin (French Foreign Minister 2002–4; Prime Minister 2005–7) could then be described 'as the main actors in cooperation between France, Germany and Russia' (De Grossouvre 2003: 5). After 2007 the three leaders met on several occasions. First, both Sarkozy and Merkel supported Medvedev's initiative of a new security treaty for Europe which was not well received by all EU members. Then the 2010 Deauville summit is particularly relevant as it was 'designed to bind Moscow more closely into a partnership with the West' (France24 2010). According to the French authorities, 'Russia seems to be looking more and more towards the West, and Deauville will be a chance to reinforce this development, which we see as positive'. For Paris, Deauville was ultimately the equivalent of a 'brainstorming' session during which no decision would be made (France24 2010).

One may argue that this comment from the French authorities may be aimed at reassuring other member states that France and Germany would not act on behalf of the EU without consulting them. Nonetheless, it may also be suggested that the existence of these summits strongly illustrates the trilateral dynamics at work between Paris, Berlin and Moscow and not the limits of what can be achieved at the bilateral level. These summits cannot be considered as interactions between Brussels and Moscow but represent discussions between three European powers. Consequently, one may wonder to what extent relations between France and Germany may impact on the formulation of a common Russia policy. Indeed, if 'France [can be considered] as one of the main representatives of Russian interests in the EU' (Dunn 2010), the same arguments can be applied to Germany. Therefore, any European policy towards Russia will first need to get the approval of both Paris and Berlin. As far as the CFSP is concerned, the French authorities consider that obstacles to France's leadership and national interest are more likely to emerge from Berlin rather than Brussels. Germany is perceived as the main challenger to France's historical influence within the EU. Consequently, if the French authorities do not see the Union completing its role as a 'multiplier of French power' (Manners and Whitman 2000: 22), Paris will focus on other partnerships to achieve such an objective: the strengthening of the relationship with Moscow could be seen as an answer to changes in the 'balance of power' within the EU and an illustration of France's political and economic competition with Germany.

To become a multiplier of French power, France needs the EU to act as one united organization implementing a strategy approved by all. As of now, this is clearly impossible to achieve as far as the EU's position on Russia is concerned because of diverging views on what the nature of such a relationship should be. France and Germany have not yet managed to convince all remaining EU member states of the benefit of a close partnership with Moscow, thus relying on strong bilateral/trilateral relations may prove more efficient to promote their own national interest in the short term rather than having to deal with uncertain European policies.

Moreau-Defarges argues that over the past couple of years, France has been 'losing its European child' (2002: 953) meaning that French influence within the EU has diminished. Currently, Paris certainly focuses on developing stronger bilateral relations with Moscow but the French authorities have not given up on influencing the EU strategy on Russia which represents another vector of power to maintain France's greatness. Sarkozy saw himself as the only European leader able to deal effectively with Russia and therefore as the one to lead the EU strategy towards a common Russia policy. The willingness of the French authorities to act as a 'push factor' between the EU and Russia could prove successful in the longer term. Nevertheless, as argued previously, the main obstacle is still to reconcile all member states' positions over the Russian issue: on one hand 'reassuring' some states like the Baltic countries and on the other perhaps 'curbing the enthusiasm' of others like Italy or Germany towards the Russian neighbour. At the 2010 Annual French Ambassadors' Conference, it was asserted that 'France will make specific proposals to Russia pertaining to its relations with the EU and NATO'. At the last conference in September 2011, Sarkozy emphasized the urgent need for the EU to commit fully to a common security and foreign policy, referring to Europe's blindness when confronted by strategic threats. Paris therefore clearly regards Moscow as a key actor and partner in the European security framework. In fact, 'our shared interests with Russia must lead us to develop, if Moscow so wishes, an unprecedented partnership to guarantee the security of the entire Euro-Atlantic space' (Sarkozy 2010). The EU therefore represents a major feature in French politics and will remain so in the long-term future. On the other hand, it is unlikely that, even with the change of President, Paris will soon cease co-operation with the Russian authorities politically and/or economically.

The French authorities do not see any contradiction between supporting both the EU and establishing further co-operation with Russia; rather, a partnership with Russia should be an element of an effective European foreign policy. Nevertheless, the conduct of bilateral relations between EU member states and Russia has often been perceived as impacting negatively on the establishment of a common Russia policy. Bilateralism and multilateralism may not be mutually exclusive and, if the policies of some member states like France may be criticized for their relations with Moscow, it is also important to recognize that the EU is lacking a common vision about its commitment to Russia and the establishment of a European foreign policy that Moreau-Defarges characterizes as geopolitical myopia. For historical, geopolitical, economic or even cultural reasons, the EU has thus far failed to assess and address the subject of Moscow. If 'Russia is looking to France to help improve strained relations with the 27 member states' (*Financial Times* 29 May 2008), Dov Lynch also rightly points out that 'Russian officials note the difficulty of dealing with the EU because of its complexity in terms of different loci of decision-making and opacity' (2003: 78). The building of a coherent and comprehensive European 'Russia' policy implies re-evaluating the role of the EU as a (global) political actor first. The Lisbon Treaty institutionalized the position of High Representative for Foreign and Security Policy, currently occupied by Lady Ashton. Nonetheless, if in theory the High Representative should enable the EU to speak and act as one in world affairs, in practice a common foreign policy fully supported by all member states simply does not exist. Whether one focuses on Russia or not, the EU remains a political dwarf by comparison with its aspirations.

White argues that three options can be found regarding European foreign policy: for some it already exists although that term may not be used, for others it does not exist yet but it should, and finally some believe it does not yet exist, never will and it never should (2001: 37). The second option is the most appropriate to describe Paris's attitudes towards the CFSP. France remains strongly attached to the EU. The French authorities are aware that relations with Russia should not eclipse this. But France has also become a vector for Russian interests to be heard within the EU. The EU–Russia Summit taking place in Paris in October 2000 was a prime example of it as the Joint Declaration gave 'priority to the development of a strategic partnership between Russia and the EU, calling for regular consultations on defence matters'. In 2008, the *Financial Times* reported that France is for a strategic partnership between Russia and the EU. Since then, the mediation in Georgia and the Mistral agreement have certainly highlighted the extent to which the French authorities wish to lead European politics on the subject of the Russian Federation. On the other hand, Moscow knows that a partnership with the EU is a crucial element in the European security logic. From Moscow's perspective, a partnership with the EU also represents a factor of recognition internationally. France and Russia benefit from bilateral contacts that allow them to further assert their power: for Russia, whose foreign policy has become more assertive, such co-operation is seen as a sign of recognition as a great power, for France, whose global influence has diminished, it is perceived as an opportunity to reassert its leadership role. Questioning the future impact of bilateral relationships and assessing how they can contribute to a stronger EU is essential because it is high time that a European foreign policy move beyond being considered an 'amalgamate mess' (Torreblanca 2008: 5).

For France to invest more energy into a potential European policy, it seems that such a policy will have to follow French guidelines. As far as a European 'Russia' policy is concerned, Peter Mandelson, former European Commissioner for Trade, rightly suggests that 'no other country reveals our differences as does Russia' (2007). It may be argued however that the Franco–Russian relationship coming to an end would not necessarily facilitate the establishment of a more efficient EU foreign policy. The 'europeanization' of member

44 *Rachel Le Noan*

states' policies is certainly a reality on numerous issues throughout the Union; however, one cannot refer to a 'europeanization' of foreign policies. Security remains a strategic field within which the EU's influence is confronted by the prevalence of national interests and already existing strategic and economic partnerships, sometimes long-established, such as the Franco–Russian relationship. The future of a common Russia policy may be rather a 'Franco–Germanization' of the Union's foreign policy framework, especially towards the Russian Federation. For Dubien (2010), the main challenge facing both countries is to preserve their 'entente' and to reinvent it in a new strategic environment. Both Paris and Berlin have significant contacts with Moscow and France is not ready to let Germany lead any EU policy and vice versa. The geopolitical environment is evolving rapidly and the EU is now faced with more challenges in the South following developments throughout the Arab world and Africa. The temptation is there for the EU to focus on these priorities and once again postpone the establishment of a common Russia policy. Nevertheless, as the 2008 war in Georgia demonstrated, the European continent itself is not immune to geopolitical transformations and the EU cannot afford to ignore Russia if it truly wants to become a global political player.

Notes

1 Governmental agency responsible for France's space policy in Europe.
2 A Mistral-class amphibious assault ship can carry up to 16 helicopters, four landing craft and a 750-strong landing force, and is equipped with a 69-bed hospital (BBC 2010).
3 Spain's Navantia shipyard had emerged as a serious rival to DCNS; and Dutch Defense Minister Eimert van Middelkoop said last year that the Russians had approached Damen Schelde Naval Shipbuilding in the Netherlands (Kralev 2010).

References

Assemblée Nationale (2011) *Grande Commission Interparlementaire France-Russie.* Available at www.assemblee-nationale.fr/international/commission-russie.asp (accessed 5 March 2012).
BBC (2010) 'Russia to buy two French Mistral-class warships'. Available at www.bbc.co.uk/news/world-europe-12076393 (accessed 20 March 2012).
Bowen, N. (2005) 'Multilateralism, multipolarity, and regionalism: the French foreign policy discourse', *Mediterranean Quarterly*, Vol. 16, No. 1, 94–116.
Braithwaite, R. (1999) 'La Russie, Pays Européen', in *Politique Etrangère*, No 2, 269–90.
Cabirol, M. (11 June 2011) 'La France signe la vente de quatre porte-hélicoptères à la Russie', *La Tribune*. Available at www.latribune.fr/actualites/20110611trib000628775/exclusif.-la-france-signe-la-vente-de-quatre-helicopteres-a-la-russie.html (accessed 15 March 2012).
CNES (2006) *Coopération spatiale franco – russe: les racines du futur.* Centre National d'Etudes Spatiales, available at www.cnes.fr/web/CNES-fr/5393-cooperation-spatiale-franco-russe.php (accessed 16 July 2010).

France   45

De Grossouvre, H. (2003) 'La Révision du Traité de l'Elysée, l'Europe et la Russie', *Revue de Défense Nationale*, No. 2, 67–77.

Donovan, J. (2007) 'France's Sarkozy takes critical stand on first trip to Moscow', Radio Free Europe/Radio Liberty, available at www.rferl.org/content/article/107889 4.html (accessed 10 July 2010).

Dubien, A. (2010) *France – Russie: des relations privilégiées?* Institut de Relations Internationales et Stratégiques, available at http://affaires-strategiques.info/spip.php? article2908 (accessed 27 September 2010).

Dunn, A. (2010) *New Format of the EU-Russia Dialogue, European Dialogue.* Available at http://eurodialogue.org/New-Format-of-the-EU-Russia-Dialogue (accessed 28 March 2012).

Euractiv (2008) *Sarkozy Steps Up Mediation Efforts over Georgia.* Available at www.euract iv.com/en/foreign-affairs/sarkozy-steps-mediation-efforts-georgia/article-174946 (accessed on 21 July 2010).

European Commission (2007) 'Energy corridors: European Union and neighbouring countries', Project Report EUR22581. Available at http://ec.europa.eu/research/energy/pdf/energy_corridors_en.pdf (accessed 15 March 2012).

Fasciaux, N. and Gornovskaya, M. (2011) 'Navire Mistral à la Russie: un jouet cher et inutile', *Le Courrier de Russie.* Available at www.lecourrierderussie.com/2011/06/21/navire-mistral-russie-jouet-cher/ (accessed 15 March 2012).

Fillon, F. (2009) *14e Séminaire intergouvernemental France-Russie à Rambouillet.* Portail du Gouvernement, available at www.gouvernement.fr/gouvernement/14e-seminaire-intergouvernemental-france-russie-a-rambouillet (accessed 20 July 2010).

Financial Times (29 May 2008) 'France hoping to broker EU deal with Russia', available at www.ft.com/cms/s/0/1ca2334a-2dcb-11dd-b92a-000077b07658.html#axzz1X5 3yR9wk (accessed 18 August 2011).

France24 (2010) *France, Germany extends hand to Russia at seaside summit.* France24 International News, 18 October 2010, available at www.france24.com/en/20101018-f rance-germany-extend-hand-russia-seaside-summit-deauville (accessed 20 March 2012).

Gomart, T. (2007a) 'France's Russia policy: balancing interests and values', *The Washington Quarterly*, Vol. 30, No. 2, 147–55.

——(2007b) 'La politique russe de la France: fin de cycle?', *Politique Etrangère*, No 1, 123–35.

Gueldry, M. (2001) *France and European Integration: Toward a Transnational Policy?* Westport, CT: Praeger.

Hassner, P. (2000) 'Towards a common European foreign and security policy?', *Journal of Common Market Studies*, Vol. 38, No. 2, 189–98.

——(2008) 'Russia's transition to autocracy', *Journal of Democracy*, Vol. 19, No. 2, 5–15.

Hoffmann, S. (1964) 'De Gaulle, Europe and the Atlantic alliance', *International Organization*, Vol. 18, 1–28.

——(2000) 'Towards a Common European Foreign and Security Policy?', *Journal of Common Market Studies*, Vol. 38, No. 2, 189–198.

Jauvert, V. (2008) 'Sarko le Russe', *Le Nouvel Observateur*, 13 November 2008, available at http://premier.gov.ru/eng/premier/press/world/1182/ (accessed 20 March 2012).

Kraft, O. (2007) 'Union Européenne – Russie: les négociations pour un nouvel accord à l'épreuve des intérêts des états membres', *Actualités de la Russie et de la CEI.* Paris: IRIS, No. 3.

46 Rachel Le Noan

Kralev, N. (2010) 'France snubs U.S., will sell ships to Russia', *Washington Times*. Available at www.washingtontimes.com/news/2010/feb/09/france-snubs-us-will-sell-ship-to-russia/?page=all (accessed 5 March 2012).

Lobjakas, A. (2008) *EU puts mediation above recriminations over Georgia crisis*. Radio Liberty/Radio Free Europe, available at www.rferl.org/content/EU_Puts_Mediation_Above_Recriminations_Over_Georgia_Crisis/1190839.html (accessed 20 March 2012).

Lynch, D. (2003) 'Russia Faces Europe', *Chaillot Paper*. Paris: Institute for Security Studies, No. 60.

Mandelson, P. (2007) *The EU and Russia: Our Joint Political Challenge*. Bologna: Speech 07/242, available at http://trade.ec.europa.eu/doclib/docs/2007/april/tradoc_134524.pdf (accessed 21 July 2010).

Manners, I. and Whitman, R. G. (eds) (2000) *The Foreign Policies of European Union Member States*. Manchester: Manchester University Press.

Menon, A. (1995) 'From Independence to Cooperation: France, NATO and European Security', *International Affairs*, Vol. 71, No. 1, 19–34.

Ministère de l'Economie, des Finances et de l'Industrie (2012a) *Pour la promotion de l'immigration professionnelle*. Available at www.immigration-professionnelle.gouv.fr/textes-de-r%C3%A9f%C3%A9rence/accords-bilat%C3%A9raux/accord-france-russie (accessed 16 March 2012).

——(2012b) *Les services economiques a L'étranger: Russie*. Available at www.tresor.economie.gouv.fr/Pays/russie (accessed 20 March 2012).

Ministère de la Défense (2008) *Défense et sécurité nationale: le livre blanc*. Paris: Odile Jacob, available at www.ladocumentationfrancaise.fr/var/storage/rapports-publics//084000341/0000.pdf (accessed 20 March 2012).

Le Monde (2011) 'La Russie formalise l'achat de deux navires Mistral à la France', available at www.lemonde.fr/europe/article/2011/06/17/la-russie-formalise-l-achat-de-deux-navires-mistral-a-la-france_1537593_3214.html (accessed 18 August 2011).

Moreau-Defarges, P. (2002) 'La France et l'Europe, l'inévitable débat', *Politique Etrangère*, No. 4, 951–66.

Naoumova, N. (2011) *De Gaulle et la Russie Éternelle*. Institut de la Démocratie et de la Coopération, available at www.idc-europe.org/fr/De-Gaulle-et-la-Russie-eternelle (accessed 31 March 2012).

Noon, C. (2009) 'Putin plays innocent with EADS stake', *Forbes,* 26 September 2009, available at www.forbes.com/2006/09/25/putin-eads-russia-face-cx_cn_0925autofa-cescan01.html (accessed 19 July 2010).

North Atlantic Treaty Organization (NATO) (2010) *Putin in Paris (with Mistral on the menu)*. Available at http://nato-russia.org/?p=344 (accessed 21 July 2010).

Parmentier, F. (2009) 'Normative power, EU preferences and Russia. Lessons from the Russian-Georgian war', *European Political Economy Review*, No. 9, 49–61.

Patten, C. (1999) 'Declaration on Chechnya', Speech/99/166, European Parliament, Strasbourg, available at www.europarl.europa.eu/sides/getDoc.do?pubRef=-//EP//TEXT+CRE+19991117+ITEM-005+DOC+XML+V0//EN (accessed 5 March 2012).

Pop, V. and Rettman, A. (2011) 'EU preparing to launch visa-free talks with Russia', *EUObserver*. Available at http://euobserver.com/22/114281 (accessed 14 March 2012).

Raudsepp, K. (2011) 'Mistral Sales Worry Baltics', *The Baltic Times*, 10 August 2011, available at www.baltictimes.com/news/articles/29248/ (accessed 5 March 2012).

RIA Novosti (2010a) *France-Russia: la longue histoire des relations bilatérales*, 1 March 2010, available at http://fr.rian.ru/france_russia_2010/20100301/186152750.html (accessed 27 September 2010).

France 47

——(2010b) *France committed to naval cooperation with Russia*, 8 June 2010, available at http://en.rian.ru/world/20100608/159348291.html (accessed 20 July 2010).

Sarkozy, N. (2007) *La vision du Président de la République pour l'Europe.* 6 May 2007, available at www.elysee.fr/president/les-dossiers/europe/la-vision-du-president-de-la-republique-pour.9580.html (accessed 18 August 2011).

——(2008a) World Policy Conference, 8 October 2008, available at www.ambafrance-uk.org/President-Sarkozy-s-World-Policy.html (accessed 18 August 2011).

——(2008b) *Discours sur la défense et la sécurité nationale.* 17 June 2008, available at www.elysee.fr/president/les-dossiers/defense/defense-et-securite-nationale.7934.html (accessed 18 August 2011).

——(2010) Annual French ambassadors' conference, available at www.ambafrance-rsa.org/Annual-French-Ambassadors.html (accessed on 29 August 2010).

Shevstova, L. and Wood, A. (2011) *Change or decay: Russia's dilemma and the West's response.* Washington, DC: Carnegie Endowment for International Peace.

Stratfor (2011) 'What's behind new levels of cooperation for Russia and France', *Forbes,* 21 June 2011, available at www.forbes.com/sites/energysource/2011/06/21/whats-behind-new-levels-of-cooperation-for-russia-and-france/ (accessed 18 August 2011).

Torreblanca, J. I. (2008) *Sarkozy's foreign policy: where do European interests and values stand?* European Council on Foreign Relations, available at http://ecfr.eu/page/-/documents/Torreblanca-Sarkozy-Foreign-Policy.pdf (accessed 16 March 2012).

United States House of Representatives (2011) *Ros-Lehtinen says French sale of assault ships to Russia threatens regional security.* Committee on Foreign Affairs, available at http://foreignaffairs.house.gov/press_display.asp?id=1871 (accessed 5 September 2011).

Vaillant, G. (2012) 'France – Russie: "Dans la continuité plus que dans la rupture"', *Le Journal du Dimanche.* Available at www.lejdd.fr/International/Moyen-Orient/Actualite/Hollande-ne-changera-pas-profondement-la-relation-franoc-russe-interview-515865 (accessed 4 August 2012).

Vernet, D. (1992) 'The dilemma of French policy', *International Affairs,* Vol. 68, No. 4, 655–64.

Waever, O. (1990) 'Three competing Europes: German, French, Russian', *International Affairs,* Vol. 66, No. 3, 477–93.

Weidmann Koop, M-C. and Vermette, R. (eds) (2009) *La France au XXI Siècle: Nouvelles Perspectives.* Birmingham, AL: Summa Publications Inc.

White, B. (2001) *Understanding European Foreign Policy,* Basingstoke: Palgrave.

4 Ireland and the United Kingdom

Maxine David

As two islands situated separately from the European mainland and at an appreciable distance from Russia, the United Kingdom and Ireland are relatively independent of Russia and its politics. That said, both are as susceptible to the pressures of the globalising world and thus, for both, Russia is a state that warrants attention, albeit in the case of each, for quite different reasons. Close geographically and historically, Ireland and the UK are nevertheless vastly different foreign policy actors, not least by virtue of the one having been colonized by the other. They are distinguished today by disparities in size, resources and global influence and inevitably these factors too result in each having quite different relations with Russia. Those differences extend to each state's relationship with the EU as well: Ireland's reputation within the EU is a positive one, that of a committed and well-adapted member state; the UK, meanwhile, is most often characterized as an 'awkward' partner, whose attitude to EU membership is ambivalent at best.

This chapter seeks first to identify the basis for and nature of Irish and British relations with Russia. In the case of Ireland, the relationship is primarily an economic rather than political one. For the UK, both economics and politics figure highly and interactions between the UK and Russia are more intensive and extensive than in the Irish case. It is of little surprise, therefore, that the UK has experienced far more problems in its relations with Russia than has Ireland. With the nature of the relationships established, I move on to consider Irish and British relations with the EU. In examining the impact of these bilateral relationships with Russia on the EU, I argue that neither case presents many problems for the EU, albeit for quite different reasons. The chapter concludes with a short discussion on the contribution of each member state to EU-level attempts to adopt a unified Russia policy.

Ireland

The story of Irish foreign policy is that of a small state (Laffan 2006; O'Regan 2010) on Europe's periphery. A former British colony, its 'tradition is largely one of dependence and adaptation to external terms of reference' (Hay and Smith 2010: 126). Ireland's sense of identity is rooted in a principled

Ireland and the United Kingdom 49

adherence to its neutrality, to the pursuit of values as well as interests, and to the upholding of human rights. The official discourse is one of an historical engagement with the rest of the world, beginning with missionaries in the sixth and seventh centuries and continuing today through trading relations and a commitment to multilateralism, as evidenced through membership of the UN, EU, OSCE and so on. Its engagement in multilateral fora is necessitated by its relative lack of economic resources, affecting its ability to conduct an independent foreign policy. In 2011, for instance, its mandatory contributions to international organizations, primarily the UN, consumed almost two-thirds of the annual budget of the Department for Foreign Affairs. It is unsurprising, therefore, that the UN and EU are considered to be of particular significance; the EU itself described as 'a central framework' through which Ireland seeks to achieve its foreign policy goals (Department of Foreign Affairs and Trade [Ireland] 2012). For much of the post-Cold War period, Ireland has been focused on its domestic economic problems. Motivated by the desire to improve its economic standing and the objective of 'rebuilding Ireland's international reputation' (Gilmore 2011), the Irish government has sought deeper, more extensive engagement with other states, particularly with the emerging economies, including Russia. As a result, although Ireland has had some historical encounters with Russia, the bilateral relationship today has to be seen in the context of Ireland's economic difficulties and the need to find new, promising markets.

What historical links there are between the two states derive mostly from their mutual revolutionary experiences, although economic ties can be traced further back to tsarist Russia. In the 1920s, the Communist International (Comintern) was instrumental in assisting the Communist Party of Ireland and was resolutely pro IRA. The Comintern saw Ireland 'as a flashpoint adjacent to the heart of British imperialism and the homeland of a diaspora spread throughout the empire and the USA' (O'Connor 2003: 117). The Comintern was active, of course, wherever it felt there might be fertile ground for Bolshevik ideas, including in respect of the UK's Trade Union movement in the 1920s. The Russo–Irish relationship would be sustained later by reason of Ireland's geostrategic significance and perception of mutually beneficial economic opportunities. Cultural links should be neither ignored nor overstated. Particularly notable are the Irish pianist and composer John Field's near-30 year stay in Russia and early nineteenth century influence over the Russian piano school; as well as the Irish poet, lyricist and singer Thomas Moore's influence on Russian poets and writers (in 2011 a statue of Moore was unveiled in St Petersburg). Russia remains keen on Irish culture today. Irish dancing is particularly popular and both Moscow and St Petersburg hold annual dance competitions (feis), in which both Russian and non-Russian dancers compete. St Patrick's Day has been celebrated in Russia since 1992, Moscow, St Petersburg, Kazan and other Russian cities hold festivities and Irish music and dance again plays a central role. Dublin also holds an increasingly well-established annual Festival of Russian Culture, which attracts visitors and participants from both countries.

50 *Maxine David*

Most emphasis must be placed on the economic relationship, however. As Cold War relations thawed in the 1970s and 1980s, Ireland provided a vital stopping point for Russian airplanes en route to the USA, Aeroflot establishing a fuel base at Shannon airport in 1980. Most famously, in 1994, President Yeltsin failed to disembark a plane at Shannon, sparking a minor diplomatic embarrassment for the Taoiseach, Albert Reynolds. But it was those links established in the late Soviet period that positioned Ireland well for the immediate post-Soviet period, translating into Irish management of Russian airports and the establishment of the first Irish bar at Moscow's Sheremetyevo airport: Aer Rianta International Duty Free (ARI) began operating at Sheremetyevo as early as 1989. It now runs duty free operations at four airports in Moscow and St Petersburg, notably winning a seven-year contract in 2007 to develop further duty-free services at Sheremetyevo's new Terminal Three. The traffic is two-way, in April 2012, for example, it was announced that the Russian airline, Transaero, had bought an airline maintenance business at Shannon airport. Co-operation literally extends through the stratosphere: in June 2012, Ireland signed an agreement with Russia on bilateral co-operation on space exploration.

Ireland experienced a high growth in exports to Russia in 2010 and 2011, a response to Ireland's domestic problems as well as the global banking crisis which made credit-raising activities very problematic. Russia has so far proved to be a fertile market for Ireland's ambitions. In 2009, the Ireland Russia Business Association (IRBA) was established. Its head, Constantin Gurdgiev, accounts for IRBA as the result of calculation of future opportunities for both states following Ireland's 2007–8 investment in Russian industries such as construction, logistics and industrial development. In 2010 and 2011, Ireland featured in the bottom five of the member states in respect of both import and export revenue, making it a relatively unimportant player in the EU–Russia relationship. However, the Irish export market to Russia grew by an impressive 46 per cent from €342 million in 2010 to €500 million in 2011 (Eurostat 2012). This growth was experienced by many other member states although Ireland was one of only a handful to maintain a trading surplus with Russia in both years. The upwards trend looks set to continue for Ireland, with reports of a 32 per cent increase in Irish exports to Russia in the first quarter of 2012 (Corcoran 2012a).

In 2012, Ireland made concerted efforts to ensure this growth continued. In February, a delegation went to Moscow to meet Russian counterparts in tourism, sales, conference and events organization in a bid to promote Ireland as a destination of choice. This was followed by an Enterprise Ireland trade mission, which in June 2012 spent five days of intensive networking in Russia, with a third mission planned for the autumn of 2012. The export market comprises many sectors: food, medical and pharmaceutical, agri-equipment and service industries. Irish companies such as PM Group, anticipating the decline of the construction industry in Ireland, focused on Russia, while Ireland is also moderately successful there in the soft drinks and alcoholic drinks industry. Although Ireland is also targeting Brazil and China, the Russian market presents more opportunities. It is noted, for instance, that Russia represents a better consumer market given its high rate of GDP per capita – more than double that of China in 2010 (Gurdgiev in Corcoran 2012b).

Part of Russia's interest in Ireland lies in the reputation it built as the 'Celtic Tiger' from the mid-1990s until the economic downturn in 2008. Ireland also provides a base from which re-exporters can conduct trading relations with other European countries and the USA (Gurdgiev in Nikitenko 2011), indeed, their links with the USA are also seen as good opportunities. Investment opportunities for Russians lie in the pharmaceuticals industry and information and communications technology (ICT), industries that are well represented by the big trans-national names. Other areas are airline leasing, financial services, and legal services. Work has already been done to ensure both states are more physically connected to each other, with the reinstatement of direct flights, for example, the Moscow to Dublin route on S7 in 2008. These physical links, coupled with the cultural links outlined above, mean that there is an increasing passage of people between each state. However, Tourism Ireland points out that Russians have 'limited understanding of what the island of Ireland has to offer as a holiday destination', their aim is therefore 'to begin building awareness in Russia of the many things to see and do' (Tourism Ireland 2012). This 'limited understanding', incidentally, is in marked contrast to the UK, which has no trouble attracting visitors or business, a fact of which Ireland seeks to take advantage. In 2011, the Irish government instituted a visa waiver scheme, making it easier for tourists from Russia (and other countries), to travel between the UK and Ireland. Tourism Ireland notes that over 24 million people are now travelling out of Russia and that in 2010 the UK received an increase of over 23 per cent of Russian visitors. The visa waiver scheme is designed to encourage those tourists to make the extra trip over to Ireland.

Ireland in the EU

Ireland is widely seen as a 'good' partner within the EU, both within the Brussels context and in respect of domestic attitudes and behaviour. Eurobarometer data consistently record the Irish people as strongly in favour of the EU (see Kennedy and Sinnott 2007 for evidence that the picture is more divided and complex than this), notwithstanding the Irish people's rejections of the Nice Treaty in 2001 and the Lisbon Treaty in 2008. Like other member states, Ireland experiences differing political party stances towards EU membership but nevertheless, the dominant political party discourse has long been a positive one. Historically, two of the larger parties, Fianna Fáil and Fine Gael, have been supportive of Irish membership of the EC/U. The Labour Party had traditionally exhibited greater concerns about membership but over time its position has softened somewhat and the attitude towards the EU today might be described more as one of a 'critical friend'. (See Devine 2009

52   *Maxine David*

for an historiographical account of Irish political parties' attitudes on neutrality and how these play out in EU interactions.)

In Brussels itself, Ireland operates with a small number of officials who have relatively high levels of autonomy in relation to their capacity to negotiate on behalf of their government. Ireland is described as a member state which accords the EU a high priority in its workload; as 'solution-oriented rather than problem-focused'; and which delivers high quality, flexible positions in a timely fashion (Panke 2010: 771, 780–82). Panke's results, it should be noted, differ from Laffan's (2006: 704–5) inasmuch as the latter speaks of Ireland as being low-skilled and with information of an average quality. On the other hand, Laffan also finds that Ireland bargains effectively by virtue of its practice of limiting its interactions to just that handful of issues which it chooses to prioritize, explaining Ireland's relative lack of involvement in the EU's Russia policy.

The United Kingdom

Examination of the UK–Russia relationship shows that over 450 years and more of history between these two countries, there remains a surprisingly high degree of continuity in their relations, notwithstanding certain periods when they stood on opposite sides in a conflict. The relationship dates back to1553 and the 'discovery' of Russia by an Englishman, Richard Chancellor, who established relations between the English monarchy and the Russian tsars; establishing also the first trading relationship (through the Muscovy Company) between a western European state and Russia. England continued to occupy a privileged trading position and maintain an active diplomatic relationship. Culture also figured highly from the beginning, the Russian connections in Shakespeare's *Love's Labour's Lost,* for instance, reflecting the high degree of public attention paid to Russia in Elizabethan England. Thus, from its very beginnings, the UK–Russia relationship was characterized by trade, diplomacy, monarchical links and culture. Only the loss of the Russian monarchy has changed this configuration, although other dynamics have been added to it.

Keen to continue trading, to share and explore cultural links and to interact at the highest diplomatic levels, the two states are nevertheless today often divided by their differing ideas about what constitutes 'appropriate' behaviour. Indeed, the very question of what constitutes legitimate behaviour and who adheres 'best' to such standards, splits the two. They meet in a range of fora, but given the comparative international status of the UN, G8 and EU, it is unsurprising that the UK sees the EU as one forum through which to manage relations with Russia, but not the most important one. Many UK foreign policy actions are defined by the close UK–US relationship, inevitably affecting Russian perceptions of the UK (see David 2011). From the UK and USA perspectives, they are ranged on opposite sides to Russia in relation to democracy, respect for law and human rights, and so in respect of what constitutes dominant international organizational thought on legitimacy. Russia,

Ireland and the United Kingdom 53

as seen clearly in the New Cold War discourse (see Sakwa 2008; Galbreath 2008), is still perceived by both as relatively unprogressive, adhering to sovereign, Westphalian norms of international organization. The 1999 Kosovo crisis, the 2003 Iraq War, Libya in 2010, the ongoing (in 2013) Syrian situation – on all of these the UK and USA have met with Russian opposition in the UN. The UK–US position is officially that such large-scale humanitarian crises cannot be ignored by the 'international community', that justice must be served; the Russians argue for the upholding of international law, respect for the primacy of the UN and state sovereignty, and proper consideration for the impact of intervention on international order. These positions go some way to explaining why much of the UK–Russia relationship is mediated through a US rather than EU lens. Add to this the UK's ambitions as a foreign policy actor and the realization forced upon it by, for instance, the 1956 Suez Crisis, that it cannot be an effective actor without the support of the USA. There are, in fact, underlying foreign policy similarities between France and the UK: neither is fully reconciled to its reduced position in the world; both realize that a fully independent foreign policy does not always make for an effective one; and both seek to align themselves with other actors that will facilitate the achievement of objectives. For the UK, the EU's relative weakness means it is not the sensible option (and increasingly as Le Noan shows, France shares the same concerns).

Despite this, there are appreciable differences between the UK's foreign policy approaches and those of others, such that a distinct British style is discernible, including in respect of Russia. The UK has steered a path between the more (arguably, overly) conciliatory Franco–German approach to Russia and the antagonism of the USA, avoiding what Russia certainly sees as the excesses of legislation such as the Jackson-Vanik amendment and the Magnitsky bill, but avoiding too the type of criticism levelled at Sarkozy over Georgia or Schröder generally (see Le Noan and Stewart in this volume). While in a global economy, it becomes increasingly difficult to separate the political from the economic, it is precisely this separation that the UK has sought to maintain in its relations with Russia, with some success as discussed below.

Differing perceptions, even values, explain the often discordant nature of the political relationship but it is also the case that the relationship is conducted at more than just the intergovernmental level and should not be reduced to that. Indeed, in the British case, business interests might be said to function as the glue that holds the relationship together, even when intergovernmental relations have come close to breaking. Business interests dominate and at the societal level too, there is a genuine, shared desire for interaction. The relationship can only be understood, therefore, through an analysis of not only the intergovernmental relationship but also those of the business community and people-to-people contacts. To an extent, this is a false division for the two societal-based groups are not completely free of government involvement. This is Russia's point: that it is disingenuous to

54 Maxine David

argue that the British government is removed from the activities of those working with and amongst ordinary Russians. Thus, Russia interprets external funding of NGOs working on its territory as an attempt to interfere in the internal affairs of Russia, symbolized by the signing in July 2012 of Russia's NGO Law, popularly dubbed in western media as the 'NGO foreign agents law'. In considering the work in Russia of actors such as the British Council and the BBC World Service, one cannot disregard the links that can be drawn between them and the British government but it is nevertheless fair to ascribe to them a good deal of agency as entities working independent of British governmental interference and oversight in terms of their day-to-day running.

UK–Russia intergovernmental relations

The intergovernmental relationship is characterized by high level diplomatic activity, directed at the pursuit of national interests and the shaping of interactions within the international system. A high point for the UK was Prime Minister Margaret Thatcher's role as interlocutor between the US President, Ronald Reagan, and the Soviet leader, Mikhail Gorbachev. However, British influence since has not been seen to serve Russian interests. A discourse of insistence that Russia must move further down the road of democratization, successive international interventions and differing ideas about what constitutes legal and legitimate intervention mean that Russia has learned to distrust the USA and UK equally. Divided as the UK and Russia are on such subjects, there is a clear imperative to co-operate: the FCO (Foreign and Commonwealth Office) refers to climate change, trade, Afghanistan, the Middle East and Iran (House of Commons Defence Committee 2009). More direct threats also necessitate co-operation, cyber security, for instance, is creeping up the UK–Russia political agenda. In late 2011, GCHQ reported it was 'disturbed' by the high number of cyber attacks against the UK, with Russia and China identified as the worst 'culprits'.

The vested nature of the UK's interest in Russia is clear. A stable, democratic Russia issues fewer challenges than an unstable, economically weak and authoritarian version. This was the immediate preoccupation for the UK as the USSR fell apart. Uncertainties lay in whether mass, economically-induced migration from Russia might ensue and of particular concern was what would happen to the Soviet arsenal of nuclear, chemical, possibly biological, as well as conventional weaponry (interview with former British ambassador 2012).[1] Today, however, Russia is not deemed to represent a direct existential threat to the UK, although the question of whether the more assertive nature of Russian foreign policy represents a threat to Europe is not dismissed (House of Commons Defence Committee 2009). In 1991, the UK was alive both to the threats and opportunities; Russia then (and today), offered a vast, unsaturated market.

As early as 1992, Alexander Shokin (Russian Minister of Labour and Employment) and Michael Heseltine (UK Secretary of State for Trade and President of Board of Trade) signed an Agreement on Economic Co-operation.

The agreement confirmed the establishment of the still extant UK–Russia Intergovernmental Steering Committee on Trade and Investment and spoke of encouraging financing mechanisms, training and exchange of knowledge and skills. Thus, as with the earliest beginnings of the relationship, economic and trading relations were high on the bilateral agenda. Early trade took the form of cosmetics, confectionery, alcohol and motor cars particularly and sales, it was anticipated, would only increase as Russians became more prosperous. Security concerns as well as trading interests ensured strong diplomatic relations were maintained from the beginning, with President Yeltsin visiting four times in eight years, British Prime Ministers the same (FCO 2000). That top level activity was mirrored by numerous ministerial visits and an increase in the traffic of ordinary people out to Russia (see David 2011).

Despite relations at the highest level of government remaining on a firm, even if sometimes shaky, footing until midway through the first decade of the new century, there were early signs that Russia had not fully reconciled itself to western ideas about Russia's (reduced) position and what the post-Cold War world should look like. Nuclear non-proliferation, disputes over the CFE Treaty, the continued existence of NATO, let alone its enlargement; all these and more would serve to upset Russia's relations with the USA, and, by association, the UK. Nevertheless, despite deep divisions between Russia and the UK over the 1999 Kosovo crisis and British concerns over Chechnya, in 2000 the UK would be the first overseas destination for the new (acting) Russian President, Putin. The early relationship between then-Prime Minister Tony Blair and Putin was a good one and seemed to bode well for the bilateral relationship, notwithstanding the second Chechen War and Blair's oft-referenced promulgation of and commitment to an 'ethical' foreign policy. For some, Blair trod the wrong side of his own commitments; both he and his Foreign Minister, Robin Cook, for instance, condemned Russian actions in Chechnya but this was insufficient for the Foreign Affairs Select Committee which roundly questioned the government's reaction in December 1999, deeming it insufficient in scope. Cook and Blair continued, outwardly at least, to speak positively of Russia, even as the Foreign Affairs Select Committee heard more and more evidence of a deteriorating relationship and of an increasing divide between the USA and Russia, which, given close Anglo–American relations, would inevitably impact negatively on the Anglo–Russian relationship (House of Commons Foreign Affairs Committee 1999). Blair's failed attempt to reconcile the US and Russian positions over the USA's proposed Strategic Defence Initiative (SDI), the Iraq War of 2003, and the burgeoning relationship between Russia and France and Germany, all contributed to the cooling of the intergovernmental relationship. The crisis when it came was in the form of an event no government could ignore.

The circumstances of the 2006 murder of Alexander Litvinenko, a former KGB/FSB agent, are the stuff of fiction. Litvinenko was granted political asylum in London after speaking out in Russia against the security forces, claiming he had been ordered by them to murder Russian oligarch, Boris

56   *Maxine David*

Berezovsky, who had himself by now fled Russia to Britain. Once in London, and soon to become a British citizen, Litvinenko made further allegations against the Russian security services, most notably accusing them of responsibility for the bombing of a Moscow apartment block. This attack had been blamed on Chechen terrorists by the Russian authorities and used, Litvinenko now claimed, as a pretext for the second Chechen War. On his death-bed in London, Litvinenko alleged his murder by polonium poisoning was the result of a Russian state-sponsored plot. The government response was robust: four Russian diplomats were expelled, visa restrictions applied and co-operation on counter-terrorism suspended. The British Police quickly established that Andrei Lugovoi, a former KGB agent himself, was a person of interest in the investigation. The Russians refused the British request for his extradition on the grounds it would violate their Constitution. The Litvinenko matter remains on the bilateral political agenda, even after the 2010 change of British government, and has the capacity to plague inter-state relations for some time to come. The official preliminary hearing for the British inquest into the death began in September 2012, the media rife with reports that the Russian state might be found guilty of state-sponsored nuclear terrorism. The hearing and the 2013 inquest that will follow may therefore derail recent attempts to restore diplomatic relations and put the relationship back on track.

The Litvinenko murder is notable also for how it visibly served to underline for the British the futility of turning to the EU for solidarity, despite the extreme circumstances. The British Ambassador to Moscow at the time, Sir Tony Brenton, was treated to what can only be described as harassment by the Russian authorities and Putin supporters, such as Nashi, the Russian youth movement. The murder was an inexcusable breach of British sovereignty and even if one accepts then-President Putin's argument that this was not state-sponsored, the bilateral relationship was not helped by the bellicose stance Russia adopted and the airtime given to Lugovoi at home. Despite British attempts to mobilize support in the EU, beyond informal messages of support to Brenton from other EU diplomats and a lukewarm (considering the circumstances) supporting statement, the UK would be offered no reason to rethink their opinion that the EU is not an effective foreign policy actor.

To return to the bilateral relationship, from the Russian perspective, the UK is hardly immune to criticism itself. Its own attempts to have persons of interest extradited have all met with failure. A case in point is the oligarch, Boris Berezovsky, who was granted political asylum following Russian extradition attempts. Like Lugovoi in Russia, Berezovsky was a prominent personality in the British media, including on extremely sensitive issues like the 2008 war in Georgia. This was despite the fact that the Crown Prosecution Service had investigated him for alleged attempts to incite violence abroad when he argued for regime change in Russia in a 2007 interview (House of Commons Foreign Affairs Committee 2007). As for Denmark and Austria (see relevant chapters in this volume), the Chechen War would have direct consequences for the UK, when in 2003 it granted political asylum to former

Chechen separatist leader Akhmad Zakayev, in defiance of Russian attempts at extradition. Even as Putin argued that such instances stood in the way of 'normal' relations (in Beeston 2008), it was clear that the Russians would or could not believe that Judge Timothy Workman's decision to refuse the request for extradition was the defining ruling in the case and that this was not a matter for the British government. This misunderstanding may be said to have stemmed from differing perspectives about democracy and the separation of powers but it was a sign too of the mistrust that pervaded the relationship. In an attempt to restore the state of the now visibly poor relations, the Foreign Affairs Select Committee 2007 recommended an appeal be made to Russia's pragmatism, that the UK adopt a less exclusive, more inclusive discourse with Russia, and that it see the need to be more reflexive in examining its own behaviour.

For just a little longer, these recommendations would not hold sway. The brief, yet pivotal, 2008 hot war in Georgia was met in Britain with severe disapprobation. Then-Prime Minister Gordon Brown (2008) accused Russia of irresponsible, unpredictable behaviour and took the opportunity to argue for the need to diversify energy supply to reduce Europe's reliance on this unreliable actor. This very critical stance was not echoed by all other European member states, most notably France (see Le Noan in this volume), and instead engagement with Russia in the EU moved to a more pragmatic footing. The shift was supported by the British then-EU Trade Commissioner, Lord Peter Mandelson (2008), by virtue of 'the strategic importance of our common interest'. The message found common voice within the UK as FCO Minister Lord Malloch-Brown spoke of the need to step into Russia's shoes and see how certain western actions looked 'provocative' (in House of Commons European Union Committee 2009). The new pragmatism, it should be noted, was not supposed to come at the expense of continuing to criticize Russia when deemed necessary. Whether the UK has stayed on the right side of this line, is debatable.

The change of British government in 2010 made it easier for relations between the two states to move on. The new Secretary of State, William Hague, had met Russian Foreign Minister Lavrov in the months leading up to the General Election. Once in power, Hague and Prime Minister David Cameron made clear from the outset that foreign policy was about the promotion of trade as much as anything else, receiving a positive response from the business world (if not everyone else). Thus, while the UK's Foreign Office may be a distinct entity from the Department for Business, Innovation and Skills, no less than in the Irish case the Foreign Minister has been at the forefront of the pursuit of British business interests. In September 2011, Prime Minister Cameron made the first British prime ministerial visit to Russia since the death of Litvinenko. Interpreted widely as a desire to move diplomatic relations on, Cameron nevertheless refused to restore links between the states' security services, visibly emphasizing instead the economic aspects of the relationship by taking along a number of high-profile business people. In November 2011,

58   *Maxine David*

the Russian Ambassador Alexander Yakovenko (in Embassy of the Russian Federation 2012) said:

> A new chapter is being written now in the history of our countries' relations. ... Certainly, some differences in approaches still remain ... But business collaboration, as a foundation for the overall system of our bilateral relationship, once again became the focal point of the discussions.

Trading and economic interests

As elsewhere in the relationship, the narrative here is one of opportunity, some successes but some disappointments. British companies of all shapes and sizes have made inroads into the Russian market. Energy companies receive most media attention but the UK is represented in the drinks and food industry, in services (most notably financial and legal), the motor industry and so on. According to the FCO's offshoot, UK Trade and Investment (UKTI), some of the best opportunities for UK companies reside in advanced engineering, financial services, ICT, power/energy, sports and leisure.

The boom period for UK exports to Russia came in the years immediately leading up to Russia's 1998 crash and subsequent devaluation of the rouble. In 1999, exports dropped by nearly 60 per cent even as import figures rose by approximately 66 per cent in the period from 1997–9 (FCO 1999). In the period leading up to Litvinenko's murder and the subsequent downturn in political relations, some recovery was experienced. By 2006 the export market was worth $1.9 billion and imports $3.6 billion. The UK was Russia's biggest foreign investor in 2006 and ranked fourth largest over the period 2001–6. BP's and Shell's presence in Russia made the UK the largest foreign investor in the energy market. By this point, 400 UK companies were involved in Russia (House of Commons Foreign Affairs Committee 2007) and the number of Russian holdings in the UK was also increasing, albeit slowly. The CBI reported some disruption to business activities as a result of worsening political relations but the Foreign Affairs Committee concluded in 2007 that the overall effect to that date was limited. By 2008, Mandelson was referring to the 1,000 plus British companies operating in Russia, evidence that poor political relations do not inevitably lead to poor economic relations. Figures for 2010 and 2011 show the UK is maintaining a negative trade balance with Russia, of minus €2,123 million for 2010 and minus €3,329 for 2011 (Eurostat 2012). This compares favourably with all of the EU's larger member states, including France, Germany and Italy.

High profile cases involving the poor experiences of British companies in Russia have dominated media headlines in the UK. Most talked-about have been BP's experiences, whose joint venture with Russia's TNK resulted in visa disputes, police raids, Interior Ministry investigations into alleged tax evasion and ultimately BP boss Robert Dudley's departure from Russia following

Ireland and the United Kingdom 59

disputes over management. This did not prevent BP seeking further involvement with Russian corporations, suggesting the risks for BP are far outweighed by the benefits. Indeed, in 2011 David Peattie, Head of BP in Russia, told the Executive Director of the Russo–British Chamber of Commerce (RBCC) he would do it all again because Russia is a great place to do business (interview with Stephen Dalziel 2012). Even following June 2012 reports that BP's time in Russia may have come to an end, media reports show Peattie remains resolutely upbeat.

Relying on the British media, it would be all too easy to assume that only extreme risk-takers would dare to do business in Russia and this unfortunately has a negative effect on British attitudes to Russia. The RBCC reports a good deal of initial interest from British businesses but conservative attitudes that favour export rather than longer-term investment mean conversion rates of interested parties are low. Given the bureaucratic problems, Russia now presents best opportunities for those looking to do business in the longer term. For those prepared to make a serious commitment – excellent prior research, contracts signed under English law and the establishment of good locally-based teams – there are many positives. The new NGO law has added a new layer of bureaucracy but does not necessarily impact detrimentally on those working in Russia (interview with Stephen Dalziel 2012). The RBCC experience is also that poor political relations do not lead inexorably to poor trading relations, rather an attitude of 'business is business' prevails. Where politics does interfere is in respect of structures. The RBCC deals with a constant stream of complaints from clients requiring help with visas. While it is quite easy for Russians to secure visas, the processes are time-consuming and the loss of a passport for two to three weeks is detrimental to business. As a result, Paris, Berlin and other continental European cities are preferred meeting places (interview with Stephen Dalziel 2012). It is the bureaucracy involved in setting up a business in Russia that is the single biggest problem, however. This is second on UKTI's (2010) list of market challenges and the problem becomes much more severe when one considers that the corruption that both the RBCC and UKTI identify as a feature of doing business in Russia is a not irrational response to problems of bureaucracy.

People-to-people contacts

Despite the more high-level problems, there can be little doubt about the attraction that the UK offers for Russians. Visa figures alone demonstrate this. The British Embassy in Moscow witnessed a rise in the issue of visas from approximately 3–5,000 in the 1980s to 20 times that by 2000 (interview with former British Ambassador 2012). The numbers of people travelling both ways are positive indicators of the possibility of gaps being bridged in a way that governments simply cannot manage, of mutual knowledge gained and relationships formed. They represent something inherently good and right in

60 Maxine David

their own right, which cannot 'but have a significant effect over time' (interview with former British ambassadors 2012). Clearly, however, governments play a role in creating the structures and environments in which different societies and individuals can connect. It is not entirely surprising, therefore, that Russian political elites do not distinguish between contacts at the level of people and those at the level of government and fear societal contacts offer all too-many opportunities for espionage and dissemination of propaganda. Clearly there exists a close connection between the interests of any state and the values it espouses. After all, as already established, a free and democratic Russia is a more stable one, reducing the threat of economic migration and offering a prosperous market in which British businesses can profit. Government-sponsored and facilitated activities include the Department for International Development's (DfID) Know How Fund (KHF), and the British Council. These British ventures in Russia serve both the UK's interests and its values, even while benefiting ordinary Russians too. As former Prime Minister Tony Blair said: 'In the end values and interests merge' (1999). However, the British are resolute that there exists a separation between state and society, and that the government role is restricted to helping construct a favourable environment and framework to facilitate exchange, eschewing interference in the day-to-day activities of non-governmental actors. The NGO law indicates Russia does not fully accept this.

For the FCO, the KHF was designed as a key facilitating instrument, a mirror to the EU's TACIS, to assist Russia in its transition to a market economy, consistent with both Russian (professed) objectives and UK values and interests. It was also about the trickle-down of technical and commercial knowledge to society. Young Russian managers were to be trained in the UK in order that they could return to Russia with increased knowledge of how business was conducted in the West. The British Council was also to play a key part in the government's activity in Russia but again with the aim of transfer of knowledge and experience to ordinary Russians. The British Council is open about its objective of promoting interest in and knowledge of the UK and open too about its administration of the scholarship programme of the FCO, which enables regional administrators to study in Britain. During Sir Roderic Lyne's time in Russia (2000–4), 15 British Council offices were established, staffed mostly by Russians, open to Russians and providing them with access to key resources, for instance, computers. The offices facilitated exposure to British culture and the English language but worked free of government interference (interview with former British Council staff member 2012). Nevertheless, ultimately staff at British Council offices in Russia would experience what the Council called 'intimidation', forcing them in early 2008 to close their offices outside Moscow on the basis of 'external pressures' (FCO 2009). The BBC World Service's experiences were hardly more promising, manoeuvrings by Russia's regulatory board effectively limiting its transmissions to larger urban areas such as Moscow and St Petersburg. In response, it concentrated efforts on online activity, encountering no obstacles in doing so (FCO 2009). However, developments since 2012 suggest the Russian government will become increasingly repressive in respect of internet usage. Effective hacking activities and campaigns of 'dis-information' are now being accompanied by tactics to restrict access, such as we have seen adopted by China for some time now.

People-to-people contacts occur outside directly government-facilitated schemes, of course. The UK enjoys a good reputation in Russia for the quality and integrity of its education, finance and judicial sectors. The UK remains the destination of choice for wealthy Russians seeking to educate their children abroad. As for finance, when Russia began to need access to money markets, London held more attraction than New York, in London Russians felt more comfortable and were condescended to less (interviews with former British ambassadors 2012). Today, the 'London Stock Exchange remains a principal international platform for [Russian] companies to access global capital markets with more than 60 Russian and Russian-focused companies listed on the International Order Book' (Embassy of the Russian Federation 2012). Meanwhile, the status accorded to the British legal system by Russians has been evident in the seeming rash of legal disputes by Russian oligarchs pursuing their cause in London's courts. It must be recognized, however, that the importance of all these links in terms of exchange is diminished somewhat by the fact that many of the Russians coming to be educated in the UK do not return home and share that knowledge. Reflecting a relative lack of opportunity, Russia is experiencing a brain drain, which is detrimental to its own economy and to the deepening of understanding between the two states.

The EU in UK foreign policy

A noticeable absence from the UK–Russia relationship is the EU. Given the close relations so many of the EU member states have with Russia and the range and extent of the EU's co-operative activities with Russia, it must be, for the uninitiated, a source of surprise that the UK does not conduct more of its relations with Russia through the multilateral resources available to it within the EU. This is particularly so given the UK has experienced some deeply troubling moments in its relations with Russia, moments which held warnings for other European states about Russia's likely transition to a democracy based on rule of law, and which should, prima facie, have evoked a far stronger and more unified approach than they did. The UK opinion of the EU as a foreign policy actor is, it is fair to say, resigned, at best. The dominant perception is that a major part of the problem is that the many and various bilateral relations present a major obstacle to the establishment of a common Russia policy. From both the UK and the wider EU perspective, it is clear the EU has reached the limits of its capacities to effect change in Russia; WTO membership is vital if Russia is to learn the importance of the rule of law and to become a more reliable partner (interviews with European Commission officials 2011[2] and former British ambassadors to Russia 2012).

62 Maxine David

Whether even WTO membership will in and of itself be enough is highly questionable.

Listening to British accounts of EU failings, however, one cannot help but reflect on that fact that unity has to begin somewhere. If the EU has failed to establish *a* Russia policy, then the UK, as one of the 27 member states, must inevitably shoulder some blame. It is true that many of the reasons that bring the EU member states together to seek joint solutions to common problems regarding Russia do not pertain to the UK: energy dependence, insufficiency of foreign policy resources and perception of direct threat. This brings benefits to the EU in that the UK does not seek regularly to upload issues to the EU, indeed it prefers to rely on its own resources (David 2011). However, the flipside of that lack of engagement is that the EU suffers losses in that the UK fails to use its diplomatic resources for the benefit of the wider European good. As for why (leaving aside the residual attitude of great power status), from the UK perspective the EU has exhibited little unity over the Russia question and has been singularly poor at defending those values for which it stands, particularly as they relate to rule of law and human rights, as the differing discourses over Georgia demonstrated. The FCO position is that the EU must negotiate a 'rules-based relationship with Russia' and seek a replacement for the PCA that is 'robust', covering the entire range of EU–Russia relations and ensure it 'will not be unconditional' (House of Commons Defence Committee 2009). In the same report, the FCO speaks of the EU's need to engage in dialogue and negotiation with Russia. What must precede that, however, is an arrangement suitable to ensure the member states can first engage in dialogue and negotiation *with each other*. No current arrangement achieves that and it is the multiplicity of voices, despite the commonality of interests, which is the biggest hindrance to an effective EU–Russia policy. The UK does not constitute the biggest headache for the EU; indeed, in a range of interviews, the states most commonly referenced as obstacles to a Russia policy were France, Germany and Italy.

Many UK officials are not unappreciative of the fact that the EU has scored some goals. In relation to Russian membership of the WTO, the EU was credited; as it was too for its progress in relation to energy policy (interviews with former British ambassadors, 2012). However, the compliments were directed at a narrow sampling of EU entities: DG Trade, DG Energy, and notably the European Parliament for its strong defence (in marked contrast to the member states and the Council) of human rights and its very outspoken record against Russia in this regard. Implicit in all conversations, but explicit rarely, was a perception of limited agency on the part of the EU, or indeed the UK. Sir Andrew Wood (Shevtsova and Wood 2011) has argued that: 'It is Russia's own historic development that will count, not the rhetoric of foreigners, and Russia is in a self-absorbed condition. Outside influence seems to me to be limited at best'.

The one exception to this is the WTO, which was consistently evoked as the most necessary step to be taken if Russia is to become a reliable partner for the West. However, the UK adheres most strongly to the view that real change will come only when there is a change of the guard within Russia. Thus, the protests seen in Russia following the parliamentary and presidential elections in late 2011 and early 2012 are vindication of an approach that criticizes Russia for human rights violations and emphasizes the importance of adherence to certain norms and standards of behaviour, but which simultaneously pursues partnerships at the various levels of state and society. In this, there is really little daylight between the EU and UK positions. For the UK, however, until other member states come to appreciate that and act accordingly, the EU will remain an ineffective foreign policy actor, affecting the willingness of the UK to act through it.

Conclusion

While Ireland and the UK are quite different foreign policy actors, in one fundamental aspect they are similar and that is in respect of their economic interconnectedness with the EU. Indeed, Hay and Smith (2010: 129) argue that they, along with the rest of the EU and Europe, 'have experienced a de-globalisation not a globalisation of [their] economic activities'. Each state does adopt a different approach, however, to this interconnectedness and has varying levels of capacity to effect change within the EU. Ireland is distinct from the UK by virtue of its relatively positive 'can-do' attitude within the EU context, albeit it is relatively protected by its status as a small state and what might fairly be regarded as the lower expectations that others have of it, and it of itself. To date, Ireland has embraced its place in Europe and the EU. Any questions of sovereignty have revolved around the issue of neutrality mainly but also other issues that reflect on Irish identity, abortion laws for instance. On the whole, however, membership of the EU has been interpreted as an enhancement of Irish sovereignty, not a loss of it, again, a story common to many of the EU's smaller member states. In respect of sovereignty, the opposite is true of the UK, where the dominant, political, media and societal discourse is of the EU tapping away at the walls of British sovereignty, of an insiders' defence against encroachment by 'outsiders'. This is a paradoxical reflection of ideas about the UK's economic and political significance relative to many EU member states, but fears also about a diminishing role for the UK in world affairs. In this, Russia and the UK have much in common. Compared to Ireland, the UK's resource base means that it has greater capacity to build bilateral relations that serve its interests well and reduce the imperative to coordinate its relations within a multilateral environment. It is perhaps telling, however, that the Irish government is directing resources and efforts into building a deeper bilateral relationship with Russia, even as the EU seeks to build a more unified Russia policy. How is this to be interpreted?

It is Ireland's economic interests that are driving its interactions with Russia. There is a close connection between the Irish government and Irish business (the Foreign Ministry is the Department of Foreign Affairs *and*

64 *Maxine David*

Trade and the Minister of State led the June mission to Moscow) so it would be surprising if we did not see government policy reflecting Irish business interests. As for that, the Chief Executive of the Irish Exporters' Association has 'urged' Irish businesses to exploit the potential of the 2012 trade missions in order 'to break away from the stagnant EU markets' (Whelan in Corcoran 2012a). This suggests that the government too will continue to court Russian trade and this will inevitably affect some of the positions Ireland will adopt in relation to the EU's relations with Russia but there is no reason to think they will impact negatively on the EU. Indeed, it may mean Ireland will play an increasingly active and constructive role. Ireland is intent on freeing up the visa regime with Russia, a subject which has long been on the EU's political agenda and its agreement on space exploration is a consequence of a wider EU initiative.

Implicit in all the criticism of the EU is the assumption that if the member states did adopt a common stance in their relations with Russia, then Russia would be brought round to 'our' way of thinking. However, it is worth remembering Sir Andrew Wood's admonition that ultimately change needs to come from within Russia itself. Events within Russia suggest that change may well be coming. The question is where the EU and its member states should position themselves in respect of it. Change is needed in the EU too, in particular for mechanisms that enable the member states to come together to share perceptions and arguments on Russia, to analyze and to agree on answers and desirable parameters of action. Without such mechanisms, and despite a wealth of excellent analysis available to the EU, the member states see the same thing differently and fail to appreciate the insights that other states have to offer (interviews with former British ambassadors, 2012). The lesson from the UK is that business is business and can be compartmentalized to a large extent from politics. After all, British trading figures with Russia rose even as the bilateral political relationship suffered, all parties recognizing the extent to which each other's prosperity was dependent on facilitating business relations. The Ireland–Russia and UK–Russia relationships will be sustained in the longer term by the mutual recognition of business and trading opportunities and the people-to-people contacts that promote a genuine cultural exchange.

Notes

1 Interviews were conducted in 2012 with three former British Ambassadors to Russia; also with representatives of NGOs and the Russo–British Chamber of Commerce.
2 Interviews were conducted in 2011 within COEST, the European Commission and the EEAS.

References

Beeston, Richard (2008) 'Putin Tells Britain: Relations Can Only Improve When You Remove Dissidents', *TimesOnline*. 12 September 2008, available at www.timesonline. co.uk/tol/news/world/europe/article4734450.ece (accessed 26 August 2009).

Ireland and the United Kingdom   65

Blair, Tony (24 April 1999) *Prime Minister's Speech: Doctrine of the International Community.* Available at http://keeptonyblairforpm.wordpress.com (accessed 20 May 2010).

Brown, Gordon (2008). 'This is How We Will Stand Up to Russia's Naked Aggression', *The Observer.* 31 August 2008, available at www.guardian.co.uk/commentisfree/2008/aug/31/russia.georgia (accessed 20 August 2009).

Corcoran, Sorcha (2012a) Trade Missions to Boost Irish Exports to Russia, *Business and Leadership.* Available at http://businessandleadership.com/exporting/item/35556-trade-missions-to-boost/ (accessed 29 June 2012).

——(2012b) 'Indigenous Irish Exports Doing Well in Russia', *Business and Leadership.* Available at http://businessandleadership.com/exporting/item/35865-indigenous-irish-exports-do/ (accessed 29 June 2012).

David, Maxine (2011) 'A Less than Special Relationship: the UK's Russia Experience', Special Issue *Journal of Contemporary European Studies,* 19, 2: 201–12.

Department of Foreign Affairs and Trade [Ireland] (2012) *Policies.* Available at www.dfa.ie/home/index.aspx?id=36 (accessed 31 May 2012).

Devine, Karen (2009) 'Irish Political Parties' Attitudes towards Neutrality and the Evolution of the EU's Foreign, Security and Defence Policies', *Irish Political Studies,* 24, 4: 467–90.

Embassy of the Russian Federation (2012) *Russo-British Economic Relations.* Available at www.rusemb.org.uk/economy/ [accessed 20 September 2012].

Eurostat (2012) *EU – Russia Summit. Strong Recovery of Trade in Goods between EU27 and Russia in 2011.* Eurostat News Release, available at http://europa.eu/rapid/pressReleasesAction.do?reference=STAT/12/82&format=HTML&aged=0&language=EN&guiLanguage=en (accessed 14 June 2012).

Foreign and Commonwealth Office (FCO) (1999) *Memorandum: The FCO's Role in Promoting British Interests in and Relations with Russia.* Available at www.publications.parliament.uk/pa/cm199900/cmselect/cmfaff/101/9120802.htm (accessed 2 September 2010).

——(2009) *Foreign and Commonwealth Office Annual Report 2007–08.* 21 January 2009, available at www.publications.parliament.uk/pa/cm200809/cmselect/cmfaff/195/19514.htm#a52 (accessed 15 March 2011).

Foreign and Commonwealth Office, Eastern Research Group (2000) *High Level Visits to and from Russia 1992–1999.* October 2000, available at http://collections.europarchive.org/tna/20080205132101/www.fco.gov.uk/Files/kfile/russiavisits.pdf (accessed 12 March 2010).

Galbreath, David (2008) 'Putin's Russia and the "New Cold War": Interpreting Myth and Reality', *Europe–Asia Studies,* 60, 9:1623–30.

Gilmore, Eamon (2011) 'Tánaiste's Meeting with Joint Committee on Foreign Affairs and Trade, 5 October 2011'. Available at www.oireachtas.ie/ (accessed 31 May 2012).

Hay, Colin and Smith, Nicola (2010) 'Horses for Courses? The Political Discourse of Globalisation and European Integration in the UK and Ireland', *West European Politics,* 28, 1: 124–58.

House of Commons European Union Committee (2009) *After Georgia – The EU and Russia: Follow-Up Report.* Available at www.publications.parliament.uk/pa/ld200809/ldselect/ldeucom/26/2604.htm#n2 (accessed 2 September 2010).

House of Commons Defence Committee (2009) *Russia: a new confrontation? Tenth Report of 2008–9.* HC 276, House of Commons, available at www.publications.parliament.uk/pa/cm200809/cmselect/cmdfence/276/276.pdf (accessed 10 October 2011).

66 *Maxine David*

House of Commons Foreign Affairs Committee (1999) *Examination of Witnesses (Questions 242 – 259)*. 8 December 1999, available at www.publications.parliament.uk/pa/cm199900/cmselect/cmfaff/101/9120807.htm (accessed 1 September 2010).

——(2007) *Global Security: Russia. Second Report of 2007–8*. HC51, 25 November 2007, available at www.publications.parliament.uk/pa/cm200708/cmselect/cmfaff/51/51.pdf (accessed 1 September 2010).

Kennedy, Fiachra and Sinnott, Richard (2007) 'Irish Public Opinion toward European Integration', *Irish Political Studies*, 22, 1: 61–80.

Laffan, Brigid (2006) 'Managing Europe from Home in Dublin, Athens and Helsinki: A Comparative Analysis', *West European Politics*, 29, 4: 687–708.

Mandelson, Peter (2008) *Russia and the EU: Building Trust on a Shared Continent*. Available at http://trade.ec.europa.eu (accessed 24 June 2010).

Nikitenko, Eugene (2011) 'Russian Investments in Ireland: A Steady Upwards Trend', *Voice of Russia*. Available at http://english.ruvr.ru/2011/03/23/47865338.html (accessed 16 June 2012).

O'Connor, Emmet (2003) 'Communists, Russia, and the IRA, 1920–23', *The Historical Journal*, 46, 1: 115–31.

O'Regan, Mary (2010) 'Political Language as a Flexible Friend: Irish parliamentary Debate on the Iraq War', *Irish Political Studies*, 25, 1: 1–21.

Panke, Diana (2010) 'Good Instructions in No Time? Domestic Coordination of EU Policies in 19 Small States', *West European Politics*, 33, 4: 770–90.

Sakwa, Richard (2008) '"New Cold War" or Twenty Years' Crisis? Russia and International Politics', in *International Affairs*, 84,2: 241–67.

Shevtsova, Lilia and Wood, Andrew (2011) *Change or Decay. Russia's Dilemma and the West's Response*. Washington, DC: Carnegie Endowment for International Peace.

Tourism Ireland (2012) *Taking Ireland to Russia – Tourism Blitz on Moscow This Week*. Available at www.tourismireland.com/Home!/About-Us/Press-Releases/2012/Taking-Ireland-to-Russia-%E2%80%93-tourism-blitz-on-Moscow.aspx (accessed 29 May 2012).

UK Trade and Investment (UKTI) (2010) *Russia Business Guide*. Available at www.ukti.gov.uk/home.html (accessed 24 June 2010).

5 Italy

Riccardo Alcaro

Italy and Russia diverge on virtually everything, from geographical location to climate, from size to strategic landscape, from history to cultural heritage and political, economic and social development. Yet, relations between the two countries have been remarkably strong historically. The roots of this peculiar relationship are not easily identifiable, in particular when Italy's relations with Russia are compared to those of other large European states. Unlike Germany, geography has not linked Russia and Italy; nor geopolitics, as is the case with France and Britain. So, what is it? Do Russia's views and ensuing policies really match with Italy's? And what are the implications for Italy as a member state of the EU, but also NATO?

This chapter answers these questions. The first section recalls the historical roots and summarizes the current state of play of Italian–Russian relations; the second section looks at the specifics of Italy's Russia policy; the third section examines the match or mismatch between Italian and Russian interests and views; and the fourth section assesses whether, taking its impact on Italy's commitment to the EU and NATO into account, Italy's Russia policy entails a consistent strategy.

Italian–Russian ties yesterday and today

In the past, Russia looked at Italy much as other European nations, big and small: a country of riches, both financial and cultural, with prominent skills in all disciplines of human knowledge and craftsmanship, but most importantly with the ability to create beautiful things. In the fifteenth century, it was Italian architects that designed and built the Kremlin walls and cathedrals. In the eighteenth century, Tsar Peter I the Great resorted again to Italian architectural prowess to give shape to a new capital that would embody Russia's European soul and, incidentally, bear his own name: St Petersburg. Throughout the eighteenth and nineteenth centuries, Italy continued to be viewed as a land of inspiration by the increasingly lavish tsarist court, as well as by members of Russia's vibrant cultural environment. Tsars and tsarinas alike dispatched envoys to Italy to buy luxury goods and works of art, while poets and writers left the cold shores of St Petersburg to accomplish their 'Grand Tour' to Italy, the must-do experience of the time for Europe's educated elite.

68   *Riccardo Alcaro*

When, towards the end of the nineteenth century, revolutions and wars in Europe gave way to a delicate balance of power among some four-five large nations, relations between Russia and Italy became more complex. By then, Italy was a young state and a would-be power determined to play a role on the European chessboard. Russia, which thanks to Peter's successors had become a major European player for well over a century, took note. Geopolitical interest added to romanticized cultural links in forging an awkward partnership between the aspirant Mediterranean power and the giant in the East. They shared, in particular, concerns for the Austro–Hungarian appetite for exploiting Ottoman weakness in the troubled Balkan region (Salleo 2009: 10–13). However, whatever benefits Italian and Russian policymakers had hoped to reap from their common antagonism to Austria–Hungary were lost in the First World War and the chaos that followed the Bolshevik seizure of power. Yet, those links would later prove to be an asset. Italy and the USSR built upon them, enabling the development of a special relationship even in the context of the Cold War.

Firms, both private and public, made a substantial contribution to shaping bilateral ties along a co-operative, dialogue-orientated track. In 1969 Italy's then state-owned energy monopoly Eni agreed to a long-term gas supply contract, making Italy one of the first Western countries to establish an energy relationship with the Soviets. In 1970 Fiat, Italy's largest carmaker, was allowed to start production in the USSR.

Most importantly, Italy was home to the most influential Western communist party (the Partito Comunista Italiano, PCI), constantly able to garner somewhere between a quarter and a third of the popular vote between the early 1950s and late 1980s. Combined with Italy's geographical location on the edge of the East–West line of demarcation, the PCI's electoral strength made the country one of the Cold War's most prominent theatres, whereby a strong preference for détente policies took hold in Italian foreign policy-making circles.

The PCI foundered amid the geopolitical revolution that followed the USSR's dissolution, but the Italian fondness for good relations with Russia was undiminished. In fact, the fall of the USSR was seen by many in Italy as a golden opportunity to re-embrace Russia as the prodigal son of the European family of nations.

This conviction has guided the Russia policy of Italy's post-Cold War ruling elites, both left-of-centre and right-of-centre. This fact has tended to be somewhat neglected in media coverage of Italy's relations with Russia, as much emphasis has been put on the personal friendship between Italy's former conservative Prime Minister Silvio Berlusconi (he held the post three times between 1994 and 2011) and Vladimir Putin, Russia's dominant political figure since 2000. Berlusconi indulged massively in celebrating the benefits of his comradeship with Putin, as if Italy's strong relationship with Russia was a by-product of it. The truth, however, was that Berlusconi found a willing partner in Putin (and vice versa) because Italy and Russia are tied by more enduring factors than the goodwill of individuals.

Today, Italy has an extensive relationship with Russia. Bilateral institutional links have grown at a speedy pace, with summits, ministerial meetings, and inter-parliamentary dialogues held on a regular basis. Economic ties have also grown deeper. The volume of Italian direct investments in Russia still places Italy behind some of its EU partners (Ministry of Economic Development of Russia 2011),[1] but trade has expanded significantly in the last decade. In 2010, bilateral trade amounting to around €21 billion[2] had partly recovered from the sharp contraction recorded in 2009, signalling that the global recession had slowed down, but not yet permanently reversed, a positive trend (ISTAT 2011a).

In spite of a difficult investment environment, Italian business operators look at Russia as a lucrative market.[3] Currently, there are around 500 Italian companies operating in Russia, most of them in the Moscow district, with energy being by far the main field of investment (De Bonis 2009: 153). This comes as no surprise since Russia is Italy's single most important energy supplier: as of April 2011 it provided 24 per cent of Italian natural gas imports and around 13 per cent of its crude oil imports. These figures put Russia at the top of the list of Italy's energy suppliers.[4] Eni, Italy's partly privatized energy company, is the main international customer of Gazprom, Russia's giant gas monopoly. Over the years, the two companies have developed a solid partnership, involved as they are in a number of co-operation projects spanning several aspects of the oil and gas industry line (extraction and production, transport, distribution) worth billions of euros. In 2007, Eni agreed to buy gas from Gazprom until 2035, meaning that this trend is likely to consolidate.

Italian companies operating in Russia have shown activism also in other sectors. Significant investments have come from energy provider Enel, which has been working on gaining access to Russia's electricity market, as well as from Fiat and Finmeccanica, Italy's largest defence and aerospace company (which often operates through subsidiaries). The number of Russian companies active in Italy is not irrelevant either. Most interestingly, Gazprom has managed to get a foot in Italy's downstream gas market.

Italy's tradition of state industrial management is looked on with interest in Russia, where free-market solutions are generally associated with the economic chaos of the 1990s and therefore do not inspire enthusiasm (Caselli 2009: 120). The Italian government is convinced that it can contribute to developing Russia's industrial base by fostering the creation of 'industrial districts' in Russia (in particular in the furniture, agriculture and food, and fashion sectors) along the model developed by Italian firms and local authorities in the peninsula's industry-rich North.

Italian–Russian proximity is discernible in other policy areas as well. In 2003 an award for individuals contributing to Italian–Russian friendship was established and a 'forum for dialogue between civil societies' created, while 2011 was proclaimed the Year of Russian Culture and Language in Italy and Italian Culture and Language in Russia. The political support given both by

70   Riccardo Alcaro

Rome and Moscow to the rapprochement sought by the Roman Catholic Church and Moscow's Orthodox Patriarchate should also be seen as serving the same purpose of fostering bilateral closeness. Given the considerable influence that both churches exert over their respective publics, policymakers from Italy and Russia (particularly conservative ones) consider good relations between the Holy See and the Russian Church as benefiting relations between Russia and Italy themselves (Morozzo della Rocca 2009).

Such closeness to Russia affects, sometimes controversially, Italy's commitment to principles and policies it has subscribed to in either the EU or NATO, the principal frame of reference of Italian post-Second World War foreign policy. A look at this EU–NATO–Russia triangle, and what is best described as Italy's contortions in it, is necessary in order to appreciate better the implications of Italy's Russia policy.

Italy's contortions in the EU–NATO–Russia triangle

The debate about the extent to which Italian post-Cold War ruling elites have innovated the country's foreign policy remains anything but consensual,[5] but no single analyst is ready to deny the structural continuity of Italy's core foreign policy choices, i.e. its staunch support for multilateral action, European integration, and NATO (Alcaro 2010a; Croci 2002, 2003, 2005, 2008a, 2008b; Nuti 2003; to a lesser extent, Romano 2009; Walston 2007).

During the 1990s and early 2000s, Italy was, of the largest EU member states, the most willing to bring foreign and security policy integration forward (Greco and Matarazzo 2003). Italy was also an early advocate of the European (now Common) Security and Defence Policy (ESDP/CSDP), to which it has lent regular support since its inception in 1998 (Foradori and Rosa 2008). The fact that Italy has never conceived of CSDP as an alternative to NATO, but rather as complementary to it, attests to the Italian foreign policy establishment's lingering conviction that the vitality of NATO and the bond with the USA, on the one hand, and the unwavering support for the strengthening of the EU, on the other hand, are mutually reinforcing policies that best serve Italy's interests (Alcaro 2010a; Romano 2009). Crucially, whenever EU member states have wrangled and split over their relationship with the USA or the CSDP's appropriate degree of autonomy from NATO, Italy has taken special care not to be associated with one camp or the other, preferring instead to keep a more centrist position and advocating compromise solutions.

When developments within the EU or NATO have encroached on what is perceived as a national priority, Italian elites have generally worked towards orientating EU and NATO action according to their special sensitivities. Sometimes, however, they have simply resisted – or ignored – such developments. Nowhere is this more evident than in the West's relations with Russia, particularly concerning three policy macro-areas: European security, energy security, and human rights and democracy.

Italy 71

When the USSR collapsed, Italy quickly embraced the idea, shared by other European countries (most notably Germany), of luring Russia into a non-confrontational course vis-à-vis the West by associating it with the West's main fora of dialogue, such as the G7. Thus, when both the EU and NATO resolved to offer membership to countries once under Soviet rule (or part of the USSR itself, like the Baltic republics), successive Italian governments qualified their support for the dual enlargement with the request that an upgrade of relations with Russia be pursued in parallel (Menotti 2001: 99–100). Accordingly, the establishment of the NATO–Russia Permanent Joint Council (PJC) in 1997, as well as its 2002 upgrade into the NATO–Russia Council (NRC), were welcomed in Italy as important foreign policy achievements.

This background sheds light on Italy's opposition to the US push to offer the prospect of NATO membership to Ukraine and Georgia in 2008. Italy was aware that NATO membership of Ukraine and Georgia – the former extending deep into European Russia, the latter fraught with territorial disputes in which Russia is actively involved – was too much to stomach for Russia's political and military leadership. On top of that, Russia was offered no measure comparable to the establishment of the PJC/NRC that could offset its perceived security loss (Giusti 2009: 92).

This strong preference for détente informed the Italian reaction to the August 2008 war between Russia and Georgia. Italy joined in the EU's formal condemnation of Russia's attack against Georgia as a 'disproportionate' response to minor clashes between Georgian forces and Russia-leaning separatists from South Ossetia. Italy also joined the condemnation of Moscow's formal recognition of Abkhazia's and South Ossetia's self-proclaimed secession from Georgia. Nonetheless, then Prime Minister Berlusconi could not help expressing his 'perplexity' over the use of the notion of proportionality in such a complex context as Georgia's (*La Repubblica* 2008b). His government refused to consider the imposition of sanctions on Russia, and worked for the prompt resumption of formal relations between NATO and Russia and the re-start of negotiations over a new EU–Russia treaty, both of which had been suspended due to the war. On another occasion, Berlusconi, with his usual inclination to emphasis, openly spoke about a series of 'provocations' suffered by Russia on the part of the West (*La Repubblica* 2008a). Apart from Ukraine's and Georgia's prospective NATO bids, the other 'provocations' were the recognition of Kosovo's independence by most Western countries (Italy included), which Russia opposed, and the George W. Bush administration's plan to install parts of a US-built missile defence system in Poland and the Czech Republic, which Russia considered a potential threat to its nuclear deterrent.

All these issues have, in fact, been the object of a lively, sometimes tense, internal debate within the EU, involving groups of member states as well as institutions. Thus, Italy has hardly been alone in advocating caution towards Russia. But on other issues its strongly Russia-friendly attitude has been singled out more critically.

72   Riccardo Alcaro

Eni's energy deals with Gazprom are a good case in point. In 2007, for instance, Eni participated in a public auction of assets owned by Yukos, the once powerful energy company that then President Putin had resolved to dismantle as part of his design of securing state control of Russia's energy resources. Eni's participation, needed to lend legality to the auction, was widely believed to be the result of a previous agreement with Gazprom's leadership. This allegation was apparently confirmed by Eni's prompt decision to sell part of its newly acquired Yukos assets to Gazprom itself. The fact that a Western company contributed to the de facto expropriation of Yukos by the Russian state did not go unnoticed in the West (*The Times* 2007).

More controversial still has been Eni's agreement with Gazprom to jointly develop a huge gas pipeline project, called 'South Stream' (to distinguish it from a sister project, 'Nord Stream', developed by Gazprom in co-operation with German and Dutch companies). South Stream, due for completion in 2015, is planned to bring up to 63 billion cubic metres from Russia to Southeast Europe through an offshore pipeline under the Black Sea (South Stream AG n.d.). Speculation has been wide that the project was an ingenious move by Russia to secure its control over Europe's gas imports from the Caspian basin. South Stream is in competition with a European Commission-championed parallel pipeline project, called 'Nabucco', for supplies from gas-producing countries such as Azerbaijan and Turkmenistan (Petersen 2009; Finon 2010).[6] Nabucco, ostensibly designed to bring Caspian gas to Europe via Turkey (therefore bypassing Russian soil), has been the highest-profile initiative the EU has taken so far to meet its objective of diversifying its energy source countries, featuring among the energy infrastructures to which the Union is expected to accord priority (European Commission 2011a: 33).[7]

South Stream has also come in for criticism because it would bypass Ukraine, currently the main transit country for Russia's gas exports to Europe. The concern is that, with gas safely flowing into the EU through South Stream (and, in the north, Nord Stream), Ukraine would be more vulnerable to Russia's influence (House of Commons Defence Committee 2009: 16). The assumption is that the EU would not feel the urgency to broker a compromise between Russia and Ukraine, should the two enter into yet another clash over the cost of Russian gas and Kiev's unpaid bills (clashes that led twice, in 2006 and 2009, to serious disruptions to several EU member states' gas imports).

Italy is not the only EU member state that has struck bilateral deals with Russia, nor is it the only EU member state involved in the South Stream project (French and German companies are also involved, and the pipeline is planned to run through Bulgaria, Greece and Austria).[8] However, given the implications for both the EU energy policy and Ukraine's ability to escape pressure from Russia, South Stream has come to symbolize the harmful tendency of EU individual member states to accord preference to what they perceive as national priorities at the expense of stated EU interests. Accordingly, it has also contributed to solidifying the image of an Italy particularly, if not excessively, keen on good relations with Moscow.

Italy 73

A similar path can be observed concerning the state of Russian democracy. Italy has been anything but vocal in respect of the Kremlin's hardly optimal record in promoting human rights and fundamental freedoms. Despite the EU having identified human rights as 'an area of concern' in its relations with Moscow (Council of the European Union, European Commission 2008), the Italian government has seemed more intent on deflecting criticism of Russia's leadership than in calling upon it to improve its standards. In 2003, Prime Minister Berlusconi baffled his European counterparts by publicly defending Russia's human rights and democratic record in the war-torn Chechnya, Russia's separatist republic, and by expressing his conviction that the case against Yukos was legitimate and entirely legal (*La Repubblica* 2003). On a later occasion, during a joint press conference with Putin, Berlusconi dismissed a question by a young Russian journalist concerning Putin's private life by mimicking the act of pointing a shotgun at her (*La Stampa* 2008); the gesture shocked the audience not so much for being bizarre and inappropriate for a prime minister (which it certainly was), as because it raised doubts about Italy's actual commitment to urging Russia to defend press freedom (according to some estimates, in the period up to 2009 violent deaths and disappearances of journalists in Russia had exceeded 300; International Federation of Journalists 2009). Even as late as 2009 US diplomats in Rome recalled that Berlusconi was 'soft' on human rights issues concerning Russia out of concern that his much-publicized special relationship with Russia's leaders might be spoilt (*Libero* 2010).

The picture drawn above shows an Italy that, in several instances, has seemed to accord preference to its relations with Russia over its commitment to being a diligent implementer of policies set at the EU or NATO level. This interpretation is shared both in European capitals and Moscow, as well as in Washington. In 2008 the Russian daily *Izvestia* put Italy into a group of EU member states categorized as 'Russia's lobbyists' (quoted in Giusti 2009: 90). In a 2007 widely circulated report on EU member states' relations with Russia, two prominent European experts assigned Italy to the camp of Russia's 'strategic partners' (Leonard and Popescu 2007: 31 and ff.). In their cables to Washington made public by WikiLeaks, US diplomats speak of an Italian government verging on passive acceptance of Russia's controversial behaviour (*La Repubblica* and *L'Espresso* 2010). Nonetheless, before rushing to the conclusion that Italy acts like a Russian proxy, its policy choices concerning Russia need to be put into perspective.

The match/mismatch In Italy's and Russia's views and interests

In recent years, on certain issues, Italy and Russia have undoubtedly happened to be close, sometimes even closer than Italy and some of its partners in the EU. Partly, this depends on the perception, at times fanned by powerful lobbies, that essential national interests are at play, and that these may warrant a policy potentially conflicting with objectives set at the EU level. It may

74　*Riccardo Alcaro*

be, and sometimes actually is, that such perceptions bring about poorly designed policies that privilege short-term gains over long-term benefits. Yet, this does not allow for defining Italy as a proxy of Russia. In fact, closeness to Russia does not necessarily imply commonality of views with Russia.

Whatever the intensity of the relationship between leaders, Italians generally do not hold an idealized view of Russia as a trustworthy ally that shares Italy's values and purposes. Off the record, several Italian diplomats and businessmen admit that Russia is something between a friend and foe or, at least, a difficult partner to deal with. Even so, very few of them infer that Russia should be treated with a heavy hand, the prevailing opinion being instead that pragmatism should guide the government's choices.[9] Italy, so the argument goes, is a mid-size country with limited resources and no autonomous capacity of military projection. Given that Russia is one of the two great powers with which Italy has well-established links (the other being the USA), Italian foreign policy-makers simply see no reason to spoil their country's relationship with Moscow. These feelings are particularly strong in the Foreign Ministry, both in the upper echelons and among the ranks and files.

Other, more concrete, factors reinforce the generic assumption that having good relations with a great power is better than the other way round. Unsurprisingly, a powerful argument is Italy's reliance on Russian energy supplies. This argument is correct, but only if 'reliance' is not made equal to 'dependence'. As shown in Figure 5.1, in the last 20 years Italy has successfully diversified its suppliers, to the extent that Russia's share of overall Italian gas imports has gone down – and significantly so – while oil imports have oscillated above and below 15 per cent after an initial surge.

True, in absolute terms energy trade has increased owing to a growing demand by Italy (due, in part, to its decision to privilege gas consumption in order to meet EU-set carbon emissions limits) and the steep rise in gas and oil prices (see Figure 5.2). Yet the depth and complexity of the Italian–Russian relationship far exceeds mere seller-buyer dynamics. The strong partnership between Gazprom and Eni, in particular, makes interdependence, rather than dependence, a more appropriate analytical category to understand Italian–Russian energy relations. Contrary to dependence, interdependence creates strong incentives to avoid clashes. As a matter of fact, while dependence unfolds according to a zero-sum logic (the more dependent one country, the more influential the other), an interdependent relationship is closer (although not necessarily equal) to a win-win situation, in that the gain of one party is often to the benefit of the other party.

In Italy, the party in question is Eni. In talks with government officials, Eni representatives have little difficulty in getting the upper hand. They can contend, with good reasons, that Italy has a strong interest in Eni's dealings with Gazprom, not only because they create profits, but also because participation in the development of Russia's lucrative energy resources contributes to balancing Italy's reliance on Russian supplies.[10] Italian policymakers are also reminded that strong ties with Russia might pave the way to a fully stabilized

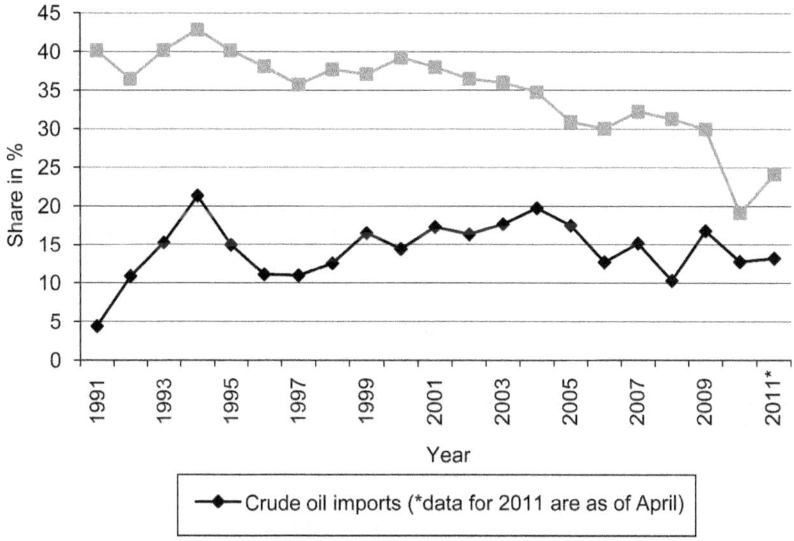

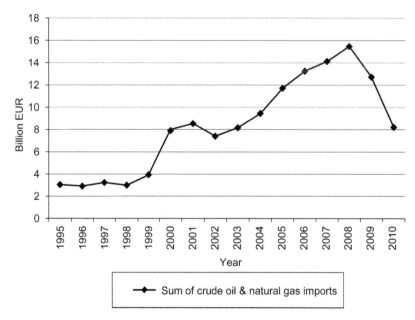

Figure 5.1 Share of crude oil and natural gas imports from Russia in Italian gas and oil imports

Figure 5.2 Italy's crude oil and natural gas imports from Russia

76   Riccardo Alcaro

EU–Russia energy relationship, which would epitomize the win-win situation that interdependence can bring about: Russia would secure long-term contracts from the energy-voracious EU and the EU would put its oil and gas imports on firmer ground. Thus, in principle, Italy is persuaded that its energy partnership with Russia can be beneficial to the EU as a whole.

The problem with this assessment is that it fails to factor in the fundamental differences between Italy's view of the energy partnership and Russia's. Italy has subscribed to an EU energy policy that aims, among other things, to reduce imports, diversify supply routes, and redefine the rules of co-operation with supplier countries to bring them closer to its competition policy standards. Since Russia is understandably unhappy with this plan, a corollary of the EU's ambitious energy policy is therefore that EU member states coalesce around a common position when dealing with Russia. Thus far, however, this has hardly happened, as several EU member states have opted for separate deals with the Russians. The South Stream pipeline project eloquently shows that Italy is no exception. Italian governments, both left and right-of-centre, have accorded preference to the immediate gains resulting from a strengthened Eni–Gazprom partnership over the more distant benefits potentially deriving from the implementation of the EU's energy agenda. In this regard, the advantages of interdependence have, at least partly, gone. On the one hand, interdependence continues to function as a brake on a potential escalation of tensions between the EU and Russia. On the other hand, however, it has turned into a sort of straitjacket (Sherr 2010), as Italy is disincentivized to re-discuss the terms of co-operation with its most important energy partner.

The importance of the energy factor in Italy's friendly approach towards Russia is the result of a confusedly processed mixture of economic calculations (largely shaped by Eni's powerful lobbying) and political considerations, rather than structural conditions. Its importance should therefore not be overestimated, as it is just one (potentially reversible) element underlying Italy's Russia-friendly attitude. Russia is too deeply enmeshed in the geopolitical context on which much of Italy's security hinges for it to be regarded exclusively as an energy partner. Strategic and security considerations matter as well.

The starting point of any such strategic considerations for Italy is the following: Europe's long-term security and stability can only be achieved with a co-operative Russia. However difficult it may be to deal with the Kremlin, confrontation is a losing option. From this perspective, opposition to NATO's eastward enlargement, or Bush's missile shield plan, had less to do with business interests than with Italy's vision of European security as, potentially, a single space. Italy has consequently expressed support for engaging in a serious EU- and transatlantic-wide discussion on former Russian President Dmitry Medvedev's idea of a new European security architecture, based on a comprehensive treaty encompassing all countries from the Urals to the Atlantic (Medvedev 2009). While stopping short of endorsing the treaty's details – which seemed to reflect Russia's interest in advancing claims rather than putting forward shared goals – former Italian Foreign Minister Franco

Italy 77

Frattini made it clear that Italy deemed the integration of Russia into an upgraded European political-security complex a strategic goal (Frattini 2009).

Italy, in other words, has found itself on the 'side of Russia' on some key European security issues because it considers stability in the European strategic balance a pre-condition to develop non-confrontational relations, which in turn should lead to a truly co-operative relationship between Russia and the EU/NATO (Arbatova 2011: 15–18).

This conviction, however, has not prevented Italy from supporting choices within the EU or NATO that were opposed (sometimes fiercely) by Russia if it calculated that they were instrumental to stabilizing Europe's security map in the long run. Italy's participation in the Kosovo war in 1999 and its prompt recognition of Kosovo's independence in 2008 are a good case in point. So are also Italy's support for the reactivation of the Treaty on Conventional Armed Forces in Europe (CFE), which the Russians suspended in 2007 in retaliation against Bush's missile shield plan; and its unwillingness to relinquish the US nuclear weapons still deployed in its territory in spite of Russia's wish that they be repatriated. Even on missile defence the Italian position has shifted. Rome has welcomed President Barack Obama's reformulated missile shield scheme because it has been designed to be integrated at a NATO level, whereas Bush's was fully US-owned. Were Russia to oppose Obama's plan openly, Italy would be unlikely to perorate its cause this time around.

In sum, Italy does not favour an alteration of the balance of power in Europe, only its evolution towards a more co-operative stage. Russia, by contrast, would like to see the US role in it reined in and its claim to having a 'privileged sphere of interest' (in former President Medvedev's own words) in the former Soviet space recognized (Medvedev 2008). Italy is far from sharing this view. Its vision for a European security architecture coincides with the Kremlin's insofar as it accords Russia a prominent role in it, but no more than that. Italy aims at building a co-operative system based on the predictability of the behaviour of all parties, and possibly on the rule of law, instead of a re-proposition of a system based on a 'spheres of influence' logic.

Moving from the European onto the global stage, the picture changes little. True, Russia and Italy at times boast of sharing the opinion that global issues should be managed by way of international co-operation in multilateral fora, in particular the United Nations Security Council (UNSC) (Arbatova 2011: 10–12;, Giusti and Ferrari 2010: 124–25). In November 2009, former Foreign Minister Frattini went as far as to co-author with his Russian counterpart, Sergey Lavrov, an op-ed presenting a common vision of a 'new world order based on interdependence and cooperation' (Frattini and Lavrov 2009). In reality, however, things stand differently. For Italy, international law means the expansion of rule-based international relations, including in hard security matters, whereas for Russia the most appealing part of it seems still to be the principle of non-interference and its veto power in the Security Council. Furthermore, Italy's point of reference in the management of global challenges is the USA, not Russia, as attested to by its decision to side with

Washington, not Moscow, on issues ranging from Kosovo to Iraq, Libya, Iran's nuclear ambitions, or the Israeli–Palestinian conflict.

When put into the right perspective, then, Italy's ties with Russia provide insufficient evidence to justify the accusation of free-riding. With the partial exception of the energy dimension, Italy's relationship with Moscow unfolds mostly within the EU and NATO frameworks. In both venues Italy tries to act more like a 'balancer' rather than a 'free-rider', although it is not always successful. The inclination to balancing derives from Italy's persuasion that the European security space cannot be permanently stabilized unless the EU and NATO find workable ways to manage issues on which they are at odds with Russia in a non-confrontational way. When this turns out not to be possible, Italy's instinct is to delay confrontation, in the hope that co-operation in other sectors (or unexpected events occurred in the meanwhile) create more favourable conditions for a settlement of unsolved questions.

In a way, Italy's Russia policy presents a measure of strategy: no action on a transatlantic, European or bilateral level should be taken that could fatally jeopardize the prospect of a co-operation-based system in Europe, involving the EU, NATO (i.e. the USA) and Russia alike. A strategic objective is nonetheless insufficient to win the name of 'strategy' to a set of policies. The question arises whether Italy is making full use of the assets at its disposal to achieve that objective or it is under-utilizing them.

Italy's Russia policy: in search of an EU-centred strategy

A strategy worthy of the name involves the ability to identify the best possible tradeoffs between conflicting priorities. Measured against these higher standards, Italy's Russia policy entails no full-fledged strategy.

Italy seems to be content with having championed the creation of West–Russia institutional settings of consultation, such as the enlarged G8 or the NRC. However, these fora were also created with the hope that Russia and the West would bridge the gap between their respective positions on issues on which they do not see eye-to-eye, especially concerning European security and the former Soviet space. In this regard, the West–Russia institutions of co-operation have failed to deliver the desired results, since both parties, deliberately or not, have taken decisions leading to tensions. Caught in the middle, countries that oppose confrontation, like Italy, have engaged in damage control, which has generally led them to favour a conservative approach. With the only exception of the recognition of Kosovo's independence in early 2008, not once has Italy in the last 10 years shown enthusiasm for unilateral proposals with the potential to alter the status quo.

It may be that, at times, damage control was the only option at hand. However, a government that boasts of having special ties with the Kremlin should be expected to come out with pro-active ideas on how to settle issues that have been dragging on since the end of the Cold War, in particular in the former Soviet space. But, given the lack of evidence to suggest otherwise, Italy seems strikingly uninterested in such undertakings. Italy has been equally timid also when the initiatives have come from Moscow. For instance, its support to discuss Medvedev's proposal of a new security architecture in Europe has remained largely rhetorical, notwithstanding the fact there might be some room for action on this matter, since other EU members, notably France, have expressed similar feelings. Thus, while in principle Italy remains opposed to the notion of spheres of influence, in practice it seems to have accepted the possibility that some light form of it be established again in Eastern Europe. It remains uncertain how this course of (in)action may contribute to realizing Italy's long-term objective of a co-operation-based system in Europe.

The other weakness of Italy's Russia policy is that its European and bilateral tracks proceed in parallel without much co-ordination. The agenda of Italian–Russian summits and ministerial meetings is usually packed with initiatives of co-operation, real or planned, while final declarations generally tend to emphasize commonalities of views, real or presumed. Issues on which Italy, as an EU and NATO member state, disagrees with Russia are also discussed, but the Italian government is generally content with paying lip-service to the official EU or NATO position before moving on to the following item. This contributes to making Russian leaders more relaxed when confronted by the EU or NATO with the urgency of addressing issues like arms control in Europe, relations with former Soviet republics, or their democracy record.

Italy's difficulty in connecting more incisively bilateral with multilateral action on Russia weakens the consistency of its position. For Italy, membership in both organizations is a key component of its Russia policy, as it provides some leverage. Italy may count on the fact that Russian leaders are likelier to give their ear to a member of powerful and wealthy organizations like the EU or NATO than to what Italy would be otherwise: a mid-size country with a modest military history and relatively limited resources. Membership in NATO has allowed Italy to support measures opposed by Russia (above all keeping the USA focused on Europe, but also the stabilization of the Balkans) as well as favoured by Russia (obstructionism to Ukraine's and Georgia's NATO bids and Bush's missile shield plan). By contrast, the potential enshrined in EU membership has remained largely unexploited. The issue of energy is particularly telling in this regard, given its political implications.

Strengthening the EU's energy policy is of interest to all EU member states not only because it would contribute to securing their energy imports. It would also reduce Russia's influence on transit and producing countries in East Europe and the South Caucasus. In so doing, it would weaken any dynamic towards the creation of de facto spheres of influence while not estranging Russia, which would remain the EU's most important energy partner. However, because the benefits accruing from a single EU energy policy are far removed in the future, jarring with more immediate priorities, Italy has preferred to strike deals with Russia on a bilateral basis.

80 *Riccardo Alcaro*

In so doing, Italy has failed to see that making use of EU membership does not necessarily imply sacrificing potentially lucrative deals such as South Stream. No doubt, the gas pipeline project is hardly in sync with the EU's energy goals, but it would be naive not to understand that South Stream was very hard indeed to oppose. The Italian government would have had to clash with Eni for the sake of Nabucco, a pipeline project in which no Italian company is involved. Clearly, there was no political expediency in doing so.[11] But the main problem with South Stream is not so much that it is in conflict with the EU-set goal of supplier diversification, as that it has not been accompanied by a significant effort by Italy's government to address the integration of EU energy markets, an arguably more important obstacle hampering an EU common energy policy. The deal on a project, such as South Stream, that would have predictably fed intra-EU tensions should have spurred the Italian government to advance a more integrationist energy agenda in the EU. Italy would have only to gain if the EU were eventually able to agree on policies, such as intra-EU regulatory harmonization and physical connection of energy grids, that would do more to increase its negotiating position than supplier diversification (Sherr 2010).

That here, as in other instances, Italy has failed to make use of the potential added leverage provided by the EU is the most lamentable because, of the three pillars of Europe's political-security architecture envisaged by Italy (the EU, NATO/USA, and Russia), the EU is the least embroiled in the bitter legacy of Cold War confrontations. Russia often indulges in chastising NATO and the USA, but is less critical of the EU, with which it interfaces on a number of non-military areas of primary concern, ranging from trade to energy and immigration. Given the strong overlap in the EU's and NATO's European membership, the Union acts as a sort of 'de-escalating' actor in NATO–Russia rivalries. Its stabilizing effect is felt all across Europe, including the Balkans and, admittedly to a much lesser extent, East Europe and the Caucasus (Alcaro 2011: 23–25, Alcaro and Alessandri 2010).

Strengthening the EU's cohesion might certainly lead to more clashes with Russia than Italy would like, as an EU common position would hardly be as accommodating as positions by single member states like Italy sometimes are. Concerns that this might compromise relations with Russia are nonetheless illplaced, because Russia cannot afford permanently alienating the EU as a whole. This EU-centric perspective is what Italy's Russia policy lacks for it to be really strategic.

Conclusion

An experienced Italian diplomat once defined Italy–Russia relations as a combination of 'attraction and strategy' (Salleo 2009: 5–6). As for 'attraction', cultural infatuation and, for Italian communists, political parentage have played a fundamental role in cementing Russia's special position in the mind of Italy's foreign policy-makers. But what about strategy? Shared or compatible

Italy 81

interests are instrumental in forging political ties, but they ought to be both long-term and structurally linked to a nation's most important objectives to be elevated to the dimension of strategy. Is this the case with Italy and Russia?

The analysis conducted in this chapter indicates that, in fact, this is not the case. Italy and Russia do agree that Russia's concerns should be duly taken into account. However, in terms of long-term goals, the two aim at different outcomes. Russia is mostly interested in regaining part of the power it lost when the USSR dissolved by exerting exclusive influence in the former Soviet space and, on this basis, re-drawing the outline of Europe's political-security architecture. Moreover, Russia would like to see the role of NATO (read: the USA) reduced. For its part, Italy, while agreeing that Europe's current political and security system is insufficiently equipped to ensure the continent's long-term security, favours an upgrade of it, not a radical change. And nothing could be more distant from Italy's vision of Europe's security than a scenario in which NATO loses relevance (Alcaro 2010b).

In envisaging Europe's future, both Russia and Italy apparently look at the Helsinki Process that in the 1970s led to reciprocal recognition of the Cold War blocs as a source of inspiration. The difference is that Russia sees it as an end result, Italy as a step in a longer process leading to a comprehensive system of political, economic and security relations based on interdependence, co-operation, and a shared view of the future.

The problem with Italy is that, with its tendency to avoid or oppose any measure that could fatally jeopardize this objective, it has backtracked towards a mostly reactive approach, apparently renouncing the possibility of challenging Russia's agenda in the former Soviet space. Incoherence and lack of capacity of initiative, reflected in Italy's inability to co-ordinate better the various dimensions (bilateral and multilateral) of its Russia policy are serious weaknesses. In particular, Italy is apparently incapable of framing its relations with Moscow from a strongly EU-centric perspective, which leads it to neglect the greater, but more long-term, benefits potentially accruing from EU cohesion vis-à-vis Russia.

In conclusion, the starting point of Italy's Russia policy – that Russia needs to be part of the European political-security equation – is commendable, as it is hard to envisage a fully stabilized Europe without Russia being a committed member of it. Italy is therefore wise to avoid unnecessary confrontation and to work toward a sustainable modus vivendi between Russia and the West. However, its inability to make better use of its leverage on Russia – enshrined in the potential of common EU policies – risks making its long-term objective unattainable. Therefore, the set of policies that make up Italy's Russia policy do not deserve the name of strategy, as bilateral action and EU action proceed on different tracks, at different speed, and sometimes even in different directions.

Notes

1 As of March 2011 Italian direct investment in Russia amounted to around €498.25 million.

82 *Riccardo Alcaro*

2 More precisely, €20,961,437,464. As of April 2011 Italian-Russian trade did not seem to have changed tack, amounting to €8,448,922,004 already (ISTAT 2011a).
3 Italian investors' most common complaints concern the difficulty of getting or extending government contracts, the poor quality of infrastructure, and the absence of financial facilities for foreign investors. The cumbersomeness of the bureaucracy also features regularly in their *cahiers de doleances*, as do the higher costs resulting from widespread corruption (De Bonis 2009: 159–60).
4 Elaboration of ISTAT data, accessed from ISTAT's website on 29 July 2011.
5 For different assessments of post-Cold War governments' foreign policy, one emphasizing flat continuity and the other relative innovations, see Croci 2005, 2008a; and Romano 2006; see also Alcaro 2010a.
6 South Stream was identified as a competitor of Nabucco also by the European Commissioner for Energy, Günther Öttinger (UPI.com 2010).
7 The European Commission reiterated the importance of diversifying energy suppliers on 9 September 2011 (European Commission 2011b: 5–6).
8 South Stream AG, the company in charge of building the Black Sea offshore section of the pipeline, was born as a joint venture by Gazprom and Eni in June 2007. Today, shares of South Stream AG are distributed as follows: 50 per cent Gazprom; 20 per cent Eni; and 15 per cent France's EdF and Germany's Wintershall each (*The Wall Street Journal*, 2011).
9 Interviews by the author with officials from the ministries of foreign affairs and defence, the office of the prime minister, and representatives from the academy, the media, and the private sector, Rome, April–June 2010.
10 For Eni's role in Italy's energy policy, see Luciani and Mazzanti 2006.
11 Even if fully operational, Nabucco would bring a fraction of the gas Europe needs to fulfil its demand, which is expected to grow in the coming years (although the economic crisis might yet dampen it for a while) (European Commission 2010). Nabucco is to transport a maximum of 31 bcm per year, over 13 times less than the 420.64 bcm of gas EU member states collectively imported in 2010, 110.43 of which came from Russia (for Nabucco's capacity, see Nabucco's website: www. nabucco-pipeline.com; for EU data, see BP 2011). It comes as no surprise that the original plan for the development of Nabucco is now being downgraded to a more limited and less ambitious proposal, 'Nabucco West', only covering the EU-based section of the pipeline.

References

Alcaro, R. (2010a) 'Catching the change of the tide. Italy's post-Cold War security policy', *The International Spectator*, Vol. 45, No. 1, pp. 131–45.
——(2010b) *The Italian government and NATO's new Strategic Concept*, Documenti IAI 10/12, July 2010, available at www.iai.it/pdf/DocIAI/iai1012.pdf (accessed 1 September 2011).
——(2011) 'Transatlantic relations in a multipolar Europe', in R. Alcaro and E. Jones (eds) *European Security and the Future of Transatlantic Relations*, Rome: Edizioni Nuova Cultura.
Alcaro, R. and Alessandri, E. (2010) 'Engaging Russia: prospects for a long-term European security compact', *European Foreign Affairs Review*, Vol. 15, No. 2, pp. 191–207.
Arbatova, N. (2011) 'Italy, Russia's Voice in Europe?', *Russie.Nei.Visioons*, No. 62, available at www.ifri.org/downloads/ifrirussieitaliearbatovaengsept2011.pdf (accessed 20 September 2011).

Italy 83

BP (2011) *BP Statistical Review of World Energy*, June.

Caselli, G. P. (2009) 'L'economia russa in simbiosi con il Vecchio Continente', *Limes*, 3/2009, pp. 111–23.

Council of the European Union, European Commission (2008) *Review of EU–Russia relations*, Memo/08/678, Brussels, 5 November, available at http://europa.eu/rapid/pressReleasesAction.do?reference=MEMO/08/678&format= (accessed 28 March 2012).

Croci, O. (2002) 'The second Berlusconi government and Italian foreign policy', *The International Spectator*, Vol. 37, No. 1, pp. 89–101.

——(2003) 'Italian security policy after the Cold War', *Journal of Modern Italy Studies*, Vol. 8, No. 2, pp. 266–83.

——(2005) 'Much ado about little: the foreign policy of the second Berlusconi government', *Journal of Modern Italy Studies*, Vol. 10, No. 1, pp. 59–74.

——(2008a) 'The second Prodi government and Italian foreign policy: New and improved or the same wrapped up differently?', *Journal of Modern Italy Studies*, Vol. 13, No. 3, pp. 291–303.

——(2008b) 'Not a zero-sum game: Atlanticism and Europeanism in Italian foreign policy', *The International Spectator*, Vol. 43, No. 4, pp. 137–55.

De Bonis, M. (2009) 'Roma e Mosca, amore e affari', *Limes*, 3/2009, pp. 153–60.

European Commission (2010) *EU energy trends to 2030. Update 2009*, Luxembourg: Publications Office of the European Union, available at http://ec.europa.eu/energy/observatory/trends_2030/doc/trends_to_2030_update_2009.pdf (accessed 5 September 2011).

——(2011a) *Energy infrastructure. Priorities for 2020 and beyond – A blueprint for an integrated European energy network*, Luxembourg: Publications Office of the European Union.

——(2011b) *Communication from the Commission to the European Parliament, the Council, the European Economic and Social Council and the Committee of Regions on security of energy supply and international cooperation – 'The EU Energy Policy: Engaging with Partners Beyond Our Borders'*, COM(2011) 539 final, Brussels, 9 September.

Finon, D. (2010) 'Nabucco versus Southstream: an economic competition behind geopolitical confrontation', *Energy Policy Blog*, 14 September, available at www.energypolicyblog.com/2010/03/01/nabucco-versus-southstream-an-economic-competition-behind-a-geopolitical-confrontation/ (accessed 28 March 2012).

Foradori, P. and Rosa, P. (2008) 'Italy and defense and security policy', in S. Fabbrini and S. Piattoni (eds) *Italy in the European Union*, Lenham, MA: Rowman & Littlefield, 173–90.

Frattini, F. (2009) *Intervento del Ministro Frattini al Foro di dialogo Italia–Russia*, Rome, 2 December.

Frattini, F. and Lavrov, S. (2009) 'Nuovo ordine mondiale', *La stampa*, 9 November.

Giusti, S. (2009) 'Le relazioni Italia – Russia: una partnership strategica', in G. Bonvicini and A. Colombo (eds) *L'Italia e la politica internazionale*, Bologna: Il Mulino, 89–101.

Giusti, S. and Ferrari, A. (2010) 'L'Italia dai Balcani alla Russia fino alle repubbliche del Caucaso meridionale', in G. Bonvicini and A. Colombo (eds) *La politica estera dell'Italia*, Bologna: Il Mulino, 121–31.

Greco, E. and Matarazzo, R. (2003) 'Italy's European policy and its role in the European Convention', *The International Spectator*, Vol. 38, No. 3, pp. 125–35.

84 Riccardo Alcaro

House of Commons Defence Committee (2009) *Russia: a new confrontation? Tenth Report of Session 2008–09*, London: House of Commons of the United Kingdom of Great Britain and Northern Ireland.

International Federation of Journalists (2009) *Partial Justice. An Inquiry into the Deaths of Journalists in Russia, 1993–2009*, Brussels: International Federation of Journalists.

Istituto Nazionale di Statistica (ISTAT) (2011a) *Serie storica (Export- Import) per Paesi. Russia*, data accessed 29 July 2011.

——(2011b) *Interscambio commerciale in valore Italia – Russia per Gruppi 'Ateco 2007'–1991–2011. Petrolio Greggio*, data accessed 29 July 2011.

——(2011c), *Interscambio commerciale in valore Italia – Russia per Gruppi 'Ateco 2007'–1991–2011. Gas Naturale*, data accessed 29 July 2011.

——(2011d), *Interscambio commerciale in valore Italia-Mondo per Gruppi 'Ateco 2007'–1991–2011. Petrolio Greggio*, data accessed 29 July 2011.

——(2011e), *Interscambio commerciale in valore Italia-Mondo per Gruppi 'Ateco 2007'–1991–2011. Gas Naturale*, data accessed 29 July 2011.

La Repubblica (2003) 'Berlusconi difende Putin e attacca la stampa', 6 November, available at www.repubblica.it/2003/k/sezioni/esteri/putinroma/berluprodi/berluprodi. html (accessed 28 March 2012).

——(2008a) 'Berlusconi: "Lo scudo spaziale una provocazione verso la Russia"', 12 November.

——(2008b) 'Mosca sbaglia ma dialoghiamo: Putin non si isoli dall'Europa', 1 September, available at www.repubblica.it/2008/08/sezioni/esteri/ossezia-bombardamenti-4/berlusconi/berlusconi.html (accessed 28 March 2012).

La Repubblica and *l'Espresso* (2010) 'L'Italia svelata dai cablogrammi', available at http://racconta.espresso.repubblica.it/espresso-wikileaks-database-italia/index.php (accessed 28 March 2012).

La Stampa (2008) 'Silvio finge di sparare in difesa di Zar Vladimir', 19 April, available at www.lastampa.it/redazione/cmsSezioni/politica/200804articoli/32045girata.asp (accessed 28 March 2012).

Leonard, M. and Popescu, N. (2007) *A Power Audit of EU – Russia Relations*, ECFR Policy Paper, available at http://ecfr.3cdn.net/1ef82b3f011e075853_0fm6bphgw.pdf (accessed 30 July 2011).

Libero (2010) 'WikiLeaks: "Putin spesso da Berlusconi, Italia morbida con la Russia"', 4 December, available at www.liberoquotidiano.it/news/545200/Wiki-Putin-spesso-da-Berlusconi-Italia-morbida-con-Russia.html (accessed 28 March 2012).

Luciani, G., and Mazzanti, M. R. (2006) 'Italian energy policy: the quest for more competition and supply security', *The International Spectator*, Vol. 61, No. 3, pp. 75–89.

Medvedev, Dmitri (2008) *Interview given by President Dmitri Medvedev to Television Channels Channel One, Rossiia, and NTV*, 31 August, available at www.kremlin.ru/eng/speeches/2008/08/31/1850_type82912type82916_206003.shtml (accessed 28 March 2012).

——(2009) *The Draft of the European Security Treaty*, 29 November, available at http://eng.kremlin.ru/news/275 (accessed 28 March 2012).

Menotti, R. (2001) 'Italy: Uneasy ally', in G. A. Mattox and A. R. Rachwald (eds) *Enlarging NATO. The National Debates*, Boulder: Lynne Rienner, pp. 91–107

Ministry of Economic Development of Russia (2011) Статистика Внешней Торговли и Инвестиционного Сотрудничества Россия– ЕС, 10 June, available at www.gosman. ru/?news=15666%3E (accessed) 28 March 2012).

Italy 85

Morozzo della Rocca, R. (2009) 'Roma – Mosca: prove tecniche d'intesa religiosa', *Limes*, 3/2009, pp. 67–74.

Nuti, L. (2003) 'The role of the US in Italy's foreign policy', *The International Spectator*, Vol. 38, No. 1, pp. 91–101.

Petersen, A. (2009) *Putin's Pipeline Pipe Dream*, The Henry Jackson Society, 14 September, available at www.henryjacksonsociety.org/stories.asp?pageid=49&id=2154 (accessed 4 September 2011).

Romano, S. (2006) 'Berlusconi's foreign policy: inverting traditional priorities', *The International Spectator*, Vol. 61, No. 2, pp. 101–7.

——(2009) 'Italian foreign policy after the end of the Cold War', *Journal of Modern Italy Studies*, Vol. 14, No. 1, pp. 8–14.

Salleo, F. (rapporteur) (2009) 'Le relazioni italo – russe', *Dialoghi diplomatici* 201/202.

Sherr, J. (2010) 'The Russia – EU energy relationship: getting it right', *The International Spectator*, Vol. 45, No. 2, pp. 55–68.

South Stream AG (n.d.) *South Stream. Europe's Energy Security*, available at http://south-stream.info/?L=1 (accessed 28 March 2012).

The Times (2007) 'Eni wins auction for Yukos, then hands it to Gazprom', 5 April, available at http://business.timesonline.co.uk/tol/business/industry_sectors/natural_resources/article1615107.ece (accessed 4 September 2011).

The Wall Street Journal (2011) 'Companies sign South Stream deal', 16 September, available at http://online.wsj.com/article/SB10001424053111903927204576574182325712222.html (accessed 28 March 2012).

UPI.com (2010) *EU: South Stream, Nabucco are competitors*, 22 November, available at www.upi.com/Business_News/Energy-Resources/2010/11/22/EU-South-Stream-Nabucco-are-competitors/UPI-97301290461570/ (accessed 28 March).

Walston, J. (2007) 'Italian foreign policy in the "Second Republic". Changes of form and substance', *Journal of Modern Italy Studies*, Vol. 12, No. 1, pp. 91–104.

6 Poland

Bartosz Cichocki[1]

Russia is Poland's largest neighbour and its main trade partner in the East. At the same time, Russia is the single most serious challenge for Poland's security, including defence, due to a deficient level of mutual trust. Key subjects of co-operation between the two countries cover energy security, common neighbourhood and the so called historical issues. The condition of Polish–Russian relations impacts on Poland's international position, both in the European Union and in Eastern Europe.

Poland and Russia are connected by a well-developed network of institutions and bilateral initiatives but their operational effectiveness depends, to a large extent, on the political climate between the two states. Polish–Russian relations have been developing in three strategic dimensions: bilateral, the EU and NATO. One of the reasons why it is impossible to separate these three entirely is because Russia considers them to be intertwined. The rich history of Polish–Russian relations also exerts no small impact upon the identity of both nations today. One of the national holidays celebrated by the Poles is the anniversary of combating the Bolshevik troops near Warsaw, on 15 August 1920, whereas one of Russia's is the anniversary of the Polish force's capitulation of the Kremlin on 4 November 1612. Hence, for understandable reasons, mutual feelings between Poles and Russians are marked by a mix of admiration, envy and disrespect, with a prevailing tone of mistrust. More recently, confidence building has gained special importance after the plane crash which cost the lives of the Polish President Lech Kaczyński and members of the Polish delegation, on 10 April 2010. Representatives of the Polish state were heading for the Katyń cemetery, located in the vicinity of the city of Smolensk, in order to pay tribute to Polish officers murdered by the Soviet secret police NKVD in 1940.

This chapter discusses the complex nature of Polish–Russian relations. It begins with an analysis of the strategies employed toward Russia by Poland after the Cold War and their international context. The analysis is followed by a detailed diagnosis of the actual Polish–Russian rapprochement – its gains, side-effects and factors of (un)sustainability, including economic and security ones. The chapter ends with some conclusions pondering the future prospects of relations.

The context of Polish–Russian relations

Eastern policies adopted and pursued by Polish governments since the fall of communism have been characterized either by lack of trust towards Russia or attempts at building it. The question of confidence was already central to the programme developed by the Polish émigré circles in Paris in the early 1970s. The legendary Polish émigré literary and political magazine *Kultura*, edited by Jerzy Giedroyc, called upon Poles, Russians, Belorussians, Lithuanians and Ukrainians to build mutual confidence, based on recognizing the Polish post-Second World War eastern border, as well as the right of the former Soviet republics for independence, in case of the collapse of the USSR. This proposal was originally considered treason by Polish pro-independence (anti-communist) circles in Poland and abroad. However, at the time of the fall of communism, in 1989, the Mieroszewski–Giedroyc concept had already become the mainstream in Poland. There was not a single political faction in the new democracy which would call for a revision of the 1945 border. Governments originating from both Solidarity as well as from the former Polish communist party recognized the independence and territorial integrity of Lithuania, Belarus and Ukraine. The momentousness of the concept is perhaps easiest to understand when one looks at the nostalgia numerous Russians feel now for their empire, lost in 1991.

In the post-Cold War era, the Mieroszewski–Giedroyc concept facilitated the avoidance of the rebirth of a centuries-long Polish–Ukrainian conflict and the establishment of good neighbourly relations between the third Polish Republic and Lithuania, Ukraine and Belarus. If it had not been for the programme of the Parisian *Kultura*, the process of disintegration of the USSR could have followed the Yugoslav scenario (Chikhotskii 2010).

The early 1990s saw a peaceful dismantling of the Yalta system, put an end to the Warsaw Pact and witnessed the withdrawal of Soviet troops from Eastern Europe. The Central and East European states became part of proper western institutions, whereas Russia found itself on the outside looking in. Still, it was granted partner status in its relations with NATO and the EU (Nowak 2011: 229–31).

In the 2000s Russia has come up with at least two mutually exclusive projects concerning a new European security architecture. The so-called Medvedev initiative, dating from 2008, seeks to subordinate the currently binding collective security treaties and create a directorate over the existing defence blocks. The other project – Sergei Karaganov's 'United Europe' – foresees entering into a new agreement between the superpowers, while maintaining both NATO and CSTO (Karaganov 2010). A common denominator of these concepts is a refusal to treat Central European countries equally, but rather as belonging to a second-class security zone (Rotfeld 2012: 144–45).

Accession to NATO and the EU has effectively protected Poland against lapsing into a grey zone between the West and Russia. Nevertheless, the third Polish Republic failed to solve another strategic problem: strengthening the

88   Bartosz Cichocki

independence of the former Soviet republics and pursuing the process of Polish–Russian rapprochement at the same time. The dilemma became acute when Russia's policy toward its neighbours entered the period of increased assertiveness after 2000 (Sherr 2008).

In the meantime in Poland the Law and Justice party led by Jarosław Kaczyński formed a government. Simultaneously Lech Kaczyński won presidential elections. Conservatives who held power in 2005–7 (Lech Kaczyński held his office until his tragic death in 2010) focused on geopolitical issues in relations with Russia. They were particularly sensitive about possible Russian expansionism and Poland's as well as the entire region's vulnerability to the use of energy resources as a policy tool (Dong 2007: 41–46, 49–54). They were also unwilling to compromise on the human rights agenda. Last, but not least, Polish conservative leaders reacted decisively whenever Russian authorities denied or questioned the accountability of the Soviet authorities for crimes committed against Poles during the Second World War and for the outbreak of the war itself (Reeves 2010).

Under the Polish conservatives' programme, Eastern policy is the key to Poland's foreign policy identity (M. A. Cichocki 2009/10). According to conservatives, Poland should not constrain its role to that of an administrator of the German–French European project. Furthermore, conservatives believe that the 'European perspective' is the only stimulus capable of triggering structural reforms in Eastern Europe and the South Caucasus. If the EU departs from the enlargement policy, its neighbours will turn to the post-Soviet model of regulating relations between the people and the government, the government and the business and relations among the nomenclature, whereas Kyiv in particular will be forced to accept an integration (incorporation) offer put on the table by Moscow. This in turn, will result in the destabilization of the EU's eastern peripheries. Conservatives believe Poland should not withdraw a membership offer for Eastern European countries and the South Caucasus, just because the EU is not able to build a consensus on the issue. Law and Justice perceived the Eastern Partnership precisely as a concession made for 'Brussels'. They are ready to support this initiative, but only as long as it constitutes a political foretaste of geopolitical changes east of the EU, rather than a simple *upgrade* of the neighbourhood policy (Waszczykowski 2012).

As a result, Polish–Russian relations reached a state of crisis. It was symbolized by the Russian two-year-long embargo imposed on Polish meat and plant products as well as by a series of batterings of Polish diplomats and journalists in Moscow to which Poland responded by blocking on the EU level the adoption of a negotiating mandate authorizing talks with Russia on a new Partnership and Cooperation Agreement (the so-called PCA-2) as well as the President Kaczyński-led mission of Central European leaders to Tbilisi threatened by Russian tanks in August 2008. In the years 2005–7, contacts between the two governments lost their dynamics and regularity on all levels, whereas those at the highest level stopped altogether.

Poland 89

During the tenure of the Law and Justice party, Russian policy became one of the axes along which the Polish political scene was split, whereas normalization of relations with Russia came to be one of the slogans of the successful election campaign of a liberal Civic Platform in the autumn of 2007. The normalization was supposed to be based on pragmatism and on assigning a priority status to economic interests. In his policy statement, delivered in the Polish Parliament in November 2007, Donald Tusk, the leader of the Civic Platform, declared a willingness to conduct dialogue with Russia 'as it is' (Sejm 2007: 24).

One major item on the political agenda of the liberal party is an assumption that in the final analysis the position of Poland in the international arena does not depend on the nature of relations between Warsaw and Kyiv, Tbilisi or Minsk. On the contrary, a condition which has to be met in order to strengthen Poland's position east of the EU, is joining the group of leading EU countries (Germany, France, Great Britain, Italy and Spain) and normalizing relations with Russia. Liberals also assume that even a moderate joint policy in the EU on Eastern issues is stronger than even the most ambitious of national strategies (hence, the establishment of the Eastern Partnership). Moreover, the EU's eastern neighbours will not be able to adopt a Western European political and economic model, even if the former is ready to enlarge. On the contrary, liberals sign up to the concept that promoting EU enlargement irrespective of the internal situation of the aspiring countries, negatively impacts the determination of national authorities to implement reforms which might not be popular, but which are necessary. Those in power in Poland since 2007 have also drawn a conclusion from the fact that unconditional support for Ukraine's euro-integration coincided with increased Ukrainian chauvinism, including one of an anti-Polish nature. When programming their policy, liberals are thinking in terms of 30–40 years ahead and they do not expect immediate results. Liberals typically narrow down the scope of actions in the field of eastern policy to the European part of the post-Soviet area. At the end of the day, liberals consider Russia a participant of the European family of nations as well, without excluding Russia's institutional integration into Europe either (Bratkiewicz 2011).

Rivalry between the two largest political forces, i.e. the Civic Platform and the Law and Justice Party, launched a discussion in Poland which brought results comparable only to the debate provoked by Mieroszewski and Giedroyc (Cichocki 2010). The discussion may weaken support for independence of the former Soviet republics in favour of the development of Polish–Russian relations. By the same token, it will be conducive to presenting a common position by the EU on Russia (Judah, Kobzova and Popescu 2011: 49–51).

The political dimension of Polish–Russian relations

The poor state of relations with Russia weakened Poland's position within the EU and NATO. Tense relations with the largest new member of the EU did

90   *Bartosz Cichocki*

not serve Moscow in its dialogue with Brussels or Washington either. What is more, relations with Poland constitute an important element of Russia's regional policy (Cichocki 2009). Following the 2007 parliamentary elections, after two years of cooling in mutual relations, a process of political normalization started between Warsaw and Moscow. Russia lifted the embargo imposed on Polish meat and plant products, while Poland cancelled its veto on the EU–Russian negotiations concerning a new legal agreement. Furthermore, the parties resumed political dialogue at a high level (reciprocal visits of Prime Ministers as well as Foreign, Economic, Agricultural Ministers, etc.) (Malgin 2010: 705–9).

Restoring institutional forms of bilateral political dialogue has become a priority of Prime Minister Donald Tusk towards Russia. One of his first decisions was to lift the veto on Moscow's accession talks with the OECD. The Jarosław Kaczyński government had been of the opinion that talks on accepting Russia as a member could only start after Russia joining the WTO (Kowal 2011: 152–53). The Russian side took note of the gesture, which led to more intensive political contacts. In February 2008, Prime Minister Tusk paid an official visit to Moscow. Resumption of the Polish–Russian Strategic Committee, presided over by Foreign Ministers, and an Intergovernmental Committee for Economic Co-operation (chaired by Ministers of Infrastructure/Transport) has been agreed. Both parties also used the opportunity to present their positions on a number of controversial issues in the area of international security: CFE regime crisis, status of Kosovo and PCA-2 negotiations, among others.

The Russian invasion of Georgia in August 2008 posed a serious challenge to the Polish–Russian rapprochement. Poland decided to adopt a double-track approach in the face of the crisis. The government strived to achieve a maximum level of EU involvement to stop Russia from continuing its military action while the Polish President, Lech Kaczyński, accompanied by the leaders of the Baltic States and Ukraine, headed for Tbilisi, where he bluntly condemned Russian aggression during a rally broadcast worldwide (see also the contribution of Lašas and Galbreath in this volume). Concurrently, Poland accelerated negotiations with the USA on Missile Defence, which had been protracted for a couple of months. The Polish government seemed to have used increased popular concern caused by Russia's actions in the South Caucasus in order to enter into agreement on the construction of a missile interceptor base in Redzikowo, in the Pomerania Region (Kowal 2011: 43–49). In addition, at the extraordinary EU Summit on 1 September 2008 Poland used the political climate created by the Russian action in Georgia to accelerate the European Commission's work on the Eastern Partnership and EU energy security policy.

At the same time, bilaterally with Russia Poland continued to demonstrate a compromise-based approach, which made it possible for Minister Lavrov to visit Poland on 11 September 2008, the first visit to a NATO country since the conflict in Georgia. Generally speaking, the Polish government assumed that the response to the Russian–Georgian conflict should focus not so much on punishing Russia, but rather on supporting Georgia and other former Soviet republics potentially threatened by Russia's assertiveness. An attempt at unfreezing Poland's relations with Belarus was based on this logic. In September 2008, Minister Sikorski met with Foreign Minister Siarhey Martynau to discuss ways out of the crisis provoked by the Belorussian regime's repressions targeted at the Polish minority. Shortly before the December 2010 presidential election, Minister Sikorski visited Minsk on a joint mission with Minister Guido Westerwelle of Germany to offer President Lukashenko EU assistance in exchange for fair elections. An attempt at breaking the self-imposed isolation of the Belarus regime failed. Presidential elections were rigged and peaceful protests became subject to brutal repression. However, Poland demonstrated its ability to play a role in the defence of democratic values in the East, irrespective of Russia's position, as proved by a donor conference organized in Warsaw on 2 February 2011, with the aim of supporting the opposition in Belarus. Joint assistance declared by participants of the meeting amounted to €87 million, with Commissioner Štefan Füle announcing a fourfold increase in EU support.

Bilateral Polish–Russian dialogue on the legal controversies related to the common past deserves separate reflection. Soon after it came to power Donald Tusk's government approached the Russian side with a proposal to renew the composition of the bilateral Group on Difficult Matters, which had been established in January 2002, with the Foreign Ministries' officials replaced by eminent representatives of scientific circles, headed by the internationally recognized Professor Adam Daniel Rotfeld and Anatoly Torkunov, Rector of the MGIMO University in Moscow. The reconstituted Group played a particular role in discussing conflicting assessments of historical events, one of the sources of crises in Polish–Russian relations in 2005–7 (Szczygło 2009: 10–11).

The work of the Group enjoyed continuing interest at high political levels in Poland and Russia. In some instances attempts were made to use the Group as an instrument to avoid or at least postpone decisions to be made by Russia on the political level concerning the legal rehabilitation of victims of the Katyń Massacre and conducting a reliable investigation against the persons responsible for the mass murder. Even so the Group's main task was accomplished when a collection called *White spots, black spots: difficult issues in Polish–Russian relations 1918–2008* was published both in Polish and Russian in 2010 (Rotfeld and Torkunow 2010). During the presentation of the Polish version Professor Rotfeld suggested that the books be included in the history curriculum in Poland, counting on the reciprocity of the Russians.

In April 2010 the Group on Difficult Matters concluded its work by issuing a joint recommendation for the Polish and Russian Prime Ministers to establish Centres for Polish–Russian Dialogue and Understanding in Warsaw and Moscow. The Centres opened in 2011 and have been supporting research into the shared past, as well as projects aimed at the intensification of human contacts. The November 2011 international conference in Brussels should be regarded as an important epilogue to the Group's work. During the meeting

92   *Bartosz Cichocki*

'Rethinking EU–Russia Relationship. Interim Report of the Polish–Russian Group on Difficult Matters' was presented to the public (Adamski *et al.* 2011). *Constructive engagement* and *accountability* were the two fundamental principles underpinning the comprehensive conclusions drawn by the authors on: building institutional basis for co-operation, strengthening the rule of law, increasing mobility, common neighbourhood, as well as a broad range of challenges for international security. In this way, the dialogue mechanism, which was initially thought to be an instrument for the development of bilateral, Polish–Russian relations, was used to revitalize relations between the EU and Russia.

This philosophy was reflected in the November 2011 joint letter to High Representative Catherine Ashton by Ministers Sikorski of Poland and Westerwelle of Germany (Sikorski and Westerwelle 2011; see also Stewart's contribution to this volume). The letter highlighted unprecedented convergence of the Polish and German diplomacies during the Civic Platform rule in Poland. Previously irritating issues, such as Nord Stream, rights of the Polish minority in Germany or the German Second World War expellee leader Erika Steinbach, have become much less public. Yet another significant traditional controversy between Poland and Germany was the balance between values and interests when it comes to the European strategy toward Russia. The Tusk government, and particularly Foreign Minister Sikorski, changed their tune. Under Civic Platform rule Warsaw insisted on Germany's leadership in the euro-zone turmoil (see Sikorski 2011). Germany showed appreciation for closer relations with Poland as well. For example, both Presidents Christian Wulff and Joachim Gauck chose Warsaw for their first visits abroad, 13 July 2010 and 26 March 2012 respectively. But it was Minister Westerwelle, during his visit to Poland 31 October 2009 (his first trip abroad after nomination), who declared his wish for Polish–German relations to be as strong as Germany's relations with western neighbours (James 2009).

As far as Polish and German positions on Russia are concerned, the constructive engagement/accountability dual-track approach enabled a reliable compromise to be built and Poland to be involved in the traditionally intensive German–Russian dialogue. Hence, trilateral Polish–German–Russian initiatives – as illustrated by regular consultations on the level of foreign affairs ministers (labelled the 'Kaliningrad Triangle'). Thus, the Civic Platform's government strategy to address key issues relating to Russia from within the EU mainstream proved its effectiveness – at least from a short-term perspective.

The process of normalization of Polish–Russian relations reached its climax when Polish and Russian Prime Ministers met in Gdansk, Poland, on the occasion of international celebrations commemorating the 70th anniversary of the outbreak of the Second World War on 1 September 2009. The speech given by Vladimir Putin during the ceremony itself, as well as his article published in *Gazeta Wyborcza* a day before, were testimony to the fact that Russia's position remained broadly unchanged. Moscow continued to put the

Katyń Massacre and the alleged extermination of Soviet prisoners of war in the Polish camps in 1920–1 on a par. This did not create conditions for meeting the Polish legal demands, i.e. making available files from the Katyń investigation, conducted by the Chief Military Prosecutor's Office of the Russian Federation in 1990–2004, and rehabilitating the murdered Polish officers. Russian courts still consider them victims of the abuse of administrative power, which falls under the statute of limitations, rather than victims of a war crime and genocide, to which the statute of limitations does not apply. Nevertheless, the presence of Putin in Poland on such a day among US and European politicians demonstrated that the Russian policy of isolating Poland in the international arena, by means of historical disputes, belongs in the past.

The Russian investigation into the crash of the Polish state aircraft near Smolensk on 10 April 2010 created yet another challenge to the Polish–Russian rapprochement. The accident killed the President and 95 senior officials, military commanders and Polish patriots. The report of the Interstate Aviation Committee (MAK) authored by General Tatiana Anodina and presented on 12 January 2011 outraged the Polish public, for its failure to examine all the circumstances of the tragedy and instead focusing on shifting the entire responsibility onto the Polish crew and even the passengers. By doing so, it squandered a wealth of trust created by the sympathetic response of the Russian people and authorities in the wake of the catastrophe. In such an atmosphere, Bronisław Komorowski, the Speaker of the Polish Parliament and acting Head of State, paid a visit to Moscow on 9 May 2010, on the occasion of international celebrations commemorating the 65th anniversary of the end of the Second World War. President Dmitry Medvedev passed to Komorowski copies of 67 files of the Katyń investigation, covering the period from 1990–2004 and announced that the process of declassifying the remaining 116 files would be continued. On the occasion of the event, the Heads of the Security Councils of Poland and Russia, Stanisław Koziej and Nikolai Patrushev, respectively, initiated a series of regular consultations on security policy. Shortly before the December 2010 return visit paid by Medvedev in Poland, the Russian Duma passed a special resolution which condemned the Katyń Massacre as a Stalinist crime and, by doing so, confirmed (contrary to the view held by the Russian courts) the political nature of the deed. In 2011, the Russian Ministry of Foreign Affairs made assurances on a couple of occasions that it was working on a formal solution to the issue of the rehabilitation of the Polish officers murdered by the NKVD.

As far as the accountability side of Russia's co-operation with the West is concerned, the European Court of Human Rights' decision concerning the Katyń case raises a major concern. On 16 April 2012, the Court stated that Russia had violated Article 3 of the European Convention on Human Rights through the 'inhumane and humiliating treatment' of the victims' relatives by classifying documents of the investigation as secret, failing to indicate the place where the murdered officers had been buried, and denying the truth about the massacre. Furthermore, the judges ruled that Russia had violated

94 *Bartosz Cichocki*

Article 38 of the Convention by refusing to co-operate with the Court (ECHR 2012). The Katyń case in Strasbourg may well serve as a litmus test for how Russia fulfils its commitments and should not be ignored when it comes to Russia's accession to the WTO as well as PCA-2 negotiations.

Despite the ambivalence of political developments between Poland and Russia throughout 2010 both countries continued their efforts to improve bilateral relations. In mid-December 2011 important progress was made in this regard, when Ministers Sikorski and Lavrov signed an agreement excluding the Kaliningrad Oblast and neighbouring Polish regions from the visa regime. Warsaw has taken advantage of EU Regulation 1931/2006, which permits bilateral visa-free agreements with neighbouring countries. Under such an agreement, inhabitants of a 30-km-wide zone on both sides of the EU external border (50 km in some cases) are allowed to move within the area without a visa. Poland has concluded similar agreements with Ukraine (ratified, entered into force in mid-2009) and Belarus (ratified, but not introduced as of early 2013). As regards the Kaliningrad Oblast, Warsaw and Moscow have jointly approached the European Commission with a request to adopt a detailed solution which would cover the entire Kaliningrad Region with a visa-free regime. Following months of diplomatic efforts the request has been approved by the EU countries.

The economic dimension of Polish–Russian relations

Russia is Poland's most important trade partner from outside the EU. The annual exchange of goods between Poland and Russia exceeds that between Russia and the USA (see Rosstat figures at gks.ru). Poland ranks fifth among the EU countries exporting their goods to Russia after Germany, France, Italy and Great Britain. Over the last decade Polish exports to the Russian market increased almost ten times from $860 million in 2000 to about $8.5 billion in 2011. The dynamic stems from the EU enlargement, which boosted Polish economic development, as well as from favourable economic conditions in Russia where bigger demand was recorded for imported goods. The economic crisis which hit Russia in late 2008 put a brake on Polish exports but the pre-crisis value is expected to be restored again in 2012.

Polish exports are dominated by electromechanical products (41 per cent), chemical (19.5 per cent) as well as farm and food stuffs (13 per cent). It is estimated that about 50 per cent of exports are covered by production generated by international companies residing in Poland. Russia mainly sells Poland mineral products (73.3 per cent). As a result of high oil and gas prices, Poland, like most of the EU countries, has recorded a negative trade balance with Russia. In 2011 the deficit may reach $17 billion, whereas in 2010 it amounted to $11.6 billion.

The cumulative value of Russian investments in Poland at the end of 2010 totalled a symbolic €25 million (National Bank of Poland data). The cumulative value of Polish investments in Russia as of the end of September 2011, amounted to a mere $688 million. Still, the vast majority of these ($452 million) are direct investments, which contribute to job creation and the production of market-demanded goods. As regards the geographical location of Polish investments, it depends on access to raw materials and to the market. Hence, it is regions not located closest to the Polish borders which rank high on the list of Polish investments, such as the Novgorod and Moscow Oblasts. Conditions for Polish investors tend to be more attractive there, rather than the customs services in the old-type special economic zones (the Kaliningrad Oblast) (mg.gov.pl).

Poland has advocated the development of the EU–Russia Partnership for Modernization (P4M) as a support mechanism for a comprehensive modernization of Russian social and economic life. Warsaw stresses the equality of the economic and political dimensions of the Partnership. At the same time, Poland, together with other EU partners, underlines the priority nature of the currently negotiated PCA-2 agreement vis-à-vis the P4M.

Poland is a major consumer of Russian gas (9 billion cubic metres a year – out of 14 billion cubic metres of consumed gas overall) and oil with more than 90 per cent of fuel processed in Polish refineries imported from Russia. Besides, Russia offers Poland exports of electricity including from the nuclear power plant currently being constructed in the Kaliningrad Oblast (see also the contribution of Lašas and Galbreath in this volume). The interests of both parties do not always overlap, as is usually the case between a supplier and a consumer. For obvious reasons, Poland tries to take advantage of its position as a transit country, whereas Russia, for reasons equally obvious, tries to make itself independent from transit countries. This gives rise to controversies regarding such projects as the Nord Stream gas pipeline and the BTS-2 oil pipeline, bypassing Belarus via the oil terminal in Ust-Luga near St Petersburg (Stępień and Zawisza 2011).

Dynamic changes on the European gas market, caused by increased availability of LNG, the shale gas revolution and the German departure from nuclear energy, might introduce new elements into Polish–Russian energy relations. Much will also depend on whether the EU succeeds in integrating its own energy policy. When Russia cut off gas supplies delivered via Ukraine's territory in January 2009, the EU governments were inclined to make efforts aimed at extending interconnectors, increasing the pace of works on regulations which would liberalize the energy sector and diversification of supplies (Jakubowski, Miland, Woźniak 2011). Poland's policy has been an integral part of the new strategy.

Broadly speaking, Poland has advocated the application of the same rules towards gas suppliers from outside the EU as are binding regarding the EU companies. This covers the so-called Third Energy Package (TEP) that was adopted in 2009 and entered into force in March 2011, which imposed an obligation of unbundling, providing third party access to transmission as well as establishing independent regulatory institutions. The TEP is concurrent with introducing competition for the Yamal Gas Pipeline, which runs through the territory of Poland. Russia demands derogations from the EU energy regulations and a privileged status for Gazprom. What has been unsettling from the Polish perspective, however, were some declarations made by Russian authorities according to which WTO mechanisms could be used to question the legitimacy of extending the EU energy liberalization package to Russia (Bryanski 2011). In practical terms, the derogations and privileges Russia has been demanding would for all intents and purposes exempt Central Europe from the TEP and thus from the EU – at least as far as its energy security dimension is concerned.

Poland unequivocally supported Russia's accession to the WTO. The conclusion of the 18-year plus negotiations in December 2011 coincided with the end of the Polish Presidency of the EU Council. Poland, as well as the entire EU, will benefit from lower customs tariffs as a result of Russia's accession to the WTO. An average consolidated tariff rate applicable to all products is scheduled to gradually drop from 10 per cent in 2011 to below 8 per cent in 2020. The European Commission estimates that the value of industrial articles exported to the Russian market will increase by €4 billion per annum. Warsaw hopes that the legal frameworks of the Organization will contribute to the stabilization of trade relations and increased predictability of rules regulating access to the Russian market, whereas a dispute settlement mechanism will provide protection against a unilateral introduction of restrictive trade policy measures. Due to its vivid memories of a two-year embargo imposed on Polish foodstuffs, Warsaw felt obliged to focus particularly on the sanitary and phytosanitary measures agreement during the process of negotiations led by the European Commission. Russia's adoption of obligations with regard to rail tariffs was also of major importance. Last, but not least, one of the top issues on the Polish agenda was that of Siberia overflight charges. A reduction of these is scheduled for 1 January 2014.

It is worth noting that during the WTO accession negotiations, the Tusk government was persistent in pushing through Polish interests by using the EU channel, rather than trying to enter into bilateral, individual compromises. Such an approach was in line with the assumption adopted by the Polish government, according to which even a moderate EU strategy would be more efficient toward Russia than an ambitious national strategy. We could see how this assumption worked in practice before, when Poland responded to the August 2008 conflict between Russia and Georgia, as well as the January 2009 Russian–Ukrainian gas crisis.

The security dimension in Polish–Russian relations

As stressed by representatives of Donald Tusk's government, never before in its history has Poland been as safe as today (PAP 2010). A challenge which remains to be faced is that of Russia refusing to come to terms with NATO member states' equal security. In 1997 NATO promised in the NATO-Russia Founding Act not to deploy *substantial* combat forces in the territories of new member states. Russia, however, would like to translate this term into very low limits on the number of weapons. For Poland, the adoption of such limits would result in creating second-class security status within NATO. A similar situation is the one regarding Moscow's proposal of establishing sectoral NATO–Russia Missile Defence System, under which Russia would be responsible for the security of the countries located between the Baltic and the Black Seas.

When discussing the future of Polish–Russian relations, the issue which has to be touched upon is the lack of transparency in the process of organizational and technical modernization of the Russian Armed Forces as well as the related matter of the role of force within Russian foreign policy (de Haas 2011: 28–34). Announcements of Iskander-M missiles to be deployed in Kaliningrad Oblast (capable of carrying tactical nuclear warheads at a distance of 500 km); a statement made by President Vladimir Putin on the artificial nature of Ukraine at the NATO Summit in Bucharest in April 2008); invading Georgia in August 2008; and the 2009 military exercises Ladoga and Zapad and Centre-2011 manoeuvres all have had a direct impact on Poland's security.

The confrontational rhetoric used by Russian diplomats in response to Polish–American military co-operation regarding threats posed by 'rogue states' or whenever it comes to Poland's initiatives toward their common neighbours, further deepens the atmosphere of mistrust. Efforts at normalizing Polish–Russian relations will not bring permanent results unless Russia discontinues its attempts at rebuilding a sphere of exclusive influence in the area of the former USSR and a buffer zone in Central Europe (for Russia testing the hypothesis of American decline, see Mitchell and Grygiel 2011: particularly 8–10).

For Poland, the current transatlantic security architecture is capable of solving all security-related problems. Russia has declared its willingness to co-operate in the area of crisis management but has done so without changing its views of NATO – of which the majority of EU states are members – as a threat. The list of controversies on the EU–Russia agenda is long: trade, education, air transportation, energy security, conflicts in Georgia and Transnistria. Hence, a sceptical view of a breakthrough in EU–Russia relations as regards security is justified. That said, one should not underestimate the positive examples of co-operation: Russia's support for the OSCE mission in Kyrgyzstan, counter-piracy operations off the Horn of Africa, the EU mission in Chad, the stabilization and reconstruction of Afghanistan. The Transnistria crisis was supposed to test the intentions of both parties. Russia's involvement in solving the crisis was supposed to open co-operation in the format of the EU–Russia Political and Security Committee (the so called Ashton–Lavrov Committee), which was proposed in Meseberg near Berlin, on the initiative of Chancellor Angela Merkel and Dmitry Medvedev in 2010 (for more about the initiative, see Stewart's contribution to this volume).

According to Poland, Russia should not feel excluded from the European security system. A perennial problem in EU–Russia relations is the discrepancy in the understanding of security. Whereas Russia keeps focusing on hard

98 Bartosz Cichocki

threats and the military toolbox, the EU tries to generate a security zone using means typically applied by the OSCE. This is one of the reasons why it is so difficult to find a common platform of action in the event of protracted conflicts on the territory of the CIS. At the same time it is necessary to begin co-operation at the working-level between NATO and Russia, be it within the OSCE framework, as regards the CFE. It is impossible to solve other security-related problems in Europe unless the CFE regime is revitalized.

Poland has been persistent in applying the strategy of constructive involvement and accountability regarding Russia. During the February 2011 Weimar Triangle Summit, held in Wilanów, President Bronisław Komorowski extended an invitation to Russia to participate in the next meeting. Also, at the September 2011 meeting of the EU Foreign Ministers, organized in Sopot in the Gymnich formula, Minister Sikorski proposed inviting the Russian Foreign Minister to join the discussions. Another example is including Russia in the Group of Friends of the Eastern Partnership (an official name reads: Co-ordination and Information Group for the Eastern Partnership). Consultations between the Foreign Ministers of Poland, Germany and Russia have acquired a regular character.

Conclusions

Poland's relations with Russia leave their mark on the overall EU–Russia relationship. Poland is just too big to ignore, too centrally located to avoid and too aware of what it has to gain and what it has to lose to stay in the backseat and let others drive. But what this chapter leaves no doubt about is that the highs and lows of Poland's relations with Russia are not all country-specific, peculiar or isolated. On the contrary, they are not easily attributed to euro-sceptic, conservative or euro-enthusiastic, liberal governments. The issues in the Polish–Russian discourse are European in nature. Poland is learning fast how to achieve its goals regarding Russia in a constructive and co-operative manner.

The future of Polish–Russian relations is not to be painted in black and white. On the one hand the normalization process is slowing down. In April 2012 Russia declared it will not make available all the Katyń investigation files President Medvedev promised to open up (Freepl.info 2012). In May 2012 the Russian army chief General Nikolai Makarov threatened MD sites in Europe (i.e. in Poland, too) with a pre-emptive strike (Atlantic Council 2012). The Polish public is increasingly frustrated by the Russian investigation into the Smolensk plane crash (Borger and Pidd 2011). On the other hand, Polish business elites understand well that the Russian market and Russian investors are not easily neglected, especially during a period of economic uncertainty. Polish political elites, for their part, are aware that the EU's strategy toward Russia must be guided by a spirit of inclusiveness – in order for Europe to realize its global ambitions.

Note

1 The views expressed in this chapter are those of the author, and are not intended to reflect the position of the National Security Bureau of the Republic of Poland.

References

Adamski, Łukasz *et al.* (2011) *Rethinking EU-Russia Relationship. Interim report of the Polish-Russian Group on Difficult Matters.* The Centre for Polish-Russian Dialogue and Understanding, Brussels, November 2011, available at www.cprdip.pl/main/file. php?id=13&w=600&h=400&bgnews=0 (accessed 21 June 2012).

Atlantic Council (2012) *Russia's military threatens preemptive strike if NATO goes ahead with missile plan.* Atlantic Council Online, 4 May 2012, available at www.acus.org/natosource/russia%E2%80%99s-military-threatens-preemptive-strike-if-nato-goes-ah ead-missile-plan (accessed 21 June 2012).

Borger, J. and Pidd, H. (2011) 'Smolensk air crash – a year on and the scars are yet to heal', *The Guardian,* 8 April 2011.

Bratkiewicz, J. (2011) 'Racja i szkoda stanu', *Gazeta Wyborcza,* 5 October 2011.

Bryanski, G. (2011) *Russia may contest EU energy rules in WTO,* Reuters, 15 November 2011.

Chikhotskii, B. (2010) 'Pomenyaetsa li paradigma vostochnoy politiki Polshi?', APN.ru, 8 February 2010, available at www.apn.ru/publications/article22370.htm (accessed 21 June 2012).

Cichocki, B. (2009) 'Polityka Polski wobec Rosji', in *Rocznik polskiej polityki zagranicznej 2009.* Warsaw: Polish Institute of International Affairs.

——(2010) 'Wilson i Popescu jak zbiorowy Chrobry', in *Polityka Unii Europejskiej i Rosji wobec wspólnych sąsiadów.* Warsaw: Stefan Batory Foundation, available at www.batory.org.pl/doc/Polityka_UE_i_Rosji_wobec_wspolnych_sasiadow_2010.pdf (accessed 21 June 2012).

Cichocki, M. A. (2009/10) 'Szkice z polskiej podmiotowości', *Teologia polityczna,* No. 5: 55–71.

Dong, X. (2007) 'The CIS Policy of Russia and Current Challenges', in A. Eberhardt and A. Iwashita (eds) *Security Challenges in the Post-Soviet Space.* Warsaw-Sapporo: PISM-SRC.

ECHR (2012) *Russia should have cooperated with the Court and treated Katyń victims' relatives humanely.* Press release issued by the Registrar of the Court, 16 April 2012, available at http://cmiskp.echr.coe.int/tkp197/view.asp?action=open& documentId= 906167&portal=hbkm&source=externalbydocnumber&table= F69A27FD8FB8614 2BF01C1166DEA398649 (accessed 21 June 2012).

Freepl.info (2012) *Russia will not give Poland documentation concerning the Katyn massacre.* Freepl.info, 6 April 2012, available at http://freepl.info/2047-russia-will-not-give-poland-documentation-katyn-investigation (accessed 21 June 2012).

de Haas, M. (2011) *Russia's Military Reforms. Victory after Twenty Years of Failure?* Clingendael Paper No. 5, available at www.clingendael.nl/publications/2011/ 20111129_clingendaelpaper_mdehaas.pdf (accessed 21 June 2012).

Jakubowski, P., Miland, R. and Woźniak, P. (2011) *Energy Supply Crisis Management Mechanisms: A Study on Existing and Proposed Solutions.* Warsaw: Foundation for European Reform, available at http://omp.org.pl/pokazZalacznik.php?idZalaczniki=30 (accessed 21 June 2012).

100 *Bartosz Cichocki*

James, K. (2009) *Poland gets special attention from top German diplomat.* DW online, 31 October 2009, available at www.dw-akademie.de/dw/article/0,4842601,00.html (accessed 21 June 2012).

Judah, B., Kobzova, J. and Popescu, N. (2011) *Dealing with a post-BRIC Russia.* London: European Council on Foreign Relations, available at www.ecfr.eu/page/-/ ECFR44_RUSSIA_REPORT_AW.pdf (accessed 21 June 2012).

Karaganov, S. (2010) 'Soyuz Yevropy: poslednii shans?', *Rossiyskaya Gazeta.* 9 July 2010, available at www.rg.ru/2010/07/09/karaganov.html (accessed 21 June 2012).

Kowal, P. (2011) *Krajobrazy z Mistralami w tle.* 28 May 2011, Kraków: Ośrodek Myśli Politycznej, available at http://omp.org.pl/ksiazka.php?idKsiazki=208 (accessed 21 June 2012).

Malgin, A. (2010) 'Stosunki polityczne między Polską a Rosją po 1990 r.', in A. D. Rotfeld and A. Torkunow (eds) *Białe plamy, czarne plamy. Sprawy trudne w relacjach polsko-rosyjskich 1918–2008.* Warsaw: Polish Institute of International Affairs: 689–717.

Mitchell, W. A. and Grygiel, J. (2011) 'The Vulnerability of Peripheries', *The American Interest*, VI: 5–16.

Nowak, J. M. (2011) *Od hegemonii do agonii. Upadek Układu Warszawskiego – polska perspektywa.* Warsaw: Bellona.

PAP (2010) 'Tusk: Poland has never been so secure', Polish Press Agency dispatch, 18 November 2010.

Reeves, C. (2010) 'Reopening the Wounds of History? The Foreign Policy of the "Fourth" Polish Republic', *Journal of Communist Studies and Transition Politics*, 25: 518–41.

Rotfeld, A. D. (2012) *Myśli o Rosji … i nie tylko.* Warsaw: Świat książki.

Rotfeld, A. D. and Torkunow, A. (eds) (2010) *Białe plamy, czarne plamy. Sprawy trudne w relacjach polsko-rosyjskich 1918–2008.* Warsaw: Polish Institute of International Affairs.

Sejm (2007) *TREŚĆ. 2. posiedzenia Sejmu.* Obrady w dniu 23 listopada 2007 r., available at http://orka2.sejm.gov.pl/StenoInter6.nsf/0/6372FE4B9619C127C125739D0053E245/ $file/2_a_ksiazka.pdf (accessed 21 June 2012).

Sherr, J. (2008) *Russia and the West: A Reassesment.* The Shrivenham Papers, Number 6, Defence Academy of the United Kingdom.

Sikorski, R. (2011) *Poland and the Future of the European Union.* Speech in Berlin, 28 November 2011, available at www.msz.gov.pl/files/docs/komunikaty/20111128BERL IN/radoslaw_sikorski_poland_and_the_future_of_the_eu.pdf (accessed 21 June 2012).

Sikorski, R. and Westerwelle, G. (2011) *Joint letter of Foreign Ministers Radosław Sikorski of Poland and Guido Westerwelle of Germany on EU-Russia relations*, 8 November 2011, available at www.msz.gov.pl/index.php?document=46734 (accessed 21 June 2012).

Stępień, T. and Zawisza, A. (2011) *Energy Security and National Sovereignty.* Warsaw: Foundation for European Reform, available at http://omp.org.pl/pokazZalacznik. php?idZalaczniki=27 (accessed 21 June 2012).

Szczygło, A. (2009) *Russian historical propaganda in 2004–2009.* Warsaw: National Security Bureau of the Republic of Poland, available at www.bbn.gov.pl/download. php?s=1&id=3081 (accessed 21 June 2012).

Waszczykowski, W. (2012) 'Polski reset z Rosją', *Gazeta Polska*, 21 March 2012: 24.

7 Portugal and Spain

Licínia Simão[1]

One of the impacts of the big bang enlargement of the European Union in 2004/07 was the creation of new peripheral areas inside the Union. With the establishment of the ENP, in 2003, the EU aimed at dealing with the creation of an external periphery, but the effects of the internal peripheries are still to be acknowledged. For Portugal and Spain, one of the first consequences of the last enlargement was a shift in EU politics towards Eastern Europe, channelling attention and funds eastwards and loading the EU agenda with issues, which both countries were (and still are) ill-prepared to address. Therefore, the contribution of both Portugal and Spain to EU relations to the East has been scant, when compared with the new member states or Germany. This tendency to reinforce dynamics leading to the establishment of intra-EU peripheries has been further enhanced during the current financial crisis, with negative effects for both countries.

Despite these limitations, there are some factors facilitating their contributions to EU's external relations with Russia and which are also crucial to understanding their foreign policy interactions with this key EU partner. First, both countries have made serious efforts to take part in all projects deepening EU integration, such as the Euro-group, Schengen or Common Security and Defence Policy. This active participation has been regarded as a way to compensate for the structural limitations both countries faced upon accession and after years of isolation (Molis 2006: 86–87). This means, naturally, that they have taken part in important EU decision-making processes, so creating the skills and the necessary knowledge to contribute to the complex and wide-ranging relations of the EU with Russia. This relates to the second aspect, as the potentially limited interest of foreign ministries and governments in developing a position towards Russia has been compensated by good qualifications and even leadership displayed by the national functionaries integrated into EU working groups, as well as into NATO and the OSCE (telephone interviews with Brussels officials, August 2010). Finally, the lack of geographical, historical and geostrategic proximity, has also facilitated a friendly and problem-free interaction with Russia; an important resource for EU–Russia relations, considering the often tense state of relations.

102 *Licínia Simão*

The biggest difference between the two countries, regarding their contributions to a European common policy towards Russia comes from the EU's internal balance of power and dynamics, more than from structural limitations in their bilateral relations with Moscow. Although, as mentioned above, there are opportunities for individual leadership at working group-level, most EU policy decisions reflect the internal balance of power among EU member states. Spain, due to its size, has been able to portray itself as one of the 'big' EU countries, and has forged a place in some of the most important EU dynamics, namely in security issues in the Maghreb and the Middle East, which have brought it closer to Russia. Terrorism has also been a central issue for Spain, and after 9/11 there was a perfect opportunity to lead the EU in its anti-terrorist efforts, as well as to work with Russia at the bilateral and multilateral level. Of course, this has at times not been properly coordinated, exposing Spain's over-ambitious and contradictory foreign policy options. On the other hand, Portugal is a small country which, despite its early good performances in managing the EU integration process and its contributions to shaping the EU agenda (e.g. the Lisbon Strategy or the Lisbon Treaty), still encounters structural problems in its foreign policy and, within the EU, has been less than able (and willing) to take a more pro-active stance. The outcome is a reinforcement of old priorities, linked to the areas where Portugal has competitive advantages and feels it can leave a distinct imprint on the EU's agenda, such as through its relations with Brazil or Africa.

Regardless of these dynamics, both countries have been in the frontline of pan-European integration processes, in the EU, NATO or the OSCE, where relations with Russia are conducted. Both countries display a pragmatic and usually favourable position towards Russia, without having sufficiently close relations to remain hostage to intertwined interests. Russia has displayed a keen interest in deepening relations even with these remote European neighbours, but EU internal dynamics remain rather conservative, with each member state looking to advance its bilateral interests, often at the expense of a more co-ordinated EU approach to its neighbours and partners.

The Europeanization of Portuguese and Spanish foreign policies

The foreign policies of the two Iberian countries have undergone significant changes over the last 25 years, ending the long period of international isolation which marked the fascist regimes, and inextricably linking their domestic and foreign policy options to European integration. This has meant, however, an added layer to their traditional areas of interest, shaped by their historical and colonial legacies, rather than a detachment from old priorities. The prioritization of Africa and Latin America in foreign assistance, as well as in both countries' participation in international fora, illustrates this close connection. Thus, in the Portuguese programme of government for 2009–13, the Portuguese-speaking countries are the main priority for co-operation along with the European integration dimension (Government of the Portuguese

Republic 2009: 125–26). This prioritization has been translated into higher levels of Official Development Assistance (ODA), but also military co-operation with the Portuguese speaking African countries and 'regional areas of strategic interest for Portugal', such as the Maghreb and the Southern Mediterranean (Government of the Portuguese Republic 2009: 120). The distribution of Portuguese ODA illustrates these patterns: Africa takes 66 per cent, Asia 18 per cent and Europe 9 per cent (Instituto Português de Apoio ao Desenvolvimento 2008).

Spain displays similar behaviour, although it has had a more considerable presence in areas traditionally not a priority, partly facilitated by integration into the EU and OSCE. Nevertheless, the Mediterranean has been Spain's biggest foreign policy priority, as its role in the Barcelona Process (now Union for the Mediterranean) and in NATO intervention in Libya illustrates (Gobierno Español 2010; Stratfor 2011). Regardless, challenges in the Maghreb region, even prior to the Arab Spring movement, including underdevelopment, the spread of radical Islam and migration have proved hard to address, leading to some disillusionment with the possibilities of Spain's foreign policy towards the region (Villaverde 2000: 144). Spain maintains close co-operation with Latin America, the Middle East and the Maghreb region, as well as Sub-Saharan Africa (Gobierno Español 2009). According to the OECD, in 2011, except for Turkey and the Palestinian Authority, Spain's ten biggest net receivers of ODA are from Latin America and the South Mediterranean (OECD 2011). Therefore, both Portugal and Spain direct their assistance and political interest to historically close areas, which usually means that economic and security interests follow closely.

However, the last 25 years have been marked by a noticeable turn towards European and Euro–Atlantic integration (Soares 2007; Torreblanca 2001). This has meant a clear Europeanization of domestic and foreign policies, understood here as the institutionalization of formal and informal rules, policy paradigms and perceptions at the national level, which are derived from European interaction (Radaelli 2000: 4). Europeanization has also developed through closer participation in EU policy formulation, a reorientation of bilateral relations towards the European partners and the prioritization of intra-EU trade. Portugal's biggest trading partners within the EU are Germany, France and Spain. For Spain it is France, Germany, Italy and Portugal, which take the biggest share of bilateral trade (Instituto Nacional de Estatística (Portugal) and General Directorate of Customs and Excise (Spain). In fact, one of the most important distinctions in Spanish and Portuguese policy options inside European politics is their view on the leadership exercised by Germany, France and the UK and the possible establishment of a European 'directoire'. Whereas Spain pushed for recognition as one of the 'big' European states and sought to develop close relations with Germany and improve relations with France and the UK, thus shaping the European agenda in a series of quid pro quo agreements (Powell 2001: 4), Portugal was openly against the idea of such a 'directoire' leading European integration and

104 *Licínia Simão*

favoured a coalition of small and medium states, which together with the European institutions should balance relations among the bigger states (Gaspar 2000: 366). This demanded full participation from both countries in all the leading initiatives of European integration and a deepening and expanding foreign policy and diplomatic capacity to respond to these new challenges.

To some extent, Europeanization has also meant a wish to upload their priorities on to the EU's agenda. For a small country like Portugal, the rotating presidencies have been the privileged instrument to upload priorities, compensating for the lack of political weight in the Council (Bunse 2009, Koukis 2001). The Portuguese EU presidency of 2000 was Portugal's first concerted attempt to shape EU policy, leading to the adoption of the EU agenda for a competitive and knowledge-based economy, known as the Lisbon Strategy. In 2007, the third presidency brought Portugal's foreign policy priorities more clearly onto the EU's agenda, when the first EU–Brazil bilateral summit and the EU–Africa summit took place (Portuguese Presidency of the Council of the EU 2007). As for Spain, its size and population have meant it has managed to upload its foreign policy interests on to the EU's agenda beyond the presidencies, namely becoming a spokesperson of the EU in Latin America and to a certain extent in the Maghreb. The last Spanish EU presidency, in the first half of 2010, also put forward areas of interest traditionally advanced by Madrid, such as social cohesion and immigration controls, this last with important implications for relations with Russia (Spanish Presidency of the Council of the EU 2010). However, illustrating the reverse process, Spain also included Central Asia as a priority in its programme, and Portugal had to address the poor state of EU–Russia relations, hosting the Mafra Summit, in 2007.

Furthermore, both countries have actively participated in the CSDP and NATO missions in Europe, namely in the western Balkans, presenting themselves as committed partners to European and global security, independently of the existence of historical connections to these conflicts (Branco 2009; Sabiote 2008). The participation in an increasing number of United Nations, NATO or EU-led international missions, by both countries, is another illustration of the Europeanization process, recognizing a shared responsibility for global peace and security (Elcano Royal Institute 2006: 128). Added motivation came in the desire to 'avoid marginalisation in European affairs through active participation in the inner circles of European integration' (Palma 2009: 3). Relations with NATO have thus also remained a central aspect of Lisbon and Madrid's security options for Europe and, following the trend established under Salazar and Franco, both countries continue to maintain close alliances with the USA (Sahagún 2000: 149). This has meant a continuous commitment to Euro–Atlantic integration, namely to NATO's eastward expansion and to the development of relations with Russia (Sahagún 2000: 162).

In the aftermath of 9/11, the support lent by both countries to the US-led war on terror was in sharp contrast to the less enthusiastic views of France and Germany. The permanence of close relations with the superpower has provided both countries with material and symbolic benefits, which are relevant to both their foreign and domestic politics. Influence and privileged contacts with the USA are important symbolic aspects of foreign policy, while there are also real interests in the American market, in military co-operation or the management of Iberian diasporas in the USA. This closeness has come at a price for these states whenever US interests do not match the overall European views, namely in such a sensitive issue as relations with Russia. Such pressures bearing on the foreign policy choices of these two states are illustrative of broader international relations and foreign policy dynamics generally, where actors sometimes struggle to maintain agency in the face of constraining structures (Carlsnaes 1992). The mounting tensions between Moscow, Washington and Brussels thus play against the integrating and co-operative views that both countries seek to develop for Europe's security. This however, also opens new possibilities for foreign policy, which the last socialist governments in Portugal and Spain have acknowledged, by trying to emancipate both countries' foreign policy from the European continent.

Regardless of these priorities, both countries have sought to widen their political action, and adapt their foreign policy to new challenges emerging in the international system. This has been achieved building on the wide international links that both countries still maintain in Asia, Africa and America. Portugal sponsors a foreign policy of universal views, meaning close relations with all areas of the globe and different cultural and civilizational groups. During the last decade, Spain has also increased its presence in Asia, raising its profile through cultural presence and assistance, in recognition of the eastward-shifting international dynamics (Gobierno Español 2010: 94). Under the previous socialist governments in Portugal and Spain, there was an attempt to reconcile European integration with the emancipation of both countries' foreign policy from the European continent. Portugal has invested in its links with the Community of Portuguese Speaking Countries, often privileging multilateral frameworks. Spain has also diversified its outlook, developing a strategic partnership with Russia, investing in the CIS and naturally keeping close relations with Latin America.

The balance of the last 25 years of EU membership for both countries' foreign policy is mixed and, it should be noted, is in flux. This means that, although a clear adherence to the EU agenda and ways of dealing is visible, as the European project runs into economic and political hurdles and as the benefits of European integration become less visible for the South of Europe, both Portugal and Spain have sought to diversify their foreign policy outlook. This is also reflecting a new and broader trend towards a distribution of power away from Europe. Moreover, Europeanization and the development of foreign relations with Russia and the CIS countries have been achieved not only through their participation in the EU, but most prominently in the OSCE. Whereas within the EU, member states have dealt with Russia on economic and commercial issues, including energy issues; in the framework of

106 *Licínia Simão*

the OSCE, both countries have learned how to deal with pan-European security issues and have engaged with distant actors in the Caucasus and Central Asia. This has brought them into the heart of European security issues and to one of EU–Russia's hardest areas of interaction, which is security in their shared neighbourhood.

Key factors influencing bilateral relations with Russia

Portugal

Bilateral relations between Portugal and Russia are characterized by a diversified range of issues. Diplomatic relations were established for the first time in the eighteenth century, and were interrupted from 1917, after the Bolshevik revolution in Russia, until the democratic revolution in Portugal in 1974 (Milhazes 2004). Nevertheless, bilateral interaction was developed in Africa, during the Cold War, as well as in the context of Soviet support to the Portuguese Communist Party (PCP), during the dictatorship of Salazar. The USSR's moderation during the Portuguese revolution of 1974, refusing to support the PCP's ambitions of armed fighting, was a fundamental reason for this being a peaceful revolution. This background of interactions provided both countries with a common set of references from which to develop closer relations after 1991. It also provides an historical and cultural link, partly resonating with a shared feeling of 'empires gone', which according to Portuguese diplomats, can make dialogue easier (email exchange with Portuguese diplomats, Ministry of Foreign Affairs, January 2008; interview with Portuguese Representative to the OSCE Parliamentary Assembly, November 2011).

It was not until the late 1990s that both countries really started to refocus on bilateral relations. In 1994, a Treaty of Friendship was signed and since 2001, high-level visits have taken place at the presidential and governmental levels. The Ministries of Defence (MoD) have met regularly since 2004, and officially, military co-operation has been a priority in bilateral relations since 2005. However, there has been little in the way of tangible outcomes, for instance, while the Portuguese embassy in Moscow established a military attaché to manage co-operation, little has objectively been achieved. There were also plans by the Portuguese Defence Company (Empordef) and its Russian counterpart to co-operate, namely in ship building, but once more these plans have not materialized. The push towards closer economic relations, including in military areas, was a fundamental aspect of the socialist government of José Sócrates, not only towards Russia, but also towards countries in the Maghreb region (Algeria and Libya, for instance) and Venezuela, in Latin America. The practical outcomes of these policies for the Portuguese economy have been limited, with some criticism arising at the domestic level on the normative choices of the Portuguese foreign policy. The new liberal government has kept a strong emphasis on economic diplomacy as a fundamental strategy to overcome the impact of the financial crisis in Portugal, creating expectations that some of the initial steps taken to promote Portuguese strategic defence companies in Russia might be reinforced and developed. Overall, however, military co-operation issues have consistently been described by Portuguese authorities as better conceived in the framework of NATO, narrowing the political dimension of bilateral co-operation with Russia on military issues.

Bilateral trade relations remain marginal for both countries. In 2009, Russia was Portugal's 31st commercial client and its 14th supplier of traded goods. The trade deficit with Russia, which Portugal was gradually correcting as of 2004, was, in 2009, accentuated, meaning that Portuguese companies found it harder to trade with Russia (AICEP 2010b: 9). Support for Russia's bid to join the WTO is therefore justified as an attempt to improve the business opportunities for Portuguese companies. Trade relations remain extremely important in two main areas: of the total Portuguese imports from Russia, oil and its derivatives formed 80 per cent of the total in 2009; and Russian tourists are important for the Portuguese market. Thus, Portugal has sought to improve its standing as a tourist destination for Russians, although structural problems remain. First and foremost, there is strong competition from other closer destinations in the Mediterranean, offering similar products and having a less restrictive visa policy towards Russia, as is the case in Spain (interview with Portuguese officials based in Moscow, August 2010). Illustrating this, in 2009 50,000 Russian tourists visited Portugal, whereas 420,000 visited Spain (AICEP 2010a). One of the most promising and very positive signs was the creation, in 2009, of a direct flight connection between Lisbon and Moscow, operated by the Portuguese airline TAP. Over the next year the rate of tickets sales was above expected and seven weekly flights were operated, also providing important links to Madeira, Brazil and Angola, with whom Russia has no direct flight connections (Milhazes 2010). Despite this increase, Portuguese gains from Russian tourism seem to rely more on contextual factors, including the Arab Spring and NATO's intervention in Libya, than on a deliberate thought-out strategy to make Russia a priority in Portuguese economic diplomacy.

Russia has also sought to invest in strategic assets in Portugal, namely the deep-water port of Sines, and Gazprom has made a bid to buy its way into the Portuguese Galp Energia (Agência Financeira 2006). As in other areas, however, neither of these issues has been properly developed. Economic relations have been suffering with the global economic crisis, especially as the Portuguese government had to suspend major infrastructural projects set to advance with Russian support (Viana 2005). The slowdown of co-operation in these strategic areas and the decrease in investment seems to have two explanations. On the one hand, the personal engagement and deliberate strategy of the socialist government and of the Prime Minister were important for the deepening of co-operation in these strategic areas. On the other hand, Portugal and Russia's vulnerability to financial interdependence and the global crisis has dictated a slowdown of these processes. Considerations about

108 Licínia Simão

Europe have been marginal to these decisions. For Russia, Portugal also represents an important door to other markets such as Brazil and the African countries. The ability of Portugal to capitalize on these issues for its foreign policy is not irrelevant, including the promotion of the Portuguese language in Russia and the development of business partnerships.

In the context of the EU, Portugal looks to 'create bridges' and to be regarded as an honest broker, facilitating dialogue over confrontation. This was particularly important in the period of high tensions in bilateral EU–Russia relations between 2004 and 2008. Under the Portuguese Presidency of the Council of the EU, in 2007, Russia was high on the agenda and the holding of the EU–Russia summit in Mafra was a high priority of the Presidency. Although there were no major breakthroughs in EU–Russia relations at the summit, namely regarding the negotiation of the successor to the PCA and Kosovo independence issues, Portugal sought to avoid further tensions, concentrating on soft politics, such as cultural exchanges. Under the previous Socialist leadership, Lisbon further sought to increase bilateral trade with Russia, driving on the momentum of the EU Presidency. The government set up a strategy under the slogan 'Mission Russia 2007' (Misssão Rússia 2007), using the bilateral meetings of preparation to the Mafra summit as a back door for increased trade relations (Beato 2007). Portugal has also expressed its support for President Medvedev's European Security Treaty proposal, arguing that a discussion of his proposals should be co-ordinated within the existing European security structures (Lavrov and Amado 2009).

Overall, diplomatic relations are robust, although they are by no means of particular relevance to each other's priorities. We can therefore say that, because Portuguese foreign policy has privileged 'cluster' areas, where the country stands at an advantage, Russia as an area of interest has been neglected. However, a multi-sectorial view of the challenges posed by an interdependent world, and of the integration processes in the EU and NATO, has made Lisbon much more aware of the importance of enlarging the scope of its foreign policy interests.

Spain

Bilateral relations between Spain and Russia have only recently started to deepen, both in terms of the number of diplomatic exchanges and with respect to the scope of co-operation issues. Over almost 40 years, until 1977, there were no bilateral relations between the two countries (the USSR at the time). As Spain normalized its external relations, USSR/Russia gradually developed into an important partner. Nevertheless, it was only after the end of the Cold War that bilateral relations were finally regarded, by both sides, as a clear possibility. In the late 1990s and during the 2000s, there were several official visits, at the level of President/King and government (Prime Ministers and Ministers of Foreign Affairs as well as Trade and Defence among others). In 2007, both countries celebrated the 30th anniversary of

Portugal and Spain 109

their re-established bilateral relations, at a time when a strategic level of interaction was being reached (Moratinos and Lavrov 2007).

Spanish foreign policy under José Maria Aznar was marked by a clear Atlanticist dimension, often translated into unconditional support for US foreign policy objectives (Selway 2006: 15). This was particularly visible after 9/11, and the US-led global war on terror, reflecting Spain's domestic concerns with terrorism, but also the recognition that, after 9/11, the context was ripe to capitalize on its support to the USA. Following the terrorist attacks in Madrid, on March 11 2004, and the coming to power of the Socialist José Luis Zapatero, Spanish foreign policy gradually changed. The return to the 'heart of Europe', meaning closer relations with France and Germany, as well as increased support for CSDP missions, was a central change in Spanish foreign policy under Zapatero. It was also marked by a desire for national affirmation, both internationally and at the European level, even if at times that exposed glaring contradictions between normative speech and realist external action, restricted by domestic policy concerns (de Areilza and Torreblanca 2009). A central feature has been the promotion of multilateral institutions and a fierce denunciation of the Bush administration foreign policy in Iraq, which has coincided with Russian interests of advancing a multi-polar agenda, seen as more suited to address global security concerns, such as global warming, illicit trade and transnational terrorism (Moratinos 2006). Official positions place Spain as a supporter of a multipolar world, where the USA is not a leading superpower, but one great power among others, namely Russia.

Under this foreign policy revision, Spain also sought to develop a Russia-specific foreign policy, leading to the signing of a 'Declaration of Strategic Partnership', in 2009 (Medvedev 2009; Declaración de Asociación Estratégica 2009). Official visits at the highest levels between the two countries took place, improving not only economic and political relations but also establishing a practice of mutual support for each other's international initiatives. The fight against terrorism brought both countries towards closer co-operation, both bilaterally and in the UN, as illustrated by their close work towards the adoption of a UN Global Strategy against Terrorism. Afghanistan was a central issue in this regard, and Spain voiced its opposition to the development of a US missile shield in Eastern Europe, partly as a quid pro quo for Russia's co-operation in the war in Afghanistan. Spain has not recognized Kosovo's unilateral declaration of independence and has voiced sympathy for Russia's position on this matter, having taken up Serb demands for faster EU integration during its 2010 presidency (Pantelic 2010). At the NATO Bucharest Summit, Spain sided with Germany and France in blocking Georgian and Ukrainian accession perspectives. Spain also opposed sanctions against Russia in the aftermath of the Georgia war in 2008. In that sense, Spain's position towards Russia has been described as one of 'unconditional support' (Pantelic 2010).

It is surprising to see relations between Madrid and Moscow reach such a high level of agreement and interaction, considering the lack of historical and/or

110   *Licínia Simão*

cultural affinities, and the only recent development of economic relations, as further analyzed below. The development of a clear Spanish interest towards Russia can be categorized in two main aspects. On the one hand, the availability of opportunities for interaction in regional security issues, such as the Middle East, where Spain has been actively engaged and where Russia remains a central actor. On the other hand, there has been an overlap of security perceptions, mainly on issues of terrorism, which the post-9/11 context further reinforced. Today, due to Spain's engagement in global settings such as Afghanistan, and Russia's increasingly vital role in NATO efforts, both countries have furthered bilateral co-operation. Under the new conservative government of Mariano Rajoy, Spain's priorities will most likely be adjusted. Of the little mentioned in terms of foreign policy during the electoral campaign, Russia was not cited as a priority and two new main trends should be visible, according to some observers. First, a re-centring of attentions in Latin America and trans-Atlantic relations, both for economic and strategic reasons (Spain's relations with the USA are badly in need of mending). Second, a new drive to take a leading role in Europe and to join the other big powers in decision-making, including on fundamental economic aspects, but also on the stabilization of the south Mediterranean (Torreblanca and Leonard 2011, Dibbert 2011).

Besides high politics in the global and EU–Russia bilateral agenda, Spanish relations with Moscow have also focused on economic co-operation, investment and cultural relations. Bilateral trade relations between the two countries have increased exponentially over the last years, reaching $9.3 billion in 2009. Spain is the 22nd largest trade partner of Russia, which is one of Spain's top 20 trade partners (Fedyashin 2009). Trade relations are marked by the entrance of Spanish brands into the Russian market, whereas Russian exports to Spain are mainly of raw materials. Russia is Spain's second biggest oil supplier after Saudi Arabia (Elorza Cavengt 2007). Russian tourism has become one of the most important for Spain, with near half a million Russians visiting Spain every year, as mentioned above. As further developed below, visa and asylum issues have featured high on the Spanish–Russian agenda and have been transferred onto the European level, in the framework of EU–Russia visa liberalization negotiations. Gazprom was also trying to buy 20 per cent of the Spanish energy company Repsol (Tremlett 2008), which is already present in Kazakhstan and is also looking to invest in Uzbekistan. This close co-operation has been translated into high level diplomatic meetings, which Spain hoped could improve its international standing with Russia.

The impact of bilateral relations on European foreign policy towards Russia

Relations between Portugal and Russia and between Spain and Russia are primarily shaped by a lack of historical and geopolitical issues on a common agenda. Geographical distance dictated that for the better part of the last 25

Portugal and Spain   111

years of European integration, the Russia–EU common agenda would be managed and shaped by the most powerful states of the EU and then by the new member states with whom Russia has historically closer relations. However, this has gradually changed, due to external and internal factors in the EU's integration process.

Externally, distance has been relativized as a relevant factor in the design of foreign policy priorities. Therefore, trade relations with Russia became an important part of both Madrid's and Lisbon's extra-EU trade, not least as a source of much needed and sought after investment and tourism-based revenue. Moreover, as tensions rose in EU–Russia relations, especially during the second mandate of President Putin, this lack of historical links was regarded as an advantage that could be used to the benefit of both bilateral and EU–Russia relations. Therefore, internally, the EU also recognized that smaller and relatively uninterested states such as Portugal could help the EU build on constructive bilateralism to improve overall relations with Moscow.

Spain's drive towards closer relations with Moscow has been made within and outside the EU. The Europeanization process of the early years of European integration has been consolidated through participation in EU and OSCE leadership positions, and this in turn has allowed for a more encompassing view of the benefits of a non-exclusive European foreign policy. Prime Minister Zapatero's foreign policy regarded closer relations with Moscow as a way to attain benefits for Spain in trade, investment and tourism, but also in terms of its international projection as a relevant world actor. The outcomes of this political option are debatable. Spain has simultaneously sought a 'committed foreign policy' (Zapatero 2008), announcing the promotion of international law as a central aspect of this new approach, while neglecting to raise human rights issues to any significant degree in its bilateral relations with Moscow. This was poorly perceived by Spanish public opinion, which is very sensitive to human rights issues. Spain has also promoted a strong multilateralism, rooted in the UN, while partly disinvesting in the European project, by not aligning itself with EU partners on important matters such as Kosovo or Afghanistan (Vogel 2009). Overall, Spain has moved from lacking a foreign policy towards Russia, which translated into support for the EU positions, to developing bilateral relations with Moscow and thus formulating more distinct foreign policy positions within the EU, in line with Spain's global agenda. Under the new Spanish leadership, and considering that Russia is also undergoing a period of introspection, the trend might be towards one that better balances Spanish interests in the Americas and its role within a fast changing EU.

The level of impact of Portugal and Spain's views in EU–Russia relations thus depends on several variables. At the domestic level, it is important to realize whether there are important constituencies pressing the governments towards a specific course of action. Spanish public opinion and opposition parties have displayed a conservative and careful approach towards the strategic partnership between Madrid and Moscow (Saíz 2008). Illustrating this is

112 *Licínia Simão*

the lack of agreement to let Lukoil buy 20 per cent of Repsol, and the active denunciation of the contradictions of former Prime Minister Zapatero's foreign policy, balancing between a principled commitment and a pragmatic approach (de Areilza and Torreblanca 2009). In Portugal, the lack of an informed and active public opinion, and the generalized lack of knowledge about Russia and the EU has left the conduct of bilateral relations very much safeguarded from criticism or major inputs from outside the government. Moreover, with respect to Portugal's positions within the EU, national representatives in Brussels enjoy some discretion to play a pro-active role, despite the existence of guidelines in many policy issues.

This has been the case during moments of crisis, namely following the war in Georgia, when the Portuguese Foreign Minister asserted that NATO should take a 'firm, but not aggressive reaction' towards Russia, and that the lines of dialogue should be kept open (*Público* 2008). Portugal, much like Spain, has been committed to maintaining dialogue with Moscow, especially at times of greatest distress in relations with the EU and NATO (email exchange with official from the Portuguese Ministry of Foreign Affairs, March 2010). Portuguese officials have characterized relations with Russia as 'pragmatic and usually favourable' and constructive (interview with Portuguese official at COEST, September 2010). They also acknowledge that Russia is a crucial partner for Europe in regional and global security issues, as it is to NATO and the USA. These are Portugal and Spain's main multilateral and security partners and therefore, Russia's engagement with them is seen as a win-win situation. Both countries have operated conservative policies regarding EU and NATO engagement with Ukraine and the South Caucasus, opposing the offer of Membership Action Plans to Ukraine and Georgia at the Bucharest Summit, in 2008 (Mahony 2008). They also opposed the deployment of US anti-missile defence batteries in Poland and the Czech Republic (*The New York Times* 2007), as well as the application of sanctions to Russia, after the 2008 Georgian war.

Portugal has tended to maintain a principled foreign policy, and it states its highest commitment to European values (also visible in its engaged participation in the OSCE and Council of Europe). Portugal has thus been committed to EU enlargements, including to the Balkans, and has contributed to the security of the region, but is happy to keep further enlargements to the Caucasus or Ukraine off the EU agenda. On divisive issues and in periods of greater tension, Portugal has opted for a pragmatic policy, following the lead within the EU and in NATO. However, and taking into account its own strategic interests and a commitment to use its modest position to act as an honest broker, Portugal has contributed to maintaining dialogue with Russia and to advancing its integration into Europe.

Spain developed its bilateral relations with Russia late, having privileged closer relations with the USA during most of the 1990s. This meant that Madrid was free from foreign policy constraints, at the time, to align itself with EU normative approaches to Russia, for instance in sanctioning Russia

Portugal and Spain 113

due to the conflict in Chechnya (Barbé 2000: 54). This changed as Spain got more engaged in deeper bilateral relations with Russia, namely in the framework of the Zapatero government's decision to balance Euro–Atlantic co-operation with a more pragmatic co-operation with Russia, in areas of bilateral interest. Russian use of energy relations as a central aspect of its foreign policy prompted the two countries to develop closer relations. Spain is highly dependent on external sources of energy and is only now investing in renewable energies to meet environmental standards. This meant that a policy towards Russia was essential, allowing for a stronger role in the context of the EU (Pérez and Vaquer i Fanés 2008). Another major area of EU–Russia relations, where Spain also has been active, is visa liberalization. The 2010 Spanish Presidency of the EU initiative on visa liberalization with Russia aimed at providing the impetus for the advancement of one of the most significant issues in EU–Russia relations. Spain has also been at the epicentre of visa and asylum issues for Russian citizens, including some high profile cases involving Caucasian Russians accused by Moscow of involvement in terrorist operations, but also high ranking figures of the Russian political elite, allegedly linked to mafia operations in Europe. From 2005, three major operations have been developed by Spanish police to uncover the illicit operations of Russians, using the Spanish real-estate market for money laundering (Harding 2010). Judicial co-operation across Europe has led to the dismantling of these criminal networks with surprisingly little damage for bilateral relations with Russia and for the prospects of visa liberalization.

Conclusions

Portuguese and Spanish foreign policies share some important similarities. This includes their views of the European project, as the main change in foreign policy formulation over the last 25 years. An interesting coincidence has led to simultaneous political tendencies in both countries: socialist governments that made the accession process to the EU a priority. Felipe Gonzales in Spain and Mário Soares in Portugal; later on, the conservatives took power in Spain, under Aznar and in Portugal, with Durão Barroso, favouring a closer alliance with the USA and the United Kingdom; followed by the socialists of José Sócrates in Portugal and Zapatero in Spain, balancing relations with Europe with a broader outlook on both countries' foreign policy. The current conservative governments in power in both countries have focused on the management of the financial and economic crisis, for which relations with the EU are fundamental. The impact on relations with Russia is still hard to predict.

Both countries have tended to align themselves with mainstream European views (France and Germany), not least regarding external relations with Russia. The divisions among French and Germans and the trend towards the 'normalization' of national foreign policies, making national interest the main priority as opposed to a commitment to deepen European integration, has

114 *Licínia Simão*

also been felt in Spain and in Portugal. This could mean that the EU will face decisive challenges to define a common approach to Russia. A factor that could limit this tendency is the acknowledgement of the problems caused by a divided position in Europe and the need to find a consensus and show solidarity. This means old member states need to engage with Russia through European structures and new member states need to redefine their views towards Russia, avoiding the trap of EU internal divisions. Portugal and Spain would benefit from this, as both have been committed participants in the European integration processes.

Finally, we can say that there is an Iberian approach to the EU, to the extent that bilateral relations between Portugal and Spain have been widening and deepening over the last 30 years, in unprecedented rhythm. The two countries co-operate on many issues, including approaches to Latin America, the Mediterranean and the Euro–Atlantic community. This does not mean however that both countries see relations with Russia in a similar way. To some extent they are competitors for investment and trade, which both countries desperately need. They have sponsored pragmatic foreign policies, based on a rational assessment of what is the national interest. Portugal has been committed to European integration and good relations with Russia, as a way to ensure that it does not find itself in the irreconcilable position of having to choose between Euro–Atlantic structures and an exclusive pan-European orientation. Spain has also regarded good relations with Russia as an important aspect of its national interest, both in economic terms and due to the prestige it brings.

In either case, the evolution of bilateral relations with Russia seems to be the product of specific circumstances, namely the governments' perceptions of market opportunities or of international affirmation, rather than a deliberate and long-term approach to the role of Russia in Europe. This means that the impact of the bilateral relations of Lisbon and Madrid with Russia in EU foreign policy remains an open ended question.

Note

1 The author is grateful to all the officials in Lisbon, Madrid, Moscow and Brussels who shared their views and knowledge on this issue.

References

Agência Financeira (2006) 'Russos da Gazprom entram no capital da Galp'. November 17, available at www.agenciafinanceira.iol.pt/empresas/iol/743075-1728.html (accessed 1 March 2011).

AICEP (2010a) *Rússia – oportunidades e dificuldades do mercado*. AICEP Mercados e Informação de Negócios, February.

——(2010b) *Rússia–Ficha de Mercado*. AICEP Mercados e Informação de Negócios, April.

Barbé, E. (2000) 'Spain and CFSP: the emergence of a "major player"?', *Mediterranean Politics*, 5(2): 44–63.

Portugal and Spain 115

Beato, C. (2007) 'A difícil missão de Sócrates', *Diário Económico*. May 30, available at www.missaorussia.gov.pt/noticias_noticia_37.asp (accessed 1 March 2011).

Branco, C. M. (2009) 'A participação de Portugal em operações de paz. Êxitos, problemas e desafios', *E-cadernos CES*, No. 6. Issue on 'Peacekeeping: Actores, Estratégias e Dinâmicas': 86–141.

Bunse, S. (2009) *Small states and EU Governance. Leadership through the Council Presidency*. New York: Palgrave Macmillan.

Carlsnaes, W. (1992) 'The agency-structure problem in Foreign Policy Analysis', *International Studies Quarterly*, 36: 245–70.

de Areilza, J. M. and Torreblanca, J. I. (2009) 'Diagnóstico diferencial, política exterior', *Foreign Policy en Español*. June–July, available at www.fp-es.org/diagnostico-diferencial-politica-exterior (accessed 1 March 2011).

'Declaración de Asociación Estratégica entre el Reino de España y la Federación Rusa' (2009) Madrid, March 3, available at www.la-moncloa.es/NR/rdonlyres/DACEA456-08 A3-4588-BEB2-F821AB17497F/94288/DECLARACIONDEASOCIACIONESTRAT EGICA.pdf (accessed 1 March 2011).

Dibbert, T. (2011) 'Post-Zapatero Spain: obstacles and opportunities', *Journal of Foreign Relations*, December 16.

Elcano Royal Institute (2006) *20 Years of Spain in the European Union (1986–2006)*, commemorative edition celebrating the 20 years of Spain's accession to the EU.

Elorza Cavengt, F. J. (2007) 'Spain – Russia: agreed approach on vital issues', Interview by the former-Spanish Ambassador to Moscow in *Diplomat*, 2. Available at www.diplomatrus.com/article.php?id=831&l=eng&phpsessid=d8a386007bf66ef383b 97e6e76dd2501 (accessed 1 March 2011).

Fedyashin, A. (2009) 'Friendship not enough to boost Russian-Spanish trade', *RIA Novosti*. March 4 (2), available at http://en.rian.ru/analysis/20090304/120417096. html (accessed 1 March 2011).

Gaspar, C. (2000) 'Portugal e o alargamento da União Europeia', *Análise Social,* XXXV (154–55): 327–72.

General Directorate of Customs and Excise (Spain). Available at www.aeat.es (accessed 12 December 2011).

Gobierno Español (2009) *Plan Director de la Cooperación Española, 2009–2012*. Approved by the Council of Ministers, 13 February 2009, available at www.casafrica.es/casafrica/Inicio/PlanDirectorCooperacionEspanola09–12.pdf (accessed 10 August 2010).

——(2010) *España hoy*. available at www.la-moncloa.es/docs/pdfs/EspaniaHoy2010/ ESP_2010_WEB.pdf (accessed 10 August 2010).

Government of the Portuguese Republic (2009) *Programa de XVII Governo Constitucional, 2009–2013*. Available at www.portugal.gov.pt/pt/GC18/Documentos/ Programa_GC18.pdf (accessed 12 December 2011).

Harding, L. (2010) 'WikiLeaks cables: Russian government 'using mafia for its dirty work'', *The Guardian*. 1 December, available at www.guardian.co.uk/world/2010/dec/ 01/wikileaks-cable-spain-russian-mafia (accessed 15 December 2011).

Instituto Nacional de Estatística (Portugal). Available at /www.ine.pt (accessed 12 December 2011).

Instituto Português de Apoio ao Desenvolvimento (2008) *Distribution of the Portuguese bilateral ODA, 2008*. Available at www.ipad.mne.gov.pt/index.php?option=com_con tent& task=view&id=200&Itemid=220 (accessed 12 December 2011).

116   *Licínia Simão*

Koukis, T. (2001) 'Europeanisation of foreign policy making. Portugal and the Presidency of the Council of Ministers', *YEN Research Seminar*. Centre of International Studies, University of Cambridge, October.

Lavrov, S. and Amado, L. (2009) 'Transcript of the Remarks and Response to Media Questions by Russian Minister of Foreign Affairs Sergey Lavrov at Joint Press Conference Following Talks with Portuguese Minister for Foreign Affairs Luis Amado'. Moscow, April 14 2009, available at www.mid.ru/bdomp/brp_4.nsf/e78a48070f128a7 b43256999005bcbb3/06b31c486099a3dec3257599002d3671!OpenDocument (accessed 27 April 2012).

Mahony, H. (2008) 'Diplomatic tussle over Georgia and Ukraine NATO bids', *EUobserver*. March 27, available at http://euobserver.com/9/25873 (accessed 1 March 2011).

Medvedev, D. (2009) 'Press conference following the Russian – Spanish talks'. Madrid, March 3, available at http://archive.kremlin.ru/eng/speeches/2009/03/03/2019_type82 914type82915_213640.shtml (accessed 1 March 2011).

Milhazes, J. (2004) 'Moscovo e Lisboa celebram 225 anos de relações bilaterais', *Público*, March 11.

——(2010) 'Resultados da TAP na Rússia acima das expectativas', *Da Rússia*. July 2, available at http://darussia.blogspot.com/2010/07/resultados-da-tap-na-russia-cima-das.html (accessed 1 March 2011).

Missão Rússia (2007) Official website. Available at www.missaorussia.gov.pt/home.asp (accessed 12 December 2011).

Molis, A. (2006) 'The role and interests of small states in developing European security and defence policy', *Baltic Security & Defence Review*, 8: 81–100.

Moratinos, M. A. (2006) 'Russian – Spain relations developing successfully', *Interfax*. September 17, available at www.interfax.com/17/308016/Interview.aspx (accessed 1 March 2011).

Moratinos, M. A. and Lavrov, S. (2007) 'España, Rusia y el Multilateralismo', joint letter by the Spanish and the Russian Ministers of foreign affairs, *El País*. February 9, available at www.maec.es/es/MenuPpal/Actualidad/Declaracionesydiscursos/Pagin as/articuloministroelpais20070209.aspx (accessed 1 March 2011).

OECD (2011) *Development co-operation report 2011. Annex A: efforts and policies of bilateral donors.* Paris.

Palma, H. (2009) *European by force and by will: Portugal and the European security and defence policy.* EU Diplomacy Papers, 7, College of Europe.

Pantelic, Z. (2010) 'EU confuses Serbian leaders who confuse Serbian people', *WAZ. euobserver.* 22 June, 2010, available http://waz.euobserver.com/887/30334 (accessed 1 March 2011).

Pérez, F. A. and Vaquer i Fanés, J. (2008) 'Spain in the genesis of Europe's new energy policy', in E Barbé (ed.) *Spain in Europe 2004–2008.* Monograph of the Observatory of European Foreign Policy, 4, February, Bellaterra (Barcelona): Institut Universitari d'Estudis Europeus.

Powell, C. (2001) 'Fifteen years on: Spanish membership in the European Union revisited', *Center for European Studies Working Paper,* 89.

Portuguese Presidency of the Council of the EU (2007) General website, available at www.eu2007.pt/ue/ven/ (accessed 12 December 2011).

Público (2008) 'Cáucaso: Luís Amado defende uma posição da NATO 'firme' e sem 'agressividade''. August 19, available at www.publico.pt/Pol%C3%ADtica/caucaso-luis-amado-defende-uma-posicao-da-nato-firme-e-sem-agressividade_1339526 (accessed 1 March 2011).

Portugal and Spain   117

Radaelli, C. M. (2000) 'Whither Europeanization? Concept stretching and substantive change' *European Integration online Paper*, 4 (8).

Sabiote, M. A. (2008) 'Does Spain fit in the European defence policy? Spain and EU crisis management operations', in Esther Barbé (ed.) *Spain in Europe 2004–2008*. Monograph on the Committee on European Foreign Policy, 4 February 2008, Bellaterra (Barcelona): University Institute for European Studies.

Sahagún, F. (2000) 'Spain and the United States: military primacy', *Mediterranean Politics*, 5(2): 148–69.

Saíz, F. (2008) 'El CNI alerta sobre la venta de Repsol', *Publico*. 20 November 2008, available at www.publico.es/espana/176260/el-cni-alerta-sobre-la-venta-de-repsol (accessed 27 April 2012).

Selway, L. (2006) *Spanish foreign policy from A(znar) to Z(apatero)*. Franklin & Marshall College students thesis, December 14.

Soares, A. G. (2007) 'Portugal and the European Union: the ups and downs in 20 years of membership', *Perspectives on European Politics and Society*, 8 (4): 460–75.

Spanish Presidency of the Council of the EU (2010) 'The Programme of the Spanish Presidency of the Council of the European Union'. Available at www.europarl.europa. eu/meetdocs/2009_2014/documents/dlat/dv/dlat220210_programa_presid_espanola_/ dlat220210_programa_presid_espanola_en.pdf (accessed 1 March 2011).

Stratfor (2011) 'Europe's Libya intervention: Spain', *Stratfor global intelligence*, March 30.

The New York Times (2007) 'Russia tests missile to penetrate U.S. shield'. May 29, available at www.nytimes.com/2007/05/29/world/europe/29iht-shield.5.5917318.html (accessed 1 March 2011).

Torreblanca, J. I. (2001) 'Ideas, preferences and institutions: explaining the Europeanisation of Spanish foreign policy', *ARENA Working Papers* 01/26. University of Oslo, Advanced Research on the Europeanisation of the Nation-State.

Torreblanca, J. I. and Leonard, M. (2011) 'Spain after the elections: the 'Germany of the South'?', *ECFR Policy memo*.

Tremlett, G. (2008) 'Gazprom seeks 20% of Spanish oil group', *The Guardian*. November 14, available at www.guardian.co.uk/business/2008/nov/14/oil-russia-gazp rom-spain-repsol (accessed 1 March 2011).

Viana, L. M. (2005) 'Russos da Gazprom querem uma petroquímica em Sines', *Diário de Notícias*. October 22, available at http://dn.sapo.pt/inicio/interior.aspx?content_id=6 26395 (accessed 1 March 2011).

Villaverde, J. (2000) 'The Mediterranean: A firm priority of Spanish foreign policy?', *Mediterranean Politics*, 5(2): 129–147.

Vogel, T. (2009) 'On a collision course over foreign policy' *European Voice*. 11 December, available at www.europeanvoice.com/article/imported/on-a-collision-course-over-foreign-policy/66663.aspx (accessed 1 March 2011).

Zapatero, J. L. (2008) *In Spain's interest: a committed foreign policy*, speech delivered at the Elcano Institute conference, Madrid, 2 July.

8 Belgium, Luxembourg and the Netherlands

Tom Casier

Traditionally the Benelux countries have been regarded as strong supporters of European integration. At the same time, Belgium, the Netherlands and Luxembourg all have export-orientated economies that are strongly dependent on global economic developments. Pursuing business opportunities is thus a substantial part of their diplomatic activity. This chapter explores how, in their relations with Russia, these factors have evolved, how they balance out and under which circumstances the Benelux countries decide to pursue their objectives alone, rather than at EU level. In other words, in their relations with Russia, does a bilateral approach prevail over a preference for EU-co-ordinated policies?

This chapter compares the policies of the Benelux states towards Russia and their willingness to co-ordinate Russia policies at EU level. Using Carlsnaes's integrative approach to Foreign Policy Analysis (Carlsnaes 2002, 2008), I will first determine the dimensions of their policies towards Russia. In particular the role of national economic interests and of pro-European attitudes will be highlighted. Next, I will evaluate the influence of the three countries on the EU's Russia policy. I will balance Jakobsen's four sources of influence of small member states (Jakobsen 2009) with the importance of ad hoc coalition formations on the basis of national interests. External energy relations will serve as a case.

The implication of focusing on the Benelux countries in a European context is that the emphasis of this chapter is on the EU perspective rather than the Russian. As far as the latter is concerned, I accept the claim that Russia prefers to deal with the individual EU member states, rather than with the EU as a whole. Moscow regards the EU as a slow and difficult negotiation partner, inhibited by strongly diverging attitudes towards Russia. Though smaller member states are often assumed to play a limited role in these bilateral relations (Schmidt-Felzmann 2008: 178), this chapter will evaluate whether this is really the case for the Benelux countries.

By looking at the preferences and influence of the Benelux countries on the EU's Russia policy, this chapter aims to contribute to research in two areas: bilateral relations between the individual EU member states and Russia and the co-ordination of national foreign policies and EU foreign policy.

The framework

Relations with Russia can be regarded as 'the most divisive factor in EU external relations policy' (Schmidt-Felzmann 2008: 170). For most EU member states considerable interests are at stake. Moreover, they have very different historical experiences which lead to diverging perceptions of the international position and intentions of Russia. The result is that opinions on a European policy towards Russia diverge widely among the 27 member states. The same divisions can be found within the EU institutions, with the European Parliament traditionally taking the harder line. As a result, it is an understatement to say that the EU's policy towards Russia is not the most coherent, targeted and vigorous of the EU's external policies:

> [T]he EU is itself struggling with contradictory approaches and interests. On the one hand, it acknowledges that new types of threats need transnational solutions and that openness and co-operation with Russia is the most effective way to address those issues. On the other hand, within the EU mistrust towards Russia prevails.
>
> (Haukkala *et al.* 2010: 49)

Notwithstanding these ambiguities and dividedness, EU–Russia relations have in many ways become more important. Until the financial crisis in 2008 at least, the trade volume between both steadily increased. This, however, has not been translated into closer institutional co-operation. In this respect the failure to agree on a new EU–Russia Agreement, to replace the Partnership and Cooperation Agreement (PCA), is symbolic.[1] A substantial part of this increased trade is the result of bilateral relations between Russia and individual member states. Governments actively chase business contracts with Russian companies or authorities. This is a substantial part of what diplomats do today, facilitating and lobbying for trade and investment opportunities for their companies. These commercial relations develop within the framework and the rules of the game of EU trade and other policies and of the PCA, but they often constitute the stakes of a fierce competition between member states, rather than the grounds for European co-operation, as will be demonstrated further.

This chapter studies bilateral relations between the Benelux states and Russia and how the preferences of the former determine their willingness to co-ordinate Russia policies or initiatives at the EU level. It also explores the circumstances under which they are successful in doing so. Rather than following Europeanization theories in a weakly Europeanized domain, the paper will start from the national foreign policies of the countries concerned. First, I will determine the foreign policy preferences of the Benelux countries and their willingness (not) to co-ordinate Russia policies at EU level. Carlsnaes (2002, 2008) suggests that foreign policy action is always 'a combination of purposive behaviour, cognitive-psychological factors and the various structural phenomena characterizing societies and their environments' (Carlsnaes

120   *Tom Casier*

2002: 342). On these grounds foreign policy action is analyzed in terms of three dimensions: a structural dimension, an intentional dimension and a dispositional dimension ('psychological-cognitive actors which have disposed a particular actor to have this and not that preference or intention', Carlsnaes 2008: 97). These dimensions are interrelated 'increasingly exhaustive ... explanations of foreign policy actions' (Carlsnaes 2008: 97).

After having determined the dimensions of foreign policy, I will explore to what extent the Benelux countries are successful either at co-ordinating policy initiatives at EU level or at preventing that from happening. To determine the influence of the Benelux states on the EU's Russia policy, I rely on Jakobsen (2009). Building on the literature on the power of small states, Jakobsen mentions four sources of influence of small states on EU policy-making. First small states must be seen as displaying leadership in the issue area. Second, they must 'back their initiatives with convincing arguments' (Jakobsen 2009: 86). Third, influence is more likely when they are perceived to build coalitions that function in the common interest rather than national interests. Finally, their initiatives require sufficient capacity, for example resources or diplomatic expertise. It goes without saying that these four sources cannot be seen in isolation. They have to be seen in interaction with other structural factors. Most importantly, do the preferences match those of other major players in the EU, not least the major member states? The extent to which an issue is considered to be a priority area by these major players is equally determining. The analysis will balance both approaches, raising the question of whether success in co-ordinating or blocking EU initiatives results from the internal sources of influence mentioned or rather from alignment with big member states.

Academic literature on relations between the Benelux countries and Russia specifically is almost non-existent, specifically in the case of Luxembourg. The analysis here will draw heavily on interviews held by the author with Dutch and Belgian diplomats (October 2009 and March 2010), on the analysis of policy documents and on general literature on the foreign policies of those countries.

Preferences in the Benelux: explaining the pragmatic policy of constructive engagement with Russia

Predisposition: still a European reflex?

The Benelux countries have traditionally had a strong European identity (Jones 2005: 180; Coolsaet 2001; van den Bos 2006; Hellema 2010). They belong to the founding members of the European Coal and Steel Community (ECSC). They share a long integrationist tradition, in which leading politicians promoted a strong supranational Europe. The latter was considered to coincide with national interests (van den Bos 2006: 430): a strong supranational EU was the best guarantee to defend the interests of a small country. Over the last years, however, we have seen substantial changes in this pro-European reflex, though least of all in Luxembourg.

Belgium, Luxembourg and the Netherlands 121

According to van den Bos (2006) the Netherlands has undergone a 'revolution' of their Europe policy, with an increasingly defensive and sceptical attitude towards Brussels. In the aftermath of the negative Dutch referendum on the Constitution, the Netherlands has chosen a foreign policy course in which bilateral relations are favoured over supranational solutions. The national interest – no longer to coincide with a strong Europe – is at the centre stage: European co-operation is only desirable 'when a national approach does not lead to the optimal promotion of the interests of Dutch society' (Foreign Minister Bot, quoted in van den Bos 2006: 431, translation by the author). The selective will to co-ordinate policies at European level can hardly be stated more clearly and fully applies to Dutch policy vis-à-vis Russia.

Belgium's policy has changed less drastically. It is still mainly pro-integrationist, but since the end of the Verhofstadt government, pragmatism replaced great visions of a European finality (Coolsaet and Nasra 2009: 30). Then Foreign Minister Karel De Gucht, pleaded for 'proactive bilateralism', establishing permanent contacts, which may form the basis for multiple coalitions (Belgische Kamer van Volksvertegenwoordigers 2004: 9). This policy was a pragmatic answer to the lack of common views among member states in certain areas (relations with Russia being one) and the expectation that diverse ad hoc coalitions would be increasingly determining. Coolsaet and Nasra (2009: 32) point out that this proactive bilateralism differs from the bilateral choice made by the Netherlands, by maintaining a preference for a supranational approach, rather than opting for pure intergovernmental co-operation.

Of course it should be noted here that Belgium holds a particular position because it hosts international institutions such as the EU and NATO. Also Russia considers this as an important aspect of its bilateral relations with Belgium (interviews with Belgian diplomats, March 2010). Arguably, the presence of these institutions and the fairly frequent visits by presidents and ministers from third countries to Brussels allow Belgium to punch above its weight. In 2006 alone, Russian and Belgian Foreign Ministers Lavrov and De Gucht met each other six times.

Since normative issues are contentious in EU–Russia relations, another element deserving attention is the normative predisposition of the Benelux countries. The Netherlands has traditionally seen itself as a country with an international responsibility. It favours multilateral co-operation and an open international economic order, based on free trade (Schrijver 2006). Considering that the Netherlands has an export-orientated economy, neither preference is necessarily disconnected from Dutch national interests. However, the Netherlands has played a prominent role in development co-operation and has often been a vocal critic of human rights violations. This is also reflected in bilateral relations with Russia. Today, the Netherlands is one of the few EU member states running a programme for funding and assistance to transform Russian civil society (the MATRA programme). Though less so over more recent years, the Netherlands has not hesitated to raise critical issues on human rights and the state of democracy in Russia. On one occasion this led to

122   *Tom Casier*

serious bilateral tensions, when then Dutch Foreign Minister Bot raised issues about the responsibility of the Russian authorities in the Beslan hostage crisis of 2004. Two elements should be noted. First, notwithstanding this normative approach, there is little evidence that Dutch policy-makers played a particularly active role in uploading issues of human rights and democracy onto the EU's Russia agenda.[2] Neither are there indications that the Netherlands have pushed for a more coercive approach towards Russia. Second, the sporadic critique of the human rights situation in Russia has never interfered with the defence of Dutch business interests (Leonard and Popescu 2007: 47).

An interview with Dutch Ambassador Jan-Paul Dirkse with the Moscow Times is quite revealing in this respect. The Ambassador claims that 'there are no real bilateral political issues'. Referring to the Prime Minister, he states: '... relations are so good that even controversial issues can be addressed, and I think that is something that is very important, that among friends, like-minded people, you can talk even about issues on which you differ'. (Dirkse 2009) The contrast with Bot's sharp critique in 2004 is noticeable. By making a distinction between 'no real issues' and still addressing 'controversial issues', this quote seems to confirm the strongly pragmatic attitude: the Dutch may stick to their predisposition to defend ethical issues, but it is clear that those will not form an obstacle for close co-operation. This suggests a clear hierarchy between commercial interests and ethical issues.

Belgium's emphasis on 'ethical' issues in foreign policy is of a much more recent date. The most spectacular example was the so-called genocide law, which was severely restricted in 2003. Belgium has also taken the lead in certain disarmament dossiers. In 2006 it was the first country to pass a law prohibiting cluster munitions. Partly due to internal political issues, Belgium largely abandoned this policy in recent years (Coolsaet and Nasra 2009: 27 ff.). In the bilateral Action Programme with Russia, issues like democracy and human rights are mentioned as a topic for dialogue, but not as a Russia-specific topic (Action Programme 2010). In general they play a rather implicit role in the bilateral relations. It appears that Belgium prefers leaving sensitive political issues to the EU.

In the case of Luxembourg, normative concerns over the political situation in Russia are hard to find. On the contrary, ambassador to Moscow Gaston Stronck called political relations with Russia 'very very stable' and 'extremely friendly'. He stated: 'Russia is a democratic state. ... Russia is able to find its own way and it does not deserve comments ... from outside. We fully respect the developments underway in Russia' (Stronck 2010).

Structural dimension: distant partners, yet close

Belgium, the Netherlands and Luxembourg are all three small states. Their economies strongly depend on export and therefore on global economic developments. In the case of the Netherlands, 60–70 per cent of the national income depends on external economic activities (Rood 2010). This is one of the main reasons behind all three countries operating predominantly pragmatic foreign policies, evincing a clear preference for international stability and a central role for commercial interests (Coolsaet 2001; Rood 2010). All three have fairly important economic relations with Russia, but there is no dependence on Russia. In the field of energy, none of the Benelux countries is strongly dependent on Russian oil and gas. While Belgium imports around 8 per cent of its gas from Russia, the Netherlands and Luxembourg import no Russian gas at all.

The Benelux is located at a relatively distance from Russia, so there are no direct border or neighbourhood issues. Arguably one may state that security relations are still influenced by certain images and stereotypes of the Cold War, leading to perceptions of Russia being 'different', but there is no sense of imminent threat on either side (interviews with Dutch and Belgian diplomats, October 2009 and March 2010). The most important tangible remnant of the Cold War in the current security architecture is NATO, of which all three Benelux countries are members. While disagreement over its enlargement may have cast a shadow over relations between the West and Russia in general, for the Benelux they have not really featured at the bilateral level. All three countries balance a pro-European attitude with Atlanticist engagement, though to different degrees. Over the last decade the Netherlands has followed a stronger pro-American course than Belgium. While the Netherlands supported the war in Iraq, Belgium was vehemently opposed to it. Belgium took the lead in an attempt to use the divisions over Iraq to strengthen the European Security and Defence Policy. Opposition to the war in Iraq put Belgium on a line with France, Germany and also publically with Russia. All three Benelux countries have actively supported the war in Afghanistan. Due to disagreement, leading to the collapse of the government, the Netherlands withdrew from Afghanistan in August 2010. The Belgium–Luxembourg contribution continues, but has always been fairly small.

Apart from the negative historical heritage of the Cold War, the peculiar historical and cultural links between the Netherlands and Russia should be mentioned. These ties date back to Peter the Great's stay in Holland, the links between Amsterdam and St Petersburg and links between the Dutch royal family and the Romanovs. This results in active cultural co-operation, inter alia the establishment of the 'Hermitage Amsterdam'. Luxembourg's historical ties date back to the Treaty of London of 1867, when Russia became one of the guarantors of the borders and neutrality of the Grand Duchy of Luxembourg.

Intentional dimension: the prevalence of economic interests

As mentioned above, commercial interests feature prominently in the external relations of all three Benelux countries. Relations with Moscow are no exception: economic and business issues dominate the bilateral agenda. Trade and investment opportunities are expected to increase even further after an agreement was reached in December 2011 on Russian accession to the World Trade

124   *Tom Casier*

Organization (WTO). All three governments actively pursue commercial opportunities with Russia. The importance of economic relations, however, differs.

First, the Netherlands has a considerably higher degree of economic involvement in and with Russia, both in trade and investments. Among the EU member states it is Russia's second trading partner (after Germany), accounting for 9.7 per cent of the trade in goods (3.3 per cent for Belgium, 0.05 per cent for Luxembourg). The country is also the most important cumulative foreign investor in Russia, while Russia is a very important investor in the Netherlands. The banking sector turns Luxembourg into an important country of origin of FDI accounting for an important share of the investments in Russia. It is part of the top three EU investors in Russia. Total Russian assets in Luxembourg investment funds are worth €2,000 billion (Stronck 2010). While this is a factor of key importance in Luxembourg–Russia relations, Russian assets only represent 1.5 per cent of the strongly internationalized investment funds in Luxembourg. In contrast to investment, trade between Luxembourg and Russia is limited.

Second, the Netherlands plays an exceptional role in the field of energy. Several Dutch companies are very active on the Russian energy market. State-controlled *Gasunie* has a stake in the Nord Stream pipeline project (9 per cent), which was launched in November 2011 in the presence of Dutch Prime Minister Mark Rutte. Royal Dutch Shell has a 40 per cent stake in Sakhalin II. There are close connections between state-controlled Gasunie and the Russian authorities, including at the personal level. Moreover, Dutch know-how for gas extraction is highly prized in Russia, for example for exploitation of gas reserves on the Siberian peninsula of Yamal. Finally, the Netherlands has ambitions to function as a hub for gas pipelines, transporting Russian gas to countries in North-Western Europe. Though also active on the energy market, Belgium has no comparable role to play. It is, however, a leader in the field of Liquefied Natural Gas (LNG).

The resulting policy: European rhetoric versus pragmatic self-interest

The Benelux countries all have a pragmatic attitude towards Russia. They share the expectation that the best strategy to follow is stepwise constructive engagement or interlacing ('vervlechting' – Belgische Kamer van Volksvertegenwoordigers 2009) with Russia in different fields: business, culture, defence, technology, space programme. All Benelux states label the relations with Russia as excellent (Dirkse 2009; Buitenlandse Zaken, Buitenlandse Handel 2010; Stronck 2010). Arguably the pragmatic attitude is strongest in Luxembourg. Its Foreign Minister Jean Asselborn (2009: 15, author's translation) stated:

> Russia does not have a veto right over the choices of countries like Georgia and Ukraine. However, it is important to take Russian concerns into account to avoid the stability and political balance in our region being endangered unnecessarily. ... The advantage of a strategic

Belgium, Luxembourg and the Netherlands 125

partnership based on mutual trust is that divergences can be approached in an open and constructive way.

All Benelux countries rhetorically claim to favour the co-ordination of Russia policies at EU level, in line with their traditional – albeit changing – pro-integrationist identities. Key foreign policy documents refer to the fact that the Russia policy is situated within the EU's policy. In practice we see that attempts to co-ordinate policies towards Russia at EU level depend on the business interest at stake (an issue that will be developed further in the next part). This is no doubt the most determining factor inhibiting or promoting co-ordination initiatives at EU level. In general Belgium and Luxembourg are more inclined to opt for European co-ordination than the Netherlands, but even with them bilateral concerns dominate. The Dutch attitude can be explained on the basis of the U-turn in its Europe policy and because of the Dutch interests in the Russian economy, which are considerably higher than that of Belgium and Luxembourg.

The Benelux experience suggests Hyde-Price (2006) and Timmins (2006) are right to argue that there is a certain division of tasks between the EU and member states. First order issues, i.e. issues related to national interests and security are by preference dealt with bilaterally, while the responsibility for second order issues, i.e. ethical concerns, is left to the EU. This ensures that tensions over human rights or democracy with Russia do not affect bilateral relations and means that: 'Only when their first order interests are not endangered are states ready to ... pursue second order issues bilaterally with Russia' (Schmidt-Felzmann 2008: 179). The occasional Dutch critique on human rights in Russia is thus not the exception to the rule, but is clearly subjugated to business interests.[3]

The capacity to influence the EU's Russia policy: sources and coalitions

The previous part dealt with the dimensions of the bilateral relations between the Benelux countries and the Russian Federation. It explained the will of the Benelux countries to co-ordinate (or not) Russia policies at EU level on the basis of several determinants, of which business interests appeared to be dominant in daily diplomatic practice, while (changing) European identities still featured selectively and mainly at the rhetorical level. In this part, I will look at the way co-ordination and coalition formations manifest themselves. First, I will sketch how co-ordination is done within the EU and the Benelux. Then, relying on Jakobsen's – interrelated – sources of influence of small member states (leadership, convincing arguments, acting in common interest, capacity) and on the role of coalition formation, I will make a pre-liminary assessment of the influence of the Benelux countries on EU policies towards Russia – or the lack thereof.

126 *Tom Casier*

Formal co-ordination of Russia policy among the Benelux countries

Prior to EU meetings, the three Benelux countries informally co-ordinate their views within the Benelux Committee of Ministers. Further, there is an informal consultation about Russia between the Benelux countries and the Baltic states (interviews with Belgian diplomats, March 2010). This is done for two reasons. One has to do with the strengthening of the position of smaller states within the EU. The second reason is mutually beneficial expertise: on the one hand the availability of specific expertise on Russia in the Baltic states, on the other the EU expertise in the Benelux countries. However, there are strong divergences in terms of the historical experience of the countries involved, their perceived interests and preferences. It is likely that the Baltic states see co-operation with the Benelux countries as an opportunity to upload certain issues to the EU agenda. Belgium also consults with the Visegrad countries and with Romania and Bulgaria.

The effectiveness of co-ordination within the Benelux must be qualified. The Benelux was established as an intergovernmental organization in 1958. The treaty, expiring after 50 years, was renewed in 2008, albeit with limited enthusiasm. Though Belgium has tried to reinvigorate the organization, its impact has waned because of growing divergences between the European policy of Belgium and the Netherlands. Moreover, new treaties such as Schengen, have eroded the Benelux. As a result, consultation within the Benelux before Council meetings has become a formality rather than a decisive moment. 'When it comes to cooperation within the EU, even if the cohesion of the Benelux has never been as strong as assumed, it has never been as limited as today' (Franck 2009: 14, author's translation). As Franck points out, there might be an occasional convergence of views in the Council, but certainly no regular common Benelux point of view. Belgium–Luxembourg co-operation as such remains more important, in particular in economic respects. The Belgium–Luxembourg Economic Union (BLEU) dates back to 1921 but was revised in a new convention signed in 2002. One of the new elements in the agreement is the reinforcement of co-operation within international organizations. Economic co-operation and investment-related matters are discussed in an Intergovernmental Committee for Economic Co-operation between Russia and the Belgium–Luxembourg Economic Union. Business interests are promoted through a joint Belgian–Luxembourg Chamber of Commerce.

Influence of the Benelux countries on the EU's Russia policy

Relying on interviews with Belgian and Dutch diplomats (October 2009, March 2010), the influence of their individual countries on EU policies towards Russia is seen by outsiders as limited. When testing potential sources of influence of small states, as summarised by Jakobsen (2009), the Benelux countries indeed score low on all four criteria.

First, none of the Benelux countries has a leadership position in the field of external relations with Russia. The Netherlands may be an important economic partner of Russia and a prominent player in the field of energy, but these are precisely areas in which there is considerable competition among EU member states. Jakobsen (2009: 87) mentions three factors to guarantee a forerunner role: persistent activism, expertise and successful national policies. With only selective references to issues of human rights and democracy, it is hard to discern a 'persistent activism to promote an issue on the international scene'. Further, none of the Benelux countries has particular Russia expertise, though in coalitions with other states their long experience with European integration may prove valuable. Finally political problems may undermine leadership potential. Belgium's credibility as a diplomatic actor successful in fostering compromises was undermined by the ongoing political problems between 2007 and 2011. After the elections of June 2010 it took 18 months to form a new coalition government. In this context Luxembourg Prime Minister Juncker noted a real danger of Belgium losing influence if the political crisis were to continue (Juncker quoted in Franck 2009: 18). A good example is Belgium's decision to actively promote good governance in its foreign policy. The internal political crisis undermined Belgium's external credibility as an advocate of this principle (Coolsaet and Nasra 2009: 29).

Jakobsen's second criterion, 'convincing argumentation', is harder to assess. The subjective view of other players is that the Netherlands and to a lesser extent Belgium are not seen to appeal to 'fundamental norms and values shared by the member states' (Jakobsen 2009: 87), but rather are seen as countries concerned about bilateral relations and trade and investment opportunities. As described in the previous section, the European reflex which once characterized the Benelux approach is no longer prevalent in the Netherlands and has undergone considerable change in Belgium. It has been replaced by a selective use of the normative or pro-integrationist arguments, which are only used when they are considered to pose no threat to the national interest. The third source of influence, engagement in 'honest broker coalition building', relates to the degree to which countries engage in coalitions which do not promote national interests, but in an impartial way aim at promoting common interests. Again, the bilateral turn in Belgium and the Netherlands, suggests differently. The Benelux countries are not seen as active builders of neutral coalitions. The co-operation with the Baltic and other new member states serves pragmatic purposes. By no means is it a strong advocacy coalition, promoting a coherent strategy towards Russia. While the Benelux states favour pragmatic constructive engagement, some of the Baltic states have voiced strongly critical opinions about Russia.

Finally, in terms of capacity, none of the Benelux countries provides above average resources to promote its European initiatives. The long diplomatic experience with European integration, may give the countries a certain advantage, but there are no specific immaterial resources – such as particular diplomatic expertise – in the field of relations with Russia.

128 *Tom Casier*

All this implies that the influence of the Benelux countries will predominantly depend on the context. With the capacity to influence low, ad hoc coalitions and compatibility of national preferences with other major players will be much more determining. Belgium and the Netherlands have displayed a different willingness to co-ordinate energy policies vis-à-vis Russia at EU level. Whereas Belgium regards itself as a proponent of a common energy policy, the Netherlands is in general more reluctant to accept European regulation and supervision, as proposed in the European Commission's Third Energy Package (see Köper 2008: 3). When it comes to external aspects of energy policy, because of its heavy involvement in Russian energy projects, the Netherlands often finds itself in line with Germany. This was most notably the case when Germany exerted pressure to weaken the 'reciprocity clause' (nicknamed the Gazprom clause), leaving the full discretion to negotiate investment clauses with Russia to the individual member states.

How rhetoric about European co-operation is used selectively, whenever it matches national commercial interests, can be illustrated by the Dutch-Belgian competition over the construction of a gas hub, linking the gas fields of Russia with North-Western Europe (Ministerie van Economische Zaken 2009). While the Dutch government promoted Rotterdam as the gas hub, Belgium supported the case of Antwerp. The Netherlands was successful in winning the contract with the Russians, using its heavy involvement in the Russian energy sector and the deal between Gasunie en Gazprom on reciprocal participation in pipeline projects as leverage. Belgium eventually gave up the ambition to create a gas hub, ostensibly for security-related reasons (interviews with Belgian diplomats, March 2010). In the aftermath Belgium proposed to form a consortium of all 27 EU states to negotiate energy deals with Russia. In doing so it appealed to the common European interest and energy solidarity, hoping to benefit from its reputation as a pro-integrationist member state and impartial broker of coalitions. The initiative was unsuccessful and did not receive support from countries such as the Netherlands and Germany, which would instead stress the individual responsibility of the member states in their external energy relations. It remains a matter of speculation, but it is doubtful whether Belgium would have been such an active promoter of a common energy policy and a consortium of the EU-27, if it had been successful in securing the contracts for a gas hub. It is more likely that it turned only to a rhetoric of energy solidarity once it saw its ambitions to form a gas hub shattered.

Conclusion

The Benelux countries favour similar pragmatic policies of constructive engagement with Russia. These reflect the different economic interests of the three export-orientated countries. The Netherlands has exceptional relations with Russia. It is the EU's second trading partner and it plays a very active role in the Russian energy sector. Together with Luxemburg it is one of the

EU's top investors in Russia. These business interests were found to be the most important determinant of the willingness to co-ordinate Russia related policies at EU level. Commercial interests tend to push the Benelux countries to favour bilateral deals over EU co-ordinated actions.

This contrasts with the traditional pro-European disposition of Belgium, the Netherlands and Luxemburg. Pro-integrationist attitudes still feature, but mainly at the rhetorical level and in a very selective way, whenever they match national commercial interests. The European reflex was found to have been reversed in the case of the Netherlands and to have undergone substantial change in the case of Belgium. Luxemburg, in turn, has de facto developed the strongest pragmatic policy of the three towards Russia.

The traditional sources of influence of small states in the EU were found to play a limited role: the Benelux countries have a limited impact on the development of an EU Russia policy. This is due to a lack of leadership in areas relevant for relations with Russia and to a decline in the credibility of these countries as impartial, pro-European actors taking the lead in the formation of a coherent Russia strategy. In contrast, there is a considerable degree of competition over commercial deals with Russia among the Benelux states. As a result, their influence is not a co-ordinated one, but is dependent on the formation of ad hoc coalitions, based on the compatibility of their national economic interests with those of major players in the EU.

Interviews

Semi-structured interview with Dutch diplomat (Moscow, October 2009).
Semi-structured interviews with Belgian diplomats (Brussels, March 2010).

Notes

1 The PCA between the EU and Russia was signed in 1994 and entered into force in 1997. It was valid for 10 years, but was – as provided for in the treaty – silently prolonged in 2007 by lack of accord over a new EU–Russia Agreement.
2 Though the EU has frequently put forwards these issues at its summit meetings with Russia, they have virtually never led to any real sanctions or pressure on Russia.
3 Foreign Minister's Bot remarks on Beslan in 2004 were the only time that this sort of critique resulted in severe political tensions and Russian sanctions.

References

Action Programme (2010) Gezamenlijk Actieprogramma 2010–11 tussen de Russische Federatie en het Koninkrijk België, zijn Gemeenschappen en Gewesten. 4 mei 2010, available at www.belgium.mid.ru/SPD2010–11_nl.pdf (accessed August 2010).
Ambassade van de Russische Federatie in het Koninkrijk België, *Informatie over de Russisch-Belgische bilateral betrekkingen.* Available at www.belgium.mid.ru/otn_ned.html (accessed March 2010).

130 Tom Casier

Asselborn, J. (2009) Déclaration de politique étrangère de M. Jean Asselborn, Vice-Premier Ministre, minister des Affaires étrangères, prononcée devant la Chambre des Députés. 17 November, available at www.mae.lu/fr/Site-MAE/Politique-etranger e-et-europeenne/Declarations-de-politique-etrangere (accessed July 2010).

Belgische Kamer van Volksvertegenwoordigers (2004) *Algemene Beleidsnota Buitenlands Beleid.* DOC 51 1371/036.

——(2009) *Algemene Beleidsnota Buitenlands Beleid.* 5 November 2009, DOC 52 2225/010.

Buitenlandse Zaken [Dutch Ministry of Foreign Affairs] [s.d.] *Rusland.* Available at www.minbuza.nl/dsresource?objectid=buzabeheer:47354&versionid=&subobjectnam e= (accessed March 2010).

Buitenlandse Zaken, Buitenlandse Handel en Ontwikkelingssamenwerking [Belgian Ministry of Foreign Affairs] (2010) *Centraal-en Oost-Europa.* Available at http://diplomatie.belgium.be/nl/Beleid/wereldregio_s/centraal–en_oost-europa/ (accessed July 2010).

Carlsnaes, W. (2002) 'Foreign Policy', in W. Carlsnaes, T. Risse and B. A. Simmons (eds) *Handbook of International Relations.* London: Sage, 331–49.

——(2008) 'Actors, structures and foreign policy analysis', in S. Smith, A. Hadfield and T. Dunne (eds) *Foreign Policy: Theories, Actors, Cases.* Oxford: OUP, 5–100.

Coolsaet, R. (2001) *België en zijn buitenlandse politiek, 1830–2000.* Leuven: Van Halewyck.

Coolsaet, R. and Nasra, S. (2009) Buitenlands beleid in België anno 2008: beleid onder binnenlandse politieke druk, *Studia Diplomatica,* LXII, Special Issue, 21–37.

De Vos, L. and Rooms, E. (2006) *Het Belgisch buitenlands beleid: geschiedenis en actoren.* Leuven: Acco.

Dirkse, J.-P. (2009) Interview with Ambassador of the Netherlands in Russia, Jan-Paul Dirkse, *Moscow Times.* 29 October, available at www.themoscowtimes.com/business/country_supplement/russia_holland/eng/article/interview-with-ambassador-of-the-netherlands-in-russia-jan-paul-dirkse/401814.html (accessed August 2010).

Franck, C. (2009) Plus de presence, moins d'influence, *Studia Diplomatica,* LXII, Special Issue, 9–19.

Haukkala, H. *et al.* (2010) 'Contours of External and Internal in EU-Russia relations', in T. Huttunen and M.Ylikangas (eds) *Witnessing Change in Contemporary Russia.* Helsinki: Kikimora, 21–55.

Hellema, D. (2010) *Buitenlandse politiek van Nederland. De Nederlandse rol in de wereldpolitiek.* Utrecht: Het Spectrum.

Hyde-Price, A. (2006) 'Normative Europe. A Realist Critique', *Journal of European Public Policy,* 13: 17–234.

Jakobsen, P. V. (2009) 'Small States, Big Influence: The Overlooked Nordic Influence on the Civilian ESDP', *Journal of Common Market Studies,* 47: 81–102.

Jones, E. (2005) 'The Benelux Countries: Identity and Self-interest', in S. Bulmer and C. Lequesne (eds) *The Member States of the European Union.* Oxford: OUP, 164–84.

Köper, N. (2008) M. Kramer, T. van Gasunie: 'We zitten in een international concurrentiestrijd om gasrotonde te worden', *Energie Nederland,* 16: 1–3.

Leonard, M. and Popescu, N. (2007) *A Power Audit of EU-Russia Relations.* Policy Paper, London: European Council on Foreign Relations.

Light, M. (2008) 'Russia and the EU: Strategic Partners or Strategic Rivals?', in U. Sedelmeier and A. R.Young (eds) *The JCMS Annual Review of the European Union in 2007.* Oxford: Wiley-Blackwell, 7–27.

Belgium, Luxembourg and the Netherlands 131

Mernier A. (ed.) (2003) 150ste verjaardag van de diplomatieke betrekkingen tussen Rusland en België. Available at www.diplomatie.be/Moscownl/media/moscownl/webversie_fr_nl_150_belgorusse.pdf (accessed July 2010).

Ministerie van Economische Zaken [The Netherlands] *Kamerbrief Gasrotonde*. 23/10/2009, available at www.rijksoverheid.nl/documenten-en-publicaties/kamerstukken/2009/10/23/kamerbrief-gasrotonde.html

Rood, J.(2010) *Nederland in een veranderende wereld: een buitenlands beleid voor de toekomst*. Den Haag: Clingendael, available at www.clingendael.nl/staff/?id=63 (accessed August 2010).

Schmidt-Felzmann, A. (2008) 'All for One? EU member states and the Union's common policy towards the Russian Federation', *Journal of Contemporary European Studies*, 16: 169–87.

Schrijver, N. (2006) Nederland in de wijde wereld. Multilateralisme als verheven ideal in eigen belang, *Internationale Spectator*, 60: 552–55.

Stronck, G. (2010) *Interview with Ambassador of Luxembourg to Russia, Gaston Stronck. Voice of Russia*. 26 November 2010, available at http://english.ruvr.ru/radio_broadcast/2249329/35704568.html

Timmins, G. (2006) 'Bilateral Relations in the Russia–EU Relationship: The British View', in: H. Smith (ed.) *Two Levels of Cooperation: Russia, the EU, Great Britain and Finland*. Helsinki: Kikimora, 49–65.

Van den Bos, B. (2006) Teloorgang van Nederlands EU-beleid: "Spruitjes-Revolutie" vermorzelt kostbare traditie, *Internationale Spectator*, 60: 430–34.

9 Denmark, Finland and Sweden

Tobias Etzold and Hiski Haukkala

The three Nordic EU member states, Denmark, Finland and Sweden, share a certain basic asymmetry in their dealings with Russia: whereas for all of them Russia is a key factor affecting their prosperity and security, the same does not apply the other way round. For Moscow the Nordics are bit players, factors but not necessarily always actors in their own right in the wider European game Russia is playing. By contrast, for the Nordics Russia is an important element of their foreign policies and their neighbourhood that places them in a special position in EU efforts to develop a joint approach towards the country. Nevertheless, despite their geographical proximity, long common history of both regional wars and co-operation with Russia and (assumed) shared 'Nordicness' (see Ingebritsen 2006), all three countries have unique characteristics, experiences and relations with Russia. To a degree they have drawn different conclusions and settled for different political/ institutional responses and approaches as will be discussed in more detail in this chapter.

First, the case of Sweden will be discussed and then the cases of Finland and Denmark will be considered in order to contrast the differences as well as to identify the similarities the three countries have in their dealings with Russia. The chapter will focus on the development of bilateral relations between Russia and these three countries and related implications for wider EU–Russia relations. It will identify the key factors influencing these countries' relations with Russia and those policy areas that are most important in respective bilateral relations, pointing out possible similarities and differences. Another central question is to what extent the three countries' relations with Russia hinder or contribute to the formulation of a common Russia policy on the EU level. In this context, the extent to which these three small countries are able and willing to make an impact on the formulation and implementation of a common EU–Russia policy will be examined. The chapter will conclude by considering the implications of the Nordic experience for EU policies towards Russia as well as pointing towards a way forward.

Sweden

In a historic perspective, the relations between Sweden and Russia have been far from peaceful. Until the early nineteenth century, the countries had engaged in several wars in repeated attempts at establishing hegemony over the Baltic Sea (Hagström Frisell and Oldberg 2009: 7). Since the early 1800s, Sweden has pursued a policy of neutrality that enabled it to largely stay out of the two world wars – a policy that was successfully continued also during the Cold War. Its position, however, was backed up by a secret co-operation agreement with the United States and NATO which was revealed only after the end of the Cold War. During the Cold War period several incidents occurred between the Soviet Union and Sweden, such as espionage affairs and the stranding of a Soviet submarine in Swedish waters in 1981 (ibid.). The latter was perceived by Sweden as a serious security problem and violation of the country's sovereignty (Silberstein 2008). These incidents formed a severe test for the countries' relations (Hagström Frisell and Oldberg 2009: 7). The end of the Cold War and the dissolution of the Soviet Union in 1991 opened up possibilities for renewed Swedish–Russian relations and changed Sweden's position in Europe fundamentally. While transforming its neutrality policy into military non-alignment with the option of neutrality in war times, Sweden stayed out of NATO but joined the EU in 1995 (see Möller and Bjerel 2010). Nonetheless, Sweden joined the 1994 established NATO programme Partnership for Peace (PfP) and the Euro-Atlantic Partnership Council in 1997, seeking closer military co-operation with the USA and other NATO members as well as non-members in an attempt to enhance its own security. Simultaneously, Sweden emphasized that it is of the utmost importance to involve Russia in confidence-building activities within the PfP, in particular in the Baltic Sea region (Freytag 2006: 30). Swedish–Russian relations improved throughout the 1990s and exchanges on all levels have increased. Russia praised the Swedish non-alignment policy as a possible alternative model for NATO candidates such as the Baltic states (Hagström Frisell and Oldberg 2009: 7).

Current Swedish–Russian relations are politically stable but characterized by a historical distrust, conflicting values and diverging views on democracy, human rights and foreign policy issues (ibid.: 4, 6). Nevertheless, Sweden has emphasized the importance of sound relations with Russia and of Russia's modernization. The Swedish government elaborated a strategy for Sweden's Russia policies in 2004 and a strategy for development co-operation with Russia 2005–8, underlining this importance (Sveriges Utrikesdepartment 2004). At the same time, Sweden has been a vocal critic of what it perceives as negative developments both in Russian domestic and foreign affairs (Leonard and Popescu 2007: 47).[1] A Swedish government report of 2007, for example, critically stated that 'Russia is a country that continuously is characterized by a growing corrupt administration, a legal system with big problems and huge gaps between the poor and the rich' (Sveriges Utrikesdepartment 2007: 1,

134 Tobias Etzold and Hiski Haukkala

authors' translation). Sweden criticized Russia's move towards authoritarianism under President Putin, restrictions on NGOs and the media, unfair elections and Russia's military operations in Chechnya. Amongst EU members, Sweden was one of the most outspoken critics of the Russian military intervention in Chechnya, calling for political rather than military solutions (Hagström Frisell and Oldberg 2009: 8). In this context, Sweden, for example, refused to extradite Chechen 'terrorists' to Russia (Nummelin 2010). Sweden also supported other states (especially the Baltic States) in their various conflicts with Russia and in their bids to join the EU and NATO. Jointly with Poland, Sweden initiated a new EU 'Eastern Partnership' to enhance EU relations with six former Soviet-bloc states in 2008. This initiative was sceptically received by Russia.

The climax of the difficulties in Swedish–Russian relations was reached in August 2008 in the context of Russia's military intervention in Georgia of which Sweden was very critical. Within the EU, Swedish Foreign Minister Carl Bildt was amongst the most outspoken critics of the Russian intervention and even compared it with Nazi-Germany's occupation of the Sudeten district in Czechoslovakia (and other parts of Eastern Europe), much to the dismay of the Russian authorities (Silberstein 2008). Initially they declared Bildt, who after a visit to Georgia wanted to visit Moscow for talks in his capacity as then Chairman of the Council of Europe, to be a persona non-grata (Neveus 2010; Hennel 2008a). In this context, the Russian government perceived Sweden as one of the most anti-Russian EU members (Hennel 2008b). Nevertheless, despite his criticism Bildt argued for resuming negotiations on a new EU-Russia partnership agreement (Hagström Frisell and Oldberg 2009: 9).

Another controversial issue in Swedish–Russian relations was the planned Russian–German gas pipeline Nord Stream that runs along Swedish territorial waters near the island of Gotland. Apart from the fact that Sweden does not need the pipeline for its own supplies, as gas only makes a up a very small part of overall energy supply that is all imported from Denmark (ibid.: 12), the pipeline raised in particular environmental concerns (Silberstein 2008) but also issues about sovereignty, security and even of Russia's potential for spying in Sweden (see Söderberg Jacobsson 2007).

Unlike the aforementioned issues, the Russian Baltic Sea exclave Kaliningrad has not formed a source of tension between Russia and Sweden. Instead, it has been perceived as an opportunity for closer co-operation. Kaliningrad was even seen as an important co-operation partner in Sweden's close neighbourhood (Sveriges Riksdag 2001). Sweden saw great possibilities and advantages for its own economy in its co-operation with Kaliningrad into which the country has invested a considerable amount of financial resources. It was a particular Swedish incentive to seek to ensure stability in the area by including Kaliningrad in the Baltic Sea co-operation framework, which was to provide a lively network of numerous people-to-people contacts, through for instance the promotion of tourism, and a wide range of projects in various issue areas. Swedish support focused on business development, administrative reform and local government, land reform and prevention of communicable diseases. Sweden was also the first EU country which opened a general consulate in Kaliningrad in 2003. Swedish government officials, however, also expressed their disappointment that Russia greeted Swedish and Nordic initiatives, such as the opening of a Nordic Council of Ministers information office in Kaliningrad, with little interest or enthusiasm (ibid.).

Swedish–Russian economic relations, trade and cultural exchanges have increased since the late 1990s. Currently, more than 400 Swedish companies are active on the Russian market and Sweden is the eighth largest investor in Russia (Brunner 2011). The Swedish furniture company IKEA is the most important Swedish investor in Russia (Embassy of Sweden Moscow 2007). Nevertheless, despite this increase – trade has quadrupled between 2005 and 2010 – and while both countries do regard each other as important economic partners (President of Russia Official Web Portal 2010; Brunner 2011), economically Sweden and Russia do not depend upon each other in any significant degree (Hagström Frisell and Oldberg 2009: 10).

While bilateral political relations reached its low in 2008, they have improved since 2009. The Swedish EU Presidency organized an EU–Russia Summit in Stockholm in October 2009 that was by both sides perceived as fairly successful (Blomgren 2010). Around the same time, Sweden gave the green light to Nord Stream, a move that was particularly appreciated by Russia (Neveus 2010). In March 2010, Sweden's Prime Minister Fredrik Reinfeldt and Foreign Minister Bildt paid a state visit to Moscow. This was the first official visit to Russia by a Swedish prime minister since 2000. Overall, the discussions were perceived as constructive and friendly but the human rights situation in Russia was raised and Medvedev expressed his bewilderment over Swedish court decisions to award asylum to Chechens claiming that Sweden was protecting Chechen 'bandits' (Nummelin 2010). On 27 April 2011, Prime Minister Vladimir Putin paid a visit to Sweden. During the visit Russia and Sweden signed a declaration of partnership of modernization. The partnership is based on the principles of democracy, rule of law and human rights and includes co-operation in the areas of environment, innovation and space exploration (The Official Site of the Prime Minister of the Russian Federation 2011). This and other declarations to foster industrial relations are hoped 'to promote deeper and stronger interaction between Russia and Sweden' (ibid.).

Overall, the current developments resulting in more frequent meetings between state leaders, a more friendly attitude and increasing economic activity, give proof of a more friendly pragmatism in Swedish–Russian relations. Sweden, however, encouraged in particular by the media (see, for example, Dagens Nyheter 2010), still tends to maintain a critical stance when it believes it is appropriate, resulting in some occasional political sensitivity on the Russian side.

Especially in the 1990s, Sweden saw itself as one of the strongest advocates of sound EU–Russia relations (Bertelman 2011). Yet, and although Sweden

136 *Tobias Etzold and Hiski Haukkala*

as a neighbour of Russia and member of the EU has a vital interest to bring these two together (Hagström Frisell and Oldberg 2009: 20), one can also conclude that more recently within the EU Sweden has kept a fairly low profile regarding the development of a joint policy towards Russia. During its 2009 EU Presidency Sweden focused on issues in which Russia as a non-EU member state is neither fully included (EU Strategy for the Baltic Sea Region) or to which Russia is critical of (Eastern Partnership). Nevertheless, in 2006 Sweden did together with Finland promote the continuation of the Northern Dimension (ND) policy by fully involving Russia in the decision-making process and turning the policy into one of the EU, Russia, Norway and Iceland (see more below). In the Swedish view, concrete co-operation with Russia should primarily take place within regional fora such as the ND and focus on regional problems such as the pollution of the Baltic Sea (Hagström Frisell and Oldberg 2009: 20). Thus, Sweden largely promotes regional practical and project-related co-operation between Russia and the EU with a view to bringing the two closer together.

Finland

If Sweden has historically had a painful relationship with Russia at times then the same can be said of Finland. Formerly a part of Sweden, Finland has shared a good deal of turbulent Swedish history with Russia and has been through many historical ups and downs with Russia on its own as well, first during the period of political autonomy in the nineteenth century and in the form of independent statehood from 1917 onwards (for a discussion, see Heikka 2005).

Compared with Sweden, Finland's contemporary relations with Russia differ in at least four important respects. First, for Finland relations with Russia are much more important than to Sweden. One might argue that in the EU Finland has one of the biggest interests in Russia, in particular in economic respect. This interest is manifested, for example, in the fact that before the financial and economic crisis of 2008–9 Russia was briefly the largest trade partner to Finland (before Sweden and Germany). The crisis has resulted in Russia falling back to third place in 2009 but the total trade turnover was still €11 billion. Finnish companies have also invested over €6 billion in the Russian market. Since 2010 trade with Russia has been growing rapidly and Russia has once again assumed the economic pole position in Finland.

A lot has been said about the role of Russia in Finland's energy security (cf. Leonard and Popescu 2007). It is true that 100 per cent of natural gas and almost all crude oil currently comes from Russia. Yet the dependence is not as radical as is often assumed. To begin with, natural gas makes up only approximately 10 per cent of Finland's energy mix and Finns have developed spare capacity based on oil and coal in case of supply disruptions. Oil comes to Finland mainly in tankers and is therefore fairly easily traded commodity on other spot markets in the world should Russia fail to satisfy Finland's needs. On the whole Finland has a fairly diversified energy mix with five different fuels each contributing more than 10 per cent to total supply (European Commission 2007). In addition, the question of energy has never been politicized between Finland and Russia. On the contrary, Finns consider Russia to be a reliable and largely problem-free provider of energy (Parpola 2004). In this respect, Finland comes quite close to Germany in its take concerning the issue (see Stewart in this volume).

Russia is of key importance to Finland in other respects as well. The two share some 1,300 kilometres of land border – by far the biggest stretch of land compared with any other EU member – meaning that the issues of border-crossings, soft security threats and regional co-operation are of significant consequence for Finland (for more about these issues, see Ojanen 2001; Moroff 2002). The intensity of interaction is reflected in the fact that Finland has become the biggest issuer of Schengen visas to the Russians with well over a million visas granted and 11 million border-crossings in 2011, with over 80 per cent of them allowing multiple entries to the Schengen zone. All in all, managing growing proximity that was simply not there during the Soviet era has become the underlying theme in Finnish–Russian relations. This even spills over to the wider EU–Russia agenda regularly, as exemplified by the fact that the Finns have sought leadership in granting visa free travel to the EU's eastern neighbours, Russia included, largely in order to facilitate border-crossings that have become too unwieldy and cumbersome under the present Schengen visa regime (see Salminen and Moshes 2009).

Second, Finland has considerably more active political relations with Russia than Sweden. It was mentioned that in 2010 Sweden ended a 10-year drought of top level visits to Moscow. By comparison, in 2010 the Finnish leaders (the President, the Prime Minister and the Foreign Minister) met their Russian counterparts altogether 11 times both in Finland and in Russia. Also other sectoral ministers meet their Russian opposites regularly. 2010 does stand out as a particularly busy year of Finnish–Russian interaction but the longer term trends point towards a very frequent rate of meetings annually. What is more, of all EU member states Finland probably has an unprecedented and unrivalled depth of contacts ranging from ordinary citizens and civil servants to parliamentarians, ministers and heads of state. Meeting, debating and solving problems with Russians is the bread and butter of Finnish foreign policy – not a rare delicacy or an optional extra.

That said, it seems peculiar and interesting that despite this high political overlay Finnish–Russian relations are largely technocratic and bureaucratic and seem to lack an overly political component. To a degree, this is made understandable by the fact that during the post-Cold War era Finland has sought to multilateralize its relations with Russia by seeking to project all the potentially difficult issues mainly onto the EU level (Haukkala and Ojanen 2011). It would seem that the period of Finlandization during the Cold War has resulted in a certain 'escape from politics' on the Finnish side. Yet it is striking that Russia does not seem to have any coherent political agenda vis-à-vis Finland either. This was manifested in a speech by President Dmitry

138 *Tobias Etzold and Hiski Haukkala*

Medvedev during his first state visit to Helsinki in April 2009. Apart from platitudes concerning good neighbourliness and some trade statistics at its beginning, the speech was void of any political content concerning Finland. In fact, the main audience was apparently assumed to be in Western Europe and across the Atlantic as the main bulk of the speech was devoted to developing Medvedev's initiative for a new security treaty in Europe (Medvedev 2009). Nevertheless, the image of Finland in Russia seems to be that of a fairly harmless neighbour with which mutual problems are pragmatically being solved together (Shliamin 2007; Voronov, 2010; Sutela 2001: 5).

Third, and possibly because of the fact that they see the Russians so frequently, Finns have tended to convey much less criticism towards Russia than their Swedish brethren. Finland playing it safe vis-à-vis Russia has of course an established pedigree, stemming from the Cold War when the country was repeatedly accused of 'Finlandization' in the West. For Finland, neutrality and the current policy of military non-alignment are largely ways of ensuring freedom from Russia's potential interference: pragmatic policy responses in the face of an overweening and at times even domineering neighbour in the East (see Möller and Bjerel 2010).

In this respect it is paradoxical that the Golden Rule of post-Cold War Finnish–Russian relations seems to be that every time there is serious turbulence between 'the West' and Russia, Finland finds itself in a position of special responsibility. Therefore during the First Chechen War in 1994–6, Finland as a new EU member state was forced to take a firm stance on the issue when in January 1995 the Finnish Prime Minister Esko Aho was the first EU politician to visit Moscow after the beginning of hostilities in Chechnya. In an ironic twist, this feat was to be repeated four years later during the first Finnish EU presidency when Helsinki was expected to co-ordinate the EU position on Chechnya during the run-up to the Helsinki European Council in December 1999 (for more about these cases, see Haukkala and Ojanen 2011: 157–58). Finally, during the brief Russo–Georgian war in August 2008 Finland, in the role of the OSCE Chairman-in-Office, was in a thankless position of trying to broker a cease-fire until it was sidelined by the French EU Presidency and its energetic President Nicolas Sarkozy (see LeNoan in this volume). Yet it is remarkable that these potential friction points do not seem to translate into political problems on the bilateral agenda between the countries. 'Bygones' seems to be the catchword in Moscow when it comes to dealing with these issues with Helsinki.

An interesting recent development has been that Finland has started to develop a wider Eastern policy that includes also other countries than Russia in the former Soviet Union (FSU). As a consequence, Finland has opened a new embassy in Astana in Kazakhstan (2009) and a Liaison Office in Minsk in Belarus (2010) as well as adopted a policy document with a view of enhancing bilateral relations with the countries in Eastern Europe, Southern Caucasus and Central Asia (Ulkoministeriö 2010). Finland has also started to channel some of its official development assistance (ODA) funds to a new Wider

European Initiative that seeks to stimulate the economic, societal and environmental development in the areas outside Russia in the FSU (Ministry of Foreign Affairs of Finland 2009). Taken together, this flurry of activity represents a radical departure for Finland that has traditionally had an almost monomaniacal obsession with its relations with Russia. In this respect Finland has started to converge with Sweden and Denmark who both have had a stronger presence in the FSU compared to Finland. But keeping in mind the jealousy with which Russia still eyes its own neighbourhood (Haukkala 2008), this is a development that has some potential to lead to increased friction between Finland and Russia in the future – if Finland in the current and increasingly depressed economic atmosphere chooses to pursue this policy any further in the future.

Finally, Finns have showed much more activism in the EU's Russia policy than Sweden – at least until recently. Indeed, it is not far-fetched to argue that EU membership has radically altered both the setting and objectives of Finnish foreign policy (Palosaari 2011). Therefore cultivating a long-term strategy and a coherent joint policy perspective on Russia has been the mainstay of Finnish EU policy (Haukkala and Ojanen 2011: 158). The preference for robust EU policies on Russia became clear in the Finnish attempts at pushing forward the so-called Common Strategy on Russia in 1999 and onwards. In this regard, the Finnish priority has been to focus the EU–Russia agenda on actual projects and deliverables, not merely programmatic statements of benign strategic intent. The Finnish initiative for the Northern Dimension of the EU's policies in 1997 should be interpreted in this light as well: as an attempt to cultivate pragmatic co-operation with Russia whilst ensuring that the Union is recognizing the importance of the region not only for Finland but the whole of the Union (for an in-depth discussion of the initiative with many references, see Haukkala 2010: Ch. 9).

But for all intents and purposes Finland has been largely frustrated in its objectives. There seems to be a growing feeling that especially since the post-Big Bang enlargement in 2004/7 the EU has been facing increasing difficulties in developing a common and united stance on Russia. For Finland a certain culmination point was its second EU Presidency in autumn 2006. Then, despite its best efforts, Helsinki was unable to secure the commencement of negotiations for a new post-PCA agreement with Russia due to Warsaw's determination to block it on account of a bilateral Polish–Russian dispute concerning the quality of meat (see Cichocki in this volume).

The Finnish attempts at uploading its interests onto the EU level have resulted in some friction in the Nordic context as well. A case in point is Sweden, which on the one hand has eyed the Finnish initiative of the Northern Dimension with suspicion as an attempt to sideline the earlier Swedish activism concerning the Baltic Sea. Similarly, Finland has been somewhat exasperated with Sweden which has pushed for a more 'southern' agenda to the Northern Dimension by stressing, for example, the role of Kaliningrad in the initiative, a region that has always been a low priority for Finland (Haukkala 2001: 41).

140   *Tobias Etzold and Hiski Haukkala*

Overall, there seems to be a growing disillusionment in Finland with the prospects of a common EU Russia policy as well as a growing concern over Russia's development. As a consequence, Finland is increasingly grasping the need to have a sound bilateral relationship with Russia while at the same time doing its very best to prod along a more unified and consistent Russia policy on the EU level. Therefore, and despite the noticeable EU accent in Finnish foreign policy during the post-Cold War era, bilateral relations with Russia have by no means lost their significance. In fact the reverse is the case, as in recent years Russia's new-found confidence and economic growth has meant that as an economic and political partner it is much more important to Finland now than it was ten or even only five years ago. Yet, and in stark contrast to most of the twentieth century, Russia is now seen more as a possibility and a challenge than an outright problem or a threat.

None of this should be taken to mean that Finns have entirely ceased perceiving Russia as a potential hard security threat, far from it (Forsberg 2006; for a still relevant discussion concerning the role of Russia in Finnish security, see Pursiainen 2001). For this reason Finns have consistently emphasized the need to keep the United States committed to Northern European security as well as encouraging the enlargement of NATO to the southern shores of the Baltic Sea as a potential balance to Russia's military preponderance (see Vaahtoranta and Forsberg 1998) – even if Finland itself has at the same time for myriad of reasons chosen to remain outside the NATO and its security guarantees itself.

All in all, Russia's development still holds several unanswered questions that could spell trouble for Finland in the future. But for the moment it seems evident that the Finns are very keen to accentuate the positive in their relationship with Russia and keep operating in the spirit of 'friendly pragmatism' (Leonard and Popescu 2007). In 2001, the leading Finnish Russia economist Pekka Sutela (2001: 5) noted that Finnish relations with Russia were 'better than ever'. A decade later the same would still seem to hold with the proviso that Russia does not collapse into angry authoritarianism or chaos and the EU does not cease to function as a credible political entity. Neither outcome is very likely – nor entirely inconceivable. This means that the age-old tensions of Finnish–Russian relations are unlikely to fully disappear in the near future.

Denmark

Unlike Sweden and Finland, Denmark and Russia have formally never been engaged in war. Yet throughout centuries there have been very close political, diplomatic, economic and cultural relations between the two (Ministry of Foreign Affairs of Denmark 2010a). In the Cold War period Denmark chose a different approach than Sweden and Finland and joined both NATO (in 1949) and the European Communities (in 1973). Thus, while Sweden and Finland were somehow 'in between' the East and the West, Denmark was located fully in the West.

The official line of the Danish Foreign Ministry is that the foundation of the current co-operation between Denmark and Russia is an intensive

Denmark, Finland and Sweden 141

dialogue on all levels concerning political, economic and commercial issues, bilateral co-operation and international issues (ibid.). But immediately after the Cold War, relations between the two developed only slowly and reluctantly. Several Danish governments, for example, chose the side of the Baltic States in their various conflicts with Russia during the 1990s (see Lašas and Galbreath in this volume).

During the early 2000s, several problems appeared that resulted in a frosty relationship between Denmark and Russia. The liberal-conservative government of Prime Minister Anders Fogh-Rasmussen (2001–9) favoured NATO membership for Ukraine and Georgia, criticized Russia for its invasion of Georgia and supported US plans to station BMD missiles in Poland and the Czech Republic (Kruse 2009). In contrast to those difficult relations with Russia, Denmark's relations with the United States of America, in particular under the Bush administration, were fairly close, demonstrated, for example, by Danish military support in Afghanistan and Iraq (EU-27 Watch 2009). Overall, during the past 10 years, sound transatlantic relations (and NATO) were among the top priorities of Danish foreign policies, while the country somewhat neglected other issues such as developments in the Baltic Sea region in which Russia is an important player.

Denmark's overall political line towards Russia has been outspokenly critical. The most controversial issue in Danish–Russian relations has been Chechnya. Like Sweden, Denmark repeatedly criticized the Russian military operations and the human rights situation in Chechnya. Perhaps the biggest crisis took place in autumn 2002 when Denmark as the EU President was tasked to find a compromise over the issue of transit to and from the Russian mainland to Kaliningrad in the context of EU enlargement. During the negotiations Denmark permitted a Chechen congress to be held in Copenhagen and refused to extradite the Chechen leader Ahmed Zakayev to Russia (Leonard and Popescu 2007: 46). Russia also perceived the Danish stance on the Kaliningrad issue as inflexible (Thastum *et al.* 2002). These events led to a severe diplomatic crisis in the bilateral relationship and a Russian threat to boycott a planned state visit to Denmark in connection with an EU–Russia Summit in Copenhagen in November 2002. In reaction to these difficulties, the Danish government first considered cancelling the bilateral part of the Russian state visit to Denmark but to keep the EU–Russia summit in Copenhagen. However, when Russia also threatened to boycott the EU–Russia Summit in Copenhagen, Denmark reacted by moving the summit to Brussels in order not to endanger the important talks between the EU and Russia concerning Kaliningrad (ibid.). The EU played the incident down as a bilateral issue between Denmark and Russia, which would not affect wider EU–Russia relations (ibid.). However, it can be seen as an example of a bilateral crisis between an EU member state and Russia that can have the potential to threaten wider EU–Russia relations and the EU's ability to negotiate with Russia as well. In any case, such bilateral problems seem to make negotiations on already complicated issues much more difficult.

142 *Tobias Etzold and Hiski Haukkala*

Kaliningrad has also become a point of irritation in its own right. In July 2002, the Danish newspaper *Jyllands Posten* wrote an article about the *oblast* labelling it as a 'desperate and poor robbers den' and suggesting it should be turned into an 'EU-District' under Lithuanian, Polish and even German rule (see Rose 2002). Russia demanded an official apology from the Danish government, arguing that such articles undermined efforts to find a compromise over Kaliningrad between Russia and the EU and provoked nervous reactions on both sides (Krasavin, cited in Rose 2002). The Danish government, taking up an old habit from the Cold War period when critical articles on the Soviet Union appeared regularly in the Danish press, did not comment on Moscow's request (Rose 2002).

More recently, despite some frictions, co-operation between Denmark and the Baltic Sea regions of the Russian Federation, especially focusing on Kaliningrad, has become an integral and important component of wider Danish–Russian relations. Kaliningrad has even become a priority of Danish development co-operation policies (Ministry of Foreign Affairs of Denmark 2010b). Also with respect to the important Kaliningrad transit question already discussed, the Danish EU Presidency did, despite the aforementioned tensions around the summit, manage to broker a compromise which took the main Russian concerns into account. Chechnya, however, has continued to be an issue of irritation and disagreement between Denmark and Russia, resulting in a 'Siberian cold front' (Kruse 2009) in Danish–Russian relations for several years. As in the Swedish case, no mutual state visits between Russia and Denmark took place for several years as a consequence of this cooling.

In an economic perspective, there has not been much interaction between the two countries. In 2007, only 1.71 per cent of Danish trade was with Russia (Leonard and Popescu 2007: 49) and even in 2008 there were only 35 Danish companies effectively operating in the country (Ministry of Foreign Affairs of the Russian Federation 2008). More recently, this number has been increasing and amounts to some 200 now (Government of the Russian Federation 2011). The fairly low level of economic relations stems from the fact that Denmark is a net exporter of gas and oil and does not depend on Russian imports. Nevertheless, once the Danish North Sea resources come to an end, the country might also become more dependent on Russian oil and gas (Larsen 2008).

More recently, the overall bilateral relationship has improved, resulting in more active business and trade relations and several meetings between foreign ministers and the heads of state/government respectively (Kruse 2009; President of Russia 2009). By and large the Russian and Danish leaders perceive the frosty period in their countries' relations as being over. President Medvedev and former Prime Minister Løkke Rasmussen met briefly in New York at the margins of a UN Summit in New York in 2009 and agreed on mutual state visits. President Medvedev subsequently visited Denmark in April 2010, and Prime Minister Putin followed suit a year later. Since 2009, the relations have increasingly been described as fairly unproblematic (Kruse 2009). The then

Danish Foreign Minister Lene Espersen even stated that Medvedev's visit to Denmark 'was a symbol of present close and well-developed relations between Denmark and Russia as well as promoted their future development' (cited in Itar-Tass 2010). Even the previously much disputed Zakayev issue (see above) is no longer relevant for the bilateral relations (Lukyanov, cited in Kruse 2009), presumably because he is currently a political refugee in the United Kingdom now and therefore rather a problem of British–Russian than of Danish–Russian relations (see David in this volume). Russian officials noted positively that Denmark was much less opposed to the construction of the Baltic Sea gas pipeline Nord Stream than the Baltic States, Poland and Sweden, although the pipeline runs along the Danish island of Bornholm and even across Danish territorial waters. Although the project has caused some environmental concerns in Denmark, Russia nevertheless sees Copenhagen as an important partner that is 'relatively willing to cooperate' with Moscow (Lukyanov, cited in Kruse 2009).

The arrival of a new left-wing government into power in September 2011 has not resulted in any fundamental changes in Denmark's Russia policy. While the new Foreign Minister of the left-wing Socialist People's Party, Villy Søvndal, openly expressed his regret that during the latest presidential elections in Russia various irregularities occurred, he recognized Putin's election and overall emphasized that Russia is an important co-operation partner for Denmark and the EU. He hoped that the co-operation with Russia, in particular on political and economic reforms in the form of modernization partnerships (both EU and bilateral), could be further developed also under newly elected President Putin (Ministry of Foreign Affairs of Denmark 2012).

In the future, the Arctic with its huge natural resources and the complicated border question around the North Pole could cause new frictions between the two countries (Larsen 2008). However, because of its vital national interest in the Arctic (Greenland) Denmark could act as a spearhead in the development of future EU Arctic policies and therefore could also take a lead role in also fostering co-operation with Russia in the High North. Already previously Denmark has taken the initiative in developing the so-called Arctic Window to the Northern Dimension, organizing a conference concerning the topic in Greenland during its EU Presidency in August 2002. As the only EU member with a legitimate geographical stake in the Arctic, Denmark can be expected to be a key player when it comes to developing an EU role in the region, a factor that will undoubtedly enhance its clout in the eyes of Russia as well.

Conclusions

The three Nordic EU members have been far from uniform in their relations with Russia. To a degree one could be forgiven for thinking that the Nordics' bilateral relations with Russia are a function of their economic ties: Finland has had the most intensive economic linkages and it has also been by far the friendliest of the three. For Denmark the opposite has applied, with Sweden

144 *Tobias Etzold and Hiski Haukkala*

lying somewhere in between in both respects. But as has been argued in this chapter, geography, history, and even individual political events have also been important in accounting for the differences in the relations the three countries have had with Russia.

More recently, however, the policies of the three have begun to converge. This is largely due to the fact that Sweden and Denmark have seen an improvement in their relations with Russia. As a consequence, the first mutual state visits for many years have taken place and several previous disagreements have been settled. Both countries, for example, approved the construction of the Nord Stream gas pipeline through the Baltic Sea after having initially been opposed to it. Overall currently the relations between Russia and all three countries seem to have become fairly friendly and pragmatic, giving grounds to an assertion that a certain positive (or at least non-hostile) stance exists in all the Nordic countries towards Russia.

At the EU level the Nordics have been less than the sum of their parts. As has been argued in this chapter the three have had conflicting priorities and interests and they have failed to speak with one voice about Russia in the EU. The case in point is the Northern Dimension where all three have been busy coming up with their own interpretations concerning the reach of the initiative – Finland Karelian oblast; Sweden Kaliningrad and the Baltic Sea; and Denmark the Arctic – instead of agreeing on and jointly promoting a genuinely shared and common Nordic template for the policy. One can argue that as a consequence the Northern Dimension has punched below its weight although its achievements otherwise are far from being negligible.

Moving up from the regional level, and regarding the development of a joint coherent overall EU policy towards Russia, Finland has probably been the most active of the three, while Sweden and Denmark have been more passive. What is more, and as the case of Denmark has shown, at times they have even uploaded tensions and instability into the wider EU–Russia agenda. That said, it is interesting to see how the re-emerging interest in closer Nordic co-operation will play out in the EU context. In recent years the Nordics – Norway and Iceland included – have pondered the possibility of developing closer co-operation in defence and military crisis-management while rekindling Nordic co-operation as a political project as well. Also, the Nordic Council and the Nordic Council of Ministers have been active in fostering regional co-operation with North-west Russia.

That said, it is too early to conclude that we could expect a more coherent Russia policy emerging from the three Nordic members at the EU level in the future, although at the same time this is not entirely to be excluded. The possibility of an Icelandic EU membership would strengthen the pragmatic and friendly caucus in the EU, albeit only marginally. More interestingly, in recent years Norway has been moving remarkably closer in its relations with Russia (although the same cannot be said of its relations with the EU, of course). As a consequence, it is possible that the Nordics – both EU and non-EU states alike – will form some kind of an *avant garde* group in fostering closer ties with Russia

Denmark, Finland and Sweden 145

on the regional level in the future. This could have the potential to spill over into positive dynamics on the wider EU–Russia relationship as well. But the reverse could hold as well: if the EU fails to develop a more coherent policy line on Russia, then we could witness a process in which the new Nordic activism in fact starts to supplant the EU level. Therefore, for both good and for ill the Nordic way could be the way forward also for the EU in its relations with Russia.

Note

1 These two sides of Sweden's Russia policy have not gone unnoticed in Russia, either. See Voronov (2010).

References

Bertelman, T. (2011) *Bilateral relations between Sweden and Russia – a personal view by Tomas Bertelman, Ambassador of Sweden to Russia.* 11 March 2009, available at www.ruseu.com/br/sweden/details_52.html (accessed 23 June 2012).

Blomgren, J. (2010) 'Reinfeldt måste vara på sin vakt', *Svenska Dagbladet.* 9 March 2010, available at www.svd.se/nyheter/utrikes/reinfeldt-maste-vara-pa-sin-vakt_4400 305.svd (accessed 23 June 2012).

Brunner, D. (2011) 'An Interview with Swedish Minister of Trade, Ewa Börling', *Investment Insider.* 5 May 2011, available at www.investmentinsider.eu/an-interview-with-swedish-minister-of-trade-ewa-bjorling (accessed 23 June 2012).

Dagens Nyheter (2010) 'Håll distansen till Moskva', *Dagens Nyheter.* 10 March 2010, available at www.dn.se/ledare/huvudledare/hall-distansen-till-moskva- (accessed 23 June 2012).

Embassy of Sweden Moscow (2007) *Economic relations between Sweden and Russia.* 20 April 2007, available at www.swedenabroad.com/Page-47757.aspx (accessed 23 June 2012).

EU-27 Watch (2009) *Denmark and the USA: allies under Bush – allies under Obama.* Available at www.eu-27watch.org/?q=node/66 (accessed 23 June 2012).

European Commission (2007) *Finland – Energy Mix Fact Sheet.* January 2007,available at http://ec.europa.eu/energy/energy_policy/doc/factsheets/mix/mix_fi_en.pdf (accessed 23 June 2012).

Forsberg, T. (2006) 'Finnish-Russian Security Relations: Is Russia Still Seen as a Threat', in H. Smith (ed.) *The Two-Level Game: Russia's Relations with Great Britain, Finland and the European Union.* Helsinki: Aleksanteri Institute, 141–54.

Freytag, R. S. (2006) 'Schwedische Neutralität zwischen Anspruch und Wirklichkeit', *Beiträge zur Internationalen Politik und Sicherheit,* Nr. 01/2006: 24–31.

Government of the Russian Federation (2011) *Prime Minister Vladimir Putin meets with Prime Minister of Denmark Lars Lokke Rasmussen.* 26 April 2011, available at http://premier.gov.ru/eng/events/news/14994/ (accessed 14 July 2011).

Hagström Frisell, E. and Oldberg, I. (2009) *'Cool Neighbors': Sweden's EU Presidency and Russia.* Russie.Nei.Visions n42, Paris: IFRI, available at www.ifri.org/download s/ifrirussiaandswedenengjune09_1.pdf (accessed 23 June 2012).

Haukkala, H. (2001) 'Succeeding Without Success? The Northern Dimension of the European Union', *Northern Dimensions – Yearbook 2001.* Helsinki: The Finnish Institute of International Affairs, 37–47.

146 Tobias Etzold and Hiski Haukkala

——(2008) 'The Russian Challenge to EU's Normative Power: The Case of European Neighbourhood Policy', *The International Spectator*, 43: 35–47.

——(2010) *The EU-Russia Strategic Partnership: The Limits of Post-Sovereignty in International Relations*. London and New York: Routledge.

Haukkala, H. and Ojanen, H. (2011) 'The Europeanization of Finnish foreign policy: Pendulum swings in slow motion', in C. Hill and R. Wong (eds) *National and European Foreign Policy: Towards Europeanization*. London and New York: Routledge, 149–66.

Heikka, H. (2005) 'Republican Realism: Finnish Strategic Culture in Historical Perspective', *Cooperation and Conflict*, 40: 91–119.

Hennel, L. (2008a) 'Carl Bildt portad i Ryssland', *Svenska Dagbladet*. 1 October 2008, available at www.svd.se/nyheter/inrikes/car-bildt-portad-i-ryssland_1810309.svd (accessed 23 June 2012).

——(2008b) 'Relationen mellan Ryssland och Sverige "kyllig"', *Svenska Dagbladet*. 2 October 2008, available at www.svd.se/nyheter/politik/relationen-mellan-ryssland-och-sverige-kylig_1817979.svd (accessed 23 June 2012).

Ingebritsen, C. (2006) *Scandinavia in World Politics*. Lanham: Rowman & Littlefield.

Itar-Tass (2010) 'Medvedev's visit – symbol of close relations', *Amberbridge News*. 23 December 2010, available at www.amberbridge.org/newstext?id=3197&lang=eng (accessed 23 June 2012).

Kruse, S. (2009) 'Tøbrud mellem Danmark og Rusland', *Berlingske Tidende*. 24 September 2009, available at www.berlingske.dk/node/1421995 (accessed 23 June 2012).

Larsen, T. (2008) 'Bjørnen vækker uro', *Analys-Norden*. 17 September 2009, available at www.norden.org/sv/analys-norden/tema/norden-og-russland/bjoernen-vaekker-uro (accessed 23 June 2012).

Leonard, M. and Popescu, N. (2007) *A Power Audit of EU-Russia Relations*. Policy Paper, European Council on Foreign Relations, December 2007, available at http://ecfr.3cdn.net/1ef82b3f011e075853_0fm6bphgw.pdf (accessed 23 June 2012).

Medvedev, D. (2009) *Speech at Helsinki University and Answers to Questions from Audience*. Helsinki, 20 April 2009, available at http://archive.kremlin.ru/eng/speeches/2009/04/20/1919_type82912type82914type84779_215323.shtml (accessed 23 June 2012).

Ministry of Foreign Affairs of Denmark (2010a) *Forholdet mellem Danmark og Rusland*. Available at www.um.dk/da/menu/Udenrigspolitik/LandeOgRegioner/Europa/Rusland/DanmarksForholdTilRusland/ (accessed 23 March 2011).

——(2010b) *Kaliningrad: Baggrund om regionen Kaliningrad, herunder økonomisk og samfundsmæssig udvikling samt forholdet til EU og Danmark*. Available at www.um.dk/da/menu/Udenrigspolitik/LandeOgRegioner/Europa/Rusland/Kaliningrad/Kaliningrad.htm (accessed 23 March 2011).

——(2012) *Søvndal om præsidentvalget i Rusland den 4. Marts*. 5 March 2012, available at http://um.dk/da/politik-og-diplomati/nyhederogpublikationer/udenrigspolitiske-nyheder/newsdisplaypage/?newsID=2A421720–23B09–4E52–58B71–206FBC8C5BE2 (accessed 23 June 2012).

Ministry of Foreign Affairs of Finland (2009) *Wider Europe Initiative: Framework Programme for Finland's Development Policy. Implementation Plan for 2009–2013*. Available at http://formin.finland.fi/public/download.aspx?ID=44782&guid=%7B5F9179AD-3D39-4CB7-82F4-C79179EC9020%7D (accessed 23 June 2012).

Ministry of Foreign Affairs of the Russian Federation (2008) *Remarks by Russian Minister of Foreign Affairs Sergey Lavrov at Joint Press Conference following talks with Prime Minister of the Kingdom of Denmark Anders Fogh Rasmussen*. Copenhagen,

Denmark, Finland and Sweden 147

27 May 2008, available at www.mid.ru/Brp_4.nsf/arh/7874ACD320A2DEC1C325745
800504F0F?OpenDocument (accessed 23 June 2012).

Moroff, H. (ed.) (2002) *European Soft Security Policies: The Northern Dimension*. Programme on the Northern Dimension of the CFSP No. 17, Helsinki and Berlin: The Finnish Institute of International Affairs and Institut für Europäische Politik.

Möller, U. and Bjerel, U. (2010) 'From Nordic neutrals to post-neutral Europeans: Differences in Finnish and Swedish policy transformation', *Cooperation and Conflict*, 45: 363–86.

Neveus, I. (2010) 'Bildt kommer in från kylan', *Dagens Nyheter online*. 9 March 2010, available at www.dn.se/nyheter/varlden/bildt-kommer-in-fran-kylan-ryssland-georgie nkriget-1.1058052 (accessed 23 June 2012).

Nummelin, W. (2010) 'Medvedev: Sverige skyddar banditer', *Svenska Dagbladet*. 10 March 2010, available at www.svd.se/nyheter/utrikes/medvedev-sverige-skydar-band iter_4399407.svd (accessed 23 June 2012).

The Official Site of the Prime Minister of the Russian Federation (2011) *Prime Minister Vladimir Putin and Swedish Prime Minister Fredrik Reinfeldt hold joint press conference following talks*. Available at http://premier.gov.ru/eng/events/news/15024 (accessed 23 June 2012).

Ojanen, H. (ed.) (2001) *The Northern Dimension: Fuel for the EU?* Programme on the Northern Dimension of the CFSP No. 12, Helsinki and Berlin: The Finnish Institute of International Affairs and Institut für Europäische Politik.

Palosaari, T. (2011) *The Art of Adaptation. A study on the Europeanization of Finland's foreign and security policy*. Tampere: Tampere Peace Research Institute.

Parpola, A. (2004) *Kaasua! Maakaasu ja Suomi 1974–2004*. Helsinki: Edita.

President of Russia (2009) *Beginning of Meeting with Prime Minister of Denmark Lars Lokke Rasmussen*. 24 September 2009, available at http://archive.kremlin.ru/eng/speeches/2009/09/24/1717_type82914_221823.shtml (accessed 23 June 2012).

President of Russia Official Web Portal (2010) *News Conference following Russian-Swedish Talks*. 9 March 2010, available at http://archive.kremlin.ru/eng/speeches/2010/03/09/2036_type82914type82915_224701.shtml (accessed 23 June 2012).

Pursiainen, C. (2001) 'Finland and Russia', in B. Huldt *et. al.* (eds) *Finnish and Swedish Security: Comparing National Policies*. Stockholm, Helsinki and Berlin: Swedish National Defence College, the Finnish Institute of International Affairs, Institut für Europäische Politik, 142–73.

Rose, F. (2002) 'Optøning i visum-strid', *Jyllandsposten*. 6 August 2002, available at http://jp.dk/udland/article552082.ece (accessed 23 June 2012).

Salminen, M. and Moshes, A (2009) *Practice what you preach: The prospects for visa freedom in Russia-EU relations*. FIIA Report 18/2009, Helsinki: The Finnish Institute of International Affairs.

Shliamin, V. (2007) 'Finland: Solving Problems Together', *International Affairs* (Moscow), 53: 79–84.

Silberstein, M. (2008) 'Ryssland skakar om svensk försvarspolitik', *Analys-Norden*. 17 September 2008, available at www.norden.org/sv/analys-norden/tema/norden-og-russland/ryssland-skakar-om-svensk-foersvarspolitik (accessed 23 June 2012).

Söderberg Jacobsson, A. (2007) *Den svenska bilden av Ryssland*, Palme Center, 26 January 2007.

Sutela, P. (2001) *Finnish relations with Russia 1991–2001: Better than ever?* BOFIT Online No. 11, Helsinki: Bank of Finland Institute for Economies in Transition, available at www.suomenpankki.fi/en/suomen_pankki/organisaatio/asiantuntijoita/Documents/b on1101.pdf (accessed 23 June 2012).

148 Tobias Etzold and Hiski Haukkala

Sveriges Riksdag (2001) *Kammarens protokoll Riksdagens snabbprotokoll*. Protokoll 2000/01:107, Onsdagen 9, May 2001, available at www.riksdagen.se/webbnav/index. aspx?nid=101& bet = 2000/01:107 (accessed 23 March 2011).

Sveriges Utrikesdepartment (2004) *Strategi för Sveriges Rysslandspolitik*. Available at www.regeringen.se/content/1/c6/02/38/16/cdd13bd1.pdf (accessed 23 March 2011).

——(2007) *Mänskliga rättigheter i Ryska Federationen 2007*. Available at www.mansk ligarattigheter.gov.se/dynamaster/file_archive/080313/b17238ab435b45d7b6619fd895 3b6120/Ryssland.pdf (accessed 23 June 2012).

Thastum, M., Sørensen, J., Rose, F. and Collignon. P. (2002) 'Topmøde flyttes til Bruxelles', *Jyllandsposten*. 27 October 2002, available at http://jp.dk/indland/article5 24844.ece (accessed 23 June 2012).

Ulkoministeriö (2010) *Suomen Itä-Eurooppa, Etelä-Kaukasia ja Keski-Aasia–poli-tiikkalinjaus*. Available at http://formin.finland.fi/public/download.aspx?ID=52901&guid =E7F2AAE5-9317-464C-BCEB-F936684DF48B (accessed 23 June 2012).

Vaahtoranta, T. and Forsberg, T. (1998) 'Finland's Three Security Strategies', in M. Jopp and S. Arnswald (eds) *The European Union and the Baltic States: Visions, Interests and Strategies for the Baltic Sea Region*. Programme on the Northern Dimension of the CFSP, No. 2, Helsinki and Bonn: The Finnish Institute of International Affairs and Institut für Europäische Politik, 191–211.

Voronov, K. (2010) 'Perceptions of Russia in the European North: Signs of the Times', *Russian Politics and Law*, 48: 35–50.

10 Estonia, Latvia and Lithuania

Ainius Lašas and David J. Galbreath

Estonia, Latvia and Lithuania began their time as members of the European Union and NATO in 2004 having accomplished their primary foreign policy objectives of the post-Soviet era. With their security dilemma 'solved' and economic growth prospects seemingly assured, the Baltic States were expected to gradually normalize their relations with the Russian Federation. Judging from growing bilateral trade volumes throughout most of the 2000s, one may indeed get an impression of normalization. However, the politics of the post-enlargement era did not bring 'the end of history' to the eastern Baltic region. As argued by Galbreath (2010), the Baltic States found themselves 'stuck between a rock and a hard place'. Although confrontations over Russian speaking minorities somewhat subsided, the unsolved borders with Estonia and Latvia, energy-related issues and broader security concerns rolled over into the post-enlargement era. All of these and other issues have been coloured by the historical-psychological legacies of the Soviet era with its diverging interpretations and experiences in Baltic and Russian collective memories.

So what is the nature of post-enlargement Baltic–Russian relations? What are the factors that ensure apparent path dependency in the politics of the eastern Baltic region? In this chapter, we argue that, while bilateral issues move up and down the Baltic–Russian agenda, historical distrust within the region as well as larger security dilemmas define the nature of Baltic–Russian relations. EU and especially NATO memberships have only exaggerated mutual tensions, as Moscow feels more and more suspicious of Western encroachment upon its 'near abroad.' At the same time, the Baltic States find fewer reasons to trust its increasingly authoritarian and Soviet-like eastern neighbour.

In addition, the Baltic States discovered that their lives in Brussels would be a 'harder place' than previously expected. The Baltic relationship with the EU would be difficult in terms of learning how to operate in Brussels as well as how to influence the Union's agenda (Galbreath, Lašas and Lamoreaux 2008). Given their limited resources, they often have a difficult time influencing the EU policy agenda during the early stages of the process, but instead step up public pressure once the agenda comes into the open. Because of this strategy, the Baltic States risk being perceived as agenda spoilers rather than setters, especially when it comes to EU relations with Russia.

150 *Ainius Lašas and David J. Galbreath*

The first five years of NATO membership also revealed some struggles and frustrations as Estonia, Latvia, and Lithuania sought to obtain a credible defence plan, to extend the coverage of the proposed missile shield, and to establish a permanent air patrol mission. Only at the beginning of 2010, NATO finally agreed on the extension of the *Eagle Guardian* plan to the Baltic States (The Guardian 2010a). While this was a major accomplishment for the Baltic States, regional tensions increased as Moscow pursued a tit-for-tat strategy.

This chapter explores the above-mentioned dynamics of the Baltic–Russian relations in greater detail. It begins with a short excursion to the pre-enlargement years. The overview of the early bilateral relations provides a sense of the initial bilateral tone and trajectory. In the second part of the chapter, we focus on the post-enlargement era. We demonstrate that despite some changes in the agenda, especially concerning troops and minority issues, the underlying trajectory and quality of the Baltic–Russian relations have not changed.

Pre-enlargement Baltic–Russian relations

Ever since the restoration of independence, the Baltic States have tried to reorientate their economic and political trajectories westward. By the end of the 1990s, the European Union replaced the Russian Federation as the largest trading partner. Following the 1998 Russian financial crisis, the Baltic States continued to import mineral resources from the East at similar levels, but their exports to Russia recovered to the pre-crisis levels only in 2005. On the political front, the Balts were increasingly preoccupied with achieving NATO and EU memberships. These two foreign policy goals were also seen as a way to escape Russia's geopolitical sphere of influence. However, at the same time, the three republics, especially Latvia and Estonia, had to manage a number of sensitive policy areas vis-à-vis Russia. Practically all of them ended up in one way or another tied with the Russian-speaking minority issues, which in turn touched upon deeper historical-psychological experiences surrounding the Second World War.

In the early 1990s, Estonia, Latvia and Lithuania had an obvious concern of once Soviet, now Russian, troops on their soil. To the frustration of Moscow, the Baltic States sought to have the troops removed immediately and lobbied the USA and Western Europe to put pressure on Boris Yeltsin. However, as time went on and tensions built up, the troop withdrawal issue became increasingly interlinked with the minority issue further complicating bilateral relations (Galbreath 2005: 195–201). Likewise, state borders became linked to the minority issue. Lithuania, which gained the Vilnius region following the Second World War, settled its border with Russia in 1992. Estonia and Latvia, on the other hand, had territory removed during the Soviet period. The Russian government made it clear to the Baltic States that it was unwilling to negotiate borders, as it would internally with Chechnya, Ingushetia and Dagestan. Moscow also did not shy away from using the issue as leverage in stalling NATO enlargement and demanding improved conditions for Russian speaking minorities. Thus, it was no surprise that Estonia and Latvia entered

Estonia, Latvia and Lithuania   151

into the EU and NATO without a ratified (although signed) border with the Russian Federation. Latvia and Russia quietly came to an agreement in 2006, while Estonia and Russia still do not have a ratified agreement.

Returning to the minority issue, the root of the problem lies in Stalin's mass deportations of the Baltic peoples on the one hand and the subsequent Soviet migration of hundreds of thousands of non-Baltic peoples to Estonia and Latvia on the other. These Soviet era migrants played two roles. First, they addressed severe labour shortages following the Second World War. Second, Soviet migrants were used as a method of political control by bringing in over a million workers and troops during the Soviet era. Thus, it was not entirely surprising that these minorities were (and are) assumed to be prima facie untrustworthy until they proved themselves otherwise. Naturally, for communities that contained many who had been born in the Baltic republics, being assumed to be untrustworthy was unacceptable as well. The result was that minorities came to dominate the relationship between the Estonian, Latvian and Russian governments. The Russians responded by linking many of its foreign policy issues with those of the status of Russian speaking minorities in the Baltic States. Russia used its position at the OSCE, the Council of Europe and the United Nations to bring attention to the status of their co-ethnics. It was also a convenient strategy for consolidating nationalist support at home and externalizing domestic frustrations (Paulauskas 2006: 12). This applies to some Baltic right-wing politicians as well.

However, underneath the minority issue (interlinked with borders and ex-Soviet troops), there were deeper existential insecurities, traumas, and dilemmas. For the Russians, the Second World War has been their claim to national greatness and pride. They cast themselves as primary victims of and liberators from the Nazi aggression. This page of history has been at the core of the post-Soviet Russian identity. For the Baltic people, the same period looks very differently. This is the time when the Soviets – the primary victimizers – occupied their countries and systematically exterminated and subjugated their populations. What the Russians perceive as liberation, the Balts perceive as occupation (Brüggemann and Kasekamp 2009: 51). Since Moscow has been very reluctant to confront the issue and many of their politicians openly dispute the fact of occupation, the Baltic States feel an existential threat coming from Russia. The minority question (like many others) only deepens a sense of national insecurity.

Post-enlargement Baltic–Russian relations

History at play

We begin this section with history-related tensions as they arguably form the core of mutual distrust locking in Baltic–Russian relations to a path with few opportunities for genuine co-operation. In contrast to the minority issue, which became increasingly off the agenda of the bilateral relationships

152 *Ainius Lašas and David J. Galbreath*

(Galbreath and Galvin 2005), historical disputes not only continued but also heightened during the second half of the decade.

The first indication of that came with the 50th anniversary of VE-Day. The Latvian President's decision to attend the festivities in Moscow drew EU-wide praise as a sign that Latvia, in the words of Tony Blair, was able 'to get together for reconciliation and for constructive relations with Russia' (quoted in Onken 2009: 47). However, President Vaike Vīķe-Freiberga arrived in Moscow not only to celebrate the bravery of the anti-Hitler coalition, but also to point out the illegal Soviet occupation of the Baltic States and to urge Russia 'to express its regret over the post-war subjugation of Central and Eastern Europe' (Vīķe-Freiberga 2005). In the same way, the Estonian and Lithuanian presidents, who declined the Russian invitation, chastised Moscow for its refusal to condemn the Molotov-Ribbentrop Pact and to acknowledge occupation. The row between Moscow and the Baltic capitals was elevated to the EU level when former enlargement commissioner Günter Verheugen came out in defence of the Baltic position and asserted that EU-Russia relations will depend on Moscow's willingness to face the historical truth (Euractiv 2005). Denmark also supported the Baltic stance (see Etzold and Haukkala in this volume). Russia's ambassador to the EU Sergei Yastrzhembsky rebuked Verheugen and accused the Baltic States of undermining EU–Russia relations. Despite hostile rhetoric on both sides, the EU–Russia summit planned for the following day accepted the Common Spaces framework, designed to enhance mutual co-operation in four broad policy areas.

Cross-border co-operation and the movement of people was an important segment of this initiative, which directly touched upon the outstanding border agreements between the Baltic States and Russia. Given Russia's interest in visa-free travel and the limited salience of the border issue in NATO and EU expansions, Moscow decided to settle long-standing accounts. However, at least for Estonia, this became an important wedge issue for domestic political and historical reasons. While the parties successfully signed the border treaty on 18 May 2005, the ratification process unravelled the agreement. The addition of a preamble with remarks about the 1920 Tartu Peace Treaty by the Estonian parliament led not only to stern reaction by Moscow, but also to its refusal to ratify the document. The quiet standoff continues as the unratified border agreement, the only outstanding one between an EU member state and Russia, remains an obstacle in facilitating EU–Russia cross-border co-operation and visa-free travel. Tallinn seems to be unfazed by this obvious hitch, while EU officials are reluctant to push this sensitive issue.

In April 2007, following his re-election as Estonian prime minister, Andrus Ansip and his government decided to move forward with the much hyped removal of the Soviet war memorial near Tallinn's Old Town, which consisted of a bronze soldier (incidentally modelled on an ethnic Estonian wrestler) and the graves of several unknown Soviet soldiers that had died taking Estonia from the Germans (and needless to say, the Estonians). The so-called 'bronze soldier' crisis ensued. As the trucks and diggers came in to begin the removal, young Russians began protesting at the site. The protests turned into riots that ran through the Old Town and the immediate surrounding city centre. Tallinn's police were reinforced by forces from other cities, partly for fear of untrustworthy Russian policemen, but for the most part because of the sheer size of the riots.

The Russian government responded with limited economic sanctions and rhetorical condemnation (see The Economist 2007). Yet, at the same time, Estonian government and commercial websites experienced a well co-ordinated 'denial-of-service' attack. For instance, the Justice and Foreign Ministry websites were shut down and defaced. The origin of this breach of cyber security was found to be in Russia although there is no conclusive evidence that it was organized by the Russian government. More likely, analysts believe that the attack was led by Russian 'hackivists'. The Estonian government pressed for help from NATO and even went so far as to link the cyber attack to Article 5, NATO's mutual defence clause (which other NATO member states rejected). NATO did, however, locate its new Centre of Excellence for Cyber Defence in Estonia (The Economist 2010). The result was an increasingly bitter tone in the Estonian–Russian relationship that has singled Estonia out markedly as having a different relationship with its neighbour than either of the other two Baltic States. Furthermore, preceding as it did Russia's invasion of Georgia in 2008, the incident represented growing unease in the Baltic States that geopolitically Russia was again exerting its influence in the 'near abroad'.

There are also regular 'rhetorical' incidents, which are usually related either to particular anniversaries (like the anniversary of the Molotov-Ribbentrop Pact) or bilateral visits. One of the latest examples was the December 2011 OSCE meeting in Lithuania, which was attended by Russian Foreign Minister Sergei Lavrov. After a bilateral meeting, Lithuanian Foreign Minister Audronis Ažubalis insisted that the topic of compensation for the Soviet occupation was not forgotten and that it would remain an important issue for Vilnius in the future. At the same time, Lavrov accused Ažubalis of having misrepresented the meeting agenda. The Russian Foreign Minister was under the impression that his Lithuanian counterpart was boasting before journalists about his alleged demands to apologize for occupation (Černiauskas 2011). While such misunderstandings may not have significant geopolitical effects, they reveal the levels of sensitivity vis-à-vis history. They also contribute to mutual distrust, which has already deepened following NATO expansion to the eastern Baltic region.

The above examples demonstrate how tightly and in a vicious circle historical experiences and memory are related to security. Without openly confronting the questions of occupation and disassociating itself from this dark chapter of the Soviet legacy, the Kremlin contributes to the Baltic perception of insecurity. Feeling an existential threat, the Balts turn to NATO as the ultimate and most reliable guarantor of their security. In turn, Moscow feels compelled to respond to what it perceives as a challenge to its 'sphere of

154   *Ainius Lašas and David J. Galbreath*

interest', which for the Balts only further confirms the necessity of a long-term NATO presence in their region.

NATO at guard

In order to ensure substantive involvement of NATO in the region, the Baltic States, following their accession, supported and lobbied for a number of defence-orientated initiatives in Europe. Like their Polish counterparts, the Balts were eager to make sure that the Article 5 guarantees would have a very concrete and preferably permanent (or long-term) expression on the ground (see also Cichocki in this volume).

First and foremost, the Baltic States urged the alliance to develop a viable defence plan for them. However, the issue turned out to be not as straight-forward as they might have hoped for. Since the mid-1990s the Euro-Atlantic community has always assured Russia that the expansion of the alliance was not aimed against it. To build mutual confidence, NATO proposed a number of policy co-ordination mechanisms before each new phase of eastern enlargement. But none of them gave Russia any real influence in NATO decision-making structures. Thus, Moscow grew increasingly suspicious of NATO's encroachment upon its 'near abroad.' Because the new and more detailed defence plan for Poland and the Baltic States might further deepen mutual distrust, some members preferred a more gradual approach with comprehensive reviews and revisions of defence plans.

The situation underwent significant changes following the 2008 Russo–Georgian war. The Baltic arguments, once seen as a bit pushy, gained new credibility and momentum (phone interview with a high-level former NATO official, 19 December 2011). Russian military assertiveness in and around Georgia as well as its disregard for sovereignty norms following the conflict made the case of detailed defence plans for the eastern Baltic region more urgent. Furthermore, from the Baltic perspective, Moscow did not shy away from unnecessarily flexing its military muscle in the vicinity. In 2009, Russia organized two joint military exercises with Belarus, which focused on countering attacks from the Baltic States and Poland (McDermott 2009). Baltic politicians spared no time in using these exercises as yet another argument for the urgent need of the regional defence plan, which was eventually accepted at the beginning of 2010 (quoted in Wikileaks 2010).

Second, the Baltic States supported both Bush's and Obama's versions of the Ballistic Missile Defence (BMD) shield in Europe. Although the shield was officially proposed to deal with the threats coming from the rogue states such as Iran, it was also capable of countering threats 'from an unforeseen direction' (The Guardian 2010b). There is no doubt that this secondary usage was of particular interest for the Central and Eastern Europeans. Otherwise, it is hard to understand why the Poles and Balts were so upset when the Bush plan seemed later on to be sacrificed on the altar of American–Russian rapprochement as part of President Obama's reset policy towards Moscow. In

Estonia, Latvia and Lithuania 155

fact, Lithuanian President Dalia Grybauskaitė even refused an invitation to meet with President Obama in Prague as she was upset with the American approach to the region (Lietuvos Rytas 2010). Accusing Washington of abandoning Central and Eastern Europe, as some Baltic and Polish politicians did, made sense only in the context of the reset policy. From the Baltic perspective, joint NATO–Russia defence projects were naïve and misguided as they engaged Russia, which was still authoritarian, aggressive, and unapologetic. The scepticism only deepened when the Kremlin proposed a sector-based missile defence plan in 2010, where Russia was to be co-responsible for shielding the airspace of its border regions, including the Baltic States and Poland. Eventually the proposal was dropped because it was simply a non-starter.

At this point the American–Russian rapprochement came under a growing strain. The Wikileaks scandal did not help it either. As some details surrounding the extension of the _Eagle Guardian_ defence plan and the missile defence shield came to light, it was evident that neither Americans nor Central and Eastern Europeans had much trust in Russia. In response to the ongoing BMD plans and other US (and NATO) initiatives in the region, Moscow opened up an anti-missile radar station in Kaliningrad in November 2011. Using this occasion, Russian President Dmitry Medvedev also threatened to deploy Iskander missile complexes in the enclave and pull out from the START treaty, if Washington continued to ignore Russian security concerns (_Pravda_ 2011).

With Moscow placing additional military installations and troops in the region, there are growing levels of anxiety and uncertainty in the Baltic capitals.[1] This may bode well for the Baltic aim to establish a long-term NATO airspace policing mission, but the overall regional militarization presents serious security challenges to these three tiny countries with very limited military capabilities of their own. It also undermines regional economic development and co-operation, which already suffers from excessive politicization as demonstrated in the next section.

The politics of trade

The overview of Baltic–Russian trade dynamics serves as a transition from military to political issues, which take up the rest of the chapter. The reason for this approach is the fact that Baltic–Russian economic co-operation has been often driven by geopolitical rather than economic logic. This is especially true of the energy sector, which relies heavily upon Russian resources (Molis 2011). As noted by Lithuanian President Dalia Grybauskaitė, energy-related issues in the region always have a 'geopolitical character' (quoted in Delfi 2011a). Given the perception of Russia's unvarnished realpolitik, Baltic political elites usually prefer to limit their economic exposure in the east.

Among the three Baltic States, Estonia has the smallest share of its total trade with Russia. In 2011 its exports to Russia reached 10.5 per cent of the total exports, while imports constituted only 4.5 per cent of the total (see

Figure 10.1). However, these modest levels of trade largely resulted from Russian punitive measures against Estonia rather than some structural factors. After the Bronze Soldier incident in 2007, Russia drastically cut down its transit flows through Estonian railways and ports. A year after the incident, Russian cargo volumes fell by about a third, resulting in lower GDP growth by up to 1.5 per cent in 2007 and up to 2 per cent in 2008 (Anderson 2008). On the other hand, Lithuania followed a reverse trend increasing the share of Russian imports and exports. 2011 was a record year with well over 30 per cent of total imports coming from the Russian Federation. Over the last decade, Latvian imports remained largely flat, while exports exhibited substantial growth reaching 15.2 per cent of the total. Again, this should be viewed in the context of recently improved Latvian–Russian political relations.

The observed import patterns are also defined by the Baltic demand in mineral products and raw materials, principal Russian exports. As will be discussed in the next section, Estonia has developed a number of alternatives to satisfy its energy needs, while Lithuania and Latvia still struggle to limit their dependence on Russian energy resources. Having a Soviet heritage of a few very large industrial plants, Lithuanian trade volumes with Russia swing wildly with the changing fortunes of these plants. Thus, when in October 2006, Mazeikiai Oil refinery was crippled by a major fire, the Russian share of total imports dropped from 28 per cent in 2005 to barely 18 per cent in 2007. Once the refinery's capacity was fully restored in early 2008, the Russian share jumped back to 30 per cent for the year (see Figure 10.1).

Unlike Russian imports, Baltic exports to Russia range widely from machinery, furniture, textiles to various food items. With its reputation rooted in Soviet times, the Baltic food industry is especially well positioned to compete in the Russian marketplace. But ever since independence Baltic exports to Russia have had a political aftertaste as Moscow has not hesitated to put

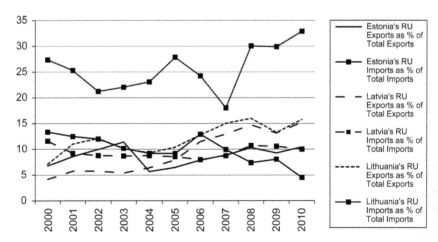

Figure 10.1 Baltic–Russian trade dynamics (2000–10)

up various trade barriers for Baltic exporters. While some strategies – like double tariffs – had to be abandoned following EU expansion, others – like excessive quality controls for food items – remain. Whether it is sprats or dairy products, Russian inspectors routinely deny export permits for Baltic companies. As noted by Ago Pärtel, the head of the Estonian Veterinary and Food Board, 'the reasons for denying the permits are *naturally* political' (quoted in Kunnas 2004, emphasis added). While politicizing food exports has relatively limited economic repercussions, it contributes to the overall mistrust of the Kremlin and its policies. At the same time, there is also a more crude way (pun intended) of politicizing bilateral trade. For this, it is necessary to turn to the analysis of the energy sector, where Russia, according to Hedenskog and Larsson (2007: 50), used coercive energy policy against the Baltic States 21 times in 1991–2006.

Energy (in)security

Since their accession to the EU, Latvia and Lithuania (and to a lesser degree Estonia) have struggled to reduce their dependence on Russian energy resources. The membership has, however, offered some opportunities in the medium term. Under the auspices of the EU Third Energy Package and EU-supported regional infrastructure projects, they may start to gradually integrate into the European energy market and reduce their dependence on Russia. At the same time, lower energy prices would boost the competitiveness of their industrial sectors and potentially attract more investment. However, at this point, brighter future prospects are tainted by a rather bleak reality on the ground. At least in the energy sector, the Baltic States still remain members of the ex-Soviet rather than European common market.

The 2004 EU accession brought mixed blessings for Baltic energy sectors. As a part of the EU accession conditionality, Lithuania had to close its Soviet-design Ignalina nuclear power plant at the end of 2009, which supplied electricity to Latvia, Estonia, Belarus, and Kaliningrad. The timing of the closure turned out to be very unfortunate since it coincided with a deep regional recession due to the global financial crisis. Although Vilnius, backed by its Baltic partners, sought to jumpstart the construction of the replacement plant, it ended up tripping over its own ambitions. In addition to delays due to fierce competition among domestic interest groups, the half-hearted involvement of Poland brought additional planning delays and complications. After a failed construction tender in 2010, the prospects for the replacement plant started to look increasingly grim. This impression was further strengthened with the acceleration of Russian plans to build a Baltic nuclear power plant in Kaliningrad and the Ostrovets nuclear plant in Belarus, both right next to the Lithuanian border. The Russians also sought to involve Poland in the Kaliningrad project since the plant's capacity would surpass the electricity needs of the Kaliningrad region. Poland rejected the offer to join the project, but conducted some preliminary negotiations over the purchase of electricity from the new plant (Warsaw Business Journal 2011; see also Cichocki in this volume). Later, at the end of 2011, Warsaw decided to withdraw from the Ignalina project altogether and announced plans to build its own nuclear power plant.[2] From a Baltic perspective, the Polish search for cheaper energy threatened to undermine their initial plans for the replacement plant and brought into question the durability of Baltic–Polish co-operation as the latter increasingly pursued narrow national interests (anonymous interview with a high-ranking Lithuanian official from the Ministry of Foreign Affairs, 22 March 2011). Despite the odds, Lithuania recently managed to attract GE Hitachi Nuclear Energy as a potential investor.

In addition to the geostrategic dimension, Lithuania (and to a lesser degree Latvia) is also worried about the safety of the two neighbouring nuclear facilities and their potential environmental impact on the region. Since both facilities will discharge cooling water into rivers that go through Lithuanian territory, Vilnius is becoming increasingly insecure and eager to involve Brussels. They also hope that the nuclear tragedy at Fukushima in Japan in 2011 might heighten EU sensitivities. However, it is doubtful whether key EU member states such as Germany and France are ready to raise the stakes with Moscow, the main player behind both projects. Having signed strategic natural gas supply and military equipment procurement agreements with Russia, both countries stand to lose too much by questioning Russian initiatives. At the same time, Estonia and Latvia weigh their options as hopes (and plans) for the replacement plant fluctuate almost monthly. Latvia is especially vulnerable as it relies on electricity imports from its southern neighbour. Estonia faces less pressure because of its native energy resources of shale oil and an electricity transmission link with Finland. In 2010, Estonia and Finland signed an agreement to build a second transmission cable. Also, the Estonian state power company Eesti Energia made strategic investments in Jordanian and recently US shale oil extraction companies (AFP 2011). Finally, seeing continuous delays with the Lithuanian project, Tallinn has been considering options for building its own nuclear power plant.

Ever since their accession to the Union, the Baltic States have been pushing the European Commission to take note of their isolation from EU energy markets and their exclusive reliance on Russian imports. With Latvian Commissioner Andris Piebalgs in charge of DG Energy since 2004, they were well positioned to make at least some inroads. In October 2008, EU Commission President Manuel Barroso established a high-level working group for the interconnection of Baltic Sea energy markets. This initiative nicely fitted into larger EU plans to liberalize the community's energy market. The first results came about in 2009 as the Commission agreed to prioritize the construction of the Nordbalt electricity transmission link between Sweden and Lithuania. The project was on hold for two years as Latvia and Lithuania argued over who would be on the receiving end of the Swedish link. The Commission played a key role in resolving the standoff by mollifying Latvia with financial resources to improve its weak electricity grid (anonymous interview with a high-ranking Lithuanian official from the Ministry of Foreign Affairs, 22 March 2011). Also, the Commission allocated funds for connecting the Polish and Lithuanian electricity grids, a key project if the Lithuanian nuclear replacement plant was to see the light of day. After the Polish pullout, the future of this project is uncertain.

Furthermore, the Third Energy Package has provided new opportunities for challenging the position of Gazprom as the only natural gas supplier and transporter to the Baltic States. With the backing of the European Commission, Lithuania took the boldest measures requiring Gazprom's subsidiary to sell its pipeline stakes in the country. It also threatened to sue Gazprom in an international arbitration court for its discriminatory pricing strategies. This step was made in response to Gazprom's decision to offer 15 per cent price discounts for Latvia and Estonia for 2011 (RIA Novosti 2010). There was little doubt that Gazprom's power play was meant to teach Lithuania a lesson in humility and split up the Baltic 'coalition'. However, for Lithuania this move is vital in order to ensure the viability of its plan to build a Liquefied Natural Gas (LNG) terminal in Klaipeda port. With Gazprom's current control of the pipelines, this facility could be easily sabotaged. The lessons of the disrupted oil supply from Russia to Mazeikiai Oil Refinery looms large in this confrontation (see below). To further complicate the picture, Latvia and Estonia are also considering building LNG facilities. However, Vilnius remains deeply sceptical of the Latvian proposal as it sees Gazprom's subsidiary Itera Latvia jostling to be in charge of the project. According to Česlovas Stankevičius, chairman of the Lithuanian Parliament's European Affairs Committee:

> if, as the word is, the builder would be a Gazprom subsidiary, it would be a Gazprom terminal, and Lithuania will not approve to [sic] this. It would not be an actual gas supplies alternative. The terminal would be intended for exports, which is clearly in line with Gazprom's interests.
> (quoted in *The Lithuania Tribune* 2011a)

Not being able to agree on the best location for the joint terminal, the Baltic States decided to ask the EU to resolve the dispute. In the meantime, Lithuania remains firmly committed to the idea of its own terminal, although recently Achema Group, one of the largest conglomerates in Lithuania and a substantial consumer of natural gas (used in fertilizer production), threw a wrench by announcing plans to build yet another LNG terminal. As with the Ignalina nuclear power plant, the plans for LNG facilities seem to change almost monthly.

If Lithuania and Estonia proposed radical steps to unbundle gas suppliers from transporters, Latvia followed a completely different route and postponed the liberalization of its gas market until 2014. This step is not only a witness to Gazprom's influence in Latvia, but also Riga's hope to play a larger role in the regional gas import-export business. Given its vast natural underground storage facilities, Latvia has not been as worried about its dependence on Russian gas supplies as Estonia and Lithuania. When the Nord Stream project acquired momentum in the second half of 2000s, Latvia offered its storage facilities for a land-based pipeline option (RIA Novosti 2009). Alternatively, it hoped to build the earlier-mentioned LNG facility for gas exports. These economic opportunities, rather than any consequences of EU membership, go a long way to explain relatively constructive Latvian–Russian relations during the second half of the 2000s. Not surprisingly, when Prime Minister Aigars Kalvītis travelled to Moscow to sign a border treaty in 2007, he also conducted negotiations with Gazprom over the development of additional gas storage capabilities in Latvia.

In comparison to Baltic electricity and natural gas markets, the EU has not had any significant impact on regional oil refining and transit sectors since 2004. There is also little substantive co-operation among the Baltic States in this area. Probably the single most important development was the acquisition of the Mazeikiai Oil Refinery by Polish state-controlled oil refiner PKN Orlen in 2006 and the subsequent disruption of oil supplies via Druzhba-1 pipeline to the refinery. Although initially Russian pipeline operator Transneft talked about a need for emergency repairs due to a leakage, over time it started questioning the overall condition of the pipeline branch and decided to close it permanently. Since from the Lithuanian perspective the closure was nothing more than a political move, Vilnius took active steps to elevate the issue to the EU level.[3] On 24 April 2008 it attempted to stall the start of EU–Russia negotiations over the new Partnership and Cooperation Agreement at the Committee of Permanent Representatives. This lonely move of desperation convinced the EU to include some of Lithuania's concerns into its negotiations mandate (for more on the Lithuanian position, see Pavilionis 2008). More importantly, Lithuania managed to draw EU attention to the isolation and vulnerability of the Baltic energy markets. The earlier-mentioned initiative of the Commission to establish a high-level working group for the interconnection of Baltic Sea energy markets should be seen as a partial result of this confrontation.

While at the time the Polish investment into the largest Lithuanian company was seen as an important move to prevent the Russian takeover of the refinery and to strengthen Polish–Baltic strategic co-operation, the situation has since changed at least twice. In 2007–10, the Lithuanian refinery, cut off from Russian oil supplies, registered annual losses. Frustrated with the financial results, the new Polish government openly admitted that it was looking for ways 'to backtrack on this cardinal mistake' (Sobczyk 2010). The Lithuanian government had little influence on the matter because of tense bilateral relations due to ethnic minority issues. Vilnius was concerned that its Western neighbour might sacrifice Lithuanian (and Baltic) interests on the altar of the Polish–Russian rapprochement. However, as the financial situation of the refinery improved in the first half of 2011, PKN Orlen changed its tone and plans. Still it remains to be seen whether the Poles will be willing to absorb a new wave of losses following the current economic slump in Western Europe.

Concerns over Russian influence in oil transit looms large in Latvia. In the background of ongoing disputes over the control of the Ventspils Oil terminal, companies with obvious and less obvious ties to Russia have repeatedly attempted to redefine the playing field. The uncertainty also continues over the fate of the Polotsk-Ventspils pipeline, once used to export oil from Russia. Recently, Belarus expressed interest in using the pipeline to import oil through Venspils port for its own needs. Around the same time, LatRosTrans, the current operator of the pipeline, announced plans to empty it of buffer oil and discontinue its use (Baltic News Network 2010). With various accusations and court proceedings in progress, the Latvian government seems to be at a loss.

Estonia has also faced oil transit disruptions from Russia. Following the Bronze Soldier crisis in 2007, there was a sharp drop in traffic from the east. Since then the volume slightly recovered, but the Russian government is warning that soon most of its oil trade will be handled by the rapidly growing Ust-Luga port near St Petersburg. This strategy of diverting transit traffic from the Baltic ports has been consistently pursued by Moscow following the EU and NATO enlargement to the region.

As demonstrated in this section, energy-related co-operation among the Baltic States may eventually have its successes, but at this point the potential is under-utilized. As always, the shadow of Russia looms large over many regional projects. Moscow continues to openly use its economic muscle to divide and rule. With rising energy prices due to instabilities in the Middle East and North Africa, Russia stands to further increase its power and influence in the region. The same development weakens the ability of the Baltic States to implement their own strategies and decrease their dependence on their Eastern neighbour. With the USA distracted and weakened by its global war on terror, the EU remains an important counterbalancing element. While the European Community is not a traditional state-like power, its legislating hand and substantial financial resources reverberate across the continent providing opportunities for the Baltic States to redefine their position vis-à-vis Russia. In addition to energy, the EU's neighbourhood policy provided yet another alluring potential for change.

The Eastern neighbourhood

Following their entry into the EU, the Baltic States began a new focus on encouraging a deeper relationship between the EU and other Western former Soviet states, such as Georgia, Ukraine and Moldova. Galbreath and Lamoreaux (2007) argue that the Baltic States were able to play the parts of 'bastion, beacon and bridge' vis-à-vis the EU and other post-Soviet states. From the Baltic States' perspective, they had a unique position to guide other post-Soviet states to the wider political, economic, and security communities. After all, they had made the path from Soviet republics to member states in a decade and a half. At the same time, this role would not be for them to decide, but would be in the hands of 'Brussels' more loosely described,

162 Ainius Lašas and David J. Galbreath

including the constellation of member-state interests more specifically. From as early as 2003, the Baltic States began to support Georgia, Ukraine and Moldova through development aid. Each of the Baltic States sought a relationship with each of the post-Soviet states. However, they also focused on specific states. For instance, Estonia focused much of its development aid and technical assistance on Georgia, Latvia predominantly on Moldova, and Lithuania on Ukraine and Georgia. Events in these states, particular the Rose and Orange revolutions, made this policy possible. In this way, the Baltic States saw themselves as being at best a 'bridge' and in the worst case a 'beacon' or shining example of how to go from post-Soviet state to member state.

These roles were being played in the context of the larger geopolitical tensions arising from the EU's European Neighbourhood Policy (ENP) and Russia's (at the time) somewhat moribund 'near abroad' policy. As the 'neighourhood' met the 'near abroad', there were considerable questions as to how far and how quickly other post-Soviet states could 'move Westward' (Aliboni 2005; Averre 2009). The ENP was a way in which to deal with what White, McAllister and Light (2002) refer to as the 'new outsiders'. For the majority of old member states, the policy became a discussion within the EU about how to engage with these states without offering them the incentive of enlargement. In other words, how can the EU produce similar conditioned results without offering the ultimate incentive (see Schimmelfennig, Engert and Knobel 2005).

The new members, especially Poland and the Baltic States, never accepted this formulation and instead pushed the EU (and NATO) to at least acknowledge the possibility of membership without offering specific dates or mechanisms (Haukkala and Moshes 2004). Their underlying motivation was two-fold. First, they sought to extend the EU frontier further to the East, stabilize the region, and open up economic opportunities. Second, they wanted to curtail Russia's geopolitical ambitions and to put more 'bastions' along the edge of 'Fortress Europe'. The rise of like-minded leaders in Ukraine and Georgia following democratic revolutions only strengthened Polish–Baltic efforts. However, traditional EU powers, especially Germany and France, were quite apprehensive about these initiatives of a decisively pro-American and at the same time anti-Russian coalition (see also Stewart and Le Noan in this volume). Grappling with post-enlargement institutional challenges and facing a Eurosceptic electorate, they put a damper on such Polish–Baltic enthusiasm and focused instead on further institutional reforms in the EU.

The divergence of the approaches reached its peak during the Russo–Georgian war in the summer of 2008. During the emergency EU Summit on 2 September 2008, the Baltic States and Poland chastised old members for their passivity and neutrality, while old members viewed the Baltic–Polish eagerness to sanction Russia with deep caution. However, by early November, Lithuania was the only one willing to further delay EU–Russia negotiations over the new PCA. Isolated from the rest, it could not prevent the resumption of the negotiations since the decision did not require unanimity. As more

Estonia, Latvia and Lithuania 163

information about the war began to emerge over time, the reservations of enlargement sceptics deepened and confirmed their fears about the EU's Eastern neighbourhood.

Russia's position on the ENP was straightforward. First, Moscow made it clear that it had no interest to be part of the EU's 'neighbourhood' (Averre 2009, 1690–91). Instead, Moscow sought an equitable relationship with the EU that would be built on EU and Russian common interests such as security and economic trade. The Four Common Spaces agreement in 2005 did exactly this. Second, Russia saw the ENP as an extension of Western engagement in its sphere of influence, illustrated by the location of Russian troops in each of the three post-Soviet states discussed. While the language of the 'near abroad' had become less fashionable in Moscow, although not so in Western academic literature, the Russian assumption remained the same: the former Soviet space is of vital interest to Russia's national security. Finally, Russia saw the ENP as capitalizing on the anti-Russian rhetoric that followed the Rose and Orange revolutions in Georgia and Ukraine respectively. In other words, the 'neighbourhood' and the 'near abroad' were perhaps overlapping but in effect mutually exclusive spaces.

All in all, the EU's focus on the Eastern neighbourhood has faltered. The glow of the Rose revolution ended as did the ceasefire status quo in Georgia with the 2008 Russian invasion. The Orange revolution was well and truly dead by the time Viktor Yanukovych was legitimately elected president in 2010. Moldova has moved no closer to being a 'normal' European state, still with a breakaway region supported by the Russian military. A glimmer of hope was recently sparked by the renewed 5+2 negotiations in Vilnius. Using its OSCE chairmanship in 2011, Lithuania managed to put the Moldovan territorial issue back on the international agenda, but any substantive progress will depend upon Russia's willingness to revise its current policy. Finally, the Eastern 'Partnership' has floundered as states like Azerbaijan and Belarus realized that political conditionality would be a part of any growing relationship with the EU (see Korosteleva 2011). At the same time, this comes at a period when the Baltic governments are unable to remain engaged in the region. State budgets have been drastically cut, with Latvia being the hardest hit. Added to this is the fact that the EU and NATO seem very unlikely to accept any states outside of Croatia anytime soon. As EU member states, the Baltics included, turn inwards, Russia's 'near abroad' appears as apt a description as ever.

Conclusions

This chapter has argued that Baltic–Russian relations continue to be defined by competing historical memories and experiences. With its 'opportunity discourse' supplementing the 'danger discourse' vis-à-vis Russia (Spruds 2009: 102), Latvia may look like an exception to the rule. However, as Baltic reactions to the 2008 Russian–Georgian conflict demonstrated, historical

164 *Ainius Lašas and David J. Galbreath*

experiences and memories tend to constrain and overrule interest-based co-operation (Muiznieks 2010: 23). Also, Moscow recently reminded the Baltic States of the 'forgotten' minority issue with its first report on human rights abroad, resulting in a new round of bilateral rhetorical 'incidents' (MID Rossii 2011). Thus, unless Russian foreign-policy-making becomes more forthcoming and transparent on the one hand, and Baltic political elites start to feel securely rooted in Europe on the other, there remains strong temptation for both sides to stick with the familiar.

In this chapter we argue that Baltic EU and NATO memberships did not reduce but largely exaggerated bilateral distrust. From a Russian perspective, which views the Baltic republics as essentially anti-Russian (Trenin 2011: 48), their access to the EU and NATO decision-making structures only complicated the pursuit of Russian regional interests. As demonstrated with the EU's Third Energy Package and Eastern neighbourhood policies, the Baltic States did not hesitate to use membership instrumentally and to confront Russian interests. In the same way, they (and Poland) sought to repeatedly strengthen NATO commitment to and involvement in the region. This is a direct challenge to what Russia has historically considered to be its sphere of influence. The unwelcome result has become the growing militarization of the region with uncertain consequences.

The repeated Baltic–Russian clashes over history provide four insights about the role of the Baltic States in European politics. First, the Baltic States have a narrow band of uploading capabilities in the EU and NATO when issues pertinent to their security and well-being are at stake. They manage to find allies not only among the new EU and NATO members, but also old ones, who also have lingering suspicions of Russia (Sweden and Denmark; see Etzold and Haukkala in this volume) or feel partial historical responsibility for the fate of the Baltic States (Germany; see Stewart in this volume). A related second, Baltic uploading is usually negative in form. Due to distrust and scepticism, the Balts seem to lack positive ideas on how to co-operate with and influence Russia. For them, the starting point is often history, which due to Russian intransigence becomes a barrier for further progress. Thus, they sometimes come to be seen as policy spoilers rather than entrepreneurs, which restricts their horizontal reach among EU and NATO member states. Third, Baltic horizontal policy co-ordination vis-à-vis Russia remains functional, but under-utilized. Only in critical situations, such as the 2008 Russo–Georgian war, do Estonia, Latvia and Lithuania manage to overcome differences and act in unison. And finally, due to their fate during and after the Second World War, the Baltic States feel an obligation and an existential necessity to educate Western Europeans about another Holocaust that took place behind the Iron Curtain. They seek to redefine and upload an expanded version of the collective European memory of the Second World War and to assert the comparability of Nazi and Soviet crimes.[4] For Russia, which builds its own national identity on the suffering and bravery of its citizens during the Second World War, such Baltic efforts raise suspicion and anger. They are

Estonia, Latvia and Lithuania 165

often seen as agents of US policy, especially under President George W. Bush, to subdue and contain the renaissance of Russian power. Sharing a largely realist conception of international relations, both sides (Baltics and Russia) view the EU as a crippled giant in terms of the CFSP. Thus, the three Baltic republics are especially keen to keep NATO involved in Europe as the ultimate guarantor of their long-term security. They do not trust that they themselves or the EU can take up this role. As long as Baltic–Russian perceptions of each other remain unchanged, the Europeanization of Baltic foreign and security policies will be limited and purely instrumental.

Notes

1 According to Estonian sources, Russia doubled its troop presence in the region next to the border with Estonia. See *The Lithuania Tribune* 2011b.
2 Since the announcement, some Polish politicians promised to reconsider the decision if better terms for Poland were assured. See Delfi 2011b.
3 As became clear from secret documents leaked by Wikileaks, US officials also believed that 'the Kremlin – specifically Igor Sechin, Rosneft's chair and Deputy Head of Russia's Presidential Administration – had ordered MN's [Mazeikiu Nafta] supply cut off and by the end-of-July pipeline "accident" near Bryansk'. See Wikileaks 2011.
4 Baltic efforts at drawing comparisons between Nazi and Soviet crimes have also been criticized as means to downplay the role of the Baltic peoples themselves in the Holocaust. See *Bernardinai* 2012.

References

AFP (2011) 'Estonia's state power firm in US oil shale deal', *AFP*, 10 March 2011.
Aliboni, R. (2005) 'The Geopolitical Implications of the European Neighbourhood Policy', *European Foreign Affairs Review*, 10: 1–16.
Anderson, R. (2008) 'Estonia pays price of defying Russia', *Business New Europe*. 19 June 2008, available at www.bne.eu/story1101 (accessed 22 June 2012).
Averre, D. (2009) 'Competing Rationalities: Russia, the EU and the "Shared Neighbourhood"', *Europe-Asia Studies*, 61: 1689–1713.
Baltic News Network (2010) 'LNT Chairman Rudolf Meroni: the Latvian State must protect its national interests', *BNN*. 9 December 2010, available at http://bnn-news.com/2010/12/09/business/lnt-chairman-rudolf-meroni-latvian-state-protect-national-i nterests (accessed 22 June 2012).
Bernardinai (2012) 'Prof. Saulius Sužiedėlis: "Svarbu ne švari, o teisinga istorija"', *Bernardinai*. 2 January 2012, available at www.bernardinai.lt/straipsnis/2012-01-02-prof-saulius-suziedelis-svarbu-ne-svari-o-teisinga-istorija/74448 (accessed 22 June 2012).
Brüggemann, K. and Kasekamp, A. (2009) 'Identity Politics and Contested Histories in Divided Societies: The Case of Estonian War Monuments', in E. Berg and P. Ehin (eds) *Identity and Foreign Policy Baltic-Russian Relations and European Integration*. Aldershot: Ashgate.
Černiauskas, Š (2011) 'S.Lavrovas: A.Ažubalis man neparodė, kur vėžiai žiemoja', *Delfi*. 7 December 2011, available at www.delfi.lt/archive/article.php?id=52633389 (accessed 22 June 2012).

166 *Ainius Lašas and David J. Galbreath*

Delfi (2011a) 'Prezidentė: Lenkija apie energetiką kalba tik komerciniais terminais, o politikoje linksta prie Rusijos', *Delfi*. 18 December 2011, available at http://verslas.delfi.lt/archive/article.php?id=53110901 (accessed 22 June 2012).

——(2011b) 'PGE neatmeta, kad gali grįžti į Visagino AE projektą', *Delfi*. 22 December 2011, available at http://verslas.delfi.lt/archive/print.php?id=53271677 (accessed 22 June 2012).

The Economist (2007) 'A cyber-riot', *The Economist online*. 10 May 2007, available at www.economist.com/node/9163598 (accessed 22 June 2012).

——2010) 'War in the fifth domain', *The Economist online*. 1 July 2010, available at www.economist.com/node/16478792 (accessed 22 June 2012).

Euractiv (2005) 'Verheugen remarks cast shadows over EU-Russia summit', *Euractiv*. 9 May 2005, available at www.euractiv.com/en/security/verheugen-remarks-cast-shad ows-eu-russia-summit/article-139151 (accessed 22 June 2012).

Galbreath, D. J. 2005) *Nation-Building and Minority Politics in Post-Socialist States: Interests, Influence and Identities in Estonia and Latvia*. Stuttgart: Ibidem Verlag

——(2010) 'Between a Rock and a Hard Place: Baltic Foreign Policy after Enlargement', in D. J. Smith, D. J. Galbreath and G. Swain (eds) *From Recognition to Restoration: Latvia's History as a Nation-State*. Amsterdam: Rodopi.

Galbreath, D. J. and Galvin, M. E. (2005) 'The Titularization of Latvian Secondary Schools: the Historical Legacy of Soviet Policy Implementation', *Journal of Baltic Studies*, 36: 449–66.

Galbreath, D. J. and Lamoreaux, J. W. (2007) 'Bastion, Beacon or Bridge? Conceptualising the Baltic Logic of the EU's Neighbourhood', *Geopolitics*, 12: 109–32.

Galbreath, D. J., Lašas, A. and Lamoreaux, J. W. (2008) *Continuity and Change in the Baltic Sea Region: Comparing Foreign Policies*. Amsterdam: Rodopi.

The Guardian (2010a) 'US embassy cables: Germany behind Nato proposal for Baltic states, says US', *The Guardian online*. 6 December 2010, available at www.guardian.co.uk/world/us-embassy-cables-documents/240187?intcmp=239 (accessed 22 June 2012).

——(2010b) 'US embassy cables: Pentagon tells Warsaw missile shield adaptable to 'hypothetical' threats', *The Guardian online*. 6 December 2010, available at www.guardian.co.uk/world/us-embassy-cables-documents/234255 (accessed 22 June 2012).

Haukkala, H. and Moshes, A. (2004) *Beyond 'Big Bang': The Challenges of the EU's Neighbourhood Policy in the East*. Helsinki: The Finnish Institute of International Affairs.

Hedenskog, J. and Larsson, R. L. (2007) *Russian Leverage on the CIS and the Baltic States*. Stockholm: Swedish Defence Research Agency Report, June 2007, available at www2.foi.se/rapp/foir2280.pdf (accessed 22 June 2012).

Kunnas, K. (2004) 'Head of Estonian food agency: Politics behind denial of licences', *Helsingin Sanomat* online. 20 September 2004, available at www.hs.fi/english/print/1076154074246 (accessed 22 June 2012).

Korosteleva, E. (2011) 'The Eastern Partnership Initiative: A New Opportunity for Neighbours?', *Journal of Communist Studies and Transition Politics*, 27: 1–21.

Lietuvos Rytas (2010) 'D.Grybauskaitė: "JAV ir Rusijos nusiginklavimo derybos galėjo pažeisti Baltijos šalių interesus"', *Lietuvos Rytas*. 5 December 2010, available at www.lrytas.lt/-12837116371283488208-d-grybauskaitė-jav-ir-rusijos-nusiginklavimo-derybos-g alėjo-pažeisti-baltijos-šalių-interesus.htm (accessed 22 June 2012).

The Lithuania Tribune (2011a) 'Lithuania afraid of Gazprom's influence if a Baltic LNG terminal built in Latvia', *The Lithuania Tribune*. 7 February 2011, available at www.lithuaniatribune.com/2011/02/07/lithuania-afraid-of-gazprom%E2%80%99s-infl uence-if-a-baltic-lng-terminal-to-be-built-in-latvia/ (accessed 22 June 2012).

——(2011b) 'Estonia's defensive options against Russia', *The Lithuania Tribune*. 15 December 2011, available at www.lithuaniatribune.com/2011/12/15/estonias-defensiv e-options-against-russia/ (accessed 22 June 2012).

McDermott, R. (2009) 'Zapad 2009 Rehearses Countering a NATO Attack on Belarus', *Eurasia Daily Monitor*, 6(179). 30 September 2009, available at www.jamestown.org/single/?no_cache=1&tx_ttnews%5Btt_news%5D=35558 (accessed 22 June 2012).

MID Rossii (2011) 'Комментарий Уполномоченного МИД России по вопросам прав человека, демократии и верховенства права К.К.Долгова в связи с заявлениями латвийского омбудсмена Ю.Янсонса', *MID Rossii*. 28 December 2011, available at www.mid.ru/brp_4.nsf/newsline/CA0479B34E81D0AF44257974004799E4 (accessed 22 June 2012).

Molis, A (2011) *Rethinking EU-Russia energy relations: What do the Baltic States want?* SPES Policy Papers. February 2011, Berlin: Institut fu?r Europa?ische Politik, available at www.iep-berlin.de/fileadmin/website/09_Publikationen/SPES_Policy_Pap ers/SPES_Policy_Papers_2011_MOLIS.pdf (accessed 22 June 2012).

Muiznieks, N. (2010) 'Latvian-Russian relations – a new thaw?' *Baltic Rim Economies*, 2/ 2010. 28 April 2010, available at www.tse.fi/FI/yksikot/erillislaitokset/pei/Documents/ BRE2010/BRE_2_2010_Artikkelit/BRE_2_2010_22.pdf (accessed 22 June 2012).

Onken, E. (2009) 'Commemorating 9 May: The Baltic States and European Memory Politics', in E. Berg and P. Ehin (eds) *Identity and Foreign Policy. Baltic-Russian Relations and European Integration.* Aldershot: Ashgate.

Paulauskas, K. (2006) *The Baltics: from nation states to member states.* The EU Institute for Security Studies, Occasional Paper Nr. 62, February 2006, available at www.iss.europa.eu/uploads/media/occ62.pdf (accessed 22 June 2012).

Pavilionis, Ž. (2008) 'Lithuanian Position Regarding the EU Mandate on Negotiations with Russia: Seeking a New Quality of EU-Russian Relations', *Lithuanian Foreign Policy Review*, 21: 174–81.

*Pravda (*2011) 'Russia and USA on verge of another Cold War', *Pravda*. 24 November 2011,available at http://english.pravda.ru/russia/politics/24-11-2011/119729-russia_usa-0/ (accessed 22 June 2012).

RIA Novosti (2009) 'Latvia set to propose alternative to Nord Stream', *RIA Novosti*. 17 April 2009, available at http://en.rian.ru/world/20090417/121186949.html (accessed 22 June 2012).

——(2010) 'Gazprom offers to cut prices 15% for Estonia, Latvia if deliveries raised', *RIA Novosti*. 24 December 2010, available at http://en.rian.ru/business/20101224/ 161916344.html (accessed 22 June 2012).

Schimmelfennig, F., Engert, S. and Knobel, H. (2005) *International Socialization in Europe: European Organizations, Political Conditionality and Democratic Change.* Basingstoke: Palgrave.

Sobczyk, M. (2010) 'Polish Finance Minister Blasts Refiner PKN Orlen's Lithuanian Investment', *Wall Street Journal*. 14 December 2010, available at http://blogs.wsj. com/new-europe/2010/12/14/polish-finance-minister-blasts-refiner-pkn-orlens-lithuan ian-investment/ (accessed 22 June 2012).

Spruds, A. (2009) 'Entrapment in the discourse of danger? Latvian-Russian Interaction in the context of European Integration', in E. Berg and P. Ehin (eds) *Identity and Foreign Policy Baltic-Russian Relations and European Integration.* Aldershot: Ashgate.

168 *Ainius Lašas and David J. Galbreath*

Trenin, D. (2011) 'Russian Policies Toward the Nordic-Baltic Region', in R. Nurick and M. Nordenman (eds) *Nordic-Baltic Security in the 21st Century: The Regional Agenda and the Global Role.* Washington, DC: Atlantic Council, 47–51, available at http://carnegieendowment.org/files/Nordic-Baltic_Security_Trenin.pdf (accessed 22 June 2012).

Vīķe-Freiberga, V. (2005) 'Declaration by H.E. Dr. Vaira Vīķe-Freiberga, President of the Republic of Latvia regarding May 9, 2005', *Personal website of Vaira Vīķe-Freiberga.* Available at www.vvf.lv/vvf/index.php?Itemid=62 (accessed 2 March 2011).

Warsaw Business Journal (2011) 'Poland to buy Russian nuclear energy?', *Warsaw Business Journal.* 14 February 2011, available at www.wbj.pl/article-53183-poland-to-buy-russian-nuclear-energy.html (accessed 22 June 2012).

White, S., McAllister, I. and Light, M. (2002) 'Enlargement and the New Outsiders', *Journal of Common Market Studies*, 40: 135–53.

Wikileaks (2010) 'Lithuanian Mod Discusses Nato Contingency Planning For The Baltics', Mission USNATO. 19 Nov 2009, available at http://wikileaks.org/cable/2009/11/09USNATO532.html (accessed 5 December 2011).

——(2011) 'Lithuania's Choice: Fight or Surrender its Refinery to the Russians', US Embassy Vilnius, 4 August 2006, available at http://wikileaks.org/cable/2006/08/06VILNIUS727.html (accessed 5 December 2011).

11 Czech Republic, Hungary and Slovakia

Martin Dangerfield

Until around the time of their EU accession, there was a rather widespread assumption that Central and East European countries (CEECs) were relatively homogeneous in their attitudes towards Russia. Two scholars wrote quite recently that many CEE states 'tend to be anti-Soviet, thus often also anti-Russia, as a result of their recent historical memory' (Bozhilova and Hashimoto 2010: 628). In the context of greater, albeit even today not extensive, scrutiny of all EU members states' bilateral relations with Russia since the 2004/7 enlargements, CEECs have actually been shown to be rather diverse when it comes to relations with Russia (as during the Soviet era). Latter-day differences have been portrayed in various ways, including a broad-based split into 'Russia-friendly' and 'Russia-hostile' camps and more specific categorizations (Leonard and Popescu 2007; Kratochvíl 2007). This chapter focuses on the Visegrad Group (VG) states, whose relations with Russia are undoubtedly distinct due to specific shared Soviet-era experiences and the early history of the VG itself. While VG states have this common context and connections with Russia follow similar patterns in many important respects, their bilateral relations nevertheless have specific characteristics. As one significant cleavage is undoubtedly between the 'small' VG states on the one hand and Poland on the other, this particular chapter concentrates on the Czech Republic, Hungary and Slovakia (and for Poland see Cichocki's chapter in this volume).

As with most CEECs, regional proximity and the communist legacy mean that there are intense and wide-ranging interactions with Russia that involve various actors in all three states and in Russia too. As is well known, a residual trepidation is ingrained which means that relations with Russia are often portrayed in a negative way. Yet many actors and interest groups in the economic, political and cultural domains maintain close relations with Russian partners and favour cordial political relations with the Russian state. Since relations with Russia are complex and also such an emotive and divisive topic, distinct 'national perspectives' are difficult if not impossible to ascertain. The aim of this chapter is to shed some light on the role that Russia currently plays in the Czech Republic, Hungary and Slovakia by analyzing the most important components of present-day multifaceted bilateral

170 *Martin Dangerfield*

relations. This should provide a framework for revealing which aspects of EU multilateral relations with Russia are likely to be most relevant for the three states and to what extent the various aspects of bilateral relations with Russia have been 'Europeanized' as a result of the EU pre-accession process and EU membership itself. The first section of the chapter focuses on why the Visegrad 4 (V4) are a specific CEE sub-group in relations with Russia. The second section summarizes the main developments in relations between Russia and the three smaller states from the end of communism until EU entry. The third section focuses on contemporary bilateral relations and is arranged thematically according to key aspects of relations with Russia, including: perceptions of Russia as a threat: energy security; the nuclear power industry; economic and business relations; foreign policy and Russia; visas; attitudes of political parties.

Visegrad states and Russia – a distinctive group

The roots of the V4's specific relationship with Russia go back to Soviet times. Despite different pre-1945 experiences with Russia, the notion of a shared identity within the Soviet bloc was captured in the narrative of *central Europe* 'revived by Czech, Hungarian and Polish writers such as Milan Kundera, György Konrad and Czeslaw Mŕlosz as a space occupied by the three nations that represented an intellectual and political alternative to the Soviet dominated "Eastern Europe"' (Garton Ash 2006: 112). As well as historical 'memories' recounted to construct this image, concrete experiences undoubtedly set 'central Europe' apart from other Soviet bloc states. First, each underwent open revolts against the communist regime and, by extension, against Soviet domination. Second, the establishment and consolidation of a radical economic reform agenda was an important consequence of this process of attempted breakaway from traditional Soviet-type state socialism. This was most openly and consistently present in Hungary where market socialism was introduced in 1968 and continued thereafter. Czechoslovakia's radical economic reform programme was mothballed in 1968 due to spill-over into political reform and rejection of Marxism-Leninism itself. In Poland reform was perpetually on the agenda but only implemented in a partial and fragmented way. Nevertheless, in all three countries a highly critical perspective on orthodox central planning and a preference for market-type reform became ingrained in pockets of the elite and intelligentsia. Despite the different trajectories of reform socialism, the key point is that all three attempted to deviate from the rigid Soviet orthodoxy whereas Romania, Bulgaria and the German Democratic Republic (GDR) did not.

These shared experiences helped to give Czechoslovakia, Hungary and Poland a head start in post-communist transformation. As Brzeziński (1992: 24) wrote: 'in the foreseeable future only three formerly communist countries – Hungary, Poland and Czechoslovakia – enjoy any likelihood of a successful transition to a market-based democracy'. They also gained a privileged trajectory in the Euro–Atlantic integration process which, in combination with the need to re-configure relations with the USSR, bound them into an exclusive alliance for regional co-operation. Personal relationships formed during the communist period were crucial. As one former Polish diplomat recalled, Polish, Czechoslovak and Hungarian dissidents had access to each others' publications and:

> met each other despite repression from the communist authorities ... (t)he new democratic authorities of our three countries consisted of people who either knew each other personally from their opposition activities during communism, or who at least had heard of each other. The Visegrad Triangle thus came to life in a very natural way.
>
> (Ananicz 2006: 28)

The Visegrad alliance was almost singularly focused on the push to join the EU and NATO with the USSR/Russia factor a key driver of this co-operation. It played an important role in securing the departure of Soviet troops, expediting the elimination of the Warsaw Pact and Council for Mutual Economic Assistance (CMEA), preventing the establishment of successor organizations and setting the VG on the path to Euro–Atlantic integration.

Early VG co-operation was in no small measure driven by the perceived need for a security guarantee vis-à-vis the USSR/Russia. This occurred, however, in the very specific historic juncture of the fall of communism and it was inevitable that the VG could not remain a player in 'high' politics. Nevertheless, common longer-term challenges might have been a basis for continued co-operation vis-à-vis Russia but other factors put the VG into cold storage anyway. Yet even after it reconvened in 1998 there was virtually no co-operation agenda vis-à-vis Russia and this 'non-policy' continues today (see Dangerfield 2011). The lack of any multilateral VG approach, either directly or as 'bloc' inputs to EU policy-making, draws attention to preferences for bilateral dealings with Russia. Leonard and Popescu's (2007) influential study of EU-Russia relations placed Poland and the Czech Republic into the broadly Russia-hostile camp and Hungary and Slovakia into the 'Russia-friendly' category. These classifications were echoed in 2010 'Wikileak' revelations (Rettman 2010). Whatever the merits of these various interpretations of attitudes to Russia, it is obvious that Poland is definitely in a different category. Compared to the other three states, Poland's relations with Russia:

> are burdened so much historically that their normalisation will always be incomplete. Issues from the past are being transferred into the present time causing a great deficit of trust in Russia. This in turn is reflected in every aspect of today's relations, not only political but also economic.
>
> (Samson 2010: 102)

We can now move to a detailed study of the Czech Republic, Hungary and Slovakia and Russia, beginning with the rather long period of transition in

172 *Martin Dangerfield*

bilateral relations which followed the end of communism and lasted until EU accession.

Relations with Russia during the EU pre-accession period

The initial 'divorce process', from early 1990 until the end of 1991, entailed a drastic adjustment of bilateral economic and political ties according to the new post-Cold War reality. Relations with Russia (also a newly independent state) developed in conditions fundamentally different from, but nevertheless involving a substantial legacy of, the Soviet era. Common key challenges of this transition period included: the need to secure stable energy supplies in the context of total supply dependency on Russia; sign bilateral agreements covering many areas; tackle large trade imbalances; deal with Russia's persistent efforts to block their NATO accession; resolve Soviet-era 'transferable rouble' debts that Russia inherited, with $1.6 billion owed to Slovakia, $1.7 billion to Hungary and $3.7 billion to the Czech Republic (Pelczyńska-Nalęcz *et al.* 2003). In addition, the states had to balance attention to Russia with the primary and massively complicated task of securing EU accession, which of course meant adjusting many elements of relations with Russia.

Since VG co-operation proved neither adaptable nor resilient enough to take on the common elements of the agenda with Russia, the three states pursued separate approaches and experienced distinct patterns in the evolution of their relations with Russia. Three key interrelated influences on the nature of bilateral relations were at work. First, the degree of commitment to the 'return to Europe' and the extent to which this was backed up by the necessary internal reforms. Second, the political background and ideologies of the party in power caused some volatility of political relations with Russia, which in turn affected the speed and ease with which the transition agenda was tackled. Third, the broad thrust of Russian foreign policy towards the three which was based on strong opposition to the plans to admit them to NATO.

After the 'velvet divorce' Czech and Slovak relations with Russia moved in opposite directions. Czech pre-occupation with NATO and EU membership coupled with a favourable geopolitical position – it no longer bordered any ex-Soviet states – meant that foreign policy towards Russia was characterized by disinterest and lack of engagement: 'Russia disappeared from the cognitive map of both the Czech political elite and the population at large' (Kratochvíl and Kuchyňková 2009: 63). Residual fear of Russia remained, however, with opposition to NATO enlargement taken as evidence of Russian ambitions to retain significant influence in central Europe. Otherwise, over this period, which endured until 1999, Czech interest was focused on economic issues. Slovakia, by contrast, became increasingly disenfranchised from Euro–Atlantic integration due to the authoritarian tendencies of the Mečiar government which:

> considered relations with Russia as an alternative foreign-policy strategy for the country ... (in) this scenario Russia was expected to provide

Czech Republic, Hungary and Slovakia 173

security guarantees to Slovakia's neutrality as well as to offer a special economic status and foreign trade regime as a sort of compensation for Slovakia's keeping out of NATO and the EU.

(Duleba 2009: 8)

Slovak and Czech relations with Russia converged after Mikuláš Dzurinda replaced Mečiar in September 1998. Slovakia's renewed commitment to EU and NATO accession did not entail an unfriendly tone in political relations with Russia. Rather, the objective was 'to have "correct", "balanced", "partner-like" and "mutually advantageous" relations with Russia ... (and) that Russia remains an important economic partner for Slovakia, particularly with regards to imports of strategic energy resources' (Duleba 2009: 16). Czech relations with Russia seemed to ease after confirmation (in 1997) that NATO enlargement would go ahead. Despite ensuing Russian aloofness, Czech attitudes towards Russia became noticeably more positive after the change of government in mid-2008. Votápek noted that 'when the minority Social Democratic cabinet took office, it declared the development of relations with Russia as one of its foreign policy priorities'(Votápek 2003: 97).

A new phase of 'warmer relations' between Russia and both the Czech Republic and Slovakia began in earnest after 2000 and President Putin's 'reset' of Russian foreign policy. The number of official visits increased markedly and political dialogue intensified. Presidential visits to Russia were symbolic of new starts in bilateral relations. Rudolph Schuster undertook the first visit of a Slovak head of state to Russia in November 2001 (Duleba 2009: 17). Given his predecessor's refusal to deal with Moscow, Czech President Vačlav Klaus's visit in March 2003 was seen as the 'ultimate reconciliation'. There was pragmatism and strong commitment on both sides towards finally resolving Soviet-era debt and matters connected to impending EU accession. Thus by the time of EU accession no serious political or economic issues hampered the progressively improving bilateral relations of either Slovakia or the Czech Republic with Russia.

Póti (2003) identifies four main phases in Hungary–Russia relations after 1990. Following the 'divorce' phase, 'peaceful co-existence' characterized the 1992–4 period. Various problematic issues were largely settled (including, for example, Russian condemnation of the 1956 Soviet invasion and agreement on settling Soviet-era financial debt). Nonetheless, 'there was a surviving element of distrust and fear of instability (on the Hungarian side) and growing opposition (on the issue of NATO enlargement) on the Russian side' (Póti 2003: 79). After 1994 the left-leaning government of Gyula Horn was much more accommodating to Russia. During this period of 'normality' high level political contact became more regular, Hungarian interest in the Russian market more pronounced and there was dialogue about Hungary's intention to join NATO. Relations deteriorated after the centre-right Fidesz/MDF government led by Viktor Orbán took office in 1998. Póti (2003: 83) remarked that this government's attitude to Russia 'was characterised by the perception

174　*Martin Dangerfield*

of a kind of cultural supremacy, a combined anti-communism/Russianism that still associated Moscow with the past, the fear of Russia's imperial resurgence, its lack of diplomatic style and the fashionable trend of neglecting Russia'. This period of 'distancing' culminated in Russia's decision to cancel Prime Minister Kasyanov's official visit in early 2001. The Hungarian Socialist Party (MSZP), in its longstanding partnership with the Alliance of Free Democrats–Hungarian Liberal Party (SZDSZ) won the 2002 elections. The new government led by Péter Medgyesi reversed course and sought to 'reset' relations with Russia, especially for trading reasons. Thus, in the context of Putin's changed approach to central Europe noted above, Hungary entered the EU in another phase of renewed engagement with Russia, favouring regular top-level political contact and regarding Russia as a strategic partner for trade and energy security.

Contemporary relations with Russia

Russia as a (traditional) security threat?

The communist past shapes perceptions of Russia, usually in a negative way. Soviet domination is held responsible for damage (economic, social, environmental) done during the communist era and of course Soviet troops invaded both Hungary and Czechoslovakia. Because of this legacy of the past, and due to some key very recent events such as threats to target nuclear weapons at CEE states in response to the proposed Ballistic Missile Defence (BMD) system, '(f)ear of Russia did not fully disappear in CEE after NATO enlargement' (Samson 2010: 42). This discourse is, however, obviously less influential when it comes to day-to day dealing with Russia and does not seem to fatally impede other close relationships at the state and sub-state level. Vital economic and energy considerations are certainly not sacrificed. Also, citizens in the three countries tend to feel safe from external threats and much more concerned about unemployment and living standards. As public interest tends to be low, foreign and security policy issues are largely neglected by the political class because they are not key election issues (Gyárfášová and Šťastný 2004; Meszerics 2004).

While Slovak-Russian and Hungarian-Russian relations have tended to be free of any serious security-related complications, after 2007 the proposed location of the radar component of the USA's Missile Defence System (MDS) weighed heavily on Czech–Russia political relations. Spill-over into debates about energy dependence and economic ties has occurred, with 'increased sensitivity of the Czech government towards Russian companies trying to buy strategic Czech firms, such as those dealing with transport (e.g. Czech Airlines–ČSA) ... or those involved in the imports and processing of raw materials (e.g. Transgas)' (Kratochvíl 2010: 197–98). The profile of Czech–Russian relations was also raised because of the serious Ukraine–Russia energy dispute that occurred in the first few days of the Czech EU Presidency and the expulsion of two Russian diplomats for alleged espionage in August 2009 and Russia's reciprocal moves. At the same time, the majority of Czech citizens opposed the BMD, showing that worries of external threats were not high on the population's priorities either. Czech business and economic relations also continued to develop positively and experienced a downturn in 2009 not because of the impact of official political tensions but rather as a consequence of the 2008 financial crisis. In sum, a discourse of Russia as a 'conventional' security threat persists, though it is clearly not the decisive influence on bilateral relations and may be even less important than threats to energy security and dangers of Russian acquisition of economic assets.

Energy security

Energy supply and security remains a major aspect of Czech, Hungarian and Slovak relations with Russia. Deep integration of the energy sector had been among the few notable successes of socialist economic integration and not so easy to undo as other communist-era linkages. The physical infrastructure for oil and gas supply and transit is still very much operational and vital today as Russia remains the principal supplier of oil and natural gas. The biggest energy security questions are focused on gas. Dependency on Russia is high in all three cases but does vary. In 2009, Russia provided 83 per cent of Hungary's total gas imports and 70 per cent of total gas consumption. The amounts were 94.5 per cent and 100 per cent respectively for Slovakia, and 69 per cent and 81 per cent for the Czech Republic. Hungary and Slovakia are supplied primarily by pipelines coming through Ukraine from Russia. Around 30 per cent of Czech gas imports come from Norway via the Olbernhauborder transfer station.[1] Supply contracts are negotiated by the main gas transmission system operators in each country – RWE Transgas Net in the Czech Republic, FGSZ Ltd in Hungary and Slovensky Plynarensky Priemysel, a.s. in Slovakia – all of which work on the basis of long term deals with Gazexport.

Gas supply became an increasingly 'hot topic' after Russia's disputes with Ukraine disrupted supplies, first in 2007 and again in 2009. The 2009 crisis, which occurred at the coldest time of year and caused public anxiety about energy security to increase considerably, shifted diversification of gas supply to the forefront of the energy policy agenda (see Nosko and Lang 2010). Shortly after the 2009 crisis the Czech Republic and Slovakia both declared their official support for the Nabucco gas pipeline project backed by the EU (see Topolánek 2009; Duleba 2009). Hungary of course was already an established proponent of Nabucco. Diversification is, however, not a short term game due to infrastructure issues and also because 'pipeline politics' are rather complex. Commercial interests of the main energy companies play a key role. Also, dependency on Russian gas coming through Ukraine may be construed as the issue rather than dependency on Russian gas per se. Hence Hungary's concomitant support for and involvement in Russia's South Stream pipeline and former Hungarian Prime Minister Gyurcsány's 2009 statement

176 *Martin Dangerfield*

that 'Hungary is interested in having as many pipelines as possible' (Euractiv 2009). In April 2012, Hungarian energy and oil company MOL announced its withdrawal from the Nabucco project. Despite speculation that this reflected Hungary's stand-off with the EU over various controversial political reforms, Orbán stated that Hungary was switching allegiance to Russia's South Stream alternative for 'very simple economic reasons' (Chazan 2012). Moreover, the Nabucco project has been flagging for some time and other major stakeholders had already expressed major doubts, including RWE of Germany (Hromadko, Hinkel and Torello 2012). Either way, diversification strategies are also fluid, with economic and political motivations not always easy to disentangle.

Nuclear power (civilian)

Nuclear electricity generation is another important, albeit lower profile, aspect of energy relations with Russia. Six reactors operate in the Czech Republic and four each in Hungary and Slovakia (Nuclear Energy Agency 2010a, 2010b, 2010c) and account for 33 per cent of domestic electricity supply in the Czech Republic and Hungary and over half – 55 per cent – in Slovakia. Nuclear energy is part of the socialist legacy. Reactors are Soviet-era, commissioned and constructed by Soviet enterprises. These days Russian nuclear energy giant Rosatom is the key partner. Its subsidiary TVEL is the exclusive supplier of nuclear fuel for the Czech Republic, Hungary and Slovakia and Russia has also in the past received spent fuel for processing on its territory. Rosatom also plays a key role in the supply of spare parts for reactors and maintenance schedules and has also been involved in certain crisis operations. In Hungary, for example, following a serious incident in April 2003 involving water contamination from the fuel rod cleaning system, TVEL specialists carried out the decontamination work with their Hungarian counterparts. As with pipeline systems, changes to this part of the energy infrastructure cannot be made except in the longer term and would be very expensive. In any case there seems to be a strong commitment to continue with current arrangements and even possibly expand Russian involvement. In 2010, TVEL replaced Westinghouse as supplier of fuel for the Czech Temelin plant until 2020. Also during 2011 Russia and Hungary held talks on Russian companies' involvement in the planned modernization of Hungary's PAKS nuclear facility. In 2009 Russia and Slovakia signed a long term deal in nuclear power engineering that involved, amongst other things, Slovakia's 'support for the participation of Russian companies in modernizing Slovakia's reactors' (RiaNovosti 2009). Rosatom subsidiary Atomstroyexport is in the consortium currently bidding to build two new reactors at the Czech Temelin plant and has strong internal support. It remains to be seen how the fear of a significant Russian presence within strategic sectors will affect the future development of nuclear power capacity. It seems clear, however, that the nuclear energy partnership is an important, stable and trouble-free (i.e. has not suffered from any equivalent of the gas crises) dimension of bilateral relations with Russia.

Business and trade relations

Economic and trade links are significant and sensitive dimensions of relations with Russia. During the 'transition' period exports of the three countries to Russia stagnated or shrank. In 1993 Czech, Hungarian and Slovak exports to Russia amounted to $593, $1,133 and $256 million respectively. By 2003 the corresponding values were $584, $653 and $267 million.[2] Since EU accession, however, exports have grown rapidly. Between 2004 and 2010 Czech exports increased by 347 per cent, Hungarian by 350 per cent and Slovak by 713 per cent (see Table 11.1).

Imports from Russia are dominated by raw materials and oil and gas, which account for 84 per cent of the imports of the Czech Republic and 90 per cent of those of Slovakia and Hungary respectively. Czech exports to Russia are in a wide range of manufactured industrial goods and mainly machinery and transport equipment (especially cars), chemicals, food products and construction materials. Slovakia's main export lines to Russia are machinery and transport equipment (especially cars), chemical and allied products, other industrial goods and fabrics. Hungary's important exports to Russia are machinery and transport equipment, pharmaceuticals, chemical and allied products and foodstuffs.

Table 11.1 Czech, Hungarian and Slovak trade with Russia 2004–10 (€ million)

	2004	2005	2006	2007	2008	2009	2010	Index 2004/10
Czech Exports	770	1132	1504	2081	2911	1877	2672	347
Czech mports	2184	3392	4224	3930	5987	3721	4885	224
Czech Balance	(1414)	(2260)	(2720)	(1849)	(3076)	(1844)	(2213)	
Hungary Exports	738	943	1617	2229	2666	2124	2583	350
Hungary Imports	2875	3962	5118	4793	6651	4091	5196	180
Hungary Balance	(2137)	(3019)	(3501)	(2564)	(3985)	(1967)	(2613)	
Slovakia Exports	271	398	549	959	1811	1416	1933	713
Slovakia Imports	2207	2980	4029	4017	5258	3473	4679	212
Slovakia Balance	(1936)	(2582)	(3480)	(3058)	(3447)	(2057)	(2746)	

Source: Eurostat.

178 *Martin Dangerfield*

Since EU accession the interplay between economic and political relations with Russia has become more pronounced, in the sense that pragmatism towards Russia seems increasingly driven by economic interests. Even in the case of the Czech Republic, where some degree of political tension with Russia has been relatively persistent over recent years, a largely 'business as usual' approach in the economic and business sphere seems to have been sustained. An important role in this has been played by the Czech Ministry of Industry and Trade, whose influence on Czech relations with Russia has grown, as Kratochvíl (2010: 206) informs us 'in direct proportion with the increasing importance of Czech–Russian trade relations'. Representatives of the Hungarian Ministry of Development also seemed to take on this mantle during the troubled early phase of the Fidesz government that came to power in 2010 (Politics.Hu 2010).

In addition to the relevant ministries, other important bilateral mechanisms support trade and economic co-operation. Various intergovernmental and other bodies bring together leading politicians, civil servants, regional actors and industrialists for extended meetings that can cover specific contracts and map out medium and long-term economic co-operation.[3] The March 2011 meeting of the Hungarian–Russian Intergovernmental Committee for Economic Co-operation that took place in Moscow discussed 'cooperation opportunities in the field of energy, agriculture, finances and transport' and signed a 'joint declaration of modernisation and partnership' that 'outlines the long-term cooperation opportunities for business organizations, and creates a framework for cooperation between the two governments in modernisation, research and development' (Government of Hungary 2011). The October 2010 Moscow meeting of the Czech–Russian Intergovernmental Commission for Economic, Industrial and Scientific Co-operation involved two days of bilateral talks and expressed 'support for important Czech–Russian projects or the utilisation of the possibilities offered by the EU–RF initiative Partnership for Modernization and Co-operation' (Vlček 2010). In a press statement during his 2009 visit to Bratislava, Vladimir Putin remarked that the Slovak–Russian Intergovernmental Commission on Co-operation in the Economy, Science and Technology had an important role in 'expanding business connections, investment partnerships, and co-operation in high-technology industries' (Government of the Russian Federation, 2009).

Foreign policy and Russia

EU membership and the accession process have exposed foreign policies to 'Europeanizing' influences that have had implications for relations with Russia. Like most CEE states, the Czech Republic, Hungary and Slovakia have declared the 'shared neighbourhood' their specialist area of EU external relations. Eastern Partnership (EaP) countries have become designated priorities for foreign and development aid policy, entailing both political support for specific countries' EU integration aspirations and provision of aid and assistance to reform and transformation processes. Country priorities are as

Czech Republic, Hungary and Slovakia 179

follows. Czech Republic: Ukraine, Georgia, Moldova and Belarus; Hungary: Ukraine and Moldova; Slovakia: Ukraine, Moldova and Belarus. The Czech Republic also made the launch of the EaP a centrepiece of its EU Presidency. The VG has also been an important multilateral vehicle for political and practical support. The three states (along with Poland) have consistently used their VG presidencies to champion key EU initiatives such as the EaP and, through the various programmes of the International Visegrad Fund (IVF), have been directly supporting democratization and reform processes in EaP countries (see Dangerfield 2009). While support for the EU (and NATO) membership aspirations of certain EaP countries is clearly a 'point of discord' in relations with Russia, this line of foreign policy (which certainly has not been couched in terms of any kind of anti-Russia strategy) does not seem to have spilt over into the key domains of bilateral relations. Indeed, certain authors have ascribed a degree of a 'Russia-first' principle to the three in that 'the smaller Visegrad countries wish to maintain good relations with Russia, and sometimes they are even willing to sacrifice their ties with other East European countries' (Kratochvíl 2007: 193). Moreover, whereas Poland has had a longstanding preoccupation with Eastern Europe, Czech, Hungarian and Slovak foreign policies only really developed this focus in earnest after 2004. This suggests that pragmatic concerns have played an important role in the choice of post-accession priorities (see Rácz 2011; Weiss 2011; Najšlova 2011).[4]

The Czech Republic is in a somewhat different category in that its relations with Russia do have some clear normative underpinnings because of the way the Europeanization of its foreign policy has reinforced a pre-existing 'values-based' foreign policy identity. Drulák (2009: 374) refers to the latter as an ideology of 'moral universalism' that argues 'for the expansion of democracy and human rights, which should be universally promoted by the actions of governments and international institutions'. This is a key context of critical rhetoric that emanates from certain Czech actors, not only in response to deeds or words that concern the Czech Republic but also towards Russia's broader foreign policy activities and internal affairs. Czech Foreign Minister Karel Schwarzenberg clearly belongs to the 'moral universalist' camp and has been one of the most strident critics of Russia. For example, Russia took a dim view of his suggestion, in April 2009, that Belarus's invitation to the Prague summit to launch the EaP could be rescinded if it chose to recognize South Ossetia and Abkhazia (Kratochvíl 2010: 202). This cannot be said to be a definitive and consistent Czech line on Russia, however, as other key actors have clear pro-Russia credentials, such as President Klaus (see below). Furthermore, the Czech Republic as well as Hungary and Slovakia do not have a conceptual/ideological approach to Russia that provides a basis for a clear foreign policy programme. Party divisions, tensions between economic interests and security concerns and alternative perspectives of various actors mean that all three countries suffer from co-ordination problems when it comes to prospects for a consistent and widely accepted foreign policy towards Russia. At the same time there are advantages in that this can have

180   *Martin Dangerfield*

the effect of keeping foreign policy towards Russia on a stable and predictable path, even when parties prone to anti-Russia rhetoric come to power.

Visas

Visa liberalization has been a regular topic of discussion at EU–Russia summits since 2003, reflecting the fact that it is one of the most important issues on the agenda but also one in which progress is slow. Since Schengen entry the three have been bound by the common rules for visa issuance and this is obviously an issue in which all three states have a particularly strong interest. They receive high, and growing, numbers of Russian visitors, especially for tourism and calls to push for more ease of entry come from certain stakeholders. Hungary's current official position is certainly in favour of visa liberalization (see Rácz 2012) while the Czech Republic tends to stress that it is bound by overall EU/Schengen regulations. Though the 2012–16 Direction–Social Democracy (SMER) government programme mentions only the intention to increase the priority given to relations with Russia, Slovak President Ivan Gašparovič, at least, has stated that 'his country fully supports removing legislative barriers in the visa regime between Russia and the European Union'(v/lex 2011). At the same time, the situation in the three reflects that of most EU member states in that preferences differ internally. Foreign ministries and those actors interested in tourism and economic and trade cooperation tend to favour a rapid move towards a visa-free regime while interior ministries and law enforcement bodies favour a slower and more rigorous approach (see Popescu 2011).

Internal divisions over Russia – political parties

Bilateral relations with Russia have developed against the backdrop of different party perspectives, and these definitely matter. During the EU pre-accession period changes in government marked turning points in the official tone of relations with Russia, willingness to engage in closer political contacts and attitudes to the importance of further developing economic and business relations. Though a key difference today seems to be that critical references to Russia are used more for domestic political purposes, these divisions clearly persist. As Kratochvíl (2010: 196) explains:

> political debate about Russia and Czech–Russian relations is characterised by a strong political polarisation ... Russia is often seen [by the Right] as a potentially dangerous and rather unstable country that has to be contained. Trade with Russia is often seen as an unfortunate necessity ... On the other hand the left sees Russia in an oddly optimistic way. It sees Russia as a great opportunity and as a partner in dialogue. No fear of the energy and economic dependence is present in this type of discourse.

As for Hungary and Slovakia, an official VG source confirms that perceptions of relations with Russia 'vary across the political spectrum and political parties' (Visegrad.Info 2010: 4). Parties in the anti-Russia or Russia-cautious camp tend to be centre-right and more committed to Atlanticism while the parties of the left/centre-left are willing to give Russia a higher priority in foreign policy and are less reserved about cultivating closer relations with Russia (usually emphasizing the importance of Russia as an economic partner). Parties that belong to the anti-Russia/Russia-cautious camp include Fidesz in Hungary, the Civic Democratic Party (ODS) in the Czech Republic and the Slovak Democratic and Christian Union-Democratic Party (SDKU-DS) in Slovakia. Those that fall into the pro-Russia camp include the Czech Social Democratic Party (ČSSD), the Hungarian Socialist Party (MSZP) and SMER in Slovakia.

Statements by officials of the various parties illustrate differing perspectives on Russia. The ODS website reveals its negativity towards Russia and also shows how the Russia issue is used to taint the main rival parties: 'It goes without saying that for the ODS any attempts of Russia to acquire larger influence in former countries of the Soviet bloc, including the Czech Republic, and moreover with help of the ČSSD and KSČM are unacceptable' (Civic Democratic Party 2011). Though the ČSSD would dispute that sentiment, its alternative attitude to Russia is plain to see, especially for the economic aspect of bilateral relations. In 2010 former (ČSSD) Prime Minister Jiří Paroubek made this clear when he said that 'under a left-leaning government, officials "would be looking for ways to improve relations, namely of a business nature, with large neighbours to the East, especially Russia"' (Carney and Rousek 2010).

A meeting between Vladimir Putin and Ferenc Gyurcsány, in which the former lauded the positive development of bilateral relations, highlighted contrasting attitudes in the rhetoric of Hungarian parties. Whereas Gyurcsány reported that 'the two countries had covered a lot of ground in order to elevate bilateral relations to the current high level' (Politics.Hu 2009), Fidesz were highly critical of the talks. One of their foreign affairs experts, Zsolt Németh, said that 'Gyurcsany was "extremely irresponsible" and that he was trying to improve the positions of his "Socialist clientele" utilising "Russian assistance"' (Politics.Hu 2009). Slovakia has been labelled (Duleba 2009) a 'quasi-Russophile' country and party variations are somewhat milder in that no major party could be classed as anti-Russia. Both major parties, for example, support close economic ties with Russia, but the centre left tends to be somewhat more accommodating and supportive of Russia's security and foreign policy concerns. Hence in October 2009 'Slovak prime minister Fico pinpointed that as long as he acts in the capacity of prime minister, the United States will not be allowed to deploy the anti-missile system in Slovakia' (Visegrad.Info 2010: 4).

The notion of distinct national perspectives on Russia becomes even more problematic when one takes into account the fact that different parties and governments are not always consistent in attitudes and rhetoric towards

182   *Martin Dangerfield*

Russia. During Medvedev's official visit to Prague in December 2011 Foreign Minister Schwarzenberg was openly critical of the Russian parliamentary elections. President Klaus, on the other hand, was reprimanded by some political commentators 'for his refusal to comment on the situation surrounding Russia's recent elections. Mr Klaus summed up the question marks over the election process and police crackdown on anti-establishment demonstrators as Russia's internal issue' (Radio Prague 2011). In 2008, the Topolánek-led ODS government and the President gave different assessments of the Russia–Georgia crisis, with Klaus taking Russia's side. Around the same time, Duleba (2009: 21) noticed similar discrepancies in the positions of the Slovak Prime Minister, Robert Fico and the Slovak Minister of Foreign Affairs, Ján Kubiš, on the deployment of the BMD system and the causes of the Russia–Georgia conflict. Finally, attitudes towards Russia can depend on whether a party is in opposition or in government. Viktor Orbán's current enthusiasm for Hungarian participation in the South Stream gas pipeline is somewhat at odds with comments made in 2008 when he accused Gyurcsány of 'treason' for signing the agreement on Hungary's participation. Rácz (2012) also notes that the Orbán government refrained from any criticism of the 2011 Russian parliamentary elections, no doubt mindful of the serious effects provocative rhetoric can have on Russia's willingness to do business. After the Orbán government took office in April 2010 various meetings of important bilateral economic co-operation committees were cancelled by the Russian side and Orbán's first meeting with Putin in November 2010 was unproductive with 'the Kremlin's mistrust and Hungary's lack of interesting assets' having had a very negative impact on the talks (Ugrosdy 2011).

Conclusions

EU accession marked the end of a distinct, and rather long, transition phase in Czech, Hungarian and Slovak relations with Russia. This was partially because the desire to deeply transform the nature of relations with Russia was a fundamental reason why EU (and (NATO) membership was so coveted. EU accession meant of course that important policies, including visa and trade arrangements, were automatically elevated from the bilateral to multilateral level. Foreign policy towards Russia has been a clear case of some 'Europeanization'. The three chose to focus on the countries of the 'shared neighbourhood' and declared themselves to be leading players in the attempt to steer the strategic orientation of EaP countries in the direction of the EU. On the other hand the discourse of Russia as a 'traditional' security threat endures and underpins the on-going commitment to NATO as the primary defence alliance and questionable degree of commitment to the EU's Common Security and Defence Policy.

There are some other clear continuities with the pre-accession period including energy dependency (and Russia's role in the nuclear power industry) and longstanding interest in the Russian market. Economic relations have become increasingly significant with exports to Russia having grown phenomenally since 2004 in all three cases. Interestingly, multilateralization of trade arrangements has actually coincided with an increased emphasis on bilateral instruments for trade promotion and economic co-operation, especially the important intergovernmental commissions with Russia. It has also meant that trade and industry ministries have become increasingly important and influential actors in bilateral relations. Energy issues have also of course been very prominent in recent years and along with economic relations represent the 'Janus' face of relations with Russia that underpins simultaneous discourses of Russia as both threat and opportunity. This links to another clear element of continuity – differing perspectives among and within the main political parties. While these clearly influenced the course of actual bilateral relations during the 1990–2004 period, this has seemed less evident since EU accession. The tone of political relations with Russia can be affected by the political complexion of the government in office but in recent years the ability to separate political issues from economic and energy interests and continue a 'business as usual' approach seems to be a feature of contemporary relations. Many aspects of Czech dealings with Russia, particularly in the critical economic and energy fields, have continued apparently undisturbed by problems at the political level. Also, when parties prone to anti-Russia rhetoric get into power, pragmatism can rapidly prevail. When entering office in 2010 the government of Victor Orbán seemed to instantly jettison its anti-Russia credentials.

Whilst tendencies towards growing pragmatism in relations with Russia have become increasingly evident since EU accession, attitudes to Russia still tend to be rather ambiguous and difficult to capture in terms of 'national perspectives' precisely because, as in the case of most of the ex-socialist bloc countries, relations are dense, complex and multifaceted and key actors involved often have contrasting perspectives and can often lack consistency. All this would suggest the impact of member states' bilateral relations on multilateralism in the EU (or in NATO) is probably best not considered in terms of a global set of relations with Russia but rather in terms of how the bilateral relations of the three would affect the prospects for effective EU multilateralism according to differentiated elements of EU–Russia relations such as trade, differentiated aspects of energy security, EU and NATO expansion, visa policy, the future of the shared neighbourhood and so on. It is also necessary to recognize that differing internal perspectives – on visa liberalization for example – mean that national positions on even the disaggregated dimensions of EU relations with Russia are not always apparent.

Notes

1 Gas statistics are taken from the Energy Delta Institute (EDI) database. Available at www.energydelta.org/mainmenu/edi-intelligence-2/our-services/Country-gas-profiles

184 *Martin Dangerfield*

2 Data provided by the National Statistical Offices of the Czech Republic, Hungary and Slovakia.
3 In 2010 the Russian government showed its disdain for the new Orban government by cancelling various scheduled meetings of the Hungarian–Russian Intergovernmental Committee for Economic Co-operation, thus suggesting at least that these are deemed to be important bodies.
4 Hungary tends to ascribe a far higher priority to the West Balkans, as does Slovakia, given that a far higher proportion of development assistance goes to West Balkan countries (especially Serbia) than to EaP states.

References

Ananicz, A. (2006) 'From the Anti-Communist Underground to NATO and the EU', in A. Jagodziński (ed.) *The Visegrad Group – A Central European Constellation.* Bratislava: International Visegrad Fund, 28–30.

Bozhilova, D. and Hashimoto, T. (2010) 'EU–Russia Energy Negotiations: A Choice Between Rational Self-interest and Collective Action', *European Security,* 19: 627–42.

Brzeziński, Z. (1992) 'The West Adrift: Vision in Search of a Strategy', reproduced in A.Jagodziński (ed.) *The Visegrad group – A Central European Constellation.* Bratislava: International Visegrad Fund, 24–25.

Carney, S. and Rousek, L. (2010) 'Czechs Seek Nuclear-Energy Partner', *Wall Street Journal.* 21 September 2010, available at http://online.wsj.com/article/SB1000142405 2748704394704575496011355102980.html (accessed 30 April 2010).

Chazan, G. (2012) 'MOL to drop share in Nabucco pipeline', *Financial Times.* 26 April, available at www.ft.com/cms/s/0/bb333a08–8fbb-11e1-beaa-00144feab49a. html#axzz1tcZG13aw (accessed 30 April 2012).

Civic Democratic Party (2011) webpages. Available at web.ods.cz/docs/dokumenty/ CR-in-Europe-and-in-the-World.pdf

Dangerfield, M. (2009) 'The Contribution of the Visegrad Group to the European Union's 'Eastern' Policy: Rhetoric or Reality?', *Europe-Asia Studies,* 61: 1735–55.

——(2011) 'Visegrad group Cooperation and Russia'. Paper presented at EUSA Twelfth Biennial Conference, Boston, 3–5 March 2011, available at http://euce.org/ eusa/2011/papers/9j_dangerfield.pdf

Drulák, P. (2009) 'Czech Foreign Policy: Ideologies, Prejudices and Co-ordination', in M. Kořan (ed.) *Czech Foreign Policy in 2007–2009: An Analysis.* Prague: Institute of International Relations, 371–84.

Duleba, A. (2009) 'Slovakia's Relations with Russia and Eastern Neighbours'. Available at www.fakprojekt.hu/docs/04-Duleba.pdf (accessed 9 December 2011).

Energy Delta Institute (2012) *Country Gas Profiles.* Available at www.energydelta.org/ mainmenu/edi-intelligence-2/our-services/Country-gas-profiles (accessed 10 January 2012).

EurActiv (2009) 'Russia wins Hungary's support for South Stream pipeline'. 11 March, available at www.euractiv.com/energy/russia-wins-hungary-supportsouth-stream-pipeline/article-180126 (accessed 11 May 2012).

Garton Ash, T. (2006) 'The Puzzle of Central Europe', in A. Jagodziński (ed.) *The Visegrad Group – A Central European Constellation.* Bratislava: International Visegrad Fund, 112–14.

Government of Hungary (2011) 'Hungarian-Russian Negotiations Concluded by Signature of Modernisation Declaration'. 22 March, available at www.kormany.hu/en/

Czech Republic, Hungary and Slovakia 185

ministry-of-national-development/news/hungarian-russian-negotiations-concluded-b
y-signature-of-modernisation-declaration (accessed 11 May 2012).

Government of the Russian Federation (2009) 'Press Conference'. 10 November, available at http://premier.gov.ru/eng/events/pressconferences/8257/ (accessed 11 May 2012).

Gyárfášová, O. and Šťastný, M. (2004) 'Priority and Sources of Security Policies – Slovakia', in T. Valášek and O. Gyárfášová (eds) *'Easternisation' of Europe's Security Policy*. Bratislava: Institute for Public Affairs, 9–21.

Hromadko, J., Hinkel, K. and Torello, A. (2012) 'RWE may reconsider Nabucco Pipeline', *Wall Street Journal*. 18 January, available at http://online.wsj.com/article/SB10001424052970204468004577166273792137122.html (accessed 10 May 2012).

Kratochvíl, P. (2007) 'The New EU Members and the ENP: Different Agendas, Different Strategies', *Intereconomics – Review of European Economic Policy*, 4:2 191–96.

——(2010) 'Russia in the Czech Foreign Policy', in M. Kořan (ed.) *Czech Foreign Policy in 2007–2009: An Analysis*. Prague: Institute of International Relations, 196–212.

Kratochvíl, P. and Kuchyňková, P. (2009) 'Between the Return to Europe and the Eastern Enticement – Czech Relations to Russia'. Available at www.fakprojekt.hu/docs/05-Kratochvil-Kuchynkova.pdf (accessed 9 December 2011).

Leonard, M. and Popescu, N. (2007) *A Power Audit of EU-Russia Relations*. Policy Paper, European Council on Foreign Relations, December 2007, available at http://ecfr.3cdn.net/1ef82b3f011e075853_0fm6bphgw.pdf (accessed 27 June 2012).

Meszerics, T. (2004) 'The Security Policy of Hungary', in T. Valášek and O. Gyárfášová (eds) (2004) *'Easternisation' of Europe's Security Policy*. Bratislava: Institute for Public Affairs, 22–31.

Najšlova, L. (2011) 'Slovakia in the East: Pragmatic Follower, Occasional Leader', *Perspectives* (Special issue: 'Identity and Solidarity in Foreign Policy: investigating East Central European Relations with the Eastern Neighbourhood', edited by Elsa Tulmets), 19: 101–22.

Nuclear Energy Agency (2010a) 'Country Profile: Czech Republic'. Available at www.oecd-nea.org/general/profiles/czech.html (accessed 10 June 2011).

——(2010b) 'Country Profile: Hungary'. Available at www.oecd-nea.org/general/profiles/hungary.html (accessed 10 June 2011).

——(2010c) 'Country Profile: Czech Republic'. Available at www.oecd-nea.org/general/profiles/slovak_republic.html (accessed 10 June 2011).

Nosko, A. and Lang, P. (2010) 'Lessons from Prague: How the Czech Republic Has Enhanced Its Energy Security', *IAGS Journal of Energy Security*, July.

Politics.Hu (2009) 'Gyurcsány, Putin hail Hungarian-Russian relations at Moscow meeting'. 11 March, available at www.politics.hu/20090311/gyurcsany-putin-hail-hungarianrussian-relations-at-moscow-meeting/ (accessed 11 May 2012).

Politics.Hu (2010) 'Minister says Hungarian-Russian relations on new footing'. 6 September, available at www.politics.hu/20100906/minister-says-hungarianrussian-relations-on-new-footing/ (accessed 24 November 2011).

Popescu, N. (2011) 'On EU-Russia visa-free travel (part 2)', *euobserver.com*. 26 October, available at http://blogs.euobserver.com/popescu/2011/10/26/on-eu-russia-visa-free-travel-part-2/ (accessed 11 May 2012).

Póti, L. (2003) 'The Good, the Bad and the Non-existent: the Hungarian Policy towards the Ukraine, Russia and Belarus, 1991–2002', in K. Pełczyńska-Nałęcz, A. Duleba, L. Póti, and V. Votápek (eds) *Eastern Policy of the Enlarged European Union*. Bratislava: Slovak Foreign Policy Association, 59–87.

186 *Martin Dangerfield*

Rácz, A. (2011) 'A Limited Priority: Hungary and the Eastern Neighbourhood', *Perspectives* (Special issue: 'Identity and Solidarity in Foreign Policy: investigating East Central European Relations with the Eastern Neighbourhood', edited by Elsa Tulmets), 19: 143–64.

——(2012) 'Hungary', in A Lobjakas and M Mölder (eds) *EU-Russia Watch 2012*. Tartu: Tartu University Press, 63–70.

Radio Prague (2011) 'Klaus draws fire for refusal to comment on Russian elections'. 8 December, available at www.radio.cz/en/section/news/news-2011-12-08 (accessed 9 December 2011).

Rettman, A. (2010) 'US cables shed light on EU 'Friends of Russia' in Georgia war', euobserver.com. 1 December, available at http://euobserver.com/9/31400/?rk=1 (accessed 3 December 2010).

RiaNovosti (2009) 'Russia, Slovakia sign long-term nuclear power deal'. Available at http://en.rian.ru/russia/20091117/156872704.html (accessed 11 May 2012)

Samson, I. (ed.) (2010) *Visegrad Countries, the EU and Russia. Challenges and Opportunities for a Common Security Identity*. Bratislava: Slovak Foreign Policy Association.

Topolánek, M. (2009) 'Speech at the Nabucco Summit'. Available at www.eu2009.cz/en/news-and-documents/speeches-interviews/speech-by-mirek-topolanek-at-nabucco-summit-7778/ (accessed 30 April 2012).

Ugrosdy, M. (2011) 'Money Alone Won't Buy Putin', *Centre for Strategic and International Studies*. January, available at http://csis.org/blog/money-alone-wont-buy-putin (accessed 10 May 2012).

Visegrad Group (2011) *About the Visegrad Group*. Available at www.visegradgroup.eu (accessed 24 January 2011).

Visegrad.Info. (2010) 'Visegrad countries and Russia'. Available at www.visegrad.info/v4-eu-russia-relations/factsheet/visegrad-countries-and-russia.html (accessed 2 December 2011).

Vlček, P. (2010) *Czech Republic and Russia to support the expansion of cooperation in high priority industrial sectors*. Press Release of the Czech Ministry for Industry and Trade. 19 October 2010, available at www.mpo.cz/dokument80139.html (accessed 18 January 2012).

v/lex (2011) 'Slovakia Supports Liberalization of Visa Regime Between EU, Russia'. 5 May, available at http://vlex.cn/vid/slovakia-liberalization-visa-regime-eu-323252827 (accessed 11 May 2012).

Votápek, V. (2003) 'Policy of the Czech Republic towards Russia, the Ukraine and Belarus', in K. Pelczyńska-Nalęcz, A. Duleba, L. Póti, and V. Votápek (eds) *Eastern Policy of the Enlarged European Union*. Bratislava: Slovak Foreign Policy Association, pp. 89–108.

Weiss, T. (2011) 'Projecting the Re-Discovered: Czech Policy Towards Eastern Europe', *Perspectives* (Special issue: 'Identity and Solidarity in Foreign Policy: investigating East Central European Relations with the Eastern Neighbourhood', edited by Elsa Tulmets), 19: 27–44.

12 Bulgaria

Diana Bozhilova

We inhabit a space governed by over 1,700 international organizations, each seeking to stimulate and enhance co-operation and co-ordination amongst nation states to an ever greater extent (Union of International Associations 2001:2586). Arguably, the role of international organizations has never been more prominent in politics than it is today, as they have come to assume the role of principal over their once traditional embodiment of an agent (Finnemore 1993). Consequently, their impact on both international relations and domestic policy formation has profoundly increased since the end of the First World War. This is especially true of the European integration project. The unprecedented role the Commission played in the integration of states into the European Communities has had an important impact on the development of cognitive structures of domestic agents through the process of socialization amongst member countries (Finnemore 1993:50–51).This incidence further increased with the end of the Cold War. The ensuing power vacuum necessitated that the political geography of the European continent be redrawn once again. The collapse of the Soviet Union and the pull of both the European Union and NATO through the carrot-and-stick approach (Buller 2000) resulted in profound foreign policy reorientations in the COMECON (Council for Mutual Economic Assistance) states of the former Soviet bloc.

In this chapter, it is argued that these processes have been felt in Bulgaria and had some visible effects, not least in resulting in a reorientation of Bulgarian foreign policy towards Russia in a manner that has the potential to benefit both the EU and Bulgaria itself. Changes since 1991 mean that the Bulgarian–Russian relationship cannot be separated from relationships between Russia and other EU member states and the EU and Russia. History and geography mean Bulgaria can be a positive mediating influence but its dependence on Russia for energy and failure to diversify to mitigate the worst effects of that dependence, mean that Europeanizing effects upon Bulgaria cannot necessarily be considered to be permanent. I begin by setting out some of the theoretical and empirical grounds for seeing Bulgaria as 'Europeanizing', before moving on to explore the historical roots of Bulgaria's relations with Russia and then the current state of the relationship. In the final part, prospects for the future of the relationship are examined.

Bulgaria and the European Union

The volume and intensity of the accession process in Central and Eastern Europe (CEE), coupled with the weakness and vulnerability of those states, as well as the advanced tools of integration that the Commission made recourse to, turned the Eastern enlargement into the most pervasive instance of export of supranational policy and institutional structures into individual nation states (Cremona 2003:1–7). Observing the dismantling of command economies through aggressive privatization, the scrapping of national champions and restitution of once nationalized property, as well as efforts towards decentralization of government and the institutionalization of civil society, scholars established a clear causal link between supranational co-operation and change in domestic institutions, public policy preferences and formation, as well as in the cognition of domestic actors.

The changes in Bulgaria have been significant, though often manifestly distorted. Freedom House indices often point to the lack of active civil society in the state, while successive Commission reports emphasize the omnipresence of corrupt practice that leads to a lag in development, pronouncing the country the poorest amongst EU member states. Former French Prime Minister, Dominique de Villepin, chairing the advisory board on Bulgaria, took little time before declaring that the pull of EU membership had failed to anchor the drive for reform in the Balkan state (Cendrowicz 2009). Such observations have raised doubt over the direction and continuity of Bulgarian foreign policy. Having once drawn a historical border between NATO allies and the Soviet sphere of influence, Bulgaria has since been called upon to balance strategic energy and trade interests in the southern energy ring (the East–West corridor). The rise of Russia since 2000 on account of its abundant natural resources and the price hikes of oil and gas has once more seen Western and Eastern interests clash on the battleground of the small South-East European state. Through projects such as South Stream and Burgas–Alexandroupolis, Russia is determined to strengthen its grip, both on upstream exploration in the Caucuses and the Near East, and on the transmission and trade of energy resources on the higher paying markets of Europe. Meanwhile, pan-European projects, such as Nabucco, have stalled for lack of resource security and cost efficiency. Russia under Putin has seen old superpower ambitions rise by restoring traditional spheres of influence in the Federation's vicinity. This, coupled with the political drift in Bulgaria, is breeding uncertainty as to the future of the EU's eastern-most boundary:

> ... without strategic direction and clear priorities on issues like security and energy, the Bulgarian state could face populist revolts. And that instability could undo the ties between the EU and Bulgaria, prompting a shift toward Russian political and economic interests.
>
> (Cendrowicz 2009)

Bulgaria 189

In the bilateral discourse between Bulgaria and Russia, the role of the EU as a supranational organization has come to be questioned. Indeed, the EU–Bulgaria relationship constitutes a good case for understanding not only the contributions but also the limits of constructivist thought. The EU has emerged as an international actor playing upon its strength as an economic giant but acknowledging its weakness as an international political actor (Jones 2005: 145). Attempting to resolve the epistemological deadlock between realists who have been rebuked for their emphasis on state-centrism where much larger interests are at stake (Ashley 1984:238) and liberal institutionalist assertions that enlargement policies promote co-operation amongst states in international organizations (Baldwin 1993:20–27), constructivism poses a two-fold quandary regarding EU policies. First, it interprets EU enlargement policy functionally, that is as premised on a substantive political consensus rationale. Second, the fact that the EU policy transfer requires a strict adhesion to supranational norms and rules by acceding states, in most cases without any derogation and transition periods, means that the latter is presupposed per se (Checkel 1998:326-ff). This far-reaching form of inter-state co-operation has likewise extensive effects on the policy formation and structural organization of EU member states. Europeanization in the instance of an external force where top-down policy transfer occurs from the supranational to the national level in order to integrate new member states, is unparalleled in its scale as compared to the practice of other international organizations (Bozhilova 2008).

Seen in the context of Europeanization, Bulgarian foreign policy vis-à-vis Russia has benefited greatly. The impact of the EU integration project on Bulgarian foreign policy has resulted in a shift away from the fears of Soviet occupation and the helplessness of small states that pervaded the discourse until the turn of the millennium. Instead, the reorientation of Bulgarian foreign policy in the course of the past decade has led to the pursuit of strategic energy and trade co-operation with Russia. Beyond the EU accession stimuli to that end, such a strategy is strongly founded in national interests since Bulgaria is dependent for its oil and gas consumption on imports from the Russian Federation. Bulgaria is further non-diversified as its only power plant at Kozluduy has reactors of Russian design, and renewable energy remains underdeveloped. The threat that so much energy dependence might lead to political pressure raises concern amongst EU member states.

On the other hand, Bulgaria's self-serving approach is also one that safeguards EU strategic interests to some significant extent. In seeking close co-operation with Russia, that is otherwise not easily achieved in the EU–Russia bilateral forum (Bozhilova and Hashimoto 2011), Bulgaria has the potential to serve as bridge over vast interests pertaining to energy security and securitization, more generally, as well as conflict mitigation and resolution in Europe's near neighbourhood and economic development on the continent as a whole. However, such substantive goals have often been threatened by unsuccessful policy transfers from the EU to Bulgaria in the post-accession

190   *Diana Bozhilova*

period. Since becoming a full member of the EU, conditionality has lost much ground in Bulgaria (Gateva 2010). This micro policy mismanagement in the Balkan state impedes bilateral EU–Russia macro policy management.

Anchored East, integrating West: Bulgaria and the Russian Federation

Western countries lacked a strategic wider vision for the continent after the end of the Cold War and had no fully fledged policy approach vis-à-vis CEE. The response of the European Commission to the aftermath of regime change in the Soviet sphere of influence was the Europe Agreements (EA). However, association with the EU did not afford any rights of co-decision. Therefore, the EAs were no substitute for EU membership (Cendrowicz 2009). The EU approach was 'in the making' for more than a decade after 1989, meandering amongst three intervening variables: (1) internal developments in the EU; (2) individual developments in the Central and Eastern European countries (CEECs); and (3) the wider context of repositioning of global players following the dissolution of the Soviet Union.

The dismantling of the Soviet sphere of influence did not result in a one-size-fits-all model for the CEE accessions (Börzel, Pamuk and Stahn 2008: 11–13). A critical distinction between the transitions in Central Europe and in Eastern Europe must be drawn. The Central European states, such as Poland, Hungary, the Czech Republic and Slovakia (Visegrad Four), had centuries-old experiences of Western acculturation prior to 1945 (Zweynert and Goldschmidt 2005; see also Dangerfield in this volume). More closely associated with the West through extensive institutional, trade and cultural linkages, the Stalinist model superimposed upon them did not succeed in undoing the effects of longer-term historical memory. By contrast, Bulgaria's historical experience was such that what civil society there was disappeared during the communist era, while all tiers of governance were subordinated to the Politburo on the example of the Soviet model. Bulgaria was known as the most faithful Soviet ally within the COMECON system of states. This legacy has left the state with scarce civic and political opposition (Rupnik 1999: 57–62). Weak democratic structures of governance notably led Bulgaria to endure one of the most severe economic crises in the 1990s. The recovery was difficult as traditional export markets in the Soviet Union were lost while fuel prices could no longer in effect be subsidized through the COMECON system of trade. In the profound economic and political turbulence of the 1990s, much of Bulgaria's natural affinity to Russia was lost. The subsequent impact of Europeanization and parallel economic strengthening of both Russia and Bulgaria since the turn of the millennium has shown that old dependencies are to be addressed through the creation of a level-playing field.

Anchored in an East–West pull of history, Bulgaria is both disadvantaged and privileged by its standing. It is disadvantaged since the geopolitical importance of the region determines its incremental economic development.

Yet, it is privileged, as the strategic significance of relations with Russia affords Bulgaria the position of a natural hub for the region.

In the Leonard and Popescu (2007) classification of EU states' relations with Russia, Bulgaria's approach was described as that of a 'friendly pragmatist'. This has evolved only in the course of the past decade and is far less appropriate when applied to the bulk of the twentieth century history of Bulgaria–Russia and Soviet relations Russia is credited as the force behind Bulgaria's liberation from the centuries' old rule of the Ottoman Empire and subsequent choice of monarchical governance. In 1945, Bulgaria fell prey to what has been theorized as the Soviet 'occupation' in Eastern Europe on account of both of the great powers' plan for division of the continent and by virtue of having lost the war. The 'swallowing' of the state by the Soviet sphere of influence was opposed little, if at all, by the West, who curbed Stalin's ambition only with respect to Greece and Northern Turkey, but little else. The critical ports of the Bosporus and the Mediterranean were secured, while the rest was left to manage its own way. In turn, Bulgaria's opposition was hardly vociferous. The country shares a Slavic heritage with Russia, a linguistic, cultural, religious and historic affinity that served to encourage its close approximation with the former Soviet Union (Obolensky 1965).

Thus, a theory of Soviet occupation in Eastern Europe is much less valid for Bulgaria than it is other countries in the Balkans, such as Romania, Yugoslavia and Albania. While communist regimes sprang up in all of these countries, they parted ways very early on, for instance, by 1948, Yugoslavia was by and large independent while Romania had carved its own domestic and foreign policy, often referred to as the 'Third Way'. Enthusiasm for and faithfulness to the Soviet Union remained symbolic primarily of Bulgaria (Brown 1984). In many respects, this stance alienated the country from other regimes, writing it off as a Soviet proxy. This was further fuelled by Bulgarian involvement alongside the Soviets in putting down the Hungarian uprising of 1956.

After 1989, Bulgarian foreign policy was re-orientated significantly not only as a result of the pull of the EU and NATO, but also because of Russia's profound weakness under Yeltsin. Bulgaria based its foreign policy on six pillars: (1) multilateralism (avoiding alliances with a regional power); (2) equidistance (no participation in specific regional conflict); (3) the de-ideologization of foreign policy (abandoning the communist understanding of the world and blind pursuit of corporatist interests); (4) European integration (applying Western European approaches and solutions to international problems); (5) the democratization of foreign policy activities (through consensus and transparency); and (6) pragmatism and rationality in the foreign policy decision-making process (Lefebvre 1994). These principles are, to a varying degree of success, still being applied to Bulgaria's foreign policy formation today.

Against these attempts at foreign policy re-orientation, Bulgaria's approach to Russia as a 'friendly pragmatist' has been the result of rational reflection on past events that are often permeated by emotion and inconsistency, and that have as a result obscured Bulgaria's overt interest in an economic

192   *Diana Bozhilova*

partnership with the Russian state. Bulgaria has over 130 years of diplomatic relations with Russia. Bulgaria's accession to NATO and the EU in the new millennium has increasingly led to calls for a measured pragmatist-realist approach in Bulgaria–Russia bilateral relations and the pursuit of a level-playing field in energy and trade negotiations, especially in light of Bulgaria's dependencies on the Russian Federation.

Bulgaria is totally dependent on Russian energy resource imports, as well as for long-term energy transmission contracts. The resource import mix is non-diversified while energy transmission is permeated by infrastructure of Soviet design. Following the dissolution of the COMECON system of states, Bulgaria has accumulated vast year on year negative trade balances with the Russian state. In a liberalized Russian market, Bulgarian produce has become non-competitive and its market share has continuously slumped since transition began. A dramatic market share loss occurred during the period of economic crisis particularly, 1996–8, and it has been only incrementally recovered since. In 2008, only some 3 per cent of total exports were destined for the Russian Federation, while Russian imports reached 14.6 per cent of total imports. Overall, 10.2 per cent of Bulgaria's cumulative trade turnover was with the Russian Federation. Given the potential of the vast Russian markets, the penetration of Bulgarian companies is limited. It is primarily hindered by the instability of the political relationship, especially the conflict over energy projects of Russian design, such as the Belene power plant and the Bourgas–Alexandropoulis oil pipeline. Such difficulties, allowed by Bulgarian political elites to linger for a long time, often offended both Russia's and Bulgaria's regional partners participating in the Russian-led projects, such as Greece and Serbia. One result of the tensions in the bilateral discourse has been the lack of easing off of prohibitively high import tariffs in both Bulgaria and Russia for mutually traded products, thereby hampering the development of bilateral trade.

Bulgaria's trade imports from Russia consist primarily of energy resources and energy by-products. Necessity-based, this is far from utilizing the potential of bilateral trade. This finding stands to disappoint proponents of 'accelerated development' theory under the auspice of which the bilateral discourse has been analyzed in the new millennium. It was thought that 'accelerated development' would facilitate the creation of a level-playing field in Bulgaria–Russia trade negotiations. Rapid growth in both states in the course of the past decade suggested that talks might increasingly occur on a more equal footing. It has also been thought that in Russia both 'accelerated' and 'braking' development may be observed since the state preserved a high degree of scientific innovation and technological growth potential in the economy despite the painful dissolution of the Soviet Union. Given Bulgaria's 'friendly pragmatist' approach, it had been anticipated that Bulgaria would stand to benefit from utilizing the economic potential of bilateral relations through know-how transfers. This was manifested in a series of proposed projects in energy and infrastructure, such a nuclear power plant at Belene and the South

Stream gas pipeline. Yet, the most recent economic crisis has squarely stalled growth in bilateral trade, putting a brake on 'accelerated development' theories. It is unlikely that that momentum can be picked up again, particularly given that political tensions between the two states have continued to rise since the 2009 parliamentary election in Bulgaria, that at times there has been an overt channelling of US interest in the state, and the discarding of high-profile projects, such as the power plant project at Belene and the Bourgas–Alexandropoulis pipeline to bring Russian oil from the Black Sea to the Mediterranean.

Against a background of conflicting interests and a significant degree of mistrust, the Eastern enlargement of the EU has served to cause an even greater impasse in the EU–Russia relationship. Nascent fears connected with the idea of a 're-birth' of the former Soviet Union continue to exist (Kaminska 2009). The promotion of democracy by the EU is often perceived of as an encroachment on what was once a traditional Soviet (ex post Russian) 'sphere of influence'. The state of the bilateral discourse has found different expressions, highlighting the many spill-over effects that have ensued often in the form of 'reactions on reactions'. A process of dislocation in the EU–Russia bilateral relationship has become ever more apparent as the Russian Federation has gradually grown aware of the lack of collective action from amongst the EU member states in their commitment to a common foreign and security policy. The 2007 enlargement of Bulgaria and Romania to the EU has thus exposed the bilateral Bulgaria–Russia relationship to a series of strains.

The EU–Russia energy forum is composed of a series of interrelated, yet significantly diverse bilateral relations. Both France and Germany participate in EU–Russia energy negotiations from a rational objective economic stance (see the relevant chapters in this volume). By comparison, many of the CEECs tend to be anti-Soviet, thus also often anti-Russian, as a result of their recent historical memory. Poland and the Czech Republic, for example, find it hard to ignore Russia's rather authoritative approach towards Ukraine and Belarus, since it evokes memories of their forced acculturation to the East after 1945. This being said, the South Stream gas pipeline project, in which Bulgaria participates, provides a collective bargaining realm with the greater number of actors amongst the CEECs, thus reducing the incidence of any one of those states remaining isolated.

The diverse positions of EU member states vis-à-vis the EU–Russia energy dialogue has led to the fact that EU–Russia bilateral relations are overwhelmingly driven by an engrained economic rational over any other. Their positions are unified in sharing two common risks as EU members engage in policy-making vis-à-vis Russia: (1) projected high future energy consumption in the EU area; and (2) increasing dependency on imports of Russian fossil fuels. This discourse exposes a significant risk in the EU–Russia energy equation, one that centres round the key question of Russia's reliability as a transmission partner, given the squabbles with Ukraine and Belarus. In energy talks with the EU, Russia consistently shows preference for bilateral

194   *Diana Bozhilova*

negotiations with individual member states rather than for negotiations with a block of states. Bulgaria is no exception to this and its recent abandoning of high-profile projects in the East–West energy corridor has certainly caused Russia much embarrassment.

Still, antagonizing Russia does not serve either Bulgarian, or EU interests. The menu of choices has expanded for the vast Russian state with economic might rising in the East, while waning in the West. Thus, neither Bulgaria, nor the EU has anything to gain from reduced trade, economic and security linkages with Russia. The process of Bulgaria–Russia and EU–Russia co-operation can be facilitated only by rational actor-building coalitions. Such an approach is supported by Germany and Italy in the main, the EU's largest importers of natural gas from the Russian Federation. Thus, vis-à-vis Russia, the level of co-operation that the EU is seeking is comparable to the level of co-operation that the six founding members of the European Coal and Steel Community have sought in the immediate post-war period. In this, Bulgaria will do well to protect both its national interest and the wider interests of the European community given that two exogenous factors are the primary determinants of EU foreign policy over and above the individual interests of member states, namely: (1) wider geo-politics and (2) state interdependence within a globalized world order.

Conclusion

There are five factors relevant for the choice between rational self-interest and collective action for participating actors in the EU–Russia bilateral forum. First, is the projection of energy consumption needs in Europe. In this, Bulgaria has increased the overall dependency of the EU on Russia. Second, the dialogue is underpinned by price indicators of energy resources. In the small Balkan state, the lack of diversification away from Russia in resource imports and the misguided privatization of state-owned energy companies have led to some of the highest energy prices in Europe. Third, the institutional coherence of the European Union needs to be taken into account as the attitudes of both old and new member states vis-à-vis Russia find common ground. In this, Bulgaria can serve as a bridge between the EU and Russia, drawing on its wealth of knowledge and linkages to the Russia state, as well as its pivotal position as the eastern-most boundary of the EU. Fourth, the political will and domestic stability of successive European presidencies are critical to maintaining the momentum in EU–Russia negotiations. Moreover, at national level, foreign policy formation needs to be both viable and consistent. Bulgaria has been often accused as lacking much of the former and none of the latter. Fifth, the degree of Russia's openness within the wider context of a multilateral world order needs to be carefully assessed against the background of the EU–Russia energy dialogue. Therefore, it is unacceptable to forego on commitments undertaken and cause public embarrassment in bilateral negotiations.

In light of these factors, rationalism with an ingrained cost-benefit orientation in Bulgaria–Russia bilateral relations is critical but can at times appear uncertain. Energy security and price levels will be affected the most. Bulgaria's national preferences must affect the aggregated interests of the European Union constructively, so as to avoid fluctuations in the coherence of the domestic and the European foreign policy. Bilateral diplomacy between Moscow and national capitals has the capacity to (re)act swiftly and flexibly in cases of disputes in the Shared Neighbourhood. Such advantages of national diplomacy, mixed with some degree of agenda setting capacity by the Presidency of the Council of the EU are key parts in the Bulgaria–Russia bilateral discourse.

The important caveat is increased politicization of bilateral relations both in Moscow and in Sofia. The primacy of economic calculations in energy transmission negotiations has been thus replaced by strategic geopolitical considerations. The EU East–West divide vis-à-vis the role of Russia in the European landscape will continue to be a key impediment in the process of Bulgaria–Russia policy negotiations. Given the obstacles lying in the way of creating a level-playing field in Bulgaria–Russia energy negotiations, as well as the large number of interdependencies, political considerations, for one, would have to play a much lesser role in energy co-operation than they have done hitherto. The overall sense of the international landscape, of which Bulgaria, the EU and Russia are a part, is one of bitterness and blame. In turn, this means that the reality of energy mapping will continue to be a strongly politicized issue for some time to come.

References

Ashley, R. K. (1984) 'The Poverty of Neorealism', *International Organisation,* Vol. 38, No. 2, pp. 225–86.

Baldwin, D. A. (1993) *Neorealism and Neoliberalism: The contemporary debate.* New York: Columbia University Press.

Börzel, Tanja A., Pamuk, Yasemin and Stahn, Andreas (2008) 'The European Union and the Promotion of Good Governance in its Near Abroad: One Size Fits All?', *SFB-Governance Working Paper Series,* No. 18, December 2008.

Bozhilova, Diana (2008) *Bulgaria's Quest for EU Membership: The Europeanization of Policies in Transition.* Milton Keynes: AuthorHouse.

Bozhilova, Diana and Hashimoto, Tom (2011) 'EU – Russia Energy Negotiations: a choice between rational self-interest and collective action', *European Security.* Special Issue: The EU, Russia and the shared neighbourhood: security governance and energy, 19, 4: 627–42.

Brown, J. F. (1984) 'The Balkans: Soviet Ambitions and Opportunities', *The World Today,* 40, 6: 244–253.

Buller, J. (2000) National Statecraft and European Integration: the Conservative Government and the European Union, 1979–97. London: Cassell.

Cendrowicz, L. (2009) 'Could the EU lose Bulgaria to Russia?', *Time World.* Available at www.time.com/time/world/article/0,8599,1912192,00.html (accessed 11 April 2012).

Cremona, M. (ed.) (2003) *The Enlargement of the European Union.* Oxford: Oxford University Press.

196 *Diana Bozhilova*

Checkel, J. T. (1998) 'The Constructivist Turn in International Relations', *World Politics,* 50, 2: 324–48.

Finnemore, M. (1993) 'International organisations as teachers of norms: the United nations Educational, Scientific, and Cultural Organisation and science policy', *International Organisation,* 47, 4: 565–97.

Jones, E. (2005) 'Idiosyncrasy and integration: suggestions from comparative political economy', Erik Jones and Amy Verdun (eds) *The Political Economy of European Integration: Theory and Analysis.* Oxon: Routledge, 54–70.

Gateva, E. (2010) 'Post-Accession Conditionality – Support Instrument for Continuous Pressure?', *KFG Working Papers,* No. p0018. Berlin: Free University Berlin.

Kaminska, J. (2009) 'Battle of Influences or Partnership? The EU, Russia and the Shared Neighbourhood'. Paper presented at the annual meeting of the ISA's 50th Annual Convention 'Exploring the Past, Anticipating the Future', New York: New York Marriott Marquis.

Lefebvre, S. (1994) 'A primer on Bulgarian security and defence issues', *Defence Analysis,* 10, 3: 243–266.

Leonard, M. and Popescu, N. (2007) *A Power Audit of EU – Russia Relations.* European Council on Foreign Relations.

Obolensky, D. (1965) 'The Heritage of Cyril and Methodius in Russia', *Dumbarton Oaks Papers,* Vol. 19: 45–65.

Rupnik, J. (1999) 'The Postcommunist Divide', *Journal of Democracy,* 10, 1: 57–62.

Union of International Associations (2001) *Yearbook of International Organisations.*

Zweynert, J. and Goldschmidt, N. (2005) 'The Two Transitions in Central and Eastern Europe and the Relation between Path Dependent and Politically Implemented Institutional Change'. HWWA Discussion Paper, No. 314.

13 Romania

Mircea Micu[1]

The past reinforced by the present

The troubled shared history of Romanian–Russian relations can be traced back to the beginnings of the eighteenth century, which saw the Russian Empire challenging Ottoman rule over the Romanian principalities of Moldova and Walachia. The first annexation of Romanian territory took place in 1812, in the aftermath of the Russo–Turkish War, when the eastern part of Moldova (Bessarabia) was ceded to Russia. Bessarabia was returned almost one century later, in 1918, to the then Kingdom of Romania, to be lost again at the end of the Second World War to the Soviet Union, together with other Romanian regions. Bessarabia was amalgamated with Transnistria into the Soviet Republic of Moldova, while northern Bukovina and the Herza county were merged with another Soviet satellite, Ukraine. Not only did Romanians have to cope with the permanent loss of territory, but they were also powerless bystanders to the tragedy of their kin in those lands, as well as to military, political and economic Soviet domination at home. It was only in the 1960s, after the withdrawal of Soviet troops, when Romania began its journey to greater autonomy from Moscow, though to the benefit of the ruthless dictatorship of Nicolae Ceauşescu. This heavily charged background naturally fuelled downbeat perceptions about Russia that persist and are reinforced to the present day.

Since the fall of the Berlin Wall, Romania's foreign policy orientation has been one of convergence with the West, embodied in accession to NATO and the EU, motivated by previously unresolved security needs spilling into the present and a desire to restore, as Romania sees it, a severely challenged European identity. Romania's traditional territorial concerns have been alleviated by NATO's much-cherished Article 5 and by an ever growing military and strategic relationship with the USA, seen by Romanians as the backbone of the transatlantic security structure. In fact, Romania's choice of a spirited westward-looking orientation can be said to have caused as many challenges as they have solved: the stationing of US troops on the Romanian Black Sea coast and the planned deployment of US missile defence elements on Romanian soil not only fuelled what some see as Russia's manifest reflex of preserving

198 *Mircea Micu*

the East–West dichotomy of the Cold War philosophy, but also pushed the prospect of a Romanian–Russian rapprochement further into the future.

Recent Romanian–Russian bilateral relations can at best be described as fragile. An attempt at normalization of relations with Russia culminated in 2003, when a treaty on friendly relations and co-operation between the two countries was signed. The most difficult items during the negotiations were the denunciation of the Molotov–Ribbentrop Pact of 1939, which caused the loss of Romanian territories to the Soviet Union, and the recovery of Romania's multibillion-worth treasure sent for safekeeping to Russia during the First World War. A separate annex to the treaty provided for mechanisms to settle the lingering historical disputes. Extremely limited high-level contacts have been testament to the low pulse of Romanian–Russian political relations. In the past 22 years, Romanian presidents travelled only four times to Moscow (the last time in 2005, for ceremonial purposes), while the Russian president visited Bucharest only once, and even then on the occasion of the 2008 NATO Summit. Also, the last trip of a Russian foreign minister to Romania occurred in 2005 (Romanian Embassy Moscow 2012). Bilateral trade has mirrored the apathetic political relationship and has boiled down to gas deliveries from Russia, which make around 75 per cent of the total volume of imports from Russia, while Romanian exports to Russia have been negligible (Romanian Department of Foreign Trade 2012; Ziarul Financiar 2012).

That the past is still present in the relationship is evident in the recurrent abrasive rhetoric employed by both sides, the last episode taking place as recently as June 2011, concerning events during the Second World War. President Băsescu's declaration that, had he been at the helm of Romania in 1941 he too would have ordered Romanian troops to fight the Soviet Union alongside Nazi Germany to recover lost territory (B1TV 2011), triggered the wrath of Moscow, which labelled the Romanian President's assertion as 'shameless bravado justifying Nazi aggression and desecrating the memory of millions of victims of Nazism' (Russian Foreign Ministry 2011). Espionage scandals have also peppered the already turbulent relationship. The last such episode came about in August 2010 when a Romanian diplomat in Moscow was accused of spying on the Russian military presence in Transnistria and was subsequently declared persona non grata and asked to leave Russia. Romania reciprocated Russia's gesture with the expulsion of a Bucharest-based Russian diplomat, a move that determined Russian authorities to declare that Romania lacked common sense since its action was unfriendly and groundless, and intentionally poisoned further the negative aspects of the relationship (Gândul 2010). Over the past seven years, the Romanian President, Traian Băsescu, has been the main driver of Romania's foreign policy, in general, and towards Russia in particular, and though the President's comments and actions regarding Russia might have been considered too daring, they have been consistent with the population's perceptions of Russia, even if, at times, they were contested by his political opponents during internal turf wars.

Romania has remained wary of Russia's re-emerging regional and global assertiveness, which has made it difficult to change the country's negative perceptions of Russia and related vulnerabilities, and for a genuine process of confidence building between the two neighbours to begin. Romanians have come to terms with the idea of never being able to reverse the loss of territories to the Soviet Union at the end of the Second World War. Instead it has been suggested that Romania and the Republic of Moldova – 'the other Romanian state' – will be 'reunited' in the EU, when the latter eventually also becomes a member state (Băsescu 2006). Romanians have long believed that pro-Moscow former communist governments in Chişinău stood in the way of Moldova's democratic destiny and reintegration with Europe. On numerous occasions, in defence of international law principles and of its kinship with Moldova, Romania has fiercely rejected the separatist tendencies of the de facto authorities of Transnistria, Moldova's breakaway region and economic Achilles' heel, and deplored the unconstructive role played by Russia by refusing to withdraw its troops from Transnistria and unequivocally support Moldova's territorial integrity. Meanwhile, Russia has remained suspicious of Romania's real intentions towards its smaller eastern neighbour, intimating that Romania is actually interested in re-establishing its sway over Moldova by employing subversive tactics. Nonetheless, Romania has expressed grave concerns about Russia's geostrategic manoeuvring in respect of Moldova and other protracted conflicts in the region. Romania has been vocal about similar developments on the eastern shores of the Black Sea and felt that its residual territorial defence worries were completely vindicated by the Russian–Georgian war of 2008, and Russia's recognition of Abkhazia's and South Ossetia's alleged statehood. The paradoxical positioning of Romania and Russia in the same Kosovo non-recognition camp emphasizes further the perceived contradiction in Russia's foreign policy discourse and its self-interested calculations.

Romania showed even greater concern when Russia announced its withdrawal as a party to the CFE Treaty in 2007, which in practice gave Russia unrestricted potential to build up its military in immediate proximity to Romania. At the same time, however, Romania played a role in Russia's CFE decision, insofar as, amongst other reasons, Russia justified its withdrawal by pointing at the US deployments of troops and missile defence elements in Romania, which were thought to breach CFE provisions, and by contesting the linkage between the ratification of the Adapted CFE (desired by Russia) and the implementation of the 1999 Istanbul commitments regarding the withdrawal of Russian troops from Moldova and Georgia (strongly supported by Romania).

Europe's energy dependence on Russia and Russia's energy tactics have been equally worrying to Romanians as they seem to have primarily targeted the former Soviet satellites which had pledged allegiance to NATO and the EU. The Romanian President, Băsescu, has spoken against energy being used as an instrument for political pressure and once compared Gazprom with the Red Army to describe Russia's attempt to exert greater political influence over

200 Mircea Micu

Europe through energy (Cotidianul 2007). Former communist countries, including Romania, have been embroiled in a large number of energy-related incidents with Russia, ranging from explicit threats of, and actual cut-offs, of oil and gas supplies, to coercive price policy and hostile takeover attempts in the national energy markets, with significant political and economic implications (Larsson 2007).

Romania's dependence on Russian energy supplies has not been as high as in the case of other European countries. For instance, in 2011, gas imports accounted for approximately 30 per cent of domestic gas consumption, all coming from Russia. More worrying has been the fact that Romania's gas imports are expected to rise to almost 70 per cent of total consumption over the next decade, as national reserves decline and gas needs soar, pushing Romania towards greater reliance on Russian gas. In addition, Romania has paid one of the highest prices for Russian gas, currently at more than \$450 per 1,000 cubic metres, as Russia chose to deliver its gas to Romania through expensive (Russian-related) intermediaries (Ziarul Financiar 2012). Romania has also been subjected to Russian covert takeovers in the energy sector (Jurnalul 2011).

The Russia–Ukraine gas dispute of 2009, while not severely damaging to Romania, exposed Romania's vulnerabilities in the face of energy supply crises. Had the dispute continued for another month or so, Romania would have experienced a severe shortage of gas supplies. Romania used this opportunity to highlight the need for greater gas storage capacity and enhanced regional pipeline interconnectedness, and also to call once again on Europe for a speedier creation of alternatives to Russian gas. Romania had been the staunchest supporter of the Nabucco pipeline project which aimed at diversifying energy supply with gas deliveries from countries in Central Asia, positioning itself in stark contrast to Russia's own proposals for future energy routes, which bypassed recalcitrant neighbours, including Romania. Furthermore, Romanian concerns about Russian energy being used as a political tool in regional affairs seemed duly justified when a year later, in 2010, Ukraine extended Russia's lease of the major naval base in the Black Sea port of Sevastopol for another 25 years in exchange for a 30 per cent drop in the price of Russian natural gas sold to Ukraine (the main point of contention in the 2009 dispute), with clear geopolitical implications for Romania's security strategy.

Against this background, Romania chose to address its Russia-related regional concerns through a comprehensive policy centred on the Wider Black Sea region, which currently occupies most of its foreign policy's agenda, while also hoping to instil more pragmatism into dealings with Russia and to bring the relationship to a minimum common denominator. To achieve these objectives, Romania sought the internationalization of its Black Sea policy through several initiatives in different multinational frameworks (mainly the EU and NATO). Wary of Russia's 'sphere of influence'-driven strategy, Romania's preference was for a policy that would keep Russia in check, but not isolated, and for engaging with Russia in a constructive and pragmatic relationship, but with clear red lines which could not be crossed. So far, Romania and Russia have interacted within the Turkish-led or driven regional initiatives of the Black Sea Naval Force and the Organization of Black Sea Economic Cooperation, but Russia (and interestingly Turkey) resisted Romania's Black Sea internationalization efforts, as evidenced by the boycott of the Romania-sponsored Black Sea Forum for Partnership and Dialogue initiative, launched in 2006.

Difficult preferences in a difficult context

The Common Foreign and Security Policy gives scope, of course, to member states to upload their preferences to the EU level in order to amplify their individual voice on the international stage. However, experience shows that the success of this endeavour is not guaranteed. In reality, such an uploading may be altered, result in only partial achievement of objectives, or be altogether fruitless. Individual foreign policy preferences can become those of the EU if they are shared by or acceptable to the other members of the club. The expectation has been that new EU member states, like Romania, would also attempt to project their (ideally palatable) national foreign policy preferences onto the European level, while also taking into account the degree of unity already reached in the area of their interest. Given the shared communist legacy of the new members from central and eastern Europe, most of their foreign and security policy concerns inevitably have a direct or indirect Russian connection. Since their territorial defence predicament had been relatively settled through accession to NATO, it has been believed that the other residual foreign and security policy concerns could be primarily addressed through the EU's evolving soft power instruments, even more so in a post-Lisbon Treaty framework.

Romania sought to advance its regional concerns and preferences by advocating Black Sea-centred policies in the EU context, with explicit and implicit references to Russia. Romania has portrayed the Black Sea region as an 'accumulation of negative energies' (Băsescu 2005), 'with active or dormant hotbeds of tension extending in an arc of crises from the Western Balkans [the disintegration of Yugoslavia] and all the way to the North [Transnistria, Chechnya] and South Caucasus [Abkhazia, South Ossetia and Nagorno-Karabakh]' (Celac 2006: 145), putting at risk Europe's security. Romania tended to emphasize the region's frozen conflicts and energy (in) security, both issues being considered to be fuelled by a rather re-assertive Russia. At the same time, the Black Sea has been promoted as a region of opportunities, which could provide alternative energy routes and thus solve the EU's energy security predicament. From a Romanian standpoint, the EU's involvement in the Black Sea region would then represent an 'excellent' test case for EU–Russia relations (Ungureanu 2006: 140).

Romania's preferences for an EU Black Sea agenda largely entailed the EU coming out in defence of Moldova's territorial integrity and its involvement in

202 *Mircea Micu*

the settlement of regional frozen conflicts (with Moldova's EU accession in sight), and EU support for alternatives to the Russian energy supplies (especially through the construction of the Nabucco gas pipeline). These new policy objectives were expected to be reflected in all EU–Russia co-operation initiatives, and in individual EU member states' bilateral relations with Russia and other neighbouring countries. In order to achieve these goals, Romania showed readiness to learn how to attract the interest of other EU member states in the Black Sea region and to apply the EU's regional expertise acquired in the Nordic dimension and Barcelona Process to its own neighbourhood (Romanian Foreign Ministry 2007).

However, the reality of the EU's supporting platform has been rather different as a result of the EU attempting to build a co-operative relationship with Russia prior to the enlargements of 2004 and 2007. In Romania's view, these attempts included an unpromising Four Common Spaces Agreement, a European Security Strategy which failed to mention Russia, and exclusivist political and economic dealings between some individual EU member states and Russia. As such, the EU did not seem sympathetic to the newcomers' lingering regional concerns (amalgamating two distinct geographical dimensions, Eastern European and Mediterranean, in one single but fragmented strategy, the ENP), and inculcating in this way a sense of despair at the lack of any coherent EU stance on Russia and of deep scepticism of the EU's desire and capacity to move towards a genuine defence and security policy (Edwards 2006).

At Romania's proposal, a new EU regional co-operation initiative for the Black Sea – the Black Sea Synergy – was launched in 2007, in which Romania's primary concerns (frozen conflicts and energy dependency) were mentioned, but not given special status or tackled with outright determination (European Commission 2007). Other issues like democracy, human rights, good governance, organized crime and illegal immigration, trade, transport, environment, maritime policy and fisheries were brought in and given equal footing. In addition, it was clearly specified that such an initiative would only be complementary to existing EU policies towards the region, encompassing elements of the ENP, the pre-accession strategy with Turkey and the unaltered strategic partnership with Russia.

In relation to regional protracted conflicts, Romania hoped to see a more spirited EU engagement. It is true that in the case of Transnistria, the EU deployed its low-politics crisis management capabilities in the form of participation with the 5+2 negotiation format (which, however, Romania tried unsuccessfully to join), an EU Border Assistance Mission to Moldova and Ukraine (EUBAM), and an EU Special Representative for Moldova. It is very likely that these would have happened even without Romania's influence. While EUBAM proved to be relatively effective in facilitating a degree of economic integration between Moldova and Transnistria, attempts to move to the high-politics of peacekeeping operations have either been thwarted by Russia or resisted by some EU member states, in order to avoid antagonising

Russia. Advances in the EU's low-politics of crisis management, for example by increasing Moldova's attraction through a clear EU membership perspective, have been persistently called for by Romania (Romanian officials lobbied to attach Moldova to the European perspective offered to the western Balkan countries), but its efforts have been opposed by or unpopular with other EU peers (Popescu 2011: 62–65). In response to the 2008 Georgia hot war, the EU has indeed been more alert and was instrumental in securing a sort of ceasefire. However, the ceasefire terms were considered flawed by Romanians and shelved by Russia later, in the absence of a guarantee mechanism. The episode served as yet more proof that territorial defence concerns in the twenty-first century were justified, vindicating Romania's 'obsolete' worries. It was not something which the EU was able to fend off convincingly and so served to expose the limits of the EU's co-operative strategy towards Russia.

In the energy field too, the EU agreed to support the construction of the Nabucco gas pipeline (fiercely supported by Romania) transporting gas from the Caspian region via Turkey to Austria, which would decrease the EU's energy reliance on Russia. However, this common endeavour seemed to be undermined by a lack of common active commitment and resolve and exclusive bilateral arrangements involving some EU countries and Russia, which included Nabucco-competing projects, as other chapters in this volume show. At times, Romania felt it was the only country fighting for Nabucco's establishment and cultivating relations with potential supply countries in Central Asia, being impelled to seek other Nabucco-like alternatives to secure greater European energy autonomy, such as the Azerbaijan–Georgia–Romania Interconnector or deliveries of Qatari liquefied natural gas through Romanian ports. Disillusioned with the progress on the creation of energy alternatives in particular and of an EU common energy policy in general, Romania turned to advocating (successfully) for an elaborate role for NATO in energy security, thus formalizing the energy stance it shared with the USA.

It is worth noting, however, that Romania's uploading of its national interests vis-à-vis Russia and the wider region to the EU has not been simply a matter of Romania being subject to external circumstances. These may not have been favourable for the creation of a coherent and firm EU Russia policy, but Romania's effectiveness has been hindered too by its need to learn to internalize European 'ways' of 'uploading' preferences: by forging alliances, setting agendas and examples, and exporting national ideas (the 'uploading' criteria used by Miskimmon and Paterson 2003).

Romania's persistent efforts to raise the international profile of the Black Sea region in previous years have been somewhat disregarded. Romania was criticized for failing to seek partnerships and build a critical mass of like-minded countries before suggesting policy options at the EU level. Because of that, its positions were considered biased and divisive (interview with EU member state diplomat in April 2008). As a result, Romania tried to look for partners who would support the idea of the Black Sea project, managing to bring Germany on their side, 'without which the adoption of the Black Sea

204   *Mircea Micu*

Synergy initiative would not have been possible' (interview with Romanian high-ranking official in April–May 2008). In turn, Romania accepted a softer wording of its two main concerns (frozen conflicts and energy security), which did not necessarily signal a higher degree of fulfilment of its regional ambitions or a shift in its overall foreign policy paradigm. At the same time, the emergence of another (apparently competing) project, the Eastern Partnership, has been seen as a failure in forging alliances, since this initiative was addressing similar regional concerns and was put forward by another neighbour from central and eastern Europe (Poland, with Sweden's support).

In respect of other EU institutions too, Romania has been stymied. The Council has not been the only alternative for projecting national preferences and influencing the EU's agenda setting: the European Parliament, for instance, is seen as an increasingly audacious and outspoken EU institution on foreign policy matters (as shown in the Polish case by Kaminska 2007). However, here, Romania has made little progress because only one Romanian Member of European Parliament (MEP) is present in the 62-strong parliamentary delegation for relations with Russia. Also, only two Romanian MEPs are members of the delegation for relations with Armenia, Azerbaijan and Georgia, three for Ukraine and none for Belarus. Nevertheless, seven of the 27 MEPs of the delegation for relations with Moldova are Romanian, one of them actually chairing it (European Parliament 2011), which may help Romania become more effective in advancing Moldova-related issues on the EU's agenda. Critics say that Romania's failure to achieve this goal was also partially due to its excessive rhetoric regarding Russia and to the lack of concrete 'constructive' proposals and actions on the ground, which did not help in setting a good example for others to follow (interview with EU member state diplomat in April 2008. Romanians were specifically advised in Brussels not to attempt to upload unreasonable or unrealistic preferences, i.e. by pursuing the two thorny issues of regional security and energy dependency (interview with EU member state diplomat in April 2008). Instead, Romania should limit itself, for the time being, to engagement with Russia in regional economic projects, encouragement of cultural exchanges, tackling of transnational crime, preventing environment degradation, etc., which would prepare the path for addressing the other, more delicate, issues in the long run.

Romania's ideational export concerning regional protracted conflicts and secessionist tendencies demanded a more vigorous and articulated EU criticism of Russia's unproductive and intimidating manoeuvres, one at odds with the EU's pre-2004 and 2007 enlargement co-operative approach towards Russia. Romania has also advanced the idea of spreading democracy in the region, but it differed from the mainstream with regard to its proposal that such democratization should be interconnected with the EU membership perspective, especially in Moldova's case. Moldova's European perspective looked far-fetched to many in Europe, given Moldova's unresolved Transnistrian problem, volatile domestic politics and poor economic standing. The idea was not even fully digested by politicians in Chişinău, mindful of

Russia's post-Cold War re-assertiveness and veiled warning that it might share Georgia's fate. Romania's proposals for alternative energy sources via the Black Sea region would have necessitated varying degrees of strength from each EU member state to withstand Russia's perceived 'divide and rule' strategy of offering tempting bilateral dealings or intimidation.

Preliminary conclusions: negative Europeanization?

The current rather undefined EU's Russia policy has inevitably allowed for member states' bilateralism to flourish, not necessarily to the benefit of Europe generally, as seen especially in the energy field, since competition for individual gains can be detrimental to any collective action. As a new member of the EU, and against this background, Romania has attempted, with little success to date, to address its neighbourhood concerns by advocating more daring EU initiatives on Russia-salient issues such as regional frozen conflicts and energy security, ideally epitomized by a vigorous EU Black Sea policy. It has been shown that Romania's capacity to upload national foreign policy preferences to the EU level has not been fully developed yet (understandably, given Romania's relatively brief post-accession exposure to European political co-operation). Its underdeveloped capacity for forging alliances with other EU member states has been particularly noticed. But it seems that even in the presence of a developed uploading capacity, the core problem may not be one of style or of the 'way' of 'uploading' preferences, but rather that of Romania's foreign policy paradigm towards Russia, which is deeply rooted in an all-too vivid historical legacy, and thus is one that cannot be easily or rapidly altered in the EU context. Given the cautious framing of EU–Russia relations, Romania's policy preferences could not have been supported by the EU's opportunity structures.

In interaction with EU institutions and other member states, Romania has learned to tone down the intensity with which it pursues its main Black Sea policy objectives by agreeing to blend them with more palatable issues such as regional economic co-operation, maritime security, trans-border crime and human trafficking, etc. Romania has softened its Russia discourse and has attempted the normalization of bilateral relations with Russia (to a bare minimum), which could eventually lead to an upgrade in the future, but the difficulty here is that mutual deep mistrust does not seem to fade away. Nevertheless, the core elements of Romania's regional policy (Moldova, protracted conflicts and energy security) have remained unaltered. Though the Romanian President is regarded as the main actor in Romanian foreign policy, Romania's Russia policy has been constant, largely unchallenged by other domestic institutions or the Romanian population at large.

It cannot be said that Romania's impact on EU–Russia relations has been negative insofar as the EU's stance towards Russia has remained relatively un-confrontational. Nor did Romania try to block other EU–Russia initiatives in order to show its discontent. On the contrary, Romania's subsequent

206 *Mircea Micu*

unilateralism could bear fruit for the EU as a whole in the long run. In the absence of a clear European membership perspective for the Republic of Moldova, Romania hopes to bring Moldovans closer to the EU by other means (for example, by granting them the natural right to Romanian citizenship, encouraging and supporting political and economic reform). In the same vein, it has embarked on an almost solitary mission of wooing energy-rich countries in Central Asia to come to the rescue of the Nabucco project, which would benefit all Europe.

But a sense of frustration and resentment generated by the EU's weak Russia performance can nevertheless be seen. In Romania's view, the EU could and should do more regarding Russia's energy politics and wider role in the troubled Black Sea region. The difficulty of formulating a robust EU–Russia policy and the preference for individually beneficial bilateralism of some EU countries in relation to Russia may give rise to centrifugal tendencies at the heart of EU foreign policy making, in the sense that the reflexive centrality of the EU, on which national foreign policies are supposedly based, especially in the Lisbon Treaty context, is being gradually replaced by other external centres of attraction and/or unilateral tendencies. This may describe a situation of retrenchment, an expression of negative Europeanization, which implies that national foreign policies become less European (Radaelli 2003: 37–38). Such a shift may occur in Romania's case, as some essential foreign policy preferences, such as those related to Russia, which cannot be satisfactorily pursued in an EU context may erode the country's already acquired reflexes of prior consultation and co-ordination on all foreign policy issues with its EU peers (in favour of the NATO/US framework, as also suggested by Bechev 2009). This tendency has been revealed by Romania's greater interest and participation in the debate about NATO's new strategic concept than in the review of the European Security Strategy, and in the apparent shielding of its strategic relationship with the USA as distinct from that with the EU. The EU framework will always matter, but its current increasing centrality in the making of Romania's foreign policy may, in future, be rolled back and replaced by an already strong co-operative framework with the USA.

Note

1 The views expressed in this chapter are those of the author, and are not intended to reflect the position of either the Ministry of Foreign Affairs of Romania or the European External Action Service.

References

Băsescu, T. (2005) *New milestones of Romanian foreign policy.* Speech at the University of Bucharest delivered on 14 June, available at www.presidency.ro/?_RID=det&tb=date&_PRID=ag (accessed 31 July 2012).

Romania 207

Băsescu, T. (2006) *Romanian President discourse at the annual meeting with Heads of Diplomatic Missions Accredited to Bucharest.* Available at www.presidency.ro/?_RID=det&tb=date&id=7320&_PRID=ag (accessed 31 July 2012).

Bechev, D. (2009) 'From Policy-Takers to Policy-Makers? Observations on Bulgarian and Romanian Foreign Policy Before and After EU Accession', *Perspectives on European Politics and Society,* 10, 2: 210–14.

B1TV (2011) *Interview with President Traian Băsescu.* Available at www.b1.ro/stiri/eveniment/traian-basescu-invitat-in-premiera-la-evenimentul-zilei-vezi-principalele-declaratii-6878.html (accessed 31 July 2012).

Celac, S. (2006) 'Romania, the Black Sea and Russia', in Phinnemore, D. (ed.) *The EU and Romania: Accession and Beyond.* London: Federal Trust, 145–51.

Cotidianul (2007) *Băsescu attacks Putin.* Available at www.9am.ro/stiri-revista-presei/2007-06-25/basescu-s-a-dat-la-putin.html (accessed 31 July 2012).

Edwards, G. (2006) 'The New Member States and the Making of EU Foreign Policy', *European Foreign Affairs Review,* 11: 143–62.

European Commission (2007) *Communication from the Commission to the Council and the European Parliament: Black Sea Synergy – A New Regional Cooperation Initiative.* Available at http://ec.europa.eu/world/enp/pdf/com07_160_en.pdf (accessed 31 July 2012).

European Parliament (2011) *European Parliament / Delegations.* Available at www.europarl.europa.eu/delegations (accessed 15 January 2011).

Gândul (2010) *The Romanian – Russian diplomatic war continues.* Available at www.gandul.info/news/razboiul-diplomatic-ruso-roman-continua-moscova-reactioneaza-si-acuza-bucurestiul-de-nepasare-6945688 (accessed 31 July 2012).

Jurnalul (2011) *RAFO refinery, the Trojan horse of Russian Mafia in Romania.* Available at www.jurnalul.ro/wikileaks-romania/rafo-calul-troian-al-mafiei-ruse-in-romania-575775.htm (accessed 31 July 2012).

Kaminska, J. (2007) 'New EU members and the CFSP: Polish foreign policy Europeanisation', *Political Perspectives,* 2, 2: 1–24.

Larsson, R. (2007) *Nord Stream, Sweden and Baltic Sea Security.* Stockholm: Swedish Defence Research Agency.

Miskimmon, A. and Paterson, W. E. (2003) 'Foreign and Security Policy: On the Cusp between Transformation and Accommodation', in K. Dyson and K. H. Goetz (eds) *Germany, Europe and the Politics of Constraint.* Oxford: Oxford University Press, 325–45.

Popescu, N. (2011) *EU Foreign Policy and Post-Soviet Conflicts – Stealth Intervention.* London: Routledge.

Radaelli, C. (2003) 'The Europeanization of Public Policy', in K. Featherstone and C. Radaelli (eds) *The Politics of Europeanization.* Oxford: Oxford University Press, 27–54.

Romanian Department of Foreign Trade (2012) *Romania: General Data.* Available at www.dce.gov.ro/Info_business/RO_flyer_apr12.pdf (accessed 31 July 2012).

Romanian Embassy Moscow (2012) *Presidential visits.* Available at http://moscova.mae.ro/index.php?lang=ro& id = 13731 (accessed 31 July 2012).

Romanian Foreign Ministry (2007) *Milestones for a Decade of Foreign Policy – Interests. Values. Instruments.* Consultation document issued on 5 September, available at http://old.mae.ro/index.php?unde=doc&id=35099&idlnk=1&cat=3 (accessed 31 July 2012).

Russian Foreign Ministry (2011) *Statement by Russian MFA Spokesman A.K. Lukashevicha.* Available at www.mid.ru/bdomp/Brp_4.nsf/arh/248D8BF99BCA4598C32578BF0039C400?OpenDocument (accessed 31 July 2012).

208 *Mircea Micu*

Ungureanu, M. R. (2006) 'The Common Foreign and Security Policy: What Can Romania Bring?', in D. Phinnemore (ed.) *The EU and Romania: Accession and Beyond.* London: Federal Trust, 135–44.

Ziarul Financiar (2012) *In eight years, Romania paid Russia's Gazprom US$ 10bn for imported gas.* Available at www.zf.ro/companii/in-ultimii-opt-ani-de-zile-romania-a-b agat-in-buzunarele-rusilor-de-la-gazprom-10-mld-dolari-pentru-gazele-importate-940 5306 (accessed 31 July 2012).

14 Austria

Martin Malek and Paul Luif

Austria is a small country in Central Europe whose present-day identity is founded in its former Habsburg identity, the two civil wars in 1934, the authoritarian corporative state of 1934–38, its experiences as a part of the Third Reich and during the Second World War, as well as in the effects of the 1945–55 four-power occupation. The key to its full independence was its neutral status, as demanded by the Soviet Union, a status that slowly seeped into the Austrian identity, maintained even after the country joined the EU in 1995. The role of the Soviet Union and other external forces in post-war Austria is therefore vital to any understanding of its relations with Russia today. This chapter deals first with the historical background to Austria's relations with the Soviet Union and then Russia. Some consideration is also given to the EU–Austria–Russia triangle. An important element of Austria's economic, but also political relations with Moscow since 1968 is the import of Soviet and then Russian gas. Because of its location, Austria has played a significant role in the import and distribution of this gas to Western Europe. Added to this, Austria is one of the main destinations for asylum seekers in Europe. A particular problem are the Chechen refugees, who have also impacted noticeably on Austria's relations with Russia. Finally, Russian views about Austria as well as Russian influence on Austria will be discussed in some detail. It is worth noting too that, to offset the overly 'rosy' picture which is regularly the stuff of diplomatic statements, this chapter aims to deliver a more 'realistic' view of Austria's position vis-à-vis Russia in the context of the EU.

Austrian–Soviet relations 1955–91

At the end of the Second World War, Austria was occupied by the four Allies and divided into four zones. As a result of the 'Grand Coalition' between the Conservatives (Österreichische Volkspartei [Austrian People's Party], ÖVP) and the Socialists/Social Democrats[1] (Sozialistische/Sozialdemokratische Partei Österreichs, SPÖ), the domestic situation stabilized after the civil strife of the 1930s and war years. Austria gained its full independence by concluding the State Treaty with the four occupying powers in 1955. As the quid pro quo, Austria had to accept the status of permanent neutrality, the precondition for

210   Martin Malek and Paul Luif

the withdrawal of Soviet troops from eastern Austria. This compromise was reached in the Moscow Memorandum of April 1955, where representatives of the Austrian government promised to establish neutrality status for Austria according to the Swiss model. In this way, the Soviet Union proscribed Austria's membership in NATO. The Federal Constitutional Law on Permanent Neutrality was passed by the Austrian National Council on 26 October 1955.

After its verbal clash with the Soviet Union in 1956, when the Austrian government strongly criticized Soviet behaviour during the anti-communist uprising in Hungary, Austrian politicians quickly tried to avoid any declarations and actions that could be interpreted by the Soviets as violation of its neutral status. This caused an estrangement in particular between Austria and the United States, about which the British Ambassador to Austria, James Bowker, commented in 1959: 'In brief, Austria is often prepared to avoid angering the Russians at the expense of irritating her Western friends' (in Gehler 2005: 296). This pattern would continue in the decades to come.

Kurt Waldheim (close to ÖVP), Foreign Minister 1968–70, went further by initiating a comprehensive policy of active neutrality; a concept which came close to the Soviet notion of peaceful coexistence. A case in point was the rather muted reaction of the Austrian government to the crushing of the Prague Spring by Soviet-led Warsaw Pact troops in August 1968. The policy of active neutrality was further intensified during the single-party Socialist government (1970–83). Austria participated in the 1980 Moscow Olympic Games, despite Western calls to boycott them due to the Soviet invasion of Afghanistan, while Bruno Kreisky (SPÖ), Chancellor 1970–83, was reluctant to condemn martial law in Poland 1981. The 'soft' Austrian attitude towards the oppressive regimes in Eastern Europe was for a long time balanced by its granting of asylum or transit visas for a large number of refugees from the East. But in 1981, two weeks before the implementation of martial law, visa requirements were reintroduced for Polish citizens.

Looking back, Peter Jankowitsch, one of the most influential Socialist foreign policy experts (foreign policy spokesperson for his party 1983–90 and Foreign Minister 1986–87), described the difference between Austria's policy of active neutrality and the policies of NATO countries in this way:

> Certainly, the nature of Austria's relations with the countries in the Soviet sphere of influence, including the USSR itself, differed greatly from the interpretation and execution of these relations by the countries of the Western military alliance. Austria abstained from many measures these states took in the context of the Cold War, e.g. in the economic field, to weaken and isolate the East, and it instead applied a policy of opening and normalization.
>
> (Jankowitsch 2010: 495, translation Malek/Luif)

Thus, the nature of Austria's relations with the states of the Eastern bloc, including the Soviet Union, diverged from the relations NATO countries had

Austria 211

with the East. Austria obviously did not participate in activities to 'weaken and isolate the East'. In contrast, it pursued a policy of 'opening and normalization' under the guise of active neutrality.

EU–Austria–Russia

Austria's position in the EU and its relations with Moscow has to be examined in the context of its neutrality. In 1955, Austrian politicians succeeded in keeping the notion of neutrality out of the State Treaty. In the early years after 1955, many politicians probably thought that with changing circumstances, Austria could renounce its neutrality unilaterally (through passing a constitutional law), without the consent of the State Treaty signatories (including the Soviet Union). However, specialists in international law saw Austria's neutrality as based on a 'quasi-treaty relationship' with the community of states, since the Constitutional Law on Neutrality was notified to all countries with which Austria had diplomatic relations. A unilateral renunciation would thus not be possible. This interpretation was accepted by most Austrian politicians.

Austria's application for membership in the EU (then EC), submitted on 17 July 1989, included a neutrality clause, the first time such a clause had been included in an application. Austrian neutrality was met with concern by some politicians in the EC member states. For instance, Belgian Foreign Minister Mark Eyskens blocked an immediate response to the application, suggesting the 'European Community could enter into negotiations about it with the Soviet Union'. This upset the Austrian government since Vienna had always asserted that it alone would interpret the country's neutrality. The EC Council of Ministers passed a declaration to reserve the right to examine Austria's neutrality, but this never happened. Austria (together with Finland and Sweden) had to sign a Joint Declaration stating that on accession the countries would, 'take on in their entirety and without reservation all the objectives of the Treaty', including the rules on the EU's Common Foreign and Security Policy (CFSP) (see Luif 1995: 198–99, 310).

When the discussions of the abandonment of Austria's neutrality intensified during the early years of the coalition government between the ÖVP and the right-wing populist Freedom Party of Austria (Freiheitliche Partei Österreichs, FPÖ), which lasted from 2000 to 2007, the question of whether Austria could abandon its status unilaterally surfaced again – basically meaning whether Austria could terminate its neutrality without Russia's consent. In an interview in January 2001, the Russian Ambassador to Austria, Alexander Golovin, maintained that the Neutrality Law and the Moscow Memorandum would bind Austria through international law, meaning that no unilateral move by Vienna would be possible (Format 2001a). But when President Vladimir Putin visited Austria a few days later, he stated that neutrality would be 'Austria's business'. However, he hastened to add that it would not be 'reasonable' for Austria to abandon its neutrality since the country would lose many 'advantages', probably the most important being the 'trust and respect' of other countries (*Kronen Zeitung* 2001). In fact, the domestic political situation meant the government could not achieve a change in Austria's status. The then Deputy Speaker of the National Council, Heinz Fischer (SPÖ), immediately made clear that his Party would not vote for a revocation of the neutrality law. Since the votes of the Social Democrats would be needed for the necessary two-thirds majority in the National Council, a change of Austria's status was not feasible for the government.

When Fischer, now Austria's President, met with Russian President Dmitry Medvedev in Moscow in September 2009, he maintained Russia was a reliable partner for Austria in all spheres. Despite the current financial crisis, Russia and Austria would continue to boost ties, including energy co-operation. Less than a month later, in a meeting in Moscow between Austria's Foreign Minister Michael Spindelegger (ÖVP) and Russia's Foreign Minister Sergey Lavrov, Russia promised to provide active support for Austria's chairmanship of the UN Security Council.

Looking at these events and statements, there can be no doubt that Austria plays, as detailed below, at least the role of a 'friendly pragmatist' in EU–Russian relations among the EU member states, abetted by its neutral status. However, it is in relation to energy that the Austrian relationship with Russia is best understood.

Austrian–Russian gas trade

A roughly 5,000 km long pipeline, crossing over Ukraine and Slovakia, connects Western Siberia with Baumgarten. In this tiny Austrian village is located one of the most important natural gas hubs in Europe. Roughly one-third of the Russian gas exports to Western Europe are transported via Baumgarten. In response to the dynamic developments on the European gas market, the partly state-owned Austrian oil and gas group OMV here established the Central European Gas Hub (CEGH) – a virtual gas trade platform – in 2005. Both South Stream and Nabucco could (if they get built) also go to Baumgarten.

But Vienna and Moscow also have long-standing links in the energy sector. In 1968 (when the ÖVP was the sole party in power), OMV became the first non-communist European company to conclude a gas supply deal with the Soviet Union. According to data provided by OMV at the beginning of 2012, Austria's annual gas consumption is currently around 9 billion cubic metres. Around 47 per cent of Austria's gas supplies come from Russia, with 38 per cent supplied by Norway and other countries. Around 15 per cent originates from Austria's own gas production. But Russia does not (although OMV and many politicians do not get tired of alleging this) grant a 'stable and secure gas supply' for Austria, but precisely the opposite: Moscow especially since 1999, when Putin rose to power, has on numerous occasions demonstrated its capabilities and willingness to use gas (and oil) supply as a political leverage in order to subdue 'disloyal' states. Even the Austrian MFA, which usually very carefully selects its phrasing, wrote in its annual report for 2007: 'Russia

Austria 213

uses its energy policy as a mighty tool of its foreign policy' (Außenpolitischer Bericht 2007: 44).

In 2006, it was agreed that a 50 per cent owned subsidiary of EconGas would be the purchaser of Russian gas instead of OMV Gas International, with the Gazprom-controlled companies GWH and Centrex Europe Energy & Gas obtaining the opportunity to sell gas directly to Austrian consumers in the provinces Carinthia, Styria, and Salzburg. In pursuance of the contracts signed, Gazprom will annually supply Austria with some 7 billion cubic metres of gas until 2027 (the earlier inked contracts for the Russian gas supply to Austria expired in late 2012). A Moscow-based daily newspaper commented that Vienna had created for Gazprom 'most favourable conditions on its domestic market' and demonstrated its 'loyalty' to the Russian company (Gurkina 2006). In fact, Gazprom officials from time to time hint at their interest to acquire OMV (or at least to take a share). Deputy Chairman of the Board of Gazprom and Director-General of the company's export arm Gazprom Export, Alexander Medvedev (who is said to be particularly fond of Vienna, after working there 1989–96 and again 1998–2002), stated that 'the time is not ripe yet' (in Wirtschaftsblatt 2007). This leaves all options open for the future.

The Nabucco pipeline is the EU's flagship project with regard to the energy resources of the Central Asia and Caucasus Region. It could bring gas from the Georgian/Turkish and/or Iraqi/Turkish border respectively to the Austrian gas hub in Baumgarten an der March (close to the Slovak border), without passing through Russia. OMV is the head company of this project; the other partners are the Bulgarian Energy Holding, Turkey's Botas, Germany's RWE, Hungary's FGSZ (a 100 per cent subsidiary of the oil and gas group MOL), and Romania's Transgaz. As initially assumed, Nabucco would cost an estimated €8 billion, a figure revised to €12–15 billion and 3,300 kilometres of pipeline should become operational by 2013 and reach a capacity of 31 billion cubic metres of gas (10 per cent of EU-27 gas imports in 2005) by 2020. But especially since the fall of 2011, prospects for Nabucco appeared to be dwindling due to several reasons. Thus, the amount of non-Russian gas needed to fill Nabucco has not yet materialized and several alternative projects with a reduced 'Nabucco West' pipeline among them are under consideration.

Moscow does not want Nabucco to be built and does its best to derail it. An important initiative in this context is the South Stream pipeline, intended to transport gas from the Central Asian and Caucasus region. This pipeline, with a capacity of 63 billion cubic metres of gas per year, is proposed to run from Southern Russia under the Black Sea to Bulgaria, then bifurcate to cross several other countries for Italy and Austria.

Russia's opposition to Nabucco is, of course, well known throughout the entire EU. Austrian Federal Chancellor Werner Faymann (SPÖ) assured Prime Minister Putin in November 2009 in Moscow that Nabucco is 'not directed against Russia'. Putin replied that it is one of the goals for South Stream to 'discipline' current transit countries like Ukraine. Faymann did not

214 *Martin Malek and Paul Luif*

enter an objection, although he could have asked why Austria (and other EU member countries) should assist Russia in its attempts to 'discipline' other countries. And when Faymann stated that Austria neither possesses a nuclear power plant nor has the intention to build one, Putin laughed and said that this is a 'very good decision for Russia as well' (in Ultsch and Steiner 2009). The reasons are obvious – Austria will remain dependent on Russian gas in the foreseeable future.

Moscow wanted to involve Austria in South Stream at all costs, and Vienna did not take long to be persuaded. In April 2010, an Austrian–Russian inter-governmental agreement and a Gazprom–OMV co-operation agreement deal in order to bring Austria into the project were signed. Putin in Vienna made it clear it would be 'realized no matter what' (in RIA Novosti 2010). At the occasion of Austria's accession to South Stream, Russian news agency RIA Novosti highlighted a 'big victory for Russia and a major blow to Nabucco' (Fedyashin 2010) – which, again, left no doubt that South Stream is, above all, a 'Nabucco-stopper'. On 21 February 2011 in Moscow, Miller announced that Gazprom and OMV had officially registered a joint venture to build and operate the Austrian section of South Stream. Its planned Austrian route practically duplicates Nabucco's (and therefore the EU's) planned route, from Hungary to the Nabucco terminus at Baumgarten.

The EU, however, has occasionally got its way. For instance, a 50/50 joint venture between OMV and Gazprom, signed in January 2008, officially aimed at expanding and further developing the CEGH into the leading trading hub of its kind in continental Europe. What OMV CEO Wolfgang Ruttenstorfer in 2008 called an 'important step for the long-term safeguarding of Europe's gas supply' would have meant a further expansion of Gazprom into strategic sectors of the EU's energy industries. But in 2011, the EU Commission blocked the acquisition of shares in the CEGH by Gazprom. Unsurprisingly, Alexander Medvedev was angry: 'The Commission's mistrust is very short-sighted. ... The conditions we would have had to fulfil were unacceptable for us. I hope that the business logic will gain the upper hand in the long run' (in RIA Novosti 2011).

It is not only in relation to energy and economics, however, that Austria sometimes looks as if it is more committed to an interest-based rather than value-based relationship, as the effects of the Chechen wars on Austria show.

Chechnya

The two wars in Chechnya, started in 1994 and 1999 respectively, when the Kremlin sent its Armed Forces to regain control of the tiny breakaway republic in the Russian North Caucasus, compelled up to 300,000 people to flee to other Russian regions or even abroad. In 1997–2006, Austria received 24,796 asylum seekers, most of them ethnic Chechens, from Russia; only Poland and Germany had more (28,906 and 24,796 respectively). With an average of 74.8 per cent, Austria had by far the highest recognition rate among the main receiving countries of Chechen asylum seekers in the EU in the period 2002–6; the highest value was recorded in 2004 with 94 per cent. In 2006, Austria hosted the largest Chechen refugee population in the EU – with a total of 8,723 recognized refugees (Hofmann and Reichel 2008: 15, 19, 22). Today, 20,000–25,000 Chechens live in Austria, about 9,000 in Vienna alone.

At the turn of the millennium Chechnya became a bone of contention between Austria and Russia. In December 1999, MPs of all four parties in the Austrian National Council, in a letter to the Russian State Duma called for an 'end to the bombardments and violence' in Chechnya, saying 'the fight against terrorism cannot justify that towns are destroyed, their inhabitants are forced to flee or that the entire population [of Chechnya] is being regarded as terrorists' (Parlamentskorrespondenz 1999). Austrian Chancellor Wolfgang Schuessel in March 2000 (when Austria headed the OSCE) urged President Putin to find a peaceful and constructive solution to the conflict in Chechnya. The then Chairperson-in-Office of the OSCE, Austrian Foreign Minister Benita Ferrero-Waldner, in April 2000 visited several areas in the republic, including the capital Grozny, and was appalled by the enormous destruction and human suffering she witnessed. After having seen Grozny, she said: 'I cannot comprehend how such a big city with so many people can be so completely destroyed' (in OSCE Press Release 2000). Representatives of the Greens and Social Democrats in meetings with Putin in Vienna in February 2001 pointed to the 'problematic situation in the realm of human rights in Chechnya' and argued in favour of a 'peaceful solution' for the republic (*Der Standard* 2001).

Aside from these examples, there were few Austrian calls upon Moscow to stop the war in Chechnya; and needless to say, the Kremlin ignored them. Austria did not further insist on Russian talks with the armed Chechen resistance. Basically, the Austrian public paid little attention to the war, and the Peace Movement (which by contrast was very active before and during the wars in Yugoslavia 1999 and Iraq 2003) kept silent. Even after the trial of three Chechens, which resulted in their conviction for participation in the killing of Umar Israilov (see below), nobody in Austria raised the question of consequences in relation to Russia. This despite a widely-held belief that Chechnya's Moscow-appointed ruler, Ramzan Kadyrov, had sent the killers to Vienna and agreement by the majority of Austrian and foreign commentators that it was difficult to imagine that could have occurred without the Kremlin's knowledge and endorsement. On the occasion of Putin's visits to Austria, there were only a few small protests, and they were hardly attended by Austrians but rather by members of the Chechen community in the country. Sometimes it seemed that during the war, the Russian side complained more than the Austrians. Thus, the Austrian Embassy in Moscow faced accusations from the Russian MFA that the Chechen refugees in Austria were 'accommodated too well' and had 'privileges'. And the Russian Embassy in Vienna attacked Austrian media outlets' hostile coverage of the Russian 'struggle against terrorism' in Chechnya. Austria, meanwhile, had suffered the consequences of a conflict that resulted in mass displacement of people.

216　*Martin Malek and Paul Luif*

Notwithstanding their narrow escape from the horrors of war in their homeland, the image of Chechens in Austria is rather negative. On many occasions, the Yellow Press has covered their – alleged or real – involvement in crimes, brutal behaviour, archaic habits, low level of education, and unwillingness to integrate into Austrian society. On the other hand, there is a widespread opinion among the Chechen refugees that Austria does not want to quarrel with Russia, which triggers in many cases mistrust against the Austrian authorities and especially the security agencies. The Chechen community in Austria is far from united, consisting of Islamic extremists as well as secular-minded people. Many Chechen refugees are intimidated due to the well-known fact that they are under constant surveillance by the Russian Embassy in Vienna and the unofficial 'foreign intelligence service' of Kadyrov which has its informants among the refugees.

Kadyrov is suspected of having ordered the murder of Umar Israilov, a Chechen refugee shot in January 2009 as he left a grocery store in Vienna. Israilov had filed a complaint with the European Court of Human Rights against Kadyrov, who he said had participated in kidnappings, torture and killings as part of his attempt to quash Chechnya's separatist movement. Kadyrov, naturally, denied all accusations, suggesting that the killers were trying to frame him. On 1 June 2011, a jury in Vienna sentenced three Chechens to varying, lengthy, terms of imprisonment. A fourth suspect believed to have fired the three shots that killed Israilov, returned to Russia after the killing, Austrian investigators said. The Austrian law-enforcement agencies' request for assistance in their attempt to interrogate five key witnesses, including Kadyrov, was ignored by Moscow.

Not everybody in Austria considers Kadyrov a despotic ruler or a criminal who hires killers in order to get rid of opponents even abroad. Thus, in February 2012, the public learned that a small FPÖ delegation had travelled to Grozny to meet with Kadyrov. Speaking to a Chechen TV station, delegation member, FPÖ foreign affairs spokesman and MP Johannes Huebner said that his team's intention was 'to make Chechnya a safer place' and that he was 'impressed' by the republic's progress. This reflected the FPÖ's eagerness to send the Chechen refugees home as soon as possible – something Kadyrov is striving for as well. The Austrian MFA branded the FPÖ's decision to visit Chechnya as 'absurd'.

Activities of Russian secret services in Austria

After the Second World War Vienna, situated near the then dividing line between East and West, became an international spy hub. Moscow's agents particularly felt 'at home' in Vienna: 'Here, they coordinated the secret services of their satellite states [in East-Central Europe] and trained agents for their missions' in Western countries (Leidinger and Moritz 2004: 156). Even after 1989, many Russian agents remained in Vienna, attracted by the high quality of life and the presence of international organizations, including the

Organization of the Petroleum Exporting Countries (OPEC), the OSCE and the UN with several sub-organizations, among them the International Atomic Energy Agency (IAEA).

In its 2001 *Report on the Protection of the Constitution* the Austrian Ministry of the Interior wrote that Russian secret services maintain one of their largest bases in Austria, which 'underlines Vienna's special importance for Russian intelligence activities in Europe' (Republik Österreich 2002: 70). According to an internal document of the Austrian State Police (then the name of the counterintelligence), leaked to the press in the same year, of the 59 diplomats at the Russian Embassy in Vienna, 32 (54 per cent) worked for secret services, and about 100 (23 per cent) of a total of 443 Russian officials in the country (Format 2001b). From time to time, the Austrian media report (covering, undoubtedly, only the tip of the iceberg) on Russian secret service activities in Austria. More often than not, these are more a source of embarrassment for Viennese politicians and officials than for the Russians. The Austrian side is usually overly keen to restore everything to normality as soon as possible: From its point of view, spy scandals must not spoil its 'good and cordial relations' with Moscow – and, especially, the natural gas supply. Two cases illustrate this.

On 11 June 2007, Vladimir Vozhzhov was detained by Austrian Police on a German warrant in Salzburg. He was accused of offering a Warrant Officer and helicopter technician of the Austrian Armed Forces €20,000 for classified information. His non-diplomatic passport identified him as a Russian government employee. Austrian investigators worked on the assumption Vozhzhov was an agent of Russian Military Intelligence, or GRU. Moscow insisted that Vozhzhov had diplomatic status as a member of the official Russian delegation attending the 50th session of the United Nations Committee on the Peaceful Uses of Outer Space, which took place in Vienna from June 6 to 14. Moscow was incensed by Vozhzhov's arrest and demanded his immediate release. It also made clear his arrest would 'damage relations' between the two countries; behind the scenes, Moscow pressured the Austrian government. The Russian MFA criticized the arrest as a breach of the UN Convention on the Privileges and Immunities. Then, the UN and the Austrian MFA investigated whether the official did in fact enjoy the diplomatic immunity that Russia asserted on his behalf. The UN subsequently confirmed that Vozhzhov had immunity because he was accredited to the Russian delegation to the Outer Space conference. This was highly doubtful, but Vozhzhov was released on 21 June. The Austrian side was obviously relieved that a pretext had been found in order to get rid of him.

In a second incident, on 14 July 2011, Mikhail Golovatov was taken into custody at Vienna International Airport. The 62 year-old former official of the Soviet Committee for State Security, or KGB, was held responsible for the death of 14 unarmed civilians when KGB's special task force *Alpha* shot into the crowd which wanted to protect the TV tower in Vilnius, Lithuania, on 13 January 1991. However, he was freed just 22 hours after his detention, although Lithuanian prosecutors had issued a European Arrest Warrant in

218   *Martin Malek and Paul Luif*

Golovatov's name in 2010. Viennese state prosecutors said evidence brought forward by the Lithuanian government was not strong enough to justify keeping Golovatov behind bars for a longer period. Unsurprisingly, the Russian MFA was very 'satisfied'. Russia, again, clearly had exerted pressure on Austria, although this was strongly denied by both governments involved. But Manfred Nowak, a former Special Rapporteur on Torture for the UN, said Austria should have taken more time to investigate the accusations brought forward by Lithuania, concluding: 'There is a certain handling – not only in Austria: don't mess with powerful Russia' (in *Austrian Independent* 2011).

Conclusions: Russian influence on Austria

Austria is one of the smaller members and does not have big influence on EU decision-making, in particular since it is not regarded as a 'specialist' for relations with Russia. In general, it tries to soften any possible disputes with Russia, since Austria is interested in good relations with Moscow. Austria as a neutral country is active in finding compromises among the EU member states in the Union's relations with Russia.

On examining EU member states' relations with Russia, Leonard and Popescu in a 2007 study opined that EU disunity allows Moscow to dominate. They identified five distinct categories of EU member countries, ranging from 'Trojan horses' (whose governments often defend positions close to Russian interests) to 'new Cold-warriors' (who have developed an overtly hostile relationship with Moscow and are willing to use the veto to block EU negotiations with Russia). Leonard and Popescu ranked Austria among the 'friendly pragmatists' who have a lukewarm but still significant relationship with Russia, in which business interests come first; their policy tends to follow pragmatic business interests, opting for a path of least resistance in political disputes (Leonard and Popescu 2007). However, one could situate Austria amongst Russia's 'strategic partners', whose relationship is closer than those of the 'friendly pragmatists'.

Truly, no-one in Austria's political elite wants to quarrel with Moscow. Russia or Austria's relations to it have never played any significant role in election campaigns, and there are no political forces in Austria which could be labelled as 'anti-Russian' by Moscow-based politicians or media outlets. The governments in Vienna and Moscow like to emphasize they are 'very close' in most of the issues of international politics, that there are very few (if any) differences between them, that their relations are 'trouble-free,' 'cordial' etc. The annual reports of the Austrian MFA are usually restrained and careful in their treatment of Russia.

In many scholarly analyses of Austria's foreign and security policy, Russia is barely mentioned, if at all. But Moscow's influence on Vienna is substantially higher than most of the incumbent Austrian politicians and diplomats (at least publicly) would admit. *Kommersant*, the probably best (and well-informed) Russian daily newspaper, wrote in 2007 that Austria, 'which is

Austria 219

a member of the EU, but not of NATO,' is 'viewed in the Kremlin as a potential lobbyist of its interests in Europe' (Yezh 2007). This means Austrian behaviour has provided official Moscow with indications that this is the case or, at least, could materialize in the near future. And, in a rare public confession, the Chief Editor of Austria's quality daily *Die Presse* stated that Austrian politicians 'are particularly proficient in the skill of anticipatory submissiveness to the "contemporary Tsar"' (Fleischhacker 2012), meaning Putin.

There is an obvious tendency in the statements of Austrian politicians, diplomats and businessmen to tell their Russian interlocutors just what they want to hear, in particular: that Austria will remain neutral (and, therefore, will not join NATO); that Russia necessarily has to be a part of a new European security system or architecture; that Moscow's interests, especially in the realm of security policy, must be respected (meaning by NATO and the USA); that Austria – like Russia – is in favour of a 'multipolar world', consisting of several equal great powers; and so on.

Austrian politicians find it difficult to say 'no' to Russia and/or to find critical words about its domestic, foreign, and security policy. Thus, Austrian media have paid some attention to increasing authoritarianism under Putin but Viennese politics rarely raise this issue. Instead, it is a widespread argument that Russia is too important as a power – and especially as supplier of energy resources – so relations must not be spoiled under any circumstances. Austrian politicians from across the political spectrums have repeatedly hailed the 'stability' and 'restoration of order' brought by Putin since 1999.

On numerous occasions, as the Vozhzhov and Golovatov cases demonstrate, it has proved quite easy for Russia to exert pressure on Austria. Usually, it is sufficient for Moscow, behind the scenes, of course, to hint at possible 'consequences for bilateral relations', and Vienna caves in without any storm of protest in Austrian politics, mass media, or public opinion. Frequently it seems Austria's foreign policy has more in common with Russia than with the United States. Austria – like many other Western European countries – on many issues ostentatiously distances itself from the USA, which brings it intentionally or inadvertently into proximity to Russia. The result is that Austria's official positions regarding many questions are closer to Moscow than Washington. And Austria's political elite as well as the media are in general much more critical towards the USA than to Russia.

Thus, while in Austria tens of thousands protested US and/or NATO interventions (especially in the 1999 Kosovo Crisis, Afghanistan in 2001 and Iraq in 1991 and 2003), there were no significant rallies against the Russian military campaigns in Georgia (2008) and Chechnya. Austrian media since 2001 have persistently reported about Guantanamo Bay, but the existence of Russian 'filtration camps' in and around Chechnya during both wars with (at least) several hundred inmates was totally unknown to the Austrian public. And several Austrian politicians showed open solidarity with Russia's position on US and NATO missile defence plans. Important departures from the pro-Russian course were Austria's rejection of the MiG-29 aircraft, which

220　Martin Malek and Paul Luif

Moscow wanted to sell (Vienna preferred the *Eurofighter Typhoon*), and the recognition of Kosovo as an independent state in 2008 (which Russia still considers a part of Serbia).

With regard to bilateral economic issues too, Russia has nothing to worry about. At first glance, it is rather difficult to understand why Austria, whose OMV is lead company on the Nabucco pipeline project, agreed to join Moscow's South Stream initiative which will further deepen EU dependence on Russian gas. The official explanation is that 'the two projects do not rule out each other' or even 'complement one another'. But this is obviously not in line with Moscow's clear intention to thwart Nabucco in order to replace it with South Stream, which would be controlled by Gazprom. Thus, the Austrian position on this question can only be explained by arguing Vienna does not wish to alienate (or even infuriate) Moscow.

This critical analysis of Austria's relations with Russia demonstrates the difficulty for the EU to 'speak with one voice' towards Russia. Just across its borders in the east, the countries of Central and Eastern Europe had rather different experiences with the Soviet Union after 1945 and thus display attitudes towards the big neighbour in the East which clearly contrast with Austria's behaviour.

Note

1 The Socialist Party of Austria was renamed the Social-Democratic Party in 1991.

References

Außenpolitischer Bericht 2008, *Jahrbuch der Österreichischen Außenpolitik*. Wien: Bundesministerium für europäische und internationale Angelegenheiten.

Austrian Independent (2011) 'Austria "acted insensitively" over Golovatov', *Austrian Independent*. 21 July 2011, available at http://austrianindependent.com/news/Politics/2011-07-21/8500/Austria_'acted_insensitively'_over_Golovatov (accessed 8 March 2012).

Der Standard (2001) 'Nato-Erweiterung führt zu neuen Barrieren', *Der Standard*. 10/11 February 2001: 3.

Fedyashin, A. (2010) 'Vladimir Putin goes to the land of Strauss and schnitzel', *RIA Novosti*. 23 April 2010, available at http://en.rian.ru/analysis/20100423/158716228.html (accessed 28 March 2012).

Fleischhacker, M. (2012) 'Entscheidungen sind gefragt, nicht nur in Russland', *Die Presse*. 3 March 2012: 2.

Format (2001a) 'Eine Bedrohung Rußlands', *Format*. No. 5, 29 January 2001: 33.

——(2001b) 'Abdeckung an der Botschaft', *Format*. No. 6, 2001: 45.

Gehler, M. (2005) *Österreichs Außenpolitik der Zweiten Republik. Von der alliierten Besatzung bis zum Europa des 21. Jahrhunderts*. Vol. 1, Innsbruck–Wien–Bozen: Studien Verlag.

Gurkina, Y. (2006) "Venskiy vals "Gazproma'. Avstriya dopustila komapniyu k konechnym potrebitelyam', *Nezavisimaya gazeta*. 2 October 2006: 4.

Hofmann, M. and Reichel, D. (2008) 'Chechen Migration Flows to Europe – a Statistical Perspective', in A. Janda, N. Leitner and M. Vogl (eds) *Chechens in the European Union*. Vienna: Austrian Integration Fund: 9–26.

Austria 221

Jankowitsch, P. (2010) 'Das Problem der Äquidistanz. Die Suche der Zweiten Republik nach außenpolitischen Leitlinien', in M. Rauchensteiner (ed.) *Zwischen den Blöcken. NATO, Warschauer Pakt und Österreich*. Wien–Köln–Weimar: Böhlau: 452–95.

Kronen Zeitung (2001) 'Putin exklusiv in der "Krone": Die Neutralität ist Sache Österreichs', *Kronen Zeitung*. 8 February 2001: 1 and 4.

Leidinger, H. and Moritz, V. (2004) *Russisches Wien. Begegnungen aus vier Jahrhunderten*. Wien–Köln–Weimar: Böhlau Verlag.

Leonard, M. and Popescu, N. (2007) *A Power Audit of EU Russia Relations*. London: European Council on Foreign Relations.

Luif, P. (1995) *On the Road to Brussels: The Political Dimension of Austria's, Finland's and Sweden's Accession to the European Union*. Vienna–West Lafayette: Braumüller–Purdue University Press.

OSCE Press Release (2000) 'OSCE to reopen office for Assistance Group to Chechnya', OSCE. 15 April 2000, available at www.osce.org/cio/52051 (accessed 5 April 2012).

Parlamentskorrespondenz (1999) 'Tschetschenien-Konflikt: Abgeordnete fordern Dialog statt Gewalt. Brief an Abgeordnete zur russischen Staatsduma', *Parlamentskorrespondenz*. Nr. 562, 16 December 1999, available at www.parlament.gv.at/PAKT/PR/JAHR_1999/PK0562/index.shtml (accessed 5 April 2012).

Republik Österreich (2002) *Verfassungsschutzbericht 2001*. Wien: Bundesministerium für Inneres.

RIA Novosti (2010) 'Putin hails Russia's gas reserves as Austria joins South Stream project', RIA Novosti. 24 April 2010, available at http://en.rian.ru/world/20100424/158729140.html (accessed 14 March 2012).

——(2011) 'EU-Kommission blockiert Gazprom-Einstieg bei Gas-Hub in Österreich', *RIA Novosti*. 20 June 2011, available at http://de.rian.ru/industry_agriculture/20110620/259512030.html (accessed 21 June 2011).

Ultsch, C. (2009) 'Putin drängt Wien zu Beteiligung an 'South Stream", *Die Presse*. 12 November 2009: 7.

Ultsch, C. and Steiner, E. (2009) 'Faymann im Kreml: Zwischen Kalaschnikow und Erdgas', *Die Presse*. 10 November 2009, available at http://diepresse.com/home/politik/aussenpolitik/520903/index.do?_vl_backlink=/home/politik/aussenpolitik/index.do (accessed 12 November 2009).

Wirtschaftsblatt (2007) 'Gazprom-Vize schließt OMV-Einstieg nicht aus: Noch Zeit nicht reif', *Wirtschaftsblatt*. 25 May 2007, available at www.wirtschaftsblatt.at/home/schwerpunkt/dossiers/omv/gazprom-vize-schliesst-omv-einstieg-nicht-aus-noch-zeit-nicht-reif-243717/index.do (accessed 28 March 2012).

Yezh, P. (2007) 'Na puti v Avstriyu vstalo televidenie', *Kommersant*. 21 May 2007: 9.

15 Slovenia

Jackie Gower

Slovenia is one of the smallest of the new member states that joined the European Union in 2004 and its foreign policy priorities are understandably focused on its immediate neighbourhood, especially the Western Balkans. However, in recent years it has developed a positive and wide-ranging bilateral relationship with Russia and also become a fairly low-key but nevertheless significant actor with regard to EU–Russia policy. Unlike most of the other post-communist member states, Slovenia's relations with Russia are almost entirely free of the painful historical legacy of the Soviet era and President Danilo Türk (2011) went so far as to say 'we share a century-long mutual affection, cultural similarities and common experiences in all areas'. The strong sense of a shared Slavic cultural identity together with mutually important economic interests, especially involving the South Stream gas pipeline project, have provided firm foundations for a significant upgrading of the bilateral relationship in recent years. That this has clearly involved Russia being willing to invest considerable diplomatic efforts at the highest political level raises the question as to whether it has a long-term strategic vision of a Russia-friendly caucus of EU member states emerging in the Western Balkans which would offset the rather negative impact on EU–Russia relations of the accession of both the Visegrad and Baltic states.

The chapter will begin with a brief assessment of the legacy of the foreign policy of the former Yugoslavia for contemporary Slovenian–Russian relations. It will then discuss the development of the foreign policy of Slovenia since its declaration of independence in 1990 and in particular its relationship with Russia, identifying the main drivers as economic and cultural factors. Although the relationship is very friendly with no significant tensions, it will be noted that it does not necessarily mean Slovenia and Russia take the same position on international issues, with both the status of Kosovo and the war in Georgia in August 2008 being prime examples. The focus will then shift from the bilateral relationship to the role of Slovenia in the conduct of EU–Russia policy at the Brussels level with a discussion of Slovenia's EU Council Presidency in 2008 and its stance on key issues on the current agenda. Finally, in the conclusion the analysis will move to the regional level, with some speculation about the potential impact on EU–Russia relations of Croatia's

Slovenia 223

accession in July 2013 and the longer term possible consequences of further enlargement to other Western Balkan states.

Yugoslavia's relations with the USSR

Slovenia, as a successor state of Yugoslavia, has very different historical memories of the end of the Second World War and the imposition of communist rule compared to those of the central and east European EU member states and this fact goes a long way in accounting for their different attitudes towards Russia even today (interview at the Permanent Representation, May 2011). Yugoslavia was very largely liberated by the indigenous partisan movement led by Marshall Tito and it was responsible for the establishment of communist rule, with very little input from either the Red Army or Soviet political agents (Headley 2008: 226; Gow and Carmichael 2010: 53). However, Slovenian politicians are happy to acknowledge the contribution the Red Army did make to liberating small parts of Slovenia, and in an interview for *Russia Today* on the 65th anniversary of the victory over Germany, President Türk (2010a) said 'we are grateful to the Red Army for the liberation contribution'. Such a statement would be inconceivable from most politicians in central and east European states. One of the important consequences is that Russia and Slovenia share an agreed historical narrative about the importance of the role of the Soviet Union in the defeat of fascism and Slovenian leaders are entirely happy to commemorate the anniversary on 8 May each year alongside their Russian counterparts, acknowledging that 'the sacrifices were enormous' and 'the Soviet Union's input to the liberation of Europe is unforgettable' (Türk 2010a). This public solidarity is very much valued by the Russians who are very sensitive to what they see as attempts in some European countries 'to rewrite history' and denigrate or deny the role of the Soviet Union in the defeat of Hitler's Germany.

Yugoslavia's experience during the Cold War was also very different from that of the members of the Warsaw Pact. There was a brief period of very strained relations with the Soviet Union following Stalin's unsuccessful attempt to impose control from Moscow and the resulting expulsion in 1948 of Yugoslavia from the Cominform. Tito's response was to go on to develop a distinctive national model of socialism and Yugoslavia was never part of the Soviet bloc. After Stalin's death in 1953, Khrushchev sought to re-establish friendly relations although the Warsaw Pact intervention in Hungary in 1956 nearly derailed the reconciliation, as did the intervention in Czechoslovakia under Brezhnev. Throughout the Cold War Yugoslavia maintained its independence from Moscow by pursuing a skilful policy of 'balancing between East and West' (Lampe 2000: 267). One of Tito's most important foreign policy contributions was to help found the Non-Aligned Movement in the 1950s which enabled Yugoslavia to derive the benefits of maintaining good relationships with both the USSR and USA/the West (Headley 2008: 22; Kullaa 2011). There is some evidence that Slovenia today draws on this

224   *Jackie Gower*

experience and reputation of playing an impartial role and maintaining good relations with both sides in the context of EU–Russia policy-making.

Slovenia's relations with Russia

Political relations

For the first decade or so after its declaration of independence, Slovenia's main foreign policy objectives were to attain membership of NATO and the EU and to settle a number of disputes with its immediate neighbours, mainly Italy and Croatia (Kajnč 2011: 203). Official diplomatic relations between Slovenia and Russia were established in May 1992 and the Slovenia–Russia Association was established in 1996 to promote closer cultural and economic co-operation, but neither party showed much interest in going beyond normal cordial interaction. However, in 2002 they adopted a Declaration on Friendly Relations and Co-operation with a commitment to strengthen bilateral co-operation in political and economic relations, science and culture with a view to enhancing political dialogue and mutual understanding. This document continues to provide the framework for political dialogue and active contact at various levels regarding all matters of mutual interest, including exchanging views on the international situation as well as security and defence issues. It is important to note that despite the positive and friendly relationship between the two countries, there have been a number of occasions when their views have diverged on important international issues such as the status of Kosovo, Georgia's territorial integrity, NATO enlargement and missile defence. However, 'the cooperation remains constructive despite at times diverging positions, which do not affect bilateral relations' (interview at Ministry of Foreign Affairs [MFA] May 2012).

The years 2010–11 were a watershed in the bilateral relationship with President Türk making his first state visit to Russia in November 2010 and signing a Declaration on Partnership and Modernization and Prime Minister Putin visiting Slovenia in March 2011 to sign a memorandum of understanding for the creation of a new joint company to construct the South Stream pipeline through Slovenia. There were also many other high-level visits which increased the intensity of the dialogue between the two states on a wide range of political, economic and cultural issues. There seem to be two main reasons for the increased activism in the Slovenia–Russia relationship. Firstly, Slovenia had held the chair in a number of international organizations (the OSCE in 2005, EU Council Presidency in 2008 and the Committee of Ministers of the Council of Europe in 2009) which required it to broaden its foreign policy horizons and adopt a more active role in international issues beyond its immediate neighbourhood, including those involving Russia (interview at MFA May 2012). It also inevitably raised its profile on the international stage and seems to have aroused a greater interest in Moscow in its potential to be a useful ally, albeit in some cases it proved somewhat of a

Slovenia 225

disappointment from Russia's perspective, most notably with regards to OSCE reform and Kosovo's status. The second reason for the recent upgrading of the relationship is the importance Russia attaches to the South Stream gas pipeline project and Slovenia's strategic position as a potential transit country through to Italy and central Europe (see below for details).

Economic relations

Russia is an increasingly important economic partner and Slovenia is one of the few EU member states to record a trade surplus with Russia (Eurostat 2012). Its main exports to Russia include pharmaceuticals, paints and varnishes, electrical goods, telecommunication equipment and consumer goods (interview at MFA May 2012). Business relations are actively supported by the Slovene–Russian Business Club under the banner 'Fostering the Slavic Bonds' and the growing Russian market is seen as increasingly attractive at a time when other export markets are under pressure from the economic recession. Special economic links have been established with a number of Russian regions and the Slovenian Embassy's section for economic co-operation is based in Kazan. The Russian tourist market is also quite important for Slovenia and numbers have been increasing significantly in recent years. Although at the moment only accounting for a relatively small proportion of tourists to the country, Russians tend to stay for more nights and also to spend more, particularly favouring health resorts and spas.

Russia's exports to Slovenia consist mainly of oil and natural gas. Slovenia depends entirely on imports for its natural gas and about 55 per cent currently comes from Russia although this figure needs to be seen in the context of natural gas only accounting for around 14 per cent of its total energy needs. After the major disruption in supply in January 2009 caused by the Russia–Ukraine gas dispute, Slovenia entered into discussions about co-operation in the construction and operation of the South Stream gas pipeline and signed an Intergovernmental Agreement with Russia in November 2009. The Slovenian energy company Plinovodi and Gazprom signed the South Stream Slovenia LLC Shareholders Agreement on 22 March 2011 to establish a joint project company with 50–50 shares to implement the South Stream project in Slovenia (South Stream 2012). Given that South Stream is generally regarded as a rival to the Nabucco pipeline favoured by the EU Commission, the government of Slovenia has been anxious to stress that their decision to support it should not be seen as disloyal to the EU. They argue that the EU's energy security depends primarily on the diversification of supply routes rather than suppliers as such and so South Stream is entirely in line with the EU's energy security goals (interview at Permanent Representation May 2011).

Further co-operation on energy and other advanced technology projects are a major objective of the Partnership for Modernization (P4M) signed in November 2011 between Slovenia and Russia. It is of course only one of a very large number of such agreements made by EU member states with

226 *Jackie Gower*

Russia in the context of the EU–Russia P4M launched at Rostov-on-Don in May–June 2010. It is however quite instructive to see where Slovenia believes it can make a contribution to the modernization programme. The main priorities are co-operation between small and medium sized enterprises and the 'fostering of an entrepreneurial environment', while they envisage a number of joint projects involving innovation, research and development.

Cultural relations

Although economic interests are becoming increasingly important drivers in Slovenia's relationship with Russia, the cultural dimension is clearly also very important. The opening sentence of the Declaration on Partnership and Modernization states it is: 'drawing on long-standing amicable relations and cooperation, which are founded on civilization, cultural and linguistic proximity and common Slavic roots … ' (Ministry of Foreign Affairs of Slovenia 2011). Official communications by both parties stress their shared Slavic identity and it is especially important in stimulating a wide range of contacts at the civil society as well as official levels. The Presidents of Slovenia and Russia jointly sponsored the foundation in 2004 of the Forum of Slavic Cultures, an international nongovernmental organization dedicated to the preservation and development of the traditions of Slavic speaking countries. Slovenia is particularly proud that Ljubljana was chosen for its headquarters and it was a focal point of the cultural programme of the Slovenian EU Presidency in 2008 which chose inter-cultural dialogue as one of its main themes. Russian Foreign Minister Sergei Lavrov opened a Russian Scientific and Cultural Centre in Ljubljana in April 2011 to give a 'fresh impetus to cultural and scientific cooperation' (Ministry of Foreign Affairs of Slovenia 2011).

An important symbolic demonstration of the importance of the cultural co-operation between the two countries takes place each year at the commemorative ceremony held at the Russian chapel in the Vršic mountain pass where some three hundred Russian prisoners of war were killed in an avalanche during the First World War. The care taken over the restoration and preservation of the chapel is highly appreciated by the Russians and the joint annual ceremony provides a regular opportunity for important Russian dignitaries to visit Slovenia and meet their counterparts. President Türk (2011) concluded his address on the occasion of the sixty-fifth anniversary by saying: 'Let the message of these gatherings gain strength every year. Long live the friendship between Slovenia and Russia'.

Slovenia and EU–Russia policy

As one of the smallest of the new member states, Slovenia's potential impact on EU-level policy towards Russia is modest but it is diplomatically active in the Council Working Group on Eastern Europe (COEST) and Alojz Peterle, MEP, is Vice-Chair of the EU–Russia Parliamentary Co-operation

Slovenia 227

Committee. Slovenia does not regularly align itself with any particular individual or sub-group of member states with regard to policy towards Russia but seeks allies on a case by case basis (interview with MFA May 2012). It generally has close diplomatic relations with Italy, Austria and Hungary but it very much depends on the issue on the agenda (Gow and Carmichael 2010; Türk 2010c). Although Slovenia co-operates quite closely with the Visegrad states on other foreign policy issues, their rather suspicious stance on Russia often makes it difficult to work with them in this area.

Slovenia's diplomatic skills (and resources) were particularly tested during the first six months in 2008 when it had the distinction of being the first of the 2004 intake of new member states to hold the EU Council Presidency. Kajnč suggests it 'kick-started Slovenia's active participation in European foreign policy' (2011: 189) and also served to raise its profile in Moscow where it was noted that this was the first Slavic state to fulfil the role. The Slovenian government set great store on successfully using their position to achieve a qualitative change in the EU–Russia relationship which had reached a very low point during the previous year. Neither of the two 2007 presidencies (Germany and Portugal) had been able to achieve a consensus on the negotiating mandate for a new EU–Russia agreement to replace the Partnership and Cooperation Agreement (PCA). Slovenia's Foreign Minister Dr Rupel took the lead in seeking a resolution to the outstanding obstacle, namely Lithuania's threatened veto over the disruption of Russian oil supplies to the Mazeikial oil refinery (see Chapter 10 of this volume and Kajnč 2008). The successful launch of the negotiations on a new agreement at the EU–Russia summit at Khanti Mansiisk in June 2008 was one of the main achievements of the Slovenian presidency and hailed as 'the start of a new age' in EU–Russia relations (Slovenian Presidency of the EU 2008). The Summit was 'marked by talks held in a friendly atmosphere' and the report explicitly claimed that 'the spirit of a new beginning' was in part due to the fact that 'Slovenia is the first Slavic country at the helm of the EU Council'.

The experience gained from the presidency has encouraged Slovenia to continue to play an active role at the Brussels level. On most policy issues its position is close to that of the majority of member states and the EU institutions and its warm bilateral relationship with Russia has not had any obvious impact on its stance on specific policy issues on the EU–Russia agenda. Although its participation in the South Stream project might be viewed as the exception, it is in the company of seven other member states so is by no means exceptional. There are two policy areas, however, where Slovenia has been noticeably active in trying to mobilise support for a more sympathetic response to Russia's position. One case is the proposal for a new European security treaty associated with former President Medvedev. The Russkiy Mir Foundation (2011) reported that 'Russia praises the fact that the Slovenian president was among the first foreign leaders to respond positively to the Russian president's initiative' and to provide specific comments on the draft. President Türk has made positive references to the initiative in

228   *Jackie Gower*

numerous speeches and interviews, urging that it is 'an opportunity Europe must not miss' (Türk 2010c; see also Türk 2010a and 2010b). However, after Putin's return to the Kremlin in 2012 it is not clear whether Russia will continue to press the idea.

The second policy area where Slovenia has been especially active is visa liberalization, which it argues is absolutely essential not only for Russia but also for the Eastern Partnership states. It believes that the very positive experience of moving towards visa free travel in the Western Balkans means that this is an area where Slovenia can make a real contribution and President Türk himself has led the diplomatic campaign to win the debate in Brussels (Türk 2010b). In addition to the usual arguments about the benefits to business, tourism and student mobility, the Slovenian government also stresses that visa liberalization is one of the most powerful tools for raising the level of contact between civil societies and direct people-to-people contact which will not only have a very beneficial effect on co-operation between the EU and Russia, but also 'raise awareness of European values' and 'facilitate more profound shifts in Russian society' (interview MFA May 2012). The argument goes some way to answering those critics of 'Russia friendly states' like Slovenia that they are unwilling to engage with the normative agenda in relation to Russia, with differences over methods rather than objectives perhaps being more accurate.

Conclusion: towards a distinctive Western Balkans perspective on Russia?

The chapter has argued that Slovenia's national perspective on Russia has been shaped by its historical experience and cultural identity with the result that it differs in important ways from that of the other new member states, especially the Visegrad and Baltic states. Its bilateral relationship with Russia is positive, co-operative and increasingly important in terms of trade and energy but it does not mean that there are not areas where the two states 'agree to differ', whether they involve international issues or domestic political developments in Russia itself. Before Slovenia's accession the Russian Foreign Minister Igor Ivanov said that 'we hope that Slovenia's entry into the European Union will aid the development of Russian relations with the EU' (Ministry of Foreign Affairs of the Russian Federation 2003). His successor Sergei Lavrov confirmed that the hope had been realized when he said in 2011 'Russia appreciates the substantial contribution of Slovenian diplomacy within the dialogue between Russia and European institutions' and specifically commented that 'mutual respect for different opinions as reflected in Slovene–Russian relations' is of key importance for successful co-operation with the EU (Ministry of Foreign Affairs of the Republic of Slovenia 2011). With the prospect of further enlargement, the question arises as to whether a distinctive regional perspective with respect to EU–Russia relations may develop in the future.

Croatia will become the 28th member of the EU in July 2013 and has a historical and cultural profile very similar to Slovenia's. It is also involved in the South Stream project and trade and tourism have both grown significantly in recent years. For four years running (2009–12) it introduced a visa free travel regime for Russians over the summer period and is expected to be a firm ally of Slovenia in pressing for the liberalization of the EU visa regime. The political dimension of its bilateral relationship with Russia has so far been rather less developed than Slovenia's and indeed until the signing of the South Stream agreement was described as rather poor (*Nacional* 2010). However, both sides have already shown interest in strengthening co-operation and Russia clearly sees Croatia as another potentially useful EU ally. Russia's expectations are probably even better founded with regard to the other three official candidate states: Serbia, Macedonia and Montenegro. They share the same historical legacy and their Slavic cultural identity is stronger with their use of the Cyrillic alphabet and adherence to the Eastern Orthodox religion. Serbia and Macedonia are involved in the South Stream project and discussions are underway about the feasibility of extending the pipeline to Montenegro. There has been significant Russian investment throughout the region which is reinforcing the perception that Russia regards the Balkans as one of its traditional spheres of influence. Russia is generally supportive of EU enlargement to include these countries and may be antici-pating that it will have a positive impact on EU–Russia relations in the future and go some way to redress the balance of the impact of the 2004 enlarge-ment. If they follow Slovenia's example of constructive engagement in the EU–Russia policy-making process, the impact may be positive from Brussels' perspective too.

Interviews

The author gratefully acknowledges the very helpful interviews granted by officials at the Permanent Representation of the Republic of Slovenia to the EU in Brussels in May 2011 and the Ministry of Foreign Affairs in Ljubljana in May 2012 (the latter by e-mail). She would also like to thank the Slovenian Embassy in London for facilitating the interviews.

References

Eurostat (2012) 'EU – Russia summit: strong recovery of trade in goods between EU27 and Russia in 2011', Europa Press Releases RAPID. 1 June 2012, available at http://europa.eu/rapid/pressReleasesAction.do?reference=STAT/12/82&type=HTML (accessed 12 July 2012).
Forum of Slavic Cultures. Ljubljana, website: www.fsk.si/ (accessed 12 July 2012).
Gow, J. and Carmichael, C. (2010) *Slovenia and the Slovenes.* London: Hurst and Company.
Headley, J. (2008) *Russia and the Balkans: Foreign Policy from Yeltsin to Putin.* London: Hurst and Company.

230 Jackie Gower

Kajnč, S. (2008) 'The Slovenian Presidency of the EU Council: How the 16th Member State Performed'. ARI 105/2008, Real Instituto Elcano, Madrid, available at www.realinstitutoelcano.org/wps/portal/rielcano_eng/Content?WCM_GLOBAL_CONTEXT=/elcano/elcano_in/zonas_in/europe/ari105–2008 (accessed 14 April 2012).

——(2011) 'Slovenia: searching for a foreign policy identity via the EU', in R. Wong and C. Hill (eds) *National and European Foreign Policies: Towards Europeanization*. London: Routledge.

Kullaa, R. (2011) *Non-Alignment and its Origins in Cold War Europe: Yugoslavia, Finland and the Soviet Challenge*. 2nd edn. London: I.B. Tauris.

Lampe, J. R. (2000) *Yugoslavia as History: Twice there was a Country*. Cambridge: Cambridge University Press.

Ministry of Foreign Affairs of the Republic of Slovenia (2011) 'Foreign Ministers Žbogar and Lavrov discuss continuation of enhanced cooperation between Slovenia and Russia'. Ljubljana, 21 April, available at www.mzz.gov.si/nc/en/newsroom/news/article/141/28687/ (accessed 6 June 2012).

Ministry of Foreign Affairs of the Russian Federation (2003) Transcript of Minister of Foreign Affairs of the Russian Federation Igor Ivanov's Remarks and Replies to Media Questions at Ljubljana Press Conference. 12 September 2003, available at www.mid.ru/bdomp/brp_4.nsf/e78a48070f128a7b43256999005bcbb3/cb14bf0681086f6c43256da200599b77!OpenDocument (accessed 11 July 2012).

Nacional (2010) 'South Stream puts Croatia back among Russia's partners'. 747, 9 March 2010, available at www.nacional.hr/en/clanak/50452/south-stream-puts-croatia-back-among-russias-partners (accessed 20 April 2012).

Russkiy Mir Foundation (2011) 'Russia and Slovenia to discuss expanding cooperation'. 16 May 2011, available at www.russkiymir.ru/russkiymir/en/news/common/news3237.html (accessed 18 May 2011).

Slovene–Russia Business Club, official website: www.slovenia-russia.com/eng/ekonomika/ (accessed 20 April 2012).

Slovenian Presidency of the EU (2008) press release, 'EU – Russia Summit: The Start of a New Age'. 27 June 2008, available at www.eu2008.si/en/News_and_Documents/Press_Releases/June/2706KPV_EU_Rusija1.html? (accessed 13 July 2012).

South Stream (2012) 'Parameters defined for South Stream in Slovenia'. Available at http://south-stream.info/index.php?id=38&l=1&tx_ttnews[tt_news]=268&cHash=8fc2ae39b2 (accessed 8 July 2012).

Türk, D. (2010a) Interview for *Russia Today*. Ljubljana, 8 May 2010, available at www.up-rs.si/up-rs/uprs-eng.nsf/dokumentiweb/75EC34FA1D2F7300C125775E0036AC54?OpenDocument (accessed 10 January 2012).

——(2010b) 'Address by the President at the Global Russia Meeting'. Brdu pri Kranju, 17 May, available at www.up-rs.si/up-rs/uprs-eng.nsf/dokumentiweb/1DC9B2B89E052B8BC125772F0047197D?OpenDocument (accessed 16 April 2012).

——(2010c) 'Slovenian foreign policy at a time of change', lecture by President of the Republic of Slovenia. Ljubliana, 3 November 2010, available at www.up-rs.si/up-rs/uprs-eng.nsf/dokumentiweb/48B4ADFBC0C29796C12577F5004B5315?OpenDocument (accessed 4 June 2012).

——(2011) 'Address at the memorial ceremony at the Russian Chapel'. Vršič, 31 July 2011, press release, speech, available at www.up-rs.si/up-rs/uprs-eng.nsf/dokumentiweb/C961CADA45E89C8EC1257942004825F4?OpenDocument (accessed 28 May 2012).

16 Malta

Arsalan Alshinawi

For Malta, an island state in the middle of the Mediterranean Sea, geography seems to imply that the government would only have a regional foreign policy focus, whereas a country like Russia extends outside its immediate points of reference and domains of interest. Relations between the two countries, however, have 'grown from strength to strength in the areas of political and diplomatic interaction, trade and economic cooperation, cultural ties, and people-to-people contacts', confirmed the Ambassador to the Russian Federation confirmed at an exhibition at the Ministry of Foreign Affairs in Valletta during a week-long celebration of the Russian–Maltese friendship in October 2010. There is a 'bilateral agenda,' explained the Ambassador, where the 'most promising areas of cooperation' are 'trade and economic ties', on the basis of a 'solid foundation of traditional friendship and mutual respect between the Russian and Maltese people' that has 'deep historical roots' (*The Malta Independent*, 31 July 2011).

This chapter seeks to assess whether this is indeed the case. The main argument is that relations with Russia need to be viewed within the twin contexts of Malta's small state identity and the wider European dynamics. Under the centre-right Christian democratic Nationalist Party, in power since 1987, the country joined the EU and NATO's Partnership for Peace (PfP) in 2004 and 2008 respectively, a few decades after gaining independence as a sovereign state within the British Commonwealth in 1964, and the termination of the military base agreement with Britain resulting in the removal of British forces in 1979.

The case of the conduct of Malta–Russia relations becomes particularly interesting considering that the government of Malta, as the smallest member state, is committed to working towards an EU common position on foreign policy and security issues towards its neighbours and beyond. Appraisals of the case of Malta's diplomacy with Russia can shed light on geography as a key factor in the interplay between bilateralism and multilateralism of member states, in theory and policy-making, which can be useful in any assessment of the relations between an organization like the EU and Russia.

This chapter seeks to provide insights into Malta's bilateralism and its implications for wider EU–Russia relations. It reviews the major developments in relations with Russia, underlines the perspective on Russia of local politicians

232 *Arsalan Alshinawi*

and foreign policy practitioners, under the Labour Party and the Nationalist Party, and elaborates on the background setting underlying the role of Malta in international relations. It draws upon academic literature, available primary documents and diplomatic communiqués, and semi-structured elite interviews conducted by the author in Valletta.

Malta and Russia

Malta has a land area of just over 300 sq. km (120 sq. miles) with no natural resources, and a population of nearly 420,000 people. At the southern edge of Europe, 60 miles south of Italy and 200 miles north of Libya, it has been 'remote from the centres of European prosperity' (Dowdall 1972: 467), and 'always had a history closely [linked] with that of great powerful nations' (Metwally 1977: ix). Its economy is small, energy-dependent and facing very high energy costs, and a variety of wealth generation activities, including serving as a freight trans-shipment point, manufacturing (foreign investment in electronics and textiles), tourism and international financial services are increasingly reliant on external sources (on Malta as a small economy, see Frendo and Bonnici 1989; Pace 2002; Briguglio 1995; Briguglio *et al.* 2008). For Malta, the sum of exports and imports of goods and services measured as a share of gross domestic product (trade as a percentage of GDP) has always been high (National Accounts of the Maltese Islands, various years).

Since securing independence, Malta has been seeking to develop its role within the international community as a viable and active partner. Its European values have been furthered during the past two decades by the Nationalist government that took office after the general elections of 1987, with a shift in the island's external relations, military alliance, trade and collaboration from the East to the West (Findlay and Wellisz 1993: 256–92; Delia 2006). Its previous socialist and non-aligned stance, mostly perceived by the West as pro-Libyan and pro-Eastern (and hence anti-Western) were espoused by the Labour Party government that ruled Malta between 1971 and 1987 (Dowdall 1972). The Nationalist government joined the PfP in April 1995, but the Labour Party withdrew from it in October 1996. The Nationalists reactivated it in March 2008, which was accepted by NATO a month later at the summit in Bucharest. The Labour Party (in opposition) is still opposed to involvement in any military alliances, recalling the significance of the island's neutrality (Pace 2002, 2009).

Malta's relations with the Russians, historically known for their interest in gaining access to the Mediterranean Sea, emerged early in time (Schembri 1990; Crowley 2008). A special association between the Knights of Malta and the Tsar of Russia (and the Russian Hospitaller tradition of St John within the Russian Empire) had developed as far back as the 16th century when Malta witnessed the arrival and liberation of Russian Christian slaves (Zolina 2002). The rulers of Malta and Russia were facing the same enemy, when in the popular imagination of Christian-Europeans, the Mongols and Turks

Malta 233

were merged after the rise of the Ottoman Turks. The interest of the Russian Empire in the Mediterranean became evident during the seventeenth century clashes with the Ottomans and attempts of Peter the Great at breaking the stranglehold of the Turks on the Black Sea (Cassar 2000; Zolina 2002). Under Catherine II, who saw herself following in the footsteps of Peter, closer links with the Maltese islands and the Mediterranean basin became an important objective for Russia (Crowley 2008). There was a brisk trade between Malta's Grand Harbour and Russia's Black Sea ports, especially in grain, during a period of flourishing overseas trade under the British rule in the nineteenth century. After the Bolshevik revolution some thousand Russian refugees, mostly urbane, highly educated and cultured, arrived in Malta during the years 1919–22 and made a positive contribution to the local social and cultural life (Zolina 2002).

After gaining independence, the Nationalist government established diplomatic relations with Russia. During the 1970s and 1980s, the Labour government moved somewhat closer towards the USSR. There was the official opening of the Maltese Embassy in Moscow in 1982, after the conclusion of an agreement in 1981 stipulating that in case of situations that 'create a threat to peace and security or the violation of international peace,' the two countries will 'coordinate their positions in order to remove the threat or to establish peace' (Cassar 2000). The aim of the Labour government was to strengthen commercial ties (through bilateral agreements on merchant shipping, air services and trade protocols), while creating a balance vis-à-vis other encroaching powers, and acquiring Soviet support for high-priority national goals such as consolidating security in the Mediterranean within the CSCE and securing Malta's neutral status (Pirotta 1997).

The Nationalist government, after winning the general elections of 1987, hosted the US–Russia Summit in December 1989, just a few weeks after the fall of the Berlin Wall. Malta, where East meets West and North connects with South (at least from a European perspective), and with its long history of foreign domination, was symbolically chosen for the meetings between Bush and Gorbachev who proclaimed the end of the Cold War, in one of the principal highlights of the island's standing on the world stage (Cassar 2000).

For the leadership of Malta, unlike for other small countries in much of Eastern and Central Europe, moving away from the Soviet Union as the former communist-period imperial master and joining the EU and NATO was not an issue. Instead, the concern has primarily been how to safeguard neutrality as a cornerstone of its foreign policy, and pursue good relations with all countries. In national diplomacy, what must be given priority is the island's geo-economic vulnerability, and its dependence within the global division of labour on other countries to produce most of the goods and services needed to sustain the welfare of the Maltese population (Frendo and Bonnici 1989). It knows that Malta, in a broad context, as one of the leading local economists pointed out, must sustain a high degree of interdependence

234   *Arsalan Alshinawi*

within the international economy to prosper or, some would argue, to survive (Briguglio 1995).

For local politicians and foreign policy practitioners from both parties, Russia constitutes a prominent factor in the equation of international stability and prosperity. Good relations with a re-emerging power like Russia are clearly advantageous. Malta, a country dependent on tourism, is one of the most popular summer destinations for Russians. Tourist arrivals from Russia in 2008 reached 23,412, an increase of almost 7,000 since 2005, and the total expenditure of Russian tourists was more than €22 million in 2009 (National Accounts of the Maltese Islands, various years). Trends for the high season for the year 2011 were, according to the Malta Tourism Authority, expected to reach the level of pre-crises years, in the region of 22,000, but the actual number of Russians visiting Malta is more than these figures indicate since the Maltese consulate in Moscow is increasingly issuing multiple entry permits (www.foreign.gov.mt).

In Malta's numerous international language schools, an increasing number of Russians attend a variety of English language courses, which is important for a country that promotes itself as a centre for teaching English to foreigners. Russian students, following courses in 37 English schools in Malta offering education to foreigners during 2010, were in fifth place among the number of students from other countries, with the top five countries accounting for almost 75 per cent of all students (National Accounts of the Maltese Islands, various years).The Russian Boarding School in Malta (RBSM), founded in 1997, remains the first and largest school in the world that follows the Russian curriculum (http://en.rbsm.ru). Exports to the Russian market, mainly pharmaceutical and plastic related products, amount to €2 million a year. In 2010, there were 307 companies registered in Malta under Russian ownership, with trading and holding as the most common type of activity. The popularity of Malta's internet casinos is on the increase among Russian customers after recently-introduced restrictions on gaming business in Russia (National Accounts of the Maltese Islands, various years).

Maltese–Russian political relations have been developing as well. Following the disintegration of the Soviet Union, the Nationalist government extended official recognition to the Russian Federation as an independent and sovereign state and continued the previous Labour government's policy of pursuing close co-operation with the country. The signing of agreements continued across a number of sectors, including tourism (1995), co-operation between the Ministries of Justice (2001), a programme of cultural and youth exchanges (2003–5), and a wide-ranging exchange programme between the University of Malta and the State University of St Petersburg in 2004.

Exchange of high-level bilateral visits by government officials have also taken place, notably the visit of the Deputy Foreign Minister of Russia to Malta in 2003, and Malta's Prime Minister to St. Petersburg in May 2003, and to Moscow in 2005, to participate in the EU–Russia summits. The flagship of the Russian Black Sea fleet cruiser *Moskva*, with the Black Sea ensemble on board, visited the Grand Harbour of Malta in September 2004, and a delegation from the Foreign and European Affairs Committee of the Maltese Parliament visited Russia in 2006. In late 2003, the Ministry of Finance of Russia announced its intention to settle the debt issue of Malta, namely $70.7 million for timber carriers ordered by the Soviet Union in 1989 (*The Times of Malta*, 5 November 2003). In July 2004, Russia participated for the first time in the Malta International Trade Fair (www.foreign.gov.mt).

On a political level the Russian government looked 'favourably towards Malta's EU membership,' even if Russians, according to an online survey by a Russian website devoted to Malta, were reportedly against Malta joining the EU (*The Malta Independent*, 31 July 2002). To allay these fears, the Russian Deputy Foreign Minister in talks in Valletta in 2003 was informed of Malta's intention to 'ensure that the adoption of the Schengen agreement does not thwart incoming tourism in any manner' (*The Times of Malta*, 19 December 2003).

The Nationalist government showed its interest in taking advantage of the opportunities resulting from Russia's economic growth and finding ways to attract a growing number of Russian tourists and language students. The Minister for Foreign Affairs in 2004, during a meeting of EU foreign ministers in Brussels, encouraged the European Commission to step up its efforts to conclude discussions with Russia over a new visa arrangement with member states,arguing that Malta 'needed to have a visa-free arrangement with Russia as soon as possible' (*The Times of Malta* 2004). The same message has been communicated to Moscow as well. For example, a delegation from the Foreign and European Affairs Committee of the Maltese Parliament, after a visit to Moscow in 2006, concluded optimistically that the Schengen agreement 'would not make things more difficult for prospective Russian visitors to Malta' (*The Sunday Times of Malta* 2006).

All in all, the Maltese government has shown that it puts national economic interests above political goals in a pragmatic approach. In EU policy-making fora it has been reluctant to confront Russia on politically sensitive issues, and tends to oppose actions it fears might irritate Moscow, even if it is not really an active promoter of Russian interests as such in Brussels. The Russians are happy that the government of Malta, unlike some EU countries, does not use EU structures to 'fight' bilateral issues with Russia.

As a consequence, the Russian government, as reported by its Ambassador, was 'highly interested in strengthening its political dialogue with Malta as a peace-loving and neutral European nation, a new member of the EU and an authoritative state playing a significant role in the Mediterranean'. For it, there is 'no doubt that Malta will continue to be one of Russia's priority foreign partner[s]' (*The Sunday Times of Malta* 2006). Russian Foreign Minister Sergei Lavrov, in talks with his Maltese counterpart in April 2007, at the margins of the General Affairs and External Relations Council (GAERC) meeting in Luxembourg, focused on how to improve co-operation on a number of bilateral issues. The Russian government wanted to build a strong partnership with Malta and to further develop relations in the context of the EU–Russia agreements. This wish was reiterated by the Deputy Minister of

236 *Arsalan Alshinawi*

Foreign Affairs responsible for European affairs in Russia, during a meeting in Malta in June 2008 with the Deputy Prime Minister and Minister of Foreign Affairs, Tonio Borg. In turn Borg made in November 2009 the first visit by a Maltese foreign minister to Russia in 20 years where he discussed with Sergei Lavrov in Moscow, the most salient bilateral issues as both sides expressed a clear willingness to work together to strengthen ties and enhance relations, as they officially opened the Maltese consulate in Moscow (www. foreign.gov.mt).

Conclusions

For Malta, the post-Cold War era has brought changes to its basic foreign policy orientation. The earlier pro-Eastern stance had been replaced with a more pro-Western course, as exemplified by the island becoming a member of the EU and NATO's PfP, while still retaining its neutrality status. With respect to its relationship with Russia, this case study has shown that the Maltese government, whether Nationalist or Labour, has sought during the past two decades to adopt a pragmatic position, largely focussing on securing its national, political and economic interests, as it witnessed the lack of unity among EU member states around a common approach to Russia.

This analysis indicates that what matters ain terms of explanation for Malta's relations with a powerful country, to which the EU is still far from having a cohesive-collective policy, is that these two countries share a history of burden of size, with a contrast between one of the largest and one of the smallest states in the world. The thrust and nature of Maltese diplomacy, conditioned by the interrelated historical and geo-political realities of the country, are determined by the interest in safeguarding neutrality and the international interdependence of the local economy. Inevitably, this results in a higher premium being placed on persuasion and consensus building than on power play.

References

Briguglio, L. (1995) 'Small Island States and their Economic Vulnerabilities', *World Development*, 23: 1615–32.
Briguglio, L., Cordina, G., Farrugia, N. and Vigilnace, C. (eds) (2008) *Small States and the Pillars of Economic Resilience of Small States*. London: Islands and Small States Institute, University of Malta and Commonwealth Secretariat.
Cassar, C. (2000) *A Concise History of Malta*. Malta: Mireva Publications.
Crowley, R. (2008) *Empires of the Sea*. London: Faber and Faber.
Delia, E. P. (2006) *Papers on Malta's Political Economy*. Malta: Midsea Books Ltd.
Dowdall, J. (1972) 'The Political Economy of Malta', *The Round Table*, 62: 465–73.
Findlay, R. and Wellisz, S. (1993) 'Malta', in R. Findlay and S. Wellisz (eds) *The Political Economy of Poverty, Equity, and Growth: Five Small Open Economies*. Oxford and New York: Oxford UP, 256–92.

Frendo, M. and Bonnici, J. (1989) *Malta in the European Community: Some Economic & Commercial Perspectives*. Valletta: The Malta Chamber of Commerce.

The Malta Independent (various editions). Malta: Standard Publications.

Malta in figures (various editions). Valletta: National Statistics Office.

Metwally, M. M. (1977) *Structure and Performance of the Maltese Economy*. Malta: A.C. Aquilina.

National Accounts of the Maltese Islands. Valletta: National Statistics Office.

Pace, R. (2002) 'A Small State and the European Union: Malta's EU Accession Experience', *South European Society and Politics*, 7: 24–42.

——(2009) *The European Union's Mediterranean Enlargement: Cyprus and Malta*. London: Routledge.

Pirotta, G. (1997) 'Politics and public service reform in small states: Malta', *Public Administration and Development*, 17: 197–207.

Schembri, G. (1990) *The Malta and Russia Connection*. Malta: Grima Publications.

The Sunday Times of Malta (various editions). Malta: Allied Newspapers.

The Times of Malta (various editions). Malta: Allied Newspapers.

Zolina, E. (2002) *A Journey through the Centuries – historical discoveries in Russo-Maltese relations*. Malta: Progress Books.

17 Cyprus and Greece

George Christou

The issue of how to move forward with EU–Russia relations has vexed many in the academic and policy-making community over the years. Indeed, whilst the broad concept of 'strategic partnership', underpinned by the rationale of a 'modernization partnership', has now been agreed as a way forward, the road map for achieving such a partnership across many policy themes remains unclear, as does what such a partnership will actually look like in its *finalité*. The historical and contemporary context of the EU–Russian relationship is, thus, a complex one. This complexity embodies many dimensions and cuts across multiple themes, of which this chapter will attempt to unravel the bilateral aspect in relation to two member states of the EU, Greece and Cyprus, with the aim of ascertaining the extent to which each influences the evolution of a common EU position on policies relating to Russia.

Academically, the literature on Greek and Cypriot bilateral relations with Russia is sparse, as is how these two (what might be characterized as) 'small' EU member states can and have impacted on policies towards Russia. This chapter takes as its starting point the work of Leonard and Popescu (2007), which, it is argued, whilst informative, requires nuancing with regard to the positions of EU member states on a number of policies that pertain to Russia. In particular, this chapter suggests that rather than characterizing Greece and Cyprus as Russian 'trojan horses' inside the EU, with the suggestion that they will dance to the jingles of the Russian balalaika (Andrianopoulos 2008) simply because they are asked to by Russia on issues that concern her, we need to consider the shades of grey that exist across different issue areas relating to Russia in order to provide a more complex picture of Greek and Cypriot action inside the EU.[1]

Beyond the above aims the chapter seeks to contribute to a deeper understanding of the bilateral relationship between Greece/Cyprus and Russia, and its impact within the multilateral EU dimension. Its main concern is to connect the domestic political drivers and factors that determine the Greek and Cypriot bilateral relationship with Russia with the subsequent positions taken up on policies towards Russia by Greece and Cyprus within the EU milieu. More precisely, it is to test whether strong bilateral relationships foster greater opportunity or create greater constraints in developing co-operation (see My

Cyprus and Greece 239

et al. 2009) and common EU positions and policies on Russia. The proposition put forth is that Greece and Cyprus, whilst having a deeper understanding of Russian concerns through bilateral contact and agreements, behave by and large in an 'Europeanized' way within EU fora on issues relating directly and indirectly to Russia. In other words, Greek and Cypriot objectives towards Russia, whilst reflecting national interest, are very much embedded in the language of a multilateral EU approach and on working towards a strategic partnership with Russia. Bilateralism and multilateralism, in this sense, are intertwined, with bilateralism an increasingly significant component of the EU multilateral order (see Bátora and Hocking 2009: 168), resulting in a complex bi-multilateral set of processes (Keukeleire 2000: 4–5).

The central questions in this respect are: What is the nature of the bilateral relationship between Cyprus/Greece and Russia? To what extent does this bilateral relationship impact on the Cypriot and Greek positions on policy towards Russia on the EU level? What are the main implications of this for the evolution of EU policies towards Russia? The chapter will proceed as follows. Section II will provide a brief outline of the foreign policy context within which we can understand Greek and Cypriot policy and positions on Russia. Section III will examine how the nature of the bilateral co-operation that exists impacts upon discussions and negotiations on policy towards Russia within the EU. In the final section conclusions will be drawn on the implications of such an analysis for the evolution of common positions and policies on Russia.

Understanding Greek foreign policy

Bilateral relations between Russia and Greece and Cyprus respectively, cannot be understood in a political vacuum, nor can the behaviour of these two member states inside the EU on policy towards Russia. This section therefore provides a brief context within which to understand the trends in the evolution of foreign policy in Greece and Cyprus in the context of 'Europeanization', as well as bilateral relations between Russia and Greece/Cyprus.

Greece has moved through various historical junctures in the Europeanization of its foreign policy. The Westernization of Greece, of course, began much before it acceded to the EC, as demonstrated by the foreign policy orientation of Karamanlis (late 1970s) and Mitsotakis (early 1990s). The general trend in Greek foreign policy,[2] however, has been towards anchoring itself to the West, with Greek membership of the EC particularly important in providing a security guarantee for Greece. In terms of the substance and style of its foreign policy, especially in the post-1996 period, Greece has become more pragmatic, proactive and outward looking in its orientation, and has multilateralized many of its foreign policy issues, effectively expressing national concerns in the language of European norms and interests (Economides 2005). Even in the context of the acute financial crisis that Greece has found itself in recent years this trend seems set to continue – even though, obviously, there are pressing challenges for Greece domestically and in the

240   *George Christou*

European and global political economy that may have implications for their European orientation in the near future. Whilst such a trend does not mitigate the pursuit of bilateral relationships for the Greek national interest, it does, in most circumstances, imply that such bilateral relationships are not contrary to EU norms and practices, and that there is some congruence between the bilateral and (EU) multilateral actions and policies on issues that are relevant to both. In the eyes of Greek policy makers, bilateralism and multilateralism are seen as complements not competitors within the broader EU space.

Bilateral relations between Russia and Greece then, must be seen first and foremost in the context of Europeanization as well as the broader processes of regionalization and globalization, and indeed, its important relationship with the USA (see Stephanou 2010 for an overview of Greece's foreign policy). In this context, although there are historical and cultural ties between Greece and Russia, there have also been ideological divisions that have created difficulties in the relationship. The rapprochement in recent years has been based mostly on national interest – strategic reactions to changes globally/regionally, and inside Russia and Greece. Indeed, as noted by Tziampiris (2010: 89) on the Greek re-alignment with Russia, 'it is ultimately explained by pragmatic and interest-based considerations and not by cultural or civilizational factors' going on to argue that 'Contemporary Greek foreign policy is simply not decided on the basis of cultural affinities. Rather, it strives … to be realist, adaptive, and finely tuned to shifts in international power relations and capabilities'. Greek bilateral relations with Russia then are significant in the context of the Greek national interest, but in an instrumental rather than normative sense. This is not to argue that Greece and Russia do not share similar views or approaches to regional and international problems (e.g. Cyprus, the Balkans), but that it does so in the broader context of its predominant Western and EU orientation.

To elaborate further, the bilateral relationship between the two has been consolidated in more recent history by a series of Agreements and Declarations. Energy, military co-operation, bilateral trade (economic co-operation) and tourism have been especially important in the relationship, and were particularly prominent in the updated Greek–Russian Action Plan signed on 31 May 2007 by the then Foreign Ministers for Greece and Russia respectively, Dora Bakoyannis and Sergei Lavrov. This Action Plan set out a framework for Greek–Russian relations between 2007–9 with the aim of strengthening and deepening co-operation on matters of mutual interest. Indeed, in December 2009, the then Greek Prime Minister, George Papandreou, and Sergei Lavrov renewed the joint Action Plan to cover the period 2009–11, with the emphasis again on enhancing economic co-operation given the global financial crisis and in particular Greece's own economic, social and financial turmoil, but with an expressed interest to enhance the strategic bilateral co-operation between the two countries on issues such as energy, trade, technology and culture, as well as in relation to the EU and NATO frameworks.

Cyprus and Greece 241

There is no doubt that the most important driving factor in Greek–Russian bilateral relations is energy co-operation. As highlighted by one Russian diplomat 'Energy is the centrepiece of our cooperation with Greece' (Chkhikvishvili 2009). Greece has also always been heavily reliant on Russia for its energy supply with over 75 per cent of its gas being supplied by Russia (Greece signed legal protocols with Russia in 1994 for delivery of natural gas from a pipeline to be extended from Bulgaria to Greece) and approximately 40 per cent of its oil. This has led to an evolving strategic partnership on energy in terms of oil and gas. With regard to the former, the Burgas–Alexandroupolis (B–A) oil pipeline deal, it could be argued, marked the beginning of the new enhanced bilateral relationship between Greece and Russia in September 2006. The B–A oil pipeline was agreed between Bulgaria, Russia and Greece – with the purpose of carrying Russian and Kazakh oil through Bulgaria and Greece to the Mediterranean. Whilst Russia has a 51 per cent ownership share, the rest being divided evenly by Greece and Bulgaria, it also involves in its construction and operation a host of private companies, and it will, in theory, at least address some, if not all, Greece's energy needs. In itself, this oil pipeline has not been controversial among European states or indeed within US diplomatic circles, but it is significant from a Greek perspective in terms of the benefits of investment in the infrastructure for such a pipeline in the regions of Thrace and Evros and Alexandroupolis port (Tziampiris 2010: 80). Moreover, it has been important as a symbol of the strategic significance of partnership with Russia in the field of energy co-operation, and remains so despite the withdrawal of Bulgaria from the project in December 2011.

As significant but arguably much more controversial was the South Stream gas pipeline proposal announced in June 2007 (Tziampiris 2010: 81). The initial idea behind South Stream was to transport gas (potentially up to 63 billion cubic metres annually) from Novorisk to Bulgaria and then to Thrace and Threspotia in Greece with the last part of the project being constructed undersea reaching Italy. Politically, however, the South Stream pipeline has caused concern and led to condemnation, especially from the USA, which has supported the competing Nabucco pipeline project – planned specifically to avoid Russian territory in order to lower Europe's dependency on Russia. One of the main initial attractions for Greece of South Stream, although making it more dependent on Russia (it will cover 77 per cent of its annual gas needs), was that it would avoid any high dependency from pipelines passing through Turkey. A series of energy agreements concluded by Putin with Turkey in August 2009, however, included that of the preliminary work to lay part of the South Stream pipeline through Turkish territorial waters, which, of course, although not highly problematic from a Greek perspective was significant, and did mean that some of the original incentive and appeal for Greece was rather lost (Tziampiris 2010: 79–83). More recently, agreement was reached on the founding charter of the joint Greek-Russian company that will undertake construction and exploitation of the South Stream pipeline.

242 *George Christou*

The agreement signed on the 7 June 2010 by Gazprom (the Russian gas monopoly) and DESFA (the Greek gas transmission operator), resulted in the company South Stream Greece SA, which will be located in Athens, and of which each side has an equal shareholding (New Europe 2010). In April 2012, and connected to the privatization programme in Greece, Gazprom expressed an interest, through tender (alongside 13 other companies), in buying the production arm of Greece's state gas firm DEPA.[3] Greece plans to sell 51 per cent of DEPA and 31 per cent of DESFA, its transportation branch (New Europe 2012).

Beyond energy, Russia has regularly supplied arms and military equipment to Greece, and has frequently supported Greece in its awkward historical relationship with Turkey. Military-technical co-operation between Russia and Greece began in 1993 when the countries signed an intergovernmental agreement. In the 1990s, Greece acquired over \$1 billion worth of Russian weapons.[4] In the context of Greek–Russian rapprochement under Karamanlis, which saw increased bilateral meetings between Putin and Karamanlis (six in 2007 as opposed to only two meetings with George W. Bush and one with Barack Obama), Greece also purchased armoured personnel carriers (420 BMP-3M) from Russia worth approximately €1.2 billion. More recently, Russia conducted aeronautical and naval exercises in Greece (2009), with future events planned for Russian and Greek servicemen, including exchanges, reciprocal visits of the countries' warships and joint naval drills as part of the Greek–Russia action plan. Greece remains the only member of NATO to purchase military hardware and material from Russia directly, with the former Greek Defence minister, Evangelos Venezelos, pointing out that 'relations in the sphere of military-technological cooperation are very constructive and they play an important role both in the development of bilateral relations between Russia and Greece and in the development of Russia–EU relations in general' (cited in RIA Novosti 2010). No doubt then, that such co-operation with Russia also sends out a political message to the neighbourhood, even though Russia has also extended such exercises to Turkey.

In addition, significant opportunities have also opened up for cultural co-operation and have been an important factor driving the development of relations between the two countries. A good example within this dimension of bilateral ties is the historical presence of a number of Russians of Greek origin, the majority of whom are found in the southernmost regions of Russia. In this context Greece and Russia have planned to celebrate 2014 as 'a Year of Greece' in Russia and 'a Year of Russia' in Greece. This has also coincided with the preparations for the Olympic Games to be held in Sochi, Russia, in 2014, which provides the opportunity not only for the enhanced activity of Greek companies in its preparation, but also of knowledge transfer (given that Greece hosted the 2004 Olympics) and shared cultural events.

The Agreements and Declarations between Russia and Greece have been supported by regular high-level contact between Ministers and governmental committees within the different dimensions of co-operation (for details see the

Ministry of Foreign Affairs of Greece 2012). This is in addition to the more regular lower level co-operation between not just government officials but also by business actors, entrepreneurs, social and religious groups and civil society. On the latter, the Russian–Greek Civil Societies Forum was established in 2008, the catalyst for which was the 180th anniversary of Greek–Russian diplomatic relations. This Forum brings together, on an annual basis, representatives from politics, arts, culture, business, religion and science (Chkhikvishvili 2009).

In summary, Greece and Russia have built a close bilateral relationship based on mutual trust and interest. It is not the case, however, that this has somehow evolved into Greece simply supporting Russia or the Russian perspective in any issue, inside or outside the EU, as this would miss the broader context within which such bilateral relations have evolved. Thus, whilst the former Greek Prime Minister acknowledged that there exists an 'excellent level of ... bilateral relations that reflect the traditional friendly relations of the two peoples throughout the centuries', there was also recognition and consideration of the 'mutual dependence and mutual supplementation between the EU and Russia' (Sofokleus10.gr 2010). For Greece, good bilateral relations with Russia are important, but they are not independent of its commitments to and membership of the multilateral EU arena.

Understanding Cypriot foreign policy

Turning to Cyprus, it can be argued that its foreign policy has been substantially Europeanized, with some evidence that Cypriot diplomats have internalized the EU way of doing things over the past six years. However, whilst the Cypriot national problem was multilateralized through Cypriot accession to the EU, this is not an issue where Cypriot diplomats have acquiesced to EU requests for compromise in all areas. Nowhere has this been more obvious than with the issue of the Direct Trade Regulation, which the Commission has consistently pressed for, supported by a coalition of member states – which would allow direct trade between the Turkish Cypriots and the EU. On this issue, the Cypriot government has remained steadfast in its rejection of any such Directive, which would, from a Cypriot national perspective, imply the recognition of the 'illegal Turkish Republic of Northern Cyprus'. Beyond this, however, and at an overarching level, it is clear that the Cypriot government has recognized the potential benefits of Europeanization – supporting the European orientation of both the Turkish Cypriots and Turkey – although with the caveat that engagement does not contravene either established international (UN) Resolutions on the Cyprus issue, or indeed, EU contractual obligations (see Christou 2010). More broadly, it has implemented substantive institutional and organizational change to facilitate the process of Europeanization and aligned itself with and engaged in EU foreign policy activity: with Cypriot diplomats learning to play the EU game in a more pragmatic rather than confrontational way.

244 *George Christou*

Within this context, Cyprus has, with its new-found political weight and status within the EU, sought to establish bilateral relations with powerful states such as China and Russia, in order to intensify their involvement and ensure their continuing and unequivocal support for a solution of the Cyprus problem through established UN parameters. Indeed, whilst Russia has always been a strong supporter of Cypriot efforts through the UN to resolve the conflict on the island, it has also in the past sought to manipulate Cypriot non-membership of NATO in order to pursue policies that divided and fostered conflict between NATO members (see Cutler 1985 for an analysis of Soviet Union policy in the 1974 Cyprus conflict). Europeanization has changed the dynamics of the relationship between Cyprus and Russia – and in particular aided continuity and the upgrading of relations between the two countries on different issues, including Russia's continuing and consistent approach to the resolution of the Cyprus issue and its support within the UN Security Council. Related to this has been the aim of counter-balancing the Atlanticist position of the majority of the member states that joined the EU alongside Cyprus, in 2004 (Sepos 2008: 127). What this has meant for Cyprus–Russia relations, according to one Greek Cypriot diplomat, is the continued enhancement of relations at the bilateral level in mutually beneficial areas of co-operation, and support for Russia within the EU, not to the detriment of establishing a multilateral EU common position on Russia but rather in tandem with realizing such a position based on mutual interest, in the context of the ongoing negotiations on the EU–Russia agreement (author's interview, anonymous, Brussels, August 2010).

Bilaterally, diplomatic relations between the Republic of Cyprus and Russia were established in 1960 and have been the subject of strengthening and deepening ever since, in particular in relation to culture and trade. In many ways the Cypriot approach to Russia has very close parallels to that of Greece, with some minor differences visible in the minutiae of certain issue areas. The institutional structure for co-operation between the two countries involves contacts between heads of state, co-operation between ministries and departments, inter-parliamentary co-operation, media interaction, as well as lower level governmental and societal/cultural links, the latter a result of the increasingly growing Russian community that has emerged in Cyprus over the last few years, estimated at almost 40,000. Indeed, the Russian Centre of Science and Education was established precisely because of this and the large number of Russians that visit Cyprus each year for holiday and leisure purposes (estimated over 150,000 in 2009). Similarly to Greece, the development of the infrastructure of Southern Russia and the construction of a modern sports and tourist complex for the 2014 Winter Olympics in Sochi has become a growth area of joint efforts. In addition to this Cyprus has concluded many legal agreements with Russia (more than two dozen), within the Intergovernmental Protocol on the Inventory of Bilateral Agreements that entered into force in 2002 (see the Embassy of the Russian Federation in the Republic of Cyprus 2012).

In terms of the economic relationship, Cypriot membership of the EU has drawn in Russian capital and Cyprus has been an attractive location for Russian business to create offshore firms. Indeed, the value of Russian business investments reached €2 billion in 2008, with the value of Cypriot investments in Russia in the same year more than €1.5 billion. Such investments were mainly in real estate and business activities, trade and repairs, financial intermediation and manufacturing. Furthermore, Cyprus has traditionally been one of the biggest investors in Russia among the EU member states. In 2007, Cyprus was the lead investor, with the UK and Netherlands second and third respectively. 2009 figures reveal that the Netherlands is the largest investor, followed by Luxembourg, Germany and Cyprus (and this in the context of an overall fall in FDI in Russia by approximately 43 per cent). In terms of trade, exports of Cypriot products to Russia in 2005–8 represented an increase of 55 per cent, with a small decline in 2009 due to the financial crisis. Total imports from Russia over the same period were nearly double the number of Cypriot exports. There is no doubt that such investments in Cyprus by Russian business are due to the favourable environment offered for business, ranging from a liberal foreign investment policy and a clear legal framework, to the lowest rate of corporation tax in the EU at ten per cent. Related to this, Cyprus and Russia signed, on 16 April 2009, a Protocol in relation to the Double Tax Treaty (DTT) – one which retains most of the favourable provisions that previously existed and which offers one of the best DTTs that Russia has with another country. In this context, Cyprus is likely to remain a prime springboard for inward and outward investment in Russia. More recently (2010), Russian company Gazprom was invited by the Cypriot government to excavate for oil in the sea south of Cyprus. No doubt from a Cypriot perspective this was a move to counter-balance Turkish protestation over the rights of the Cypriot government to do so. From a Russian perspective, Turkish protestations would not be a reason for them not to take part, even though in the current context, they do not see any such excavation as commercially viable (author's interview, anonymous, Brussels, 2010).

Cultural and economic relations aside, Cypriot bilateral relations with Russia are primarily driven by the Cyprus problem. Russia has traditionally supported the Cypriot government in the search for a just, viable and fair settlement of the Cyprus problem based on the relevant UN Security Council decisions and the high level agreements between the leaders of the two communities in Cyprus of 1977 and 1979. These agreements provide for the evolution of the unitary state of the Republic of Cyprus into a bicommunal, bizonal federation, with a single sovereignty, a single citizenship, and one international personality which will incorporate political equality. Whilst Russia's relations with Turkey have more recently been strengthened in the field of energy and economy, this position, despite the rhetoric of certain politicians in Russia and Turkey, has not changed. Indeed as one Russian diplomat put it on Cyprus, 'this position did not change and it is still very valid, and we, as a permanent member of the Security Council, are doing

246 *George Christou*

everything we can to bring a settlement' (PSEKA 2009), with another adding that 'you cannot underestimate adherence to UN principles ... you cannot change these without the risk of losing your integrity' (author's interview, anonymous, Brussels, August 2010). In this context, Russia has provided support for the government of Cyprus through use of its veto within the UN, to block a draft UN Security Council resolution that proposed the condemnation of the Cypriot government for rejecting the Annan peace plan in April 2004. Indeed, Russia demonstrated its disapproval of the way in which the UN plan was constructed (rather than its content) through a demarche at the UN rejecting the Reunification Plan which the majority of Greek Cypriots then rejected in a referendum on the island in April 2004 (Torbakov 2004). Russia has also supported Cyprus in the military sphere – the selling of surface-to-air S-300 missiles to the Cypriot government in 1996 a prime example here under the pretext of the right to self-defence against any potential aggressor. Broader co-operation also exists on the basis of the Russian–Cypriot Agreement on military and technical co-operation signed in March 1996.

Cyprus has also been able to forge excellent relations because it has less conflict with Russia ideologically and historically, especially given that it is not a member of NATO, and that the current President in Cyprus and his Party (AKEL – the Communist Party) have a historical affinity. The excellent bilateral relations between Russia and Cyprus, however, contrary to certain claims (Leonard and Popescu 2007), do not lead to automatic support for Russian positions inside the EU. What it does do, however, is allow Cyprus, because of its greater understanding of Russian concerns, to take a more pragmatic stance on issues relating to Russia. In this sense, because there is a certain convergence between Cyprus and Russia bilaterally, where it is in the Cypriot national interest to do so, it will project or defend positions that might well also be compatible with Russian thinking, e.g. on energy unbundling. As with Greece, however, it is not the only country that does this – it does not see its relationship as 'special', above and beyond other member states that it also sees as pragmatists (such as France, Italy and Germany) – and furthermore, neither does Russia within the EU milieu. Indeed, whilst Cyprus is seen as an important country, it is seen as one of many that project Russia's concerns, rather than representing any Russian views directly (author's interviews, anonymous, Brussels, July 2010). Moreover, the bilateral and the multilateral, for Cypriot diplomats, are seen as mutually reinforcing in the Russian case – in order to try and move the relationship between the EU and Russia to the next level (ibid.).

Greece and Cyprus: inside the EU

It has been argued (Leonard and Popescu 2007) that the close bilateral relationships between Greece/Cyprus and Russia have led to a situation where they veto, block and take the lead inside the EU where proposed policy is counter to that of Russia, or indeed, could potentially lead to tensions within the bilateral relationships. The argument in this chapter is that such a representation misses the complexity of the EU decision-making milieu on issues relating to Russia, and that, whilst Cyprus and Greece certainly have an excellent understanding of Russian concerns through their enhanced bilateral relations, which they have projected within the EU, it does not entail unconditional representation of Russian interests in Council deliberations on Russia. Indeed, the evidence suggests that differentiation must be made between Greek/Cypriot national interests that simply coincide with Russian positions, and unreserved support of Russian positions on any issue.

Greece has played a strategic political game in its projections on Russia within the EU milieu. There is no doubt that Greece has had an advantage in any such deliberations because of its bilateral ties, but also historically, because Greece held the Presidency of the EU in 1994 when the EU–Russia Partnership and Cooperation Agreement (PCA) was signed, and again in 2003, when a new approach through the Four Common Spaces was taken. However, whilst this, according to one Greek diplomat, provided Greece with the opportunity to be more open with the Russians in political dialogue, it did 'not mean that the Russians always see our perspective, as they are a large country and they have many of their own interests' (author's interview, anonymous, Brussels, July 2010). So from a Greek perspective, this simply provided an EU platform for discussion with Russia which they could then build upon – but it did not imply that they had a 'special' or unique relationship with Russia – or any specific role to play in defending Russian ideas inside the EU. Indeed, both Russian and Greek diplomats acknowledge that among diplomatic elites, the relationship is more of a pragmatic nature, based on political and economic interests (ibid.).

Greece, as with Cyprus, is part of a coalition of member states within the EU that Greek diplomats see as the 'pragmatists'. In this sense, 'Greece is part of the group that wishes to see closer relations with Russia evolve – alongside Germany, France and Italy – they are the strongest larger member state advocates of developing such relations with Russia' (author's interview, anonymous, Brussels, July 2010). This is also the case for Cyprus, where its main aim is to 'encourage deeper relations between EU–Russia' through 'moving beyond national positions in order to build a strong strategic partnership with Russia' (ibid.). Furthermore, from a Greek and Cypriot perspective progress cannot be made 'by telling Russia what is best for them' – as ideas for this must emanate from Russia – with the EU as a facilitator within the process of Russian engagement with and the reinvention of Russia as an actor within the international community.

Within this general context then, the conclusions that can be drawn about Cypriot and Greek projections on Russia are not particularly controversial. It is clear that within the framework for discussing EU–Russia relations in the Council – that is, the negotiations for the new EU–Russia Agreement – Cyprus and Greece support a deeper and more comprehensive relationship with Russia. However, even though both are supportive, the important finding here is that this is a consequence of a pragmatic approach and a more positive environment – which is not exclusive to Cyprus and Greece alone, but rather a much broader coalition of member states that, in the words of one EU diplomat, 'see the glass as half-full and not half-empty' in relation to Russia (ibid.). In this sense, from a Cypriot perspective, it sees itself as having an important role to play within the EU, 'as a bridge between the EU and Russia' that can 'contribute to the intensification of constructive dialogue between both partners' (Neophytou 2010). Greece also perceives itself as able to provide an important link between the EU and Russia but it does not see itself as having 'a special or particular role to play in the Council when it comes to issues related to Russia. We are one of the countries, among many, that have and support a positive relationship with Russia'. Indeed, both Cyprus and Greece acknowledge (as indeed, does Russia) that, first, this is not exclusive to either country, and second, that even if Cyprus and Greece wanted to play a leadership role in proposing initiatives (or indeed blocking them) for Russia 'it is very difficult for like-minded states – Cyprus and Greece – to propose such things and overcome the constraints in the Council' (author's interview, anonymous, Brussels, July 2010).

On the question of Cypriot and Greek positions on specific issues that are directly and indirectly related to Russia, this very much depends on the compatibility of their own national interests with that of Russian views, and the coalition dynamics within the Council. On a broader level, it is also dependent on the dynamics between the EU institutions in their approach to issues related to Russia, and the external environment within which initiatives are proposed. Thus, whilst it is claimed by Leonard and Popescu (2007: 26–27) that both Greece and Cyprus have utilized their veto on initiatives concerning, for example, the Eastern neighbourhood or the EU's involvement in the CIS space, evidence suggests that this, again, needs to be nuanced. Indeed, as one Greek diplomat put it, 'we are not a country that will simply support Russia on our own ... this has not happened. *This has never happened ... Greece has not used a veto*, only Lithuania and Poland have used the veto' (author's interview, anonymous, Brussels, July 2010, emphasis added). There is a similar story with Cyprus, where there is no evidence, at least since 2009,[5] that it 'has been in a minority or taken the lead on an issue relating to Russia. Because all the issues we supported it as a group – the pragmatists – France, Greece, Spain, Italy, Germany' (ibid.). In other words, even where Cyprus and Greece have opposed certain proposals in the past, such as those of the Commission for unbundling large energy companies into energy providers and transit companies, they have not done this alone, but as part of a coalition of member states with similar perspectives and objections. Thus, whilst such positions certainly coincided with Russia's own view (Gazprom's rejection of unbundling and liberalization) the overriding factors for opposition were related to domestic politics and member state national interests, rather than any unconditional support for Russian positions per se.

Furthermore, on the issue of the Eastern Partnership (EaP), whilst Greece has not expressed much enthusiasm about such an initiative and is obviously aware of Russia's objections, it has not blocked or voted against any aspects of it – it has remained neutral on this issue, and would only consider any such moves on issues that impact directly or indirectly on the Cyprus issue. The Cypriots, on the other hand, have been supportive of the Eastern Partnership, and they have also been supportive of greater transparency within the EaP and indeed increased Russian participation in it. However, Cyprus has also been cautious about being vocal on the issue of automatic participation, mainly because of what this also implies for Turkey's role in the EaP. In the words of one Cypriot diplomat:

> On the one hand, we need Russia to be interested in the EaP ... we, Cyprus. But nobody can go to Moscow and say you need to show greater interest in the EaP – this is normal, nobody can force them. On the other hand, we have the issue of Turkey ... we cannot vote to have Russia without having Turkey automatically, so we do not have any view on this. If Russia wants to participate it will find a way; they will officially express an interest. Russia is not clear yet if she wants to participate, so it is not up to us to intervene in this.
>
> (Author's interview, anonymous, Brussels, July 2010)

Another issue that has caused controversy in negotiations on the new EU–Russia Agreement within the Council is that of visa liberalization. In this case the split has not simply been between pragmatists and sceptics – rather, it has led to division within the pragmatist camp. Cyprus and Greece both support such an initiative within the context of strengthening and deepening relations with Russia, but there has been no need for either to take the lead on the issue, as the French have been very vocal in supporting and promoting this proposal at all levels, which, as acknowledged by one diplomat, makes it much easier for the likes of Cyprus and Greece if a larger member state leads where they also support an initiative. This has not been the case for Germany, however, which remains highly sceptical because of the fear of a Russian influx, despite its enhanced bilateral relations with Russia and its positive stance on closer economic, security and energy co-operation. For those that sit in the sceptics coalition, the same fear of influx is put forward as an argument against liberalizing the visa regime with Russia, but there is also a strategic and political element to their thinking, in that they see it as a significant bargaining chip in negotiations with Russia that should not easily be given away until further political reforms are forthcoming or visible. Thus, the discussion in the Council at the moment is difficult on this issue because there is no agreement, but a secondary and related problem is that there are no 'standards' in order for the debate on this to be able to move forward in the Council among those that do support it. Russia, in this sense, has to improve its technical standards if any progress at all is to be made in the first instance. In this sense, 'it is not

250   *George Christou*

just about the EU doing something – we have the Visa Facilitation and Readmission agreement – but it is difficult to agree on liberalization in the current context' (author's interview, anonymous, Brussels, July 2010).

An issue that Cyprus has been pro-active on in relation to Russia both within the EU and in its bilateral discussions with Russian officials in Brussels is enhanced participation and co-operation in crisis management operations (that is, building on operations that it has already been involved in such as Chad). In this context, the Cypriots have engaged with Russian officials in order to explain the potential benefits to them of showing a solid interest for participation and contribution to EU missions and operations. The reasons for this have been twofold from a Cypriot perspective. First, because of the recognition that the EU has limited resources and capability – and thus there is a need from an EU perspective for Russian involvement. Second, for the Cypriots, Russian involvement in such missions and operations is a way of bypassing the NATO problem. A more involved Russia automatically eliminates the problem with having an operation under Berlin Plus, where Cyprus is excluded (because of Turkey). Beyond this, there is clearly also a desire on the part of the pragmatists to enhance security co-operation multilaterally and bilaterally, with Germany and Russia, following a meeting in Meseberg in June 2010, proposing (bilaterally) the establishment of a committee involving the EU and Russia which was similar to that of the EU's Political and Security Committee (see Stewart in this volume). Greece and Cyprus, in this context, are also supportive of the 'Corfu process' and the further discussion and consideration of Medvedev's proposals for a new European security framework.

Finally, the issue of Georgia is one that demonstrates both support for and the limits to such support for Russian views and positions, both within the EU milieu, but also within the UN. First, in September 2009, Cyprus rejected a proposed EU common position in support of a UN General Assembly Resolution on the 'Status of Internally Displaced Persons and Refugees from Abkhazia and South Ossetia and the Tskhinvali Region/South Ossetia, Georgia'. This Resolution, despite being passed with 48 countries in favour (one of which was Greece, even though they rejected the first proposed Resolution in 2008), was rejected by Russia, which argued that it:

> falls behind the existing reality on the ground. And the reality is that two independent states – Abkhazia and South Ossetia – have emerged in the region and both the Georgian leadership and its foreign patrons will sooner or later have to reckon with this fact.
>
> (Nesterenko, cited in Civil.ge 2009)

From a Cypriot perspective, they rejected the EU common position in support of such a Resolution arguing that 'it was not done for humanitarian but political reasons' and that it 'was bad timing five days before the Geneva Summit and five days before the official report on the independent enquiry into the Georgia conflict'. Finally, Cyprus in principle, because of the Cyprus problem, has always supported the territorial integrity of Georgia, and rejected any proposal or initiatives for recognition of secessionist states. In this sense then, it is not the case that Cyprus will automatically align itself and support Russian positions or views, especially when it comes to issues that could potentially have an impact on the Cyprus problem. It is not either the case that Russia will look to Cyprus across all EU-related issues to project its position within the EU arena. In the words of one Cypriot diplomat:

> We have our national interests, our issues, so we try to help Russia as much as possible, but not doing it in a way that might be interpreted or misinterpreted by our partners. We try to help Russia when there is a need to do it, when there is a reason and when it is justified, when Russia itself helps itself and *by avoiding being the Russian trojan horses inside the EU.* We know in Brussels when and where to support Russia, from a Cypriot perspective.
> (Author's interview, anonymous, Brussels, July 2010, my emphasis[6])

Conclusions

This chapter set out to critically engage with the assertion that Greece and Cyprus are Russia's 'trojan horses' within the EU through investigating the bilateral and (EU) multilateral dimensions of influence, and in particular the relationship between the two. A significant conclusion is that despite what might be termed excellent bilateral relations this does not automatically lead to unconditional support for Russia by Greece and Cyprus inside the EU on policies that relate directly or indirectly to them. Indeed, although Greece and Cyprus are definitely 'on the same page' when it comes to Russia, they are part of a coalition of member states that take a pragmatic approach to the EU's developing relations with Russia. Moreover, once the role of Greece and Cyprus is contextualized within the broader environment within which their foreign policy has evolved, it is clear that whilst their bilateral relations with Russia provide a platform for a better understanding of Russian positions and thus their support for Russia inside the EU (i.e. it is constructive), this is not in contradiction to the EU goal of achieving progress on the new EU–Russia Agreement. In other words, the bilateral and multilateral processes at play are seen to complement rather than compete – even though, as admitted by one diplomat:

> if somebody was looking at this from the outside, there is a certain discord – you can say that we are helping you, we are opening up opportunities to cooperate – but the problem is – are we trying to pursue a common EU position on Russia or are we saying that whenever it is in our individual interest we are simply going to pursue bilateral relations? I think there is a tension here.
> (Author's interview, anonymous, Brussels, July 2010)

252　*George Christou*

As far as Cyprus and Greece are concerned, however, their approach can be characterized as 'Europeanized' and pragmatic at a general level, with little evidence of taking the lead or indeed unilaterally blocking or vetoing proposals *inside* the EU (only within a UN context in the case of Cyprus). This does not imply that Cyprus and Greece are not supportive, or do not indeed 'help' Russia – however, they do this with a consideration of their commitments to the EU milieu, and their own national concerns primarily, rather than any cultural, historical or diplomatic obligation to Russia and its interests. Thus, whilst bilateral relations with Russia might place Cyprus and Greece in a better position in discussions on Russia in the EU, it is also clear that there is a limit (author's interview, anonymous, Brussels, July 2010). Furthermore, Greece and Cyprus, as individual member states cannot, and have not, impacted significantly on constraining or indeed enhancing EU policy on Russia – they have been supportive of the initiatives such as visa liberalization, but the complexity of the coalition dynamics even on an issue where the lead has been taken by France, mitigates against an agreement in the near future. The conclusion we can draw from this is that Cyprus and Greece have a limited impact unless they are supported by a broader coalition which includes the larger and more influential member states within the Council. Indeed, whilst Greece and Cyprus clearly have a role to play in forging a common policy towards Russia within the EU, the success or failure of EU policy towards Russia is dependent on so much more than the positions of two of the EU's 'smaller' member states. Moreover, whilst they are quite happy to dance to the jingles of the Russian balalaika, this is only if it is in tune with the tunes of the Greek/Cypriot bouzouki, and more importantly, the instructions of the European orchestra conductors.

Notes

1 Primary material for the first phase of this research was collected mainly through formal interviews and informal conversations with Greek, Cypriot and Russian diplomats in Brussels in June/July 2010.
2 I say general because of course there are exceptions to this 'general' trend. There are examples where Greece has clearly not aligned itself to the EU position or succumbed to EU pressure to reach agreement or compromise on an issue (the issue of FYROM), because of bureaucratic and domestic political reasons (see Agnantopoulos 2010: 12–13).
3 Gazprom provides a large amount of the natural gas used by DEPA. Gazprom exported 2.9 billion cubic metres of natural gas to Greece in 2011. See *New Europe* 2012.
4 Russian TOR-M1 air defence systems, Kornet and Fagot antitank weapons, as well as air cushion landing craft Zubr are in service with the Greek Armed Forces. See RIA Novosti 2010.
5 I stipulate so because that was the year that the Cypriot representatives that I talked to in Brussels had taken up their posts.
6 Confirmed in a telephone interview with Cypriot official at the Ministry of Foreign Affairs, Cyprus, July 2010.

References

Agnantopoulos, A. (2010) 'The Europeanization of National Foreign Policy: the Case of Greece'. Paper presented at the GARNET Conference, 'The European Union in International Affairs II', Brussels, 22–24 April 2010.

Andrianopoulos, A. (2008) 'Greece and Russia: Dancing to the tunes of Bouzouki or Balalaika?'. Available at www.andrianopoulos.gr/0010000260/greece-and-russia-dancing-to-the-tunes-of-bouzouki-or-balalaika-.html (accessed 22 June 2012).

Bátora, J. and Hocking, B. (2009) 'EU Oriented Bilateralism: Evaluating the Role of Member State Embassies in the European Union', *Cambridge Review of International Affairs*, 22: 163–82.

Chkhikvishvili, I. V. (2009) 'Russia, Greece: strategic partnership based on common historical, spiritual heritage'. Embassy of the Russian Federation in the Greek Republic, 21 May 2009, available at www.greece/mid.ru/news_e_03.html (accessed 22 June 2012).

Christou, G. (2010) 'The European Union, Borders and Conflict Transformation: The Case of Cyprus', *Cooperation and Conflict*, 45: 55–79.

Civil.ge (2009) 'UNGA Passes Georgia IDP Resolution' *Civil.ge*, 10 September 2009, available at www.civil.ge/eng/article.php?id=21447 (accessed 22 June 2012).

Cutler, M. R. (1985) 'Domestic and Foreign Influences on Policy Making: The Soviet Union in the 1974 Cyprus Conflict', *Soviet Studies*, 37: 60–89.

Economides, S. (2005) 'The Europeanisation of Greek Foreign Policy', *West European Politics*, 28: 471–91.

The Embassy of the Russian Federation in the Republic of Cyprus (2012) *Relations between Russia and Cyprus*. Available at www.cyprus.mid.ru/en/ru_cy.htm (accessed 22 June 2012).

Keukeleire, S. (2000) 'The European Union as a Diplomatic Actor'. DSP Discussion Paper No 71, Leicester: Centre for the Study of Diplomacy.

Leonard, M. and Popescu, N. (2007) 'A Power Audit of EU-Russia Relations'. Policy Paper, London: European Council on Foreign Relations, available at www.ecfr.eu/content/entry/commentary_pr_russia_power_audit (accessed 22 June 2012).

The Ministry of Foreign Affairs of Greece (2012) *Bilateral Relations between Greece and Russia*. Available at www.mfa.gr/en/blog/greece-bilateral-relations/russia/ (accessed 22 June 2012).

My, B. K., Verchere, A. and Bertrand, S. (2009) 'Does Bilateralism Foster Cooperation in Europe? An Experimental Approach of Comparative Merits of Bilateralism and Multilateralism', *Journal of Common Marker Studies*, 47: 891–910.

Neophytou, A. (2010) Intervention by Mr. Averof Nephytou, Chairman of the House Standing Committee on Foreign Affairs of the Republic of Cyprus. Available at www.ruseu.com/br/cyprus/details_508.html (accessed 22 June 2012).

New Europe (2010) 'Papandreou, Putin discuss economy, trade and energy', *New Europe*. Issue 874, 21 February 2010, available at www.neurope.eu (accessed 22 June 2012).

——(2012) 'Gazprom cleared to bid for DEPA', *New Europe*. 15 April 2012, available at www.neurope.eu/article/gazprom-cleared-bid-depa (accessed 22 June 2012).

PSEKA (2009) 'Russia-Cyprus problem', PSEKA. 7 August 2009, available at http://news.pseka.net/index.php?module=article&id=10487 (accessed 22 June 2012).

RIA Novosti (2010) 'Russia, Greece to hold joint naval drills in 2010', RIA Novosti. 30 March 2010, available at http://en.rian.ru/mlitary_news/20100330/158365114.html (accessed 22 June 2012).

254 *George Christou*

Sepos, A. (2008) *The Europeanization of Cyprus: Polity, Policies and Politics.* Basingstoke: Palgrave Macmillan.

Sofokleus10.gr (2010) 'PM Papandreou arrives in Moscow', Sofokleus10.gr. 19 August 2010, available at www.sofokleous10.gr/portal2/greek-news-in-english/greek-news-in-english/pm-papandreou-arrives-in-moscow-2010021519902/ (accessed 22 June 2012).

Stephanou, A. C. (2010) *The Foreign Policy of Greece.* Available at http://video.minpress.gr/wwwminpress/aboutgreece/aboutgreece_foreign_policy.pdf (accessed 22 June 2012).

Torbakov, I. (2004), 'UN Veto Sparks Debate on Russian policy aims', *Eurasia Daily Monitor.* 1(3), 4 May 2004, available at www.jamestown.org/single/?no_cache=1&tx_ttnews[tt_news]=26456 (accessed 22 June 2012).

Tziampiris, A. (2010) 'Greek Foreign Policy and Russia: Political Realignment, Civilizational Aspects and Realism', *Mediterranean Quarterly,* 21: 78–89.

18 Conclusion

Maxine David, Jackie Gower and Hiski Haukkala

This book has set out to capture and analyze the multitude of EU member state bilateral relations – what we also call national perspectives – with one of the EU's main 'strategic partners', the Russian Federation. This mapping exercise then enabled us to assess the extent to which bilateral member state relations constitute a challenge to the development of a coherent and effective EU Russia policy. Certainly, there is ample evidence in the chapters supporting the dominant assumption in the literature that tensions exist between bilateral initiatives and multilateral approaches. However, there is also sufficient evidence to suggest that in certain aspects of the EU–Russia relationship the bilateral relationships do play a constructive role.

A 'universe' of national perspectives

The onus in our analysis has been on contemporary relations but in practically every chapter longer and deeper historical and cultural undercurrents have also been touched upon. This suggests that the EU's relations with external partners should not be examined in too 'presentist' terms, that is in isolation from the historical background (see Jørgensen 2006), but that such an endeavour will benefit from the application of a longer time frame analysis as well. Indeed, although EU relations with Russia date back to the early 1990s, most of the bilateral relations discussed in this book are steeped in much older history. Obviously there is no shared 'EU take' on the role and relevance of this history, and indeed what that history is and how it should be interpreted. On the contrary, there exist 27 national perspectives concerning the issue, with the quality of historical experiences varying from benign to malign to indifferent and the same also applies to the relative importance and intensity that the countries attach to them. Therefore, for example, the affinity the Maltese seem to have for their first contact with Russians during the sixteenth century is merely a pleasant background to their contemporary attempts to develop bilateral relations whereas the repulsion the Baltic states still feel towards their forcibly shared history during the twentieth century has the potential to mar not only the bilateral but at times also the wider EU–Russia agenda. The varied nature of the historical experiences of Russia in the

EU is therefore a fact that matters and registers and should be kept in mind when discussing the multitudinous contemporary agenda between the EU, its member states and Russia.

It should not be forgotten either that the background to the bilateral relations with Russia is not confined to the intra-EU dynamics alone. On the contrary, in addition to the EU level other actors are salient and in this respect the role of the United States should be highlighted. For the Central and Eastern Europeans especially – above all the Baltic states and Poland – the USA's policies towards Europe and Russia in particular are important. For example the scrambling in Central and Eastern Europe initially for a co-ordinated protestation against the 'reset' initiated by President Barack Obama in 2009 and then the individual policy changes vis-à-vis Russia in response to it is an illustrative case in point. To a certain degree it is not too far-fetched to argue that at times and in certain cases Washington seems to hold a stronger sway over individual EU member states than 'Brussels' does.

In fact, there is a whole array of intervening variables that must be considered with the role of history, geography and culture being the chief among them. However, as all the chapters show, these must be understood as intervening rather than key variables. First, they do not always impact the countries in the same way, for example, proximity does not alone explain good or bad relations in itself – it is the combination of variables that matters. Bulgaria and Romania constitute a relevant case, close geographically but with vastly different historical and contemporary relations with Russia, as do Finland and Estonia. Ireland and the UK, Portugal and Spain are some of the most distantly located member states but, again, have very different relations with Russia. Second, in some cases, it is clear that some of the more negative lasting impacts of history have the potential to be overcome to the extent of building deeper more co-operative relationships (Poland), while for others history remains a defining impediment (Estonia and Lithuania).

The place of culture, of religion and identity is a difficult one. It has been somewhat surprising that Slavic identity has not figured more highly in more of the chapters, being a significant explanatory variable in relation to Bulgaria and Slovenia only. Religion, Orthodoxy specifically, has been invoked in certain relationships, notably Cyprus and Greece, but even here it is not a decisive factor in our understanding. Where culture plays its part and therefore needs to inform analysis more extensively, is its role in building and sustaining people-to-people contacts. These are manifested in the exchange of different cultural forms (Ireland), as well as celebration of what is shared (Italy, the Netherlands, Slovenia).

Taken together, the existence of these intervening variables make it very problematic to draw firm conclusions concerning the stances of individual member states on Russia on the basis of economic and/or political interests alone, although obviously these must form the major part of the analysis. At first sight, and as the case-studies in this collection show, this profusion of issues does not readily suggest any hard and fast conclusions. Indeed one conclusion we can draw from this book relates to the very vastness of different national stakes the EU member states have with Russia, such that one could refer to a 'universe' of national perspectives. One way of illustrating this variance is to consider two key variables, the relative individual economic and/or political importance that Russia has for the member states. We can envisage an axis whereon we plot the positions (in significance terms) of the member states' economic and political relations with Russia. Thus we see, for example, that for some states, it is the political, rather than economic, relationship that is most important (Estonia, Finland, Greece) whereas for others it is the reverse (Luxembourg, Netherlands), although, as the chapters show, the situation is far more complex than this and it is also more dynamic.

We have countries that see Russia as an important political partner (Austria, Cyprus, Finland, France, Germany, Greece, Italy, Spain) and whose relationships are more easily characterized as partnerships. We also have countries for which political relations are undeniably important but which have also been beset by problems (Poland, the UK and perhaps to a lesser degree Denmark and Sweden) and countries that have had a hard time to develop any meaningful interaction with Russia despite the fact that on a priori grounds they would have a lot to be gained from it (the Baltic states). For most EU members Russia is no longer perceived as a potential military adversary but we also have a small group of countries which do still consider that a distinct possibility (the Baltics, Finland and Poland in particular). As so many of the chapters show, these relationships experience pressures which act as the catalyst for change (Poland, Romania, Spain). We also have a significant number of countries for which the political relationship is significant only when and if it impacts on the economic and trading relationship (Ireland, Luxembourg, Malta and Portugal). One thing to note particularly in respect of economics is the need to think not only about variance in trading figures between the member states, whereby on pure value in trade statistics, for instance, Germany, France and Italy account for nearly half of all EU trade with Russia, but also to look at what these figures represent in purely national terms. To illustrate the point, Germany has by far the largest share of EU–Russia trade, accounting in 2011 for 32 per cent of the exports and 19 per cent of the imports. However, in absolute terms (for Germany), Russia in fact only ranks eleventh in terms of importance, considerably behind China and the USA. This contrasts interestingly with Poland where the total value of trade with Russia is far less (€24 billion for Poland relative to Germany's €72 billion) but Russia is Poland's most important extra-EU trading partner. For some of the smaller member states the value of trade with Russia looks relatively modest but Russia actually constitutes a major trading partner.

There is, of course, another key variable, energy, that is present in a significant number of the chapters. The main outcome of the analysis is that although energy is indeed the umbilical cord tying most member states and Russia together, it is misleading to try to read the member state relations with Russia solely through the prism of energy dependence. Although the cases of,

258   *Maxine David, Jackie Gower, Hiski Haukkala*

for example, Austria and Italy show energy is far from insignificant, we also have other cases, such as the Baltic states and Finland, where even a relatively high energy dependence on Russia does not necessarily play the leading role in framing their very different relations with Moscow. Or in other words, the national perspectives on Russia are not a function or solely the outcome of levels of differing energy dependence on Russia in the member states.

All in all, these key variables highlight the differences – the variance – between the member states and underline why any crude typologies of member states into either sheep or wolves are fraught with problems. This is, first of all, the case because we are dealing with genuinely *national* perspectives on Russia. The member states have developed and continue to develop their relations with Russia on the basis of their national interests and starting points and the analyses in this book show little evidence of kow-towing before Moscow for its own sake. To a degree, this challenges Leonard and Popescu's (2007) notion of the existence of Russian-inspired 'Trojan horses' within the EU. That said, the strong economic and political links that some member states have with Russia obviously do play a role but there is no reason to assume that they play a role beyond the extent that any other significant economic and/or political interest would do. Whether this results in undue Russian influence, and whether that influence will have a benign or a malign impact on the common policy at the EU level, largely depends on Russia's objectives and intentions, the analysis of which, however, remains outside the remit of this collection.

Both sets of variables, intervening and key, also highlight the changing nature of the bilateral relationships. What is clear is that the member states do not have any fixed takes on Russia, either through time or in relation to specific issue areas, such that one can identify *two* major themes emerging: variance and change. The variance in national perspectives goes some way towards explaining the persistent problems in generating a single coherent policy on Russia at the EU level. That said, the other interesting and perhaps even somewhat paradoxical finding stemming from the country chapters is that the received wisdom of drastically differing national takes on Russia and on the EU's overall strategic objectives when it comes to the member state as the root cause of the EU's problems is largely erroneous. In fact, we conclude that there exists a surprising element of commonality between the member states concerning the overall analysis of Russia's current trajectory as well as the need to keep constructively engaging the country despite the problems associated with the process. Much of this commonality is a reflection of shifting positions. Perhaps apart from the three Baltic states – and even they have seemed to be converging with the EU mainstream position on Russia recently – practically none of the member states object to the objectives and instruments of the EU's common Russia policy *at the strategic level*.

While there are relative differences in respect of tangible economic and political outcomes and imperatives, what we have seen is that for all member states Russia offers at the very least economic opportunities and, for many,

Conclusion   259

political opportunities, even imperatives. After all, if taken from a European security perspective, it is not in the interest of any of the member states for Russia to be economically reduced, politically marginalized or destabilized. On the contrary, there is a clear common interest to engage constructively with Russia to resolve not only its internal problems (terrorism, nuclear proliferation, cyber-security) but also those of its neighbours (Belarus, Georgia, Moldova, Ukraine and others). It is evident from interactions at the member state and EU levels that all states understand this. Where there is divergence is in relation to perception of direct (and immediate) threat and perception of how best to achieve objectives. After all, Poland, like France, Germany and Italy wants to build, and for the EU to build, a constructive partnership with Russia. Even those states with most reason to fear and distrust Russia have recognized the necessity of engaging with rather than isolating Russia (the Baltic states, Poland and Romania). The divergence is in respect of method and priorities, not the underlying strategic objectives.

The member states in the EU

The story of national perspectives on Russia and their impact on the EU level obviously cannot be told by looking at the dynamics between the EU member states and Russia alone: the internal member state and EU institutional dynamics are also highly significant. Turning to the internal EU level game, as set out in the Introduction to this volume Europeanization was one of the analytical frameworks employed by the contributors. Certain chapters have provided evidence that some convergence of foreign policy towards Russia has occurred (Poland and Romania) and that, as already discussed, there is broad consensus today on what constitutes the most appropriate strategy. In this section, we will consider the three aspects of loading (down, up and cross) central to Europeanization; as well as discussing briefly the need to account for 'framing' in any analysis of the CFSP.

As many of the chapters reveal, the EU has impacted directly on individual member states' relations with Russia. EU membership extends the foreign policy community of any member state and so changes interests and, sometimes, behaviour. One of the most interesting cases is Poland, which according to Bartosz Cichocki has been forced to rethink its relations with Russia basically in its entirety. As Cichocki writes, Poland has drawn the conclusion that its own standing within the EU (but notably also within NATO) is crucially dependent on the quality of its bilateral relations with Russia. This has resulted in a sea change in Poland's Russia policy which has become more pragmatic and less belligerent towards it in recent years – a change that has been to a degree reciprocated by Russia and that has resulted in some advances between the EU and Russia as well. Another example is Romania, where Micu argues that Romania too has learned it had to adhere to EU norms of behaviour if it was to be taken seriously in respect of its problems with Russia. Romania's attempts to upload its political agenda vis-à-vis Russia to Brussels were unsuccessful, causing Romania instead to modify its own behaviour and to downgrade what it sought to achieve in respect of Russia. As a result, Romania has adopted a more constructive relationship with Russia (although the longer-term effects of that should not be over-estimated currently). Also, the Iberian states' relations with Russia are a perhaps unexpected but nevertheless good example of how Europeanization might be said to have had an effect. EU membership has brought Russia into their foreign policy orbit and they have been a positive voice on Russia within the EU – a counterbalance even to some of the more negative voices. Spain and Portugal can to date, therefore, be seen as examples of constructive bilateral relationships with Russia.

Seemingly in answer to calls for the EU to engage with Russia on a more realistic, pragmatic basis (Barysch *et al.* 2007; Mandelson 2008), in more recent times, EU, or at least European Commission, interactions with Russia have moved closer to the approaches of certain member states (Finland, France, Germany, Italy) who have long conducted a relationship with Russia that has, if not ignored, certainly sidestepped, difficult issues, particularly relating to the normative agenda, where it was felt that this impeded co-operation on key issues concerning trade, energy, visas and security. One of the most obvious changes has come in the shift from a discourse of democratization to modernization (through the P4M), with its emphasis on practical, technical co-operation, notwithstanding the EU's view that the rule of law agenda is an essential step in Russia's modernization.

Crossloading effects are more complex, impacting as they do potentially on the very identity of actors. At this stage, it is difficult to argue for evidence of change running that deep. What we do see is a growth in the type of institutional mechanisms and structures, both formal and informal, which might eventually lead to such change. Politically, the chapters have uncovered some interesting dynamics in this respect, particularly as regards co-ordination of member state positions prior to formal EU negotiations, for example the Benelux, Nordics, Visegrad (to some extent) and, more recently the apparent resurrection of the Weimar Triangle (France, Germany and Poland). Co-ordination in this type of regional locus has positive effects for the EU inasmuch as it may facilitate more effective and prompt decision-making, although admittedly it may also lead to the entrenchment of positions. This does, however, answer to some extent the criticisms the EU attracts for the absence or ineffectiveness of its own co-ordinating mechanisms.

The CFSP generally has attracted a good deal of criticism, not least for the perceived absence of a 'common' policy. Much of the criticism is justifiable but it is also the case that the EU is sometimes held up to standards that would be unreasonable in the state context, where institutional and ideological differences abound. The member states themselves are not unitary actors and internal cleavages matter. For example, the case of the UK highlights certain differences of opinion on the 'proper' approach to Russia between the government and Parliament. This difference is reflected in the EU context as well, where the European Parliament has always been the most outspoken

Conclusion 261

critic of Russia, especially with regards to human rights, while the Commission adopts a more pragmatic approach. Additionally, in some member states, the Czech Republic, Hungary, Poland and Slovakia, for instance, party political differences betray the lack of a national consensus and account for the vacillations/contradictions evident in their policy towards Russia. Moreover, we see in several member states a failure to co-ordinate, agree, compromise and concede. Problems of cohesion were not invented by or in Brussels. How issues are framed therefore matters.

In this section, we have demonstrated that EU–member state and member state–Russia relations should be viewed as existing within a circular dynamic, each relationship impacting upon the other. By looking at just one or two instances, it is very easy to see that analysis is dependent first and foremost on the assumptions made and expectations held about the EU and the manner in which an issue is framed. Take, for instance, Georgia. Sarkozy and (given France's then-Presidency of the EU) the EU's response to Georgia did not reflect all the member state's views (Baltics, Poland, Sweden and the UK) and certainly it did not reflect well on the EU's reputation as a normative actor. It is not uncommon either to read that the Kremlin's agreement to let the EU conduct a monitoring mission reflected not the EU's influence or power, but Russia's desire to keep NATO out of the region. The alternative view is that France's pre-existing strong and positive bilateral relationship with Russia meant it was well-placed to engage in dialogue with the Kremlin, to negotiate a ceasefire and to deploy, remarkably swiftly, a monitoring mission (EUMM), where no other entity would have been accepted by Moscow. Seen from this latter perspective, the bilateral relations *can* be viewed as constituting a positive resource.

The impact of bilateralism

Nevertheless, progress at the EU level has, on occasion, undeniably been impacted negatively by the priority placed by member states on their own bilateral relations with Russia rather than the common European good. Effects have been felt in a variety of ways. For instance, there is the simple and well-documented uploading of bilateral disputes to the EU level, essentially making a member state's particular problems with Russia those of the whole Union (the Estonian Bronze Soldier statue, Poland's meat embargo, the suspension of oil deliveries to Mazeikiai refinery in Lithuania). This has the effect, essentially, of hijacking a previously agreed agenda. There is the equally well-documented practice of concluding bilateral deals, most notably and damagingly in relation to energy, with scant regard for the interests of other member states and even the previous commitment to pursue a common policy. In addition and perhaps more insidiously, the widespread suspicion persists that at the many high-level bilateral meetings, the Russians are led to believe that the EU's normative agenda very much plays second fiddle to the pursuit of economic and other more material interests.

Pessimism underpins much analysis of the wider bilateral relationship and is evident in a great deal of the discourse of member states, revolving most obviously around perceptions of identity. A force for continuity in the present imperfect quality of relations is the normative agenda. At bottom, it seems the EU and Russia simply disagree on the question of values and norms and this inevitably impacts on how they define their interests. This problem also impacts on the question of the extent to which bilateralism is a hindrance to multilateralism. Despite the fact that interests and values are not separate from each other, indeed that values can *be* interests still, too often, values and interests are looked at as competing goals. Even where member states agree that pragmatic engagement with Russia is desirable, they can disagree about the extent to which the wider European normative agenda should be subordinated to economic interests, as many of the chapters show. Thus, despite the often seemingly transactional bases to both the national and EU-level relationships, a strong normative current is evident. This is, perhaps, one reason to be optimistic about the EU's relations with Russia. It suggests that on all sides there is a desire to seek something more, to find something that will bind the EU to Russia and Russia to the EU, something more than the mere promise of strategic and economic gains.

This leads us to the question of 'constructive bilateralism' that was one of our initial hypotheses when we started this project. To be frank, it proved difficult to find instances of undeniable constructive bilateralism, not least because of the assumptions, expectations and framing issues discussed above. Arguably, the role of Germany in launching the P4M is an instance where an initially purely bilateral initiative and dealing with Russia has spilled over into an eventual EU level policy that has itself resulted in not just the original member state (Germany) but 24 other member states signing Modernization Partnerships with Russia. While effects to date are small, they are all positive and have resulted in better political dynamics between 'Brussels' and Moscow. Arguments can be made for constructive bilateralism in respect of agenda-setting and the transfer of knowledge and experience. An early example of this was the Northern Dimension where Finland played a pivotal role in building on its own experiences of constructive cross-border co-operation with Russia to help the EU establish a policy framework for addressing a host of regional soft security issues. More recently, several member states have taken the lead in pressing for progress on the heavily disputed question of visa liberalization. Poland has shown how such controversies can be negotiated through small, limited but nevertheless significant and effective steps, solving problems for those living in the border regions of the Kaliningrad oblast.

The relative lack of instances of genuine constructive bilateralism does not deter us from turning the issue the other way round as there is perhaps something to be said about the potential benefits of a lack of a single EU voice when it comes to relations with Russia. As Kissack (2012) has argued, sometimes the EU seems to use the lack of a unified single voice strategically to engage its partners. Although it would be a bit of a reach to argue that the

Conclusion 263

EU has been strategic in its lack of coherence when it comes to its relations with Russia, the point can at least be entertained that the fact that the EU has verily lacked such a single voice has had some potentially fortuitous political effects as well. For example, during the second Chechen War in the early 2000s it was the slippage from the common EU stance on the part of certain key member states that kept the lines of communication open with Moscow, quite possibly preventing a bigger disruption in relations in the process. In fact, one can only imagine what the political relations between the EU and Russia would be today, had the EU been able to insist with all its full economic, institutional and normative power on the application of its own post-sovereign principles with Russia.

Here, as in the member states, institutional differences come into play in a positive, even if not calculated, way. The EP, like some national parliaments, has been the voice of conscience for the EU, the Commission the voice of strategy. For the EU as an international actor, the building and maintenance of good relations with its partners/other actors is fundamental to the pursuit of its two main objectives: stability and prosperity. The EU continues to pursue a strategic partnership with Russia precisely in order to achieve these. The member states play the central, essential role in an extremely difficult context. The New Cold War discourse, the hot war in Georgia, Russia's internal electoral controversies, the 2012 NGO (foreign agents) law, the Syria crisis in which Russia pitted itself against the West, the rhetoric of now-President Putin that decries external interference in Russia's sovereign affairs and Russia's pointed turn to the East: this is the operational milieu in which the EU has been working. It is not unremarkable that the EU and its member states have maintained the level and intensity of relations with Russia that they have.

What is so striking about the findings of every chapter, from Germany to Malta, the UK to Slovenia, is the breadth, density and intensity of the interaction with Russia, not only at the higher political level, not even only at the level of business elites, but at the level of ordinary people through tourism, cultural exchange, education and research. Regardless of the size of the political stake at play, it seems that Russia is able to cast its special charm or spell on practically all the member states: Russia is still perceived – and in the European context perhaps rightly so – as a Great Power, and political relations, diplomatic exchanges and high level visits and other photo opportunities with Russia seem to be a sought after commodity practically throughout the Union. The chapters also suggest that this seems to be a feature recognized and highly appreciated by Moscow as well and it quite cleverly manages to play on the vanity of member states by rhetorical flourishing concerning the level, quality and importance of individual member states for Russian foreign policy to its own benefit. However, the people-to-people contacts also reveal relationships that are more than those conceived of, sometimes manipulated by, political leaders.

Final thoughts and future agenda

In interviews conducted in Brussels as well as in those member states for which we have responsibility, we the editors have asked officials what needs to change if the EU–Russia relationship is to develop and improve. There is a good deal of acknowledgement that much has already changed, as is evident in the individual chapters, but there is a general consensus too that further change must occur in relation to the following. First, that member states will have to work much harder to ensure proper consultation with the EU occurs in order to avoid the worst examples of contradiction that we have seen to date, especially in relation to energy. A European Commission official argued (interviews July 2011) that changes were necessary within the EU: that more solidarity between the member states and consistent notification of bilateral developments (which some member states engage in currently) would be helpful.

Second, that the EU's structures, although the subject of ongoing change, must be made more effective if *a* Russia policy is to be achieved. The same Commission official argued in 2011 that institutional change was necessary to fill the vacuum left by DG RELEX and until that time unsuccessfully bridged by the External Action Service (interviews with European Commission July 2011). This was echoed in a different way in other interviews (for example with former British ambassadors to Moscow) where it was felt that there was a big failure to engage the member states in dialogue with each other in Brussels itself, that information and experience exchange did not feature enough – a rather surprising comment in light of the existence of a fairly extensive EU–Russia related machinery already discussed in the Introduction.

Finally, Russia itself must change if relations with the EU are to be put on a more robust and certain footing. A good deal of pessimism prevails, however, about prospects for change within Russia as long as Putin and his circle remain in power. Russia's long overdue WTO accession that finally took place in August 2012 is one potential opening. Indeed, much was said in interviews within member states and in Brussels about the importance of Russia's membership of the WTO. This seems to signal that the EU players feel that without further, wider structural constraints Russia cannot be brought into line. Here the EU is much more realistic about its capacities than are some of its critics, whose expectations of the EU are often unrealistic. External actors have limited ability to bring about change in another state, and particularly a large and relatively powerful state, such as Russia. Nor can the EU alone achieve change in Russia, which says something about the limitations of the EU's power.

When it comes to making a difference to the EU's Russia policy all eyes are usually on Germany. It is true that Berlin is an indispensable part of any attempts at taking EU–Russia relations forward. But if all that was required was for Berlin to take the lead, then surely a fully working EU policy on Russia would have been achieved by now? On the contrary, more policy entrepreneurship (and at times less policy-spoiling) is required from several member states. Therefore we should look beyond Germany to other member states and groupings of member states which may have significant untapped potential in this respect. A case in point is Italy which to date has often acted as a defender of the Russian position within the EU, often to the detriment of the EU and even Italy itself when assessed in wider strategic terms. Both the EU and Italy have failed to exploit the potential that Italy's close relations with Russia bring, such that in respect of possible catalysts for change, Italy is one to watch. The same would seem to apply to Poland which has already taken strides to revamp its relations with Russia on a more constructive and self-assured footing and which due to its location and size alone has the potential to emerge as a regional leader in Central and Eastern Europe in the future. The Westerwelle-Sikorski letter represents a very recent and potentially important step in the development of a more coherent and effective EU Russia policy. Additionally on the regional level, the attempts at deepening co-operation between the Nordics as well as their attempts at embracing the Baltic states is an interesting development that should be followed.

This book has shown that at the national level there is much more than meets the eye in EU–Russia relations. The 'national perspectives on Russia' are the obvious basis on which attempts to develop a common EU Russia policy rest. They are also the reason for many tensions and contradictions in that very project as well as a source of surprising commonality and vast future potential. This does not mean that this book manages to explore and exhaust all avenues. At least three further fields of fruitful study spring to mind: first, this study highlights that the actual encounter of national perspectives and the EU's machinery in Brussels is still under-studied. Second, we lack a comparable account of Russia's bilateral relations with EU member states. Finally, there is some merit to thinking about a longitudinal approach to the national perspectives: the book has shown that significant changes have taken place and there is no need to assume that this process will grind to a halt: the EEAS has only just begun its operation and indeed the new 'European foreign policy' is still at a relatively early stage. It seems likely that some of the dynamics of variance and change uncovered in this book have only just been set in motion and their effects on the national perspectives and eventually on the EU policy on Russia still merit further investigation.

References

Barysch, Katinka, Coker, Christopher and Jesień, Leszek (2007) *EU–Russia Relations. Time for a Realistic Turnaround.* Centre for European Reform.

Jørgensen, K. E. (2006) 'Overview: The European Union and the World', in K. E. Jørgensen, M. Pollack and B. Rosamond (eds) *Handbook of European Union Politics.* London: Sage, 507–25.

Kissack, R. (2012) *The Single Voice Problematique: Pragmatic policy or intergovernmental handmaiden?* Paper presented at the EUIA III Conference, Brussels, 3 May 2012.

266 *Maxine David, Jackie Gower, Hiski Haukkala*

Leonard, M. and Popescu, N. (2007) *A Power Audit of EU-Russia Relations*. Policy Paper, European Council on Foreign Relations, December 2007, available at http://ecfr.3cdn.net/1ef82b3f011e075853_0fm6bphgw.pdf (accessed 23 June 2012).

Mandelson, Peter (2008) 'Russia and the EU: building trust on a shared continent', Conference 'Russia in the 21st century'. Available at http://europa.eu/rapid/pressRel easesAction.do?reference=SPEECH/08/343&format=HTML&aged=0&language=E N&guiLanguage=en (accessed 18 September 2012).

Index

Abkhazia 24, 71
Achema Group 159
Aer Rianta International Duty Free
  (ARI) 50
Aeroflot 50
Afghanistan 109, 123
Africa 102, 103, 104
Aho, Esko 138
aid 102
Alcaro, R. 8
Alshinawi, A. 11
Ananicz, A. 171
Ansip, Andrus 152
Arctic 143
Ashton, Catherine 3–4, 23, 25, 26, 92
Ashton–Lavrov Committee 97
Asselborn, Jean 124–25
Austria: accession 211; Chechnya 209,
  214–16; diplomatic relations 217, 219;
  energy field 212–14, 220; historical
  ties 209–11; neutrality 209–12;
  overview 10, 209, 218–20; Poland 210;
  political parties 209, 210, 211–12;
  Russian secret services 216–18
Austria–Hungary 68
automobile industry 17, 68
aviation industry 38, 50, 51
Azerbaijan 72
Aznar, José Maria 109, 113
Ažubalis, Audronis 153

Băescu, Traian 198
Bahr, E. 14
Ballistic Missile Defence (BMD) shield
  154, 174–75
Baltic Sea co-operation framework
  134–35
Baltic States see also Estonia; Latvia;
  Lithuania: accession 15–16; Benelux

126; Eastern neighbourhood 161–63,
  164; energy field 157–61;
Europeanization 165; Georgia 162,
  163–64; historical ties 151–54, 164;
Moldova 162, 163; overview 9–10,
  149–50, 163–65; Poland 162; pre-
  enlargement 150–51; security 153–55,
  164–65; Soviet migrants 151; Sweden
  134; trade and economic interests 150,
  155–57; USA 256
Barcelona Process 102
Barroso, Durão 113
Barroso, Manuel 158
Baumgarten 212
BBC World Service 60
Belarus 20, 24, 27, 87, 90, 91, 138
Belgium see also Benelux: diplomatic
  relations 127; energy field 123, 124,
  128; EU and 121; genocide law 122;
  influence of 127; Iraq war 123;
  overview 9; security 122
Belgium–Luxembourg Economic Union
  (BLEU) 126
Benelux see also Belgium; Luxembourg;
  Netherlands: constructive bilateralism
  120–22; energy field 123; formal co-
  ordination 126; geographical position
  123; influence of 126–28; overview
  128–29; pragmatic attitude 124–25;
  security 123; trade and economic
  interests 123–24, 126, 128–29
Berezovsky, Boris 55–56
Berlin Wall 14
Berlusconi, Silvio 68, 71, 73
Beslan hostage crisis 122
Bessarabia 197
bilateralism: constructive bilateralism 2,
  111, 120–22, 262–63; impact of
  261–63; multilateralism and 2, 262

268 *Index*

Bildt, Carl 134, 135
Black Sea Forum 201
Black Sea Naval Force 201
Black Sea region 201–2
Black Sea Synergy 202, 203–4
Blair, Tony 32, 55, 60, 152
Boenisch, Peter 18
Bowker, James 210
Bozhilova, D. 10
BP 58–59
Brandt, Willy 14
Brazil 104
Brenton, Tony 56
British Council 60
Brown, Gordon 57
Brzeziński, Z. 170
BTS-2 oil pipeline 95
Bulgaria: civil society 188, 190; diplomatic relations 195; energy field 189, 192–93, 241; EU and 188–90; Europeanization 189, 190; geographical position 190–91, 256; historical ties 190–91; overview 10, 187, 194–95; pragmatist-realist approach 191–92; trade and economic interests 192–93
Burgas–Alexandroupolis pipeline 241
Bush, George 233
Bush, George W. 71, 77, 109, 141, 154, 165

Cameron, David 57
Carlsnaes, W. 118, 119–20
Casier, T. 9
Catherine II 233
Cendrowicz, L. 188
Central and East European countries (CEECs) 169–70
Central Asia strategy 22
Central European Gas Hub (CEGH) 212, 214
Centre National d'Etudes Spatiales (CNES) 37
Centres for Polish–Russian Dialogue and Understanding 91–92
Centrex Europe Energy 16; Denmark 141, 142; EU and 263; Finland 138; Germany 18–19; human rights 73; refugees 214–16; Sweden 134, 135; UK 55–57
Chirac, Jacques 18, 32, 34, 41
Christou, G. 11
Cichocki, B. 8, 259
Civic Democratic Party (ODS) 181

Civic Platform 89–90, 92
civil society dialogues 17–18, 19, 20, 21, 121–22, 226, 243
Cold War: Benelux 123; Denmark 140; EU 80; Finlandization 137, 138; Italy 68; Portugal 106; Sweden 133; West Germany 13–15; Yugoslavia 223
Committee of Permanent Representatives to the EU (COREPER II) 4
Common Foreign and Security Policy (CFSP) 3, 41, 43, 70, 201, 260–61
Common Security and Defence Policy (CSDP) 3, 104
Common Strategy on Russia 42, 139
Commonwealth of Independent States (CIS) 98, 105
Communist International (Comintern) 49
Communist Party of Ireland 49
conflict resolution 35
constructive bilateralism 2, 111, 120–22, 262–63
Conventional Armed Forces in Europe (CFE) Treaty 54–55, 77, 98, 199
Cook, Robin 55
Coolsaet, R. 121
Copenhagen summit 141
Council Working Group on Eastern Europe (COEST) 226
creeping integration 31
crisis management 38, 97, 113, 144, 202–3, 250
Croatia 229
cross-loading 5, 260
cyber attacks 54, 61, 153
Cyprus: crisis management 250; cultural ties 256; Cyprus problem 245–46; diplomatic relations 244, 246; in EU 246–51; Europeanization 239, 243–44; foreign policy 243–46; overview 11, 238–39, 251–52; political parties 246; security 244, 246, 250; trade and economic interests 243, 245; visa liberalization 250–51
Czech Republic *see also* Visegrad Group (VG): diplomatic relations 174–75; Europeanization 179; historical ties 170; missile defence systems 71; overview 10; political parties 180–82, 261; trade and economic interests 172
Czech–Russian Intergovernmental Commission 178
Czech Social Democratic Party 181

Index 269

Dangerfield, M. 10
David, M. 8
de Gaulle, Charles 30–31, 32, 33, 36
De Gucht, Karel 121
de Villepin, Dominique 41, 188
Deauville summit 41
Denmark: Chechnya 141, 142;
  diplomatic relations 141; energy field
  143; historical ties 140; overview 9,
  132; political parties 143; Presidency
  141, 142, 143; security 144; trade and
  economic interests 142, 143
DESFA 242
Dirkse, Jan-Paul 122
Double Tax Treaty (DTT) 245
down-loading 5
Drulák, P. 179
Druzhba-1 pipeline 160
Dubien, A. 31, 44
Duleba, A. 173, 182
Dzurinda, Mikuláš 173

Eagle Guardian plan 150, 155
East Asian economic crisis 16
Eastern neighbourhood 161–63, 164
Eastern Partnership 88, 89, 90, 98, 163,
  178–79, 204, 250
EconGas 213
economic migration 37
Electricité de France (EDF) 38
Enel 69
energy field: Austria 212–14, 220; Baltic
  States 157–61; Belgium 123, 124, 128;
  Benelux 123; Bulgaria 189, 192–93,
  241; Denmark 143; Estonia 157–61;
  European foreign policy 257–58;
  expansion of contracts 14, 19;
  Finland 136–37; France 37–38;
  Germany 14, 17, 19–21, 26; Greece
  241–42; Hungary 175–76; Italy 68, 69,
  72, 74–76, 75, 79–80; Latvia 157–61;
  Lithuania 157–61, 227; Luxembourg
  123; Netherlands 123, 124, 128;
  Poland 94, 95–96, 157–58, 159, 160;
  Portugal 107; Romania 199–200, 203;
  Russia 72; Slovenia 225; Spain
  111–12, 113; Sweden 134;
  Turkmenistan 72; UK 58; Ukraine
  72, 200; Visegrad Group (VG)
  175–76
Eni 68, 69, 72, 74–75, 80
Enterprise Ireland 50
Erler, Gernot 20
Espersen, Lene 143

Estonia *see also* Baltic States: bronze
  soldier crisis 152–53; energy field
  157–61; geographical position 256;
  overview 9–10; trade and economic
  interests 155–56
Etzold, T. 9
EU–Africa summit 104
EU Border Assistance Mission 202–3
EU–Brazil summit 104
EU foreign policy: bilateralism 261–63;
  Chechnya 263; co-ordination 4–5,
  260; cultural ties 256; definition 2;
  diplomatic relations 119; energy field
  72, 90, 128, 158–59, 257–58; future
  agenda 264–65; geographical position
  256; historical ties 255–56;
  interpretation 3; member states
  259–61; national perspectives 255–59;
  overview 1–2, 43–44, 119–20; security
  257, 259; Slovenia 226–28; trade and
  economic interests 119, 257; UK
  61–62; visa liberalization 94
EU–Russia Agreement 119, 134, 227,
  247–48
EU–Russia energy forum 193–94
EU–Russia Parliamentary Co-operation
  Committee 226–27
EU–Russia Summit (2000) 43
Euro-Atlantic Partnership Council 133
Europe Agreements (EA) 190
European Aeronautic Defence and
  Space Company (EADS) 38
European Commission 72, 96, 128, 158–
  59, 187, 190, 214, 235, 243, 260, 263
European Council 3, 4–5, 126, 204, 211,
  247, 248, 249 *see also* Presidency
European Court of Human Rights
  93–94, 216
European 'directoire' 103–4
European External Action Service
  (EEAS) 1, 3–4
European Football Championship 24–25
European Neighbourhood Policy (ENP)
  22, 101, 162–63
European Parliament 119, 204, 260–61,
  263
European Security Strategy 202
European Security Treaty 108, 227–28
European Space Agency 37
European Union members 2, 171, 191,
  218
Europeanization: Baltic States 165;
  Bulgaria 189, 190; Cyprus 239, 243–
  44; Czech Republic 179; definition 5;

270 *Index*

Greece 239–40; overview 43–44, 178, 189, 259–61; Poland 259; Portugal 8–9, 102–6; Romania 205–6, 259–60; Spain 8–9, 102–6, 111; Visegrad Group (VG) 182
extraditions 56–57
Eyskens, Mark 211

Faymann, Werner 213–14
Fiat 68
Fico, Robert 182
Fillon, François 37
Financial Times 43
Finland: Chechnya 138; constructive bilateralism 262; diplomatic relations 138–39; energy field 136–37; Finlandization 137, 138; geographical position 137, 256; historical ties 136; ODA 138–39; overview 9, 132; Presidency 138, 139; security 140, 144; trade and economic interests 136, 143; visa liberalization 137
Finmeccanica 69
First World War 68, 187, 198, 226
Fischer, Heinz 211
Fischer, Joschka 20, 21
Foreign Affairs Council (FAC) 4
Foreign and Commonwealth Office (FCO) 54, 60, 62
Four Common Spaces Agreement 163, 202, 247
France: cultural ties 36–37; diplomatic relations 33, 36–37, 40; energy field 37–38; foreign policy 31–33; Georgia 261; German competition 40–44; historical ties 33; overview 7–8, 30–32; Presidency 24, 34; Russia strategy 33–36; security 30–32, 36–40; trade and economic interests 37–38; visa liberalization 37
Franck, C. 126
Frattini, Franco 76–77
French Ambassadors' Conference 42
friendly pragmatists 140, 191, 218, 248, 252

G8 22, 78
Galbreath, D. 9, 149, 161
Galp Energia 107
gas *see also* Gazprom; Nord Stream project; South Stream project: Austria 212–14; Belgium 123; Denmark 142; Finland 136–37; Italy 74; Luxembourg 123; Netherlands 123;

overview 14, 17, 212; Poland 95; Romania 199–200; Slovenia 225; Visegrad Group (VG) 175–76
Gašparovic, Ivan 180
Gazexport 175
Gazprom: Austria 213, 214; Baltic States 159; Gazprom clause 128; Greece 242; Italy 68, 69, 72, 74–75; overview 96; Portugal 107; Spain 110
Genscher, Hans-Dietrich 15
Georgia: accession 109; Baltic States 162, 163–64; Cyprus 250–51; Denmark 141; France 261; Greece 250–51; Membership Action Plan (MAP) 23, 26, 112; NATO 71; overview 261; Poland 90–91; Portugal 112; Rose revolution 163; Russian war 23–24, 26, 34–36, 57, 71, 138, 141, 154; Sweden 134; Visegrad Group (VG) and 182
German Democratic Republic (GDR) 14
Germany: Chechnya 18–19; constructive bilateralism 262; diplomatic relations 23; energy field 14, 17, 19–21, 26; French competition 40–44; future agenda 264–65; geographical position 13, 40; grand coalition replaced 24; historical ties 13–15; under Merkel 21–26; overview 7, 26–27; Poland 22–23, 24, 26, 27, 91, 92; political parties 24; Presidency 22; reunited 15–16; under Schröder 16–21; trade and economic interests 17, 257; visa liberalization 250
Giedroyc, Jerzy 87
Golovatov, Mikhail 217–18
Golovin, Alexander 211
Gomart, T. 36
Gonzales, Felipe 113
Gorbachev, Mikhail 15, 18, 54, 233
Gower, J. 10
Grande Commission Inter-Parlementaire France–Russie 36–37
Greece: civil society dialogues 243; cultural ties 240, 242, 256; diplomatic relations 247; energy field 241–42; in EU 246–51; Europeanization 239–40; foreign policy 239–43; historical ties 239–40; overview 11, 238–39, 251–52; Presidency 247; security 242; visa liberalization 250–51
Greek–Russian Action Plan 240
Group of Friends of the Eastern Partnership 98

Index 271

Group on Difficult Matters 91–92
Grybauskaite, Dalia 155
Gueldry, M. 30
GWH 213
Gyurcsány, Ferenc 181

Hague, William 57
Hassner, P. 33
Haukkala, H. 9, 119
Hay, C. 63
Helsinki Process 80–81
Hermes guarantees 17
Heseltine, Michael 54–55
High Representative of the Union for
    Foreign Affairs and Security Policy 1,
    3–4, 43
Hill, C. 5
Hoffmann, S. 36
Hollande, François 34
Honecker, Erich 15
human rights 6, 18–19, 21, 62, 93–94,
    261; Austria 215, 216; Baltic States
    164; Chechnya 73; Denmark 141;
    Italy 73; Netherlands 121–22, 125;
    Poland 88; Spain 111; Sweden 135;
    UK 63
humanitarian crises 53
Hungarian–Russian Intergovernmental
    Committee 178
Hungarian Socialist Party (MSZP) 181
Hungary *see also* Visegrad Group
    (VG): diplomatic relations 174;
    energy field 175–76; historical ties
    170; overview 10; phases in relations
    173–74; political parties 174,
    180–82, 261; trade and economic
    interests 172
Hyde-Price, A. 125

Iceland 144
ICT 51
IKEA 135
IRA 49
Iraq war 16, 18, 41, 123
Ireland: cultural ties 49; diplomatic
    relations 50; in the EU 51–52;
    geographical position 48, 256;
    overview 8, 48–51, 63–64; political
    parties 49, 51–52; tourism 51; trade
    and economic interests 50–51, 64; visa
    liberalization 51, 64
Ireland Russia Business Association
    (IRBA) 50
Israilov, Umar 215, 216

Italy: cultural ties 69; diplomatic
    relations 74; energy field 68, 69, 72,
    74–76, *75*, 79–80; future agenda 265;
    geographical position 67, 68; match/
    mismatch 73–78; overview 8, 67–70,
    80–81; political parties 68; religion
    69–70; Russia policy 78–80; security
    70–73, 76–78; trade and economic
    interests 69
Ivanov, Igor 228

Jackson-Vanik amendment 53
Jakobsen, P.V. 118, 120, 125, 127
Jankowitsch, Peter 210
Jauvert, V. 35

Kaczynski, Jaroslaw 88, 90
Kaczynski, Lech 88, 90
Kadyrov, Ramzan 215, 216
Kaliningrad Oblast 94, 95, 97, 134–35,
    141–42, 144, 157–58
Kalvītis, Aigars 160
Karaganov, Sergei 87
Katyń Massacre 91, 93–94, 98
Kazakhstan 138
Khanti Mansiisk Summit 227–28
Khrushchev,Nikita 223
Kissack, R. 262
Klaus, Václav 173, 182
Knights of Malta 232
Know How Fund (KHF) 60
Kohl, Helmut 15, 16
Kommersant 218–19
Komorowski, Bronisaw 93, 98
Kosovo 71, 77, 109
Kratochvíl, P. 178, 180
Kreisky, Bruno 210
Kremlin, building of 67
Kubiš, Ján 182
Kultura 87

Laffan, B. 52
Lamoreaux, J.W. 161
Lašas, A. 9
Latin America 102, 103
LatRosTrans 161
Latvia *see also* Baltic States: energy field
    157–61; military co-operation 39–40;
    overview 9–10; trade and economic
    interests 156
Lavrov, Sergei 25, 57, 77, 94, 121, 153,
    226, 228, 235, 236, 240
Law and Justice Party 88–90
Le Noan, R. 7

272 *Index*

Leonard, M. 2, 171, 191, 218, 238, 248, 258
Link, Michael 24
Lisbon Strategy 104
Lisbon Treaty 1, 3–5
Lithuania *see also* Baltic States: energy field 157–61, 227; Ignalina nuclear power plant 157–58; KGB 217–18; overview 9–10; Poland 87, 160; Soviet occupation 153; trade and economic interests 156
Litvinenko, Alexander 55–56
LNG 95, 124, 159, 160
London Stock Exchange 61
Lugovoi, Andrei 56
Luif, P. 10
Lukoil 112
Luxembourg *see also* Benelux: cultural ties 123; energy field 123; historical ties 123; overview 9, 122; pragmatic attitude 124–25; trade and economic interests 124, 128–29
Lynch, D. 43

Macedonia 229
Mafra Summit 104, 108
Maghreb region 102, 103
Magnitsky bill 53
Makarov, Nikolai 98
Malek, M. 10
Malta: cultural ties 234; diplomatic relations 233–34; geographical position 232; historical ties 232–33, 255; overview 11, 231–32, 236–37; political parties 231, 232, 233; schools 234; security 233–34; tourism 234, 235; trade and economic interests 231, 233, 234
Malta International Trade Fair 235
Mandelson, Peter 1–2, 42, 57, 58
Martynau, Siarhey 91
Mazeikiai Oil Refinery 160, 227
McAllister, I. 162
Medgyesi, Péter 174
Medvedev, Alexander 213, 214
Medvedev, Dmitry: anti-missile radar station 155; Austria 211; in Czech Republic 182; in Denmark 142–43; in Finland 137–38; France 41; Germany 23; Italy 76, 79; Mistral ships 39; NATO summit 26; Portugal 108; security 87; Transnistria 25
Membership Action Plans (MAPs) 23, 26, 112

Merkel, Angela 21–26, 41
Meseberg initiative 25
Micu, M. 10
Middle East 103, 110
Mieroszewski–Giedroyc concept 87, 89
military co-operation: France 31, 38–40; Germany 40; Greece 240; Italy 69; Latvia 39–40; Portugal 103, 106, 107
missile defence systems 77, 90, 97, 109, 112, 141, 154, 155, 174–75
Mistral ships 31, 38–39
Mitterrand, Francois 34, 40
Moldova: Baltic States 162, 163; Germany 25; Romania 197, 199, 201–3, 205–6
Molotov–Ribbentrop Pact 198
Montenegro 229
Moore, Thomas 49
Moreau-Defarges, P. 42
Moscow Memorandum 210, 211
multipolarity 31, 32

Nabucco pipe line 38, 72, 80, 175–76, 188, 200, 203, 213–14, 220, 241
Naoumova, N. 33
Nasra, S. 121
national foreign policies, definition 2–3
national perspectives 255–59
NATO: Baltic States 150–51, 153–55, 164–65; Benelux 123; Bucharest summit 23; CSFP 70; Cyprus 244; *Doppelbeschluss* 14–15; Estonia 153; Greece 242; Italy 77, 79, 80; Partnership for Peace (PfP) 133; Poland 87–88, 96–97; Portugal 104, 112; Russia 81; Spain 104, 112; Visegrad Group (VG) 172–73, 183
NATO–Russia Council (NRC) 24, 71
NATO–Russia Missile Defence System 97
NATO–Russia Permanent Joint Council 71
near abroad policy 149, 153, 154, 162
Netherlands *see also* Benelux: civil society dialogues 121–22; cultural ties 123; energy field 19, 123, 124, 128; EU 121; historical ties 123; human rights 121–22; overview 9; trade and economic interests 121, 122–23, 124, 125, 128; USA 123
New Cold War 53, 263
new Cold-warriors 218
new world order 77, 79, 87
NGOs 54, 59

Noon, C. 38
Nord Stream project: Denmark 143, 144; Germany 19–20, 21, 25; Latvia 160; Netherlands 124; Poland 95; Sweden 134, 135, 144
Nordbalt electricity transmission link 158–59
Nordic countries 132, 143–45 *see also* Denmark; Finland; Sweden
Northern Dimension (ND) 136, 144
Norway 144
Nowak, Manfred 218
nuclear missiles 14–15, 55, 97
nuclear power 37–38, 95, 157–58, 176–77, 192

Obama, Barack 77, 154–55, 256
OECD 90
Official Development Assistance (ODA) 103
oil: Baltic States 156, 160–61; Denmark 142; EU 160; Finland 136–37; France 38; Germany 14, 17; Greece 241; Italy 69, 74, 76; Latvia 161; Poland 95; Portugal 107; Spain 110; Visegrad Group (VG) 175
Olbernhauborder transfer station 175
OMV 212–13, 214, 220
Orange Revolution 20, 163
Orbán, Viktor 173–74, 182, 183
Organization for Security and Co-operation in Europe (OSCE) 49, 97, 98, 215
Ostpolitik 14, 21
Ottoman empire 232–33
Outer Space conference 217

Pabriks, Artis 39–40
Panke, D. 52
Papandreou, George 240
Paroubek, Jiří 181
Pärtel, Ago 156
Partito Comunista Italiano (PCI) 68
Partnership and Cooperation Agreement (PCA) 22, 23, 62, 88, 90, 94, 119, 160, 162–63, 238, 247, 262
Partnership for Modernization (P4M) 26, 37, 95, 143, 225–26, 260
Partnership for Peace (PfP) 133, 231, 232
Peattie, David 59
perestroika 15
perspectives, definition
Peter the Great 33, 67, 123, 233

Peterle, Alojz 226
Petersburger Dialogue 17–18, 19, 20, 21
pharmaceuticals industry 51
Piebalgs, Andris 158
pillar system, removal of 3
PKN Orlen 160
Plinovodi 225
Poland *see also* Visegrad Group (VG): air crash 93; Austria 210; Baltic States 162; context 87–89; diplomatic relations 88, 92, 97; energy field 157–58, 159, 160; Europeanization 259; geographical position 94, 95; Georgia 90–91; Germany 22–23, 24, 26, 27, 91, 92; historical ties 170; Lithuania 160; missile defence systems 71; Nord Stream project 19–20, 25; overview 8, 86, 98; political parties 88–89, 261; Presidency 96; security 90, 93, 96–98; trade and economic interests 88, 90, 94–96, 257; Ukraine 87, 89; USA 256; visa liberalization 94, 262
Polish–Russian Strategic Committee 90
Political and Security Committee (COPS) 4
Polotsk-Ventspils pipeline 161
Popescu, N. 2, 171, 191, 218, 238, 248, 258
Portugal: constructive bilateralism 111; cultural ties 108; diplomatic relations 106, 108; Europeanization 8–9, 102–6; geographical position 101, 110–11, 256; Official Development Assistance 102–3; overview 8–9, 101–2, 106–8; political parties 106; Presidency 104, 108; revolution 106; security 104–5, 106; Spain 113–14; tourism 107; trade and economic interests 103, 106–8, 111
Portuguese Communist Party (PCP) 106
Portuguese Speaking Countries 105
Póti, L. 173–74
Power Audit of EU-Russia Relations (Leonard and Popescu) 2
Prague Spring 210
Presidency: Denmark 141, 142, 143; Finland 138, 139; France 24, 34; Germany 22; Greece 247; Poland 96; Portugal 104, 108; Slovenia 227; Spain 109, 113; Sweden 135, 136
President of the European Council 1, 3
press freedom 73

274 *Index*

Putin, Vladimir: in Austria 211–12;
  Austria 219; Berlusconi and 68;
  Chechnya 215; energy field 72;
  external interference 263; in France
  34; gas supplies 212, 213–14;
  Germany 17; Hungary 182;
  Litvinenko murder 56; Malta 236; in
  Poland 92–93; reforms 16; in Slovakia
  178; in Slovenia 224; in Sweden 135;
  third term 25; in UK 55; in Visegrad
  173; Visegrad Group (VG) 181

Rajoy, Mariano 110
Rasmussen, Anders Fogh-141
Reagan, Ronald 54
refugees 214–16
Reinfeldt, Fredrik 135
religion 69–70, 256
Repsol 110, 112
Romania: diplomatic relations 198;
  energy field 199–200, 203;
  Europeanization 205–6, 259–60;
  geographical position 256; historical
  ties 197; Moldova 199, 201–3, 205–6;
  overview 10, 191, 197–201, 205–6;
  preferences 201–5; security 197–98,
  199, 201–3; trade and economic
  interests 198; up-loading 201, 205
Rosatom 176
Rotfeld, Adam Daniel 91
Royal Dutch Shell 124
Russia: anti-missile radar station 155;
  debts 17; foreign policy 43; future
  agenda 264; secret services 216–18;
  trade and economic interests 17, 50–51
Russian Centre of Science and
  Education 244
Russian–Greek Civil Societies Forum 243
Russkiy Mir Foundation 227
Russo–British Chamber of Commerce 59
Rybkine, Ivan 36

Sakhalin II 124
Samson, I. 171
Sarkozy, Nicolas 33, 34–36, 39, 41, 42,
  138
Schengen 137, 235
Schmidt, Helmut 14–15
Schröder, Gerhard 16–21, 26
Schuessel, Wolfgang 215
Schuster, Rudolph 173
Schwarzenberg, Karel 179
Second World War 88, 92, 151, 164,
  197, 198, 209

secret services 216–18
Seguin, Philippe 36
September 11 terrorist attacks 16
Serbia 229
Shevardnadze, Eduard 15
Shevchuk, Yevgeny 25
Shevstova, L. 39
Shokin, Alexander 54–55
Siberia overflight charges 96
Sikorski, Radosaw 23, 24, 26, 91, 92, 94,
  98, 265
Simão, L. 8
Slovakia: historical ties 171; overview
  10; political parties 180–82, 261;
  security 172–73; trade and economic
  interests 172
Slovenia: civil society dialogues 226;
  cultural ties 224, 226; diplomatic
  relations 222, 224, 227, 228; energy
  field 225; EU–Russia policy 226–28;
  historical ties 222; overview 10–11,
  222–23, 228–29; Presidency 227;
  security 227–28; tourism 225; trade
  and economic interests 224, 225–26;
  visa liberalization 228; Yugoslavia
  223–24
small states 120, 125, 126–27
Smirnov, Igor 25
Smith, N. 63
Soares, Mário 113
Sócrates, José 106, 113
Solidarity 87
South Ossetia 24, 71
South Stream Greece SA 242
South Stream project: Austria 214, 220;
  Bulgaria 193; Croatia 229; France 38;
  Greece 241; Hungary 175–76, 182;
  Italy 72, 76, 80; Slovenia 225
Søvndal, Villy 143
space co-operation 37
Spain: diplomatic relations 108; energy
  field 111–12, 113; Europeanization
  8–9, 102–6, 111; geographical position
  101, 110–11, 256; human rights 111;
  Official Development Assistance 103;
  overview 8–9, 101–2, 108–10;
  Portugal 113–14; Presidency 109, 113;
  security 102, 104–5, 109–10; terrorism
  109, 110; tourism 110; trade and
  economic interests 103, 110, 111; visa
  liberalization 110, 113
Spanger, H.-J. 18
Spindelegger, Michael 211
St Malo accord 32–33

Index 275

Stankevičius, Česlovas 159
Steinbach, Erika 92
Steinmeier, Frank-Walter 21, 22, 23, 24
Stewart, S. 7, 40
strategic partners 73, 218
Stronck, Gaston 122
Sutela, Pekka 140
Sweden: Chechnya 134, 135; cultural
    ties 135; energy field 134; historical
    ties 133; overview 9, 132; Presidency
    135, 136; security 133, 144; trade and
    economic interests 135, 143–44

Tagliavini Commission 24
terrorism 102, 104–5
Thatcher, Margaret 54
Third Energy Package (TEP) 95–96,
    157, 159, 164
Timmins, G. 125
Timofti, Nicolae 25
Tito, Marshall 223
TNK 58–59
Torkunov, Anatoly 91
tourism: Ireland 51; Malta 234, 235;
    Portugal 107; Slovenia 225; Spain 110
Trans-European Energy Network 19
transferable rouble debts 172
Transnistria 25, 97, 197, 199, 202–3
Trojan horses 218, 238, 251, 258
Tskhinvali 24
Türk, Danilo 222, 223, 224, 227–28
Turkey 241, 242, 250
Turkish Cypriots 243
Turkmenistan 72
Tusk, Donald 89, 90, 91, 96
TVEL 176
Tymoshenko, Yulia 24
Tziampiris, A. 240

UK Trade and Investment (UKTI) 58
Ukraine 20, 24; accession 109; Baltic
    States 162; energy field 72, 200;
    historical ties 197–98; Membership
    Action Plan (MAP) 23, 26, 112;
    NATO 71; Orange Revolution 20,
    163; Poland 87, 89
UN Global Strategy against Terrorism 109
UN Security Council 245–46
Union for the Mediterranean 102
United Europe 87
United Kingdom: Chechnya 55–57;
    cultural ties 52, 60; diplomatic
    relations 52, 54, 55, 56; energy field
    58; EU in foreign policy 61–63;

geographical position 48, 256;
    intergovernmental relations 54–58;
    overview 63–64; people-to-people
    contacts 59–61; trade and economic
    interests 54–55, 58–59; United States
    and 53–54; visa liberalization 56, 59
United Nations Security Council
    (UNSC) 77
United States: Austria 219; Baltic States
    154–55; Benelux 123; Denmark 141;
    Germany 18; influence of 31, 256;
    missile defence systems 71, 77, 90, 97,
    109, 112, 141, 174; Portugal 105;
    Spain 105, 109; Sweden 133; United
    Kingdom 53–54
up-loading 5, 201

Van den Bos, B. 121
Venezelos, Evangelos 242
Ventspils Oil terminal 161
Verheugen, Günter 152
Vernet, D. 35
Vīke-Freiberga, Vaike 152
visa liberalization: Cyprus 250–51;
    Finland 137; France 37; Germany
    250; Greece 250–51; Ireland 51, 64;
    liberalization 3, 37, 113; overview
    262; Poland 94, 262; Slovenia 228;
    Spain 110, 113; United Kingdom 56,
    59; Visegrad Group (VG) 180
Visegrad Group (VG) see also Czech
    Republic; Hungary; Poland; Slovakia:
    accession 190; Eastern Partnership
    178–80; energy field 175–76;
    Europeanization 182; geographical
    position 169; historical ties 170–72;
    nuclear power 176–77; overview
    169–70, 182–83, 194–95; political
    parties 172, 180–82; pre-accession
    period 172–74, 180, 182–83;
    Presidency 179; security 172–73,
    174–75; Slovenia 227; trade and
    economic interests 174, 177, 177–78,
    182–83; visa liberalization 180
Votápek, V. 173
Vozhzhov, Vladimir 217

Waever, O. 32
Waldheim, Kurt 210
West Berlin 14
West Germany 13–15
Westerwelle, Guido 23, 24, 26, 91, 92, 265
White, S. 162
Wider European Initiative 139

276 *Index*

Wikileaks scandal 155, 171
Wong, R. 5
Wood, Andrew 62, 64
Working Party on Eastern Europe and
Central Asia (COEST) 4
World Trade Organisation 61–63, 96,
107, 264

Yakovenko, Alexander 58
Yalta system 87
Yamal Gas Pipeline 96

Yanukovych, Viktor 163
Yastrzhembsky, Sergei 152
Year of France in Russia 37
Yekaterinburg Triangle 41
Yeltsin, Boris 15, 16, 50
Yugoslavia 223–24
Yukos 72, 73

Zagorsky, A. 18
Zakayev, Akhmad 57, 141, 143
Zapatero, José Luis 109, 111, 113

Taylor & Francis
eBooks
FOR LIBRARIES

ORDER YOUR FREE 30 DAY INSTITUTIONAL TRIAL TODAY!

Over 23,000 eBook titles in the Humanities, Social Sciences, STM and Law from some of the world's leading imprints.

Choose from a range of subject packages or create your own!

Benefits for you
- ▶ Free MARC records
- ▶ COUNTER-compliant usage statistics
- ▶ Flexible purchase and pricing options

Benefits for your user
- ▶ Off-site, anytime access via Athens or referring URL
- ▶ Print or copy pages or chapters
- ▶ Full content search
- ▶ Bookmark, highlight and annotate text
- ▶ Access to thousands of pages of quality research at the click of a button

For more information, pricing enquiries or to order a free trial, contact your local online sales team.

UK and Rest of World: online.sales@tandf.co.uk
US, Canada and Latin America:
e-reference@taylorandfrancis.com

www.ebooksubscriptions.com

A flexible and dynamic resource for teaching, learning and research.

CPSIA information can be obtained
at www.ICGtesting.com
Printed in the USA
JSHW011319201219
3107JS00002B/32

9 781138 898